Foreign Policy of the
European Union

Published in association with
the Institut für Europäische Politik, Bonn, and
the Trans European Policy Studies Association, Brussels

Foreign Policy of the European Union

From EPC to CFSP and Beyond

edited by

Elfriede Regelsberger
Philippe de Schoutheete de Tervarent
Wolfgang Wessels

LYNNE
RIENNER
PUBLISHERS

BOULDER
LONDON

Published in the United States of America in 1997 by
Lynne Rienner Publishers, Inc.
1800 30th Street, Boulder, Colorado 80301

and in the United Kingdom by
Lynne Rienner Publishers, Inc.
3 Henrietta Street, Covent Garden, London WC2E 8LU

Library of Congress Cataloging-in-Publication Data
Foreign policy of the European Union :   from EPC to CFSP and beyond
  edited by Elfriede Regelsberger, Philippe de Schoutheete de Tervarent, and
  Wolfgang Wessels.
    Includes bibliographical references and index.
    ISBN 1-55587-705-2 (hardcover : alk. paper)
    1. European Union countries—Foreign relations.   2. Europe—
Foreign relations.   I. Regelsberger, Elfriede.   II. Schoutheete de Tervarent,
Philippe de, 1932–   .   III. Wessels, Wolfgang.
JX1542.F675   1996
327.4—dc20
                                                                    96-26135
                                                                        CIP

British Cataloguing in Publication Data
A Cataloguing in Publication record for this book
is available from the British Library.

Printed and bound in the United States of America

        The paper used in this publication meets the requirements
  ∞   of the American National Standard for Permanence of
        Paper for Printed Library Materials Z39.48-1984.

    5 4 3 2

Contents

Part 4   The Future: Challenges and Limitations

Foreword

Jacques Delors

I very much welcome this opportunity to produce a study that brings together the views of both practitioners and academic experts on the Common Foreign and Security Policy (CFSP) of the European Union (EU). Such studies are most valuable in creating an awareness of the problems surrounding the external policies of the Union and make an important contribution to the very necessary reflections that we need as we move forward.

It is deeply regrettable that any assessment of the early operations of the CFSP cannot be described as positive. Despite the lofty language in Title V of the Treaty on European Union, it is difficult to observe any significant improvement in the EU's coherence or increased influence on the world stage. This is all the more unfortunate on the eve of enlargement of the Union and given the increased array of challenges facing the Union, many of which are on the immediate horizon.

During the Intergovernmental Conference (IGC) negotiations in 1991, I argued strongly for a coherent approach to external relations, for a single structure rather than the pillar structure that was eventually agreed to. I also cautioned against complete reliance on the unanimity rule and argued for all member states to accept a mutual defense obligation as part of the basic rights and responsibilities of a political union. I stand by these positions today.

The experience of CFSP in practice has demonstrated the impossibility of separating the political and economic strands of external relations and the difficulties of operating partly under the proven community system and partly under the intergovernmental system.

The successful outcome of the GATT negotiations (General Agreement on Tariffs and Trade) was a good demonstration of the EU effectively promoting its common interests by acting together and speaking with one voice. The contrast with our handling of the conflict in former Yugoslavia could not be greater.

There are a number of important lessons to be drawn from the Balkan crisis. First is the need to develop the political will to function as a coherent political actor. This may involve some institutional changes to enable one political figure to speak in the name of the Union. The "Troika" system may have worked in the era of European Political Cooperation (EPC), but I believe that we now need a more visible and continuous presence on the world stage. Second is the need to create a planning and analysis capability at the European level. This could be modeled along the lines of the U.S. National Security Council, which holds responsibility for preparing and reviewing strategy as well as for crisis management. Third is the need to develop a military component to support our diplomacy.

One of the most significant changes since the 1991 IGC has been the change in attitude of the U.S. government toward closer European cooperation on defense. This has been due partly to the reduction in U.S. forces in Europe following the end of the Cold War and partly to President Clinton's concentration on domestic issues. The January 1994 NATO summit, with its strong endorsement of a European Security and Defence Identity (ESDI), now allows the Western European Union (WEU) to be strengthened as the European pillar of the alliance. As U.S. forces are reduced in Europe, so Europeans will have to do more for their own defense. The advantages of cooperation, particularly in weapons procurement, are huge, and it is encouraging to see moves in this direction—for example, the Eurocorps and the establishment of the Western European Armaments Group (WEAG).

The enlargement of the Union since 1995 will also have an impact on CFSP. I am convinced that this will be a positive impact because the new members will not only bring additional resources to the CFSP but also a proud record in the provision of development assistance and UN peace-keeping forces. Furthermore, they are already fully committed to supporting EU policies toward the Commonwealth of Independent States (CIS), Central and Eastern Europe, and elsewhere.

But no one can doubt that decisionmaking in an enlarged Union will be more difficult. Hence the need to reflect on the institutional changes that will be necessary to ensure that the Union is able to maintain its effectiveness after further enlargements.

The Union agenda for 1996 includes a review of the CFSP and institutional change among the top priorities. As the Union approaches the twenty-first century, it cannot afford to retreat into itself. Its economic weight demands that it play a commensurate political role in world affairs. The rest of the world has high expectations for the Union. There is no doubt that we have the resources and capability—but do we have the vision?

Preface

This book is an endeavor to describe and analyze the European Union's Common Foreign and Security Policy (CFSP). It constitutes an attempt to portray the transition from European Political Cooperation (EPC) to CFSP, to examine institutional developments in the second pillar of the European Union (EU), to evaluate the first experiences with CFSP since the entry into force of the Treaty on European Union, and finally to discuss the challenges and limitations of any future CFSP.

The book was made possible after extensive exchanges of opinion on the occasion of several conferences on CFSP, organized by the Institut für Europäische Politik, Bonn, in collaboration with the Trans European Policy Studies Association (TEPSA) in Brussels. These meetings brought together both scholars, many of whom are members of a group of researchers who have been analyzing the emerging developments in political cooperation since the late 1970s, and practitioners, who are actively involved in the EU's foreign policy activities.

We would like to emphasize that this book could not have been published without the commitment and encouragement of many individuals and institutions to which we extend our gratitude. In particular, we thank the German Ministry for Foreign Affairs, which generously supported both the conferences and the preparation of this volume. We want to express our gratitude to Lynne Rienner Publishers for making this publication possible. We are especially indebted to the Trans European Policy Studies Association and its president, Jacques Vandamme. Finally, we would like to thank Bettina Döser and Janis A. Emmanouilidis for their assistance in editing this volume.

Elfriede Regelsberger
Philippe de Schoutheete de Tervarent
Wolfgang Wessels

1

From EPC to CFSP: Does Maastricht Push the EU Toward a Role as a Global Power?

Elfriede Regelsberger, Philippe de Schoutheete de Tervarent, and Wolfgang Wessels

Europe's Role in the World: The Rising Gap Between Demands and Offers

The Demands for a European Role in the World

Foreign policy has always been an integral part of the gradual process of integration in which Western European states have been engaged since the late 1940s. The "founding fathers" promoted reconciliation between former enemies, aiming at peace, and accelerated economic development, aiming at prosperity. The European construction was thus a cornerstone of the foreign policy perception of each of them. But the founding fathers also had in mind the collective defense of the external interests and influence of the European states, which were weakened by the war and the gradual demise of colonial empires.

First the European Community (EC) and now the European Union (EU) have always had a double foreign policy agenda: First, it is of vital national interest for each member state to link its own fate with that of other European states in "an ever closer Union." Second, the EU is to serve as some kind of common coalition group to pursue common interests in the regional and global systems. The demands set by the member states are high. Article J.1 of the Treaty on European Union (TEU), setting the objectives of the EU's Common Foreign and Security Policy (CFSP), calls upon the Union and its member states "to safeguard the common values, the fundamental interests, and the independence of the Union." The CFSP shall moreover "strengthen the security of the Union and its member states in all ways," it shall "preserve peace and strengthen international security," "promote international cooperation and develop and consolidate democracy and the rule of law and respect for human rights and fundamental freedoms."

1

In spite of many controversies, the demands for a Common Foreign and Security Policy are rather widely shared inside the EU.[1] Even skeptical British conservatives are generally voicing a strong interest in a stronger role for Europe in the world. U.K. prime minister John Major, for example, underlined that "steps which have been taken towards joint actions in foreign policy strike us as no more than a modest beginning. . . . We should be more ambitious."[2] However, we need to be wary of following rhetoric: The public perception that the external threat from the East has disappeared might lead to a more inward-looking Europe. The continent might consequently evolve toward something like a large Switzerland, guided by a neo-isolationist approach, following world events but not perceiving real needs to get involved.

Expectations regarding a strengthened capacity for external action of the Union,[3] however, derived only from internal interest calculations and perceptions. Other states are also putting forward demands, especially to enter into well-defined and, if possible, privileged relations with the Union.[4] Europe, more specifically the EC/EU, was and is perceived as an economic, and to a slighter degree political, power. The post-1989 changes in the global architecture increased the demands on West Europeans to shape their international role independently and without acting in a simple superpower constellation.[5] The complexity of the international system has grown considerably. The challenges have increased in number and in kind. This is obvious for the regional Eastern and Southern environment of Europe, with particular emphasis on the establishment of stable security structures and a deepening of relations with Russia, Ukraine, and Turkey as well as with regard to the numerous applicant countries,[6] but it is also visible in the global context. To shoulder only regional responsibilities seems insufficient; Europeans must recall what Henry Kissinger described in his "Year of Europe" speech and take on their share of global responsibilities.[7] The EU needs to be a global player if it wants to shape "its own destiny" and "assert its identity on the international scene, in particular through the implementation of a Common Foreign and Security Policy" (Title I, Article B, TEU).

The Offers for a Serious Policy

Foreign policy has been one of the most difficult areas in which to cooperate. It raises immediately, and most visibly, issues of national sovereignty. It has to accommodate differing historical traditions, to consider specific sensitivities and prejudices in public opinion. In the peoples' collective consciousness, foreign policy, defense, and currency are basic ingredients of the nation-state in a way that coal, steel, and the economy, however important, are not.

This explains, at least in part, the successive failures of efforts to federalize foreign policy. The innovative ideas of Monnet and Schuman, accepted for coal and steel, were rejected in 1954 when applied to defense and foreign policy. The second attempt, the so-called Fouchet Plan—a concept following a strictly intergovernmental strategy—was also unsuccessful.

The very different ideas of de Gaulle and Fouchet could not mobilize consensus, but the aspiration to communitarize the fields of defense and foreign policy persisted. The then six member states' next attempt was that of European Political Cooperation (EPC), which commenced as a trial-and-error process in 1970. By 1975, Leo Tindemans, who was touring Europe to prepare his report on European integration, had discovered that common action in the field of foreign policy had become the single most frequently quoted justification of the integration process. Arguing that the peoples of Europe expected a union to make Europe's voice heard, his report called upon the EPC member states to present a united front to the outside world.[8]

The low-key development of political cooperation from 1970 onward was the answer to this aspiration. It initiated a pooling of information and mutual reflection that spread gradually to most areas of diplomatic activity, with the clear exclusion of defense. It resulted in an increasing number of diplomatic démarches and policy statements that were agreed upon by all members, which gradually gave the European Community and its member states the appearance and some of the advantages of a collective diplomacy, accepted as such by the international community. Its development, however, left public opinion largely indifferent. The academic community took some time to show interest, but by the late 1970s a small group of researchers, many of whom are contributors to this volume, had begun to analyze emerging developments in political cooperation.

This analysis demonstrated the advantages and the limits of this new activity, both of which are described in this book.[9] Foremost among the limits was the absence of a legal foundation, with resulting doubt about the obligations and constraints accepted by member states and ambiguous relations with Community activities and institutions. This was partly remedied by Title III of the Single European Act in 1986. Nevertheless, the feeling was widely shared that political cooperation, as it stood, could hardly cope with a challenging new European environment. As Jacques Delors appeals to us in the foreword to this book, the Union, approaching the twenty-first century, cannot afford to retreat into itself. The EU's economic weight demands that it play a commensurate political role in world affairs. These words show the manner in which foreign policy gradually gained particular importance at precisely the moment that a new European treaty was to be negotiated.

An Explanation: The Credibility Gap[10]

The history of EPC proved to be a phenomenon that can well be analyzed as a credibility gap. A strong European role in the regional and international system is something like a "common good" from which each member state profits if it produces results in the interest of every state of the EC/EU. Each member country is aware that the synergy of pooling resources strengthens its own position. The demands inside the EU and the aspirations for a unified foreign policy are thus quite obvious.

The character of a "public good" that offers something to everyone (without excluding any member) leads immediately to the issue of "free riders": Whenever it looks more profitable to do so, member states might try to reduce their contribution into the common endeavor. The institutional and material burden-sharing among member states, which includes the perennial issue of making a sacrifice or at least limiting national sovereignty, turned out to be of major importance. Without efficient and effective institutions, the EC/EU member states fell into the "trap" of creating procedures and structures that suited their national perceptions and apparently offered possibilities to pursue the common good without, however, really being prepared to offer adequate means for the common undertaking.

With clear illusions about their own willingness to follow their own rules, their attempt at political cooperation led to a vicious circle (see Figure 1.1). The lack of individual "investments" into mutual endeavors favored parallel approaches of member countries, which in time created the external and internal credibility gap.

The weaknesses are only too apparent. They are described in detail in the following chapters that deal with institutions and with specific failures of policy.[11] These defects are known not only to the participants, politicians and diplomats, and academic researchers but also to the average citizen whose exposure to foreign policy occurs mostly via television. In the daily or nightly description of crises around the world—in Bosnia, Rwanda, Chechnya, Somalia, or the Gulf—the listener or viewer practically never observes the Union to be a major single actor.[12] He sees or hears about the United States or Russia—and sometimes one or more members of the Union—but not the EU as such. He is understandably tempted to conclude that Europe has no common foreign policy or that it is irrelevant to world affairs.

Since the epochal changes of 1989, the deficits have turned out to be even more visible within their "regional responsibilities"—to use Kissinger's term from his "Year of Europe" speech;[13] in former-Yugoslavia[14] and in the southern part of the Mediterranean, the EU did not come up with a credible policy that would match the Europeans' own ambitions. A new global role is hardly perceivable. Thus, the overall objectives of common European activities were clear and present, but no efficient and effective actions were taken. The visibility of the joint efforts was and is very limited.

Figure 1.1 The "Vicious" Circle (before Maastricht)

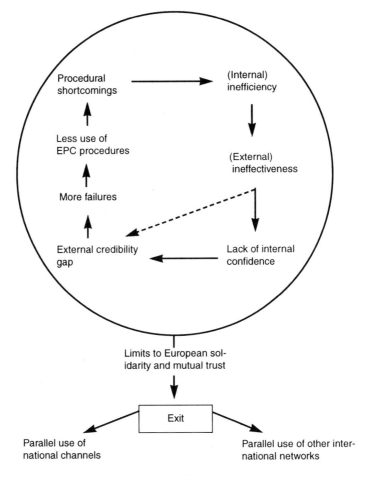

The CFSP: Does Maastricht Matter?

The Maastricht Answer:
From Political Cooperation to Common Policy[15]

From the outset, the Maastricht negotiation was dominated by the ambitious goal set out in the Mitterrand-Kohl letter of April 1990. In the foreign and security field, the member states should make a quantum jump: Switch from mere cooperation to a common policy. In substance, the aim was to pass from a situation in which the limitations of political cooperation were paralyzing its development and privileging other international channels, to a situation in which, on a new basis, an effective common foreign policy would generate its own dynamism. The implication was that routine diplomatic consultations and general policy outline, with only "soft" political consequences, were insufficient. The objective was "high politics" and "hard obligations." The Twelve were to abandon a vicious circle (see Figure 1.1), accentuating the limits of their external solidarity, and enter into a virtuous one (see Figure 1.2), leading to an upgrading of their collective efforts on the international scene. The perennial issue of the construction of a step toward communitarization, as the Dutch proposal had in mind, or by a reinforced governmentalization is not clearly defined in the Maastricht Treaty. The TEU suggests several interpretations by establishing, on the one hand, the CFSP as an "independent" pillar of its own and by creating, on the other hand, a "single" institutional framework.[16] In addition, the treaty provisions were to be understood as preliminary ones open to change in the next IGC (Intergovernmental Conference) to be opened in 1996.[17]

A Performance Test

Following the entry into force of the Treaty on European Union, the scope of topics on the agenda of the second pillar now also include the security dimension and defense perspectives of foreign policy. Thus, it sets even higher standards for its own work, but at the same time offers more possibilities to act. However, if you consider the procedural aspects of Article J (TEU), it is evident that the *saut qualitatif* in the definition of objectives is not matched by the creation of resources or instruments appropriate to those objectives. The Treaty creates a single institutional framework, it strengthens slightly the role of the Commission, it introduces the possibility of majority voting (an unpopular development among diplomats), and it proposes something called "joint actions"—but the impact of these modifications on practical performance seems to be rather minor.

Moreover, the application of the new provisions turned out to be more laborious than expected.[18] Uncertainties over an appropriate division of labor between the Political Committee and the Committee of Permanent Representatives (COREPER), confusion over the instruments, and a massive dispute both inside CFSP and with the European Parliament over the financing of the CFSP were but the most obvious problem areas. Although the use of joint actions enabled the Twelve/Fifteen to show greater visibility, the impact on a given problem—for example, former-Yugoslavia, Russia, South Africa, the Middle East—remained limited. The new provisions do not necessarily put the EC/EU into the position of being a new regional and global player. Other well-known deficiencies, such as the presidential overload and the lack of continuity in the EU's external representation, added up to a very mixed picture of the CFSP's performance in the period 1993–1995.

It seems as if the Maastricht Treaty has not broken the "vicious" circle and turned it into a "virtuous" one.

Figure 1.2 The "Virtuous" Circle (after Maastricht)

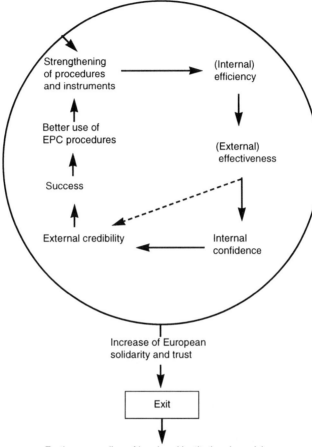

Whether or not the results of the ongoing new IGC that opened on 29 March 1996[19] will work toward the virtuous circle remains to be seen. At least attempts are being made to both improve CFSP's internal efficiency and external effectiveness as well as the EU's security identity.[20]

Incremental Reform and Global Responsibilities

Regarding global responsibilities[21] the options range from WEU (Western European Union) becoming a part of the EU as a merged second or separate fourth pillar of the Union to less ambitious proposals to improve the WEU/EU relationship.[22] In the first case the Union would undergo fundamental changes. The "civilian power" trademark would be replaced by defense-oriented features, such as a mutual assistance clause to defend the EU territory, military capacities to do so, et cetera. Such a fundamental change from the present situation would, however, require an in-depth debate about repercussions on NATO and the United States, on relations with Russia, on existing military capacities and equipment, on applicant countries, et cetera. Given the tremendous obstacles that such an approach implies for those EU members with an observer status in the present WEU and the consequences of a somehow fused institutional setup, less far-reaching models might prevail in the IGC debate. Providing that WEU preserves its independence, a sensible division of labor has to be sought with the EU in the broader area of collective security measures, which traditionally link military means to political/diplomatic and economic ones that are available in the second and first pillar.

Proposals[23] to enable the EU to respond more rapidly and more effectively to international challenges refer to all stages of the decisionmaking and implementation process.[24] One central element under discussion focuses on ways to improve the process of decision preparation inside CFSP. Though acknowledged as a fundamental need, suggestions differ on ways to improve CFSP analysis and the evaluation of international events in the perspective of essential common interests. To entrust the European Commission (and here, in particular, its DG 1A—directorate-general 1A) with this task would immediately produce opposition on principle from member states. Entrusting a separate organization with this function seems to be more promising. In order to exploit the information available to the national diplomatic services, the group would have to be composed of diplomats chosen from the national foreign ministries to serve in this unit (plus Commission participation) in Brussels. An alternative solution could be to charge the CFSP counselors already in office in the various permanent representative member states with this function, because the CFSP unit inside the Council secretariat—at least, as it stands today—seems to be caught up in daily CFSP business. The creation of such a new body immediately raises questions of hierarchy in the CFSP infrastructure and what its relationship to the other CFSP levels would be—particularly to the Political Committee and the Committee of Permanent Representatives. The situation would be even more complicated, to the extent that such a unit would be presided over by a high-ranking personality nominated by the European Council, as was suggested in the report submitted by the high-level expert group on CFSP selected by Commissioner van den Broek.[25] Consistency in the EU's external posture would require Commission participation and, possibly, the inclusion of WEU representation.

Another point under discussion refers to the use of the appropriate means to prepare decisions in CFSP. Clarification particularly has to be sought between the application of "common positions" (Article J.2 [2]) and "joint actions" (Article J.3), whereby the former would give clear guidance on the position of the Fifteen on a given subject while the latter would contain concrete issues for immediate action. Such an approach might run counter to the initial idea of Maastricht of achieving greater visibility toward the outside via joint actions, but it might possibly reduce the potential of conflict with community business. The proposed distinction might also facilitate majority voting, which has not yet been applied, although it was foreseen in Article J.3—that is, the guidelines to be laid down in the common position would be based on unanimity while joint actions resulting from that could be taken and implemented by majority voting.

The last aspect refers immediately to the level of decisionmaking. Here, the key remains: How will it be possible to overcome the member states' recourse to unanimity? Perhaps the above-mentioned distinction of different kinds of decisions might help, as could the introduction of a new "safeguard clause" in the form of a double majority vote—that is, a vote that represents a majority of the member states and of the population.

A further problem area in which a solution seems to be difficult to find is a result of the pillar structure of the EU, which is in contrast to the nature of international problems and the Union's ability to manage them. Practical experience with CFSP so far suggests the viability of an increased interconnectedness between the second and first pillars, with increased prominence for Community groups and, in particular, for the European Commission and Parliament, especially regarding the financial implications of CFSP. Such a factual upgrading might require new arrangements that respond, for example, to the EP's demands to get involved in the decisionmaking process at an early stage, thus superseding the provisions of Article J.7. If the assumption is true that community-type elements will gain in importance, this might also have an effect on the relationship between the Political Committee and COREPER, giving the latter more importance, which might facilitate the "clearing" of the provisions in Article J.8 (5).

One more field of ample hybrid debate and dispute concerns the level of decision implementation. Here, the principle of rotating presidencies is at stake. In order to compensate for the often lamented discontinuity and confusion of CFSP's outside representation, fundamentally different models from the existing one have to be considered. These center around a politically credible and experienced "figure"—for example, a secretary-general who would be analogous to the one in NATO—who would be nominated by the European Council and approved or even elected by the EP, and who could act as a spokesperson toward the outside world for an extended period of time. For the sake of homogeneity, this person would also have to be in charge of the external relations emanating from the first and third pillar—given the diversity of subjects and the existing Council structure, this would be a considerably demanding function. Such an approach would have immediate effects on the Commission's participation in the EU's external representation and could possibly reduce its involvement in CFSP. If entrusting an eminent personality with overseeing the conduct of CFSP were to be limited to the second pillar in the form of a Mr./Ms. CFSP and the present rotating system were to be preserved for the first pillar, the fact that certain subjects overlap could create new forms of a *bicephalous* or even a triple outside representation, which might appear as confusing as the present situation.

Additionally, the question arises as to whether or not one single outside representation is compatible with a similar approach on the CFSP "domestic" level—for example, via the Council secretariat. Other models, such as entrusting certain countries with specific CFSP-related tasks internally (and possibly externally because of specific merits, traditions, etc.) might look promising in terms of the division of labor, but they do not respond to a homogeneous external representation. It also seems somewhat awkward that EU member states would accept such an internal division of labor without "selling" the results of their work outside the EU borders. Any move toward a new distribution of tasks among the present Fifteen, on an individual basis or even within various groups—and if so, how the groups will be composed—requires much greater internal coordination efforts and probably additional staffing for the Council secretariat.

Experiences from previous reform debates let one conclude that the complexity of CFSP, both in scope and procedures, will increase in the late 1990s—an effect that does not necessarily respond to the constant call for greater clarity in the EU and does not promote the support of the populations. Any modification of the existing provisions should also bear in mind the EU's commitment to the applicant countries in Central and Eastern Europe, as well as in the Mediterranean, and should consider what these enlargements could mean for the CFSP.

When and Where Does the Second Pillar Matter?

More interesting than even the general question is the issue: When and where does EPC/CFSP matter? For this purpose, we identify certain factors or characteristics that can be utilized for a "matrix of typology" (see Table 1.1). These factors also assist in elucidating the selection of topics in this book.

A typology: First parameter of the matrix. If "essential European interests"—especially in the regional neighborhood—are involved, then the level of internal interactions in the second pillar framework is high and the output might be innovative in diplomatic terms, but in crisis situations the external effectiveness is widely limited to merely reacting to events. Reasons for explaining this record of EPC/CFSP are:

Table 1.1 Matrix of Typology

Essential European Interests	Consultations in an Institutionalized Framework	Ad Hoc Crisis Management
High	CSCE: Heinrich Schneider	Soviet Union/CIS/Russia: David Allen
	Trans-Atlantic Relations: Roy Ginsberg	Former-Yugoslavia: Geoffrey Edwards
	WEU: Mathias Jopp	
	CEEC: Barbara Lippert	
Low	Political Dialogue: Jörg Monar	Somalia: Patrick Keatinge

1. In the case of "high" foreign politics, member states' interests tend to diverge or, at least, larger member states want to demonstrate their sovereignty.
2. If the "stakes are high," member states still value EPC/CFSP. Since they are not "crisis proof," they like to hide "behind a big brother" (the United States as the hegemon or leader) or at least want to be allied with a strong "winning coalition."
3. In crisis situations concerning "high" politics, procedural inefficiencies are felt more strongly.
4. Earlier failures produce uncertainties about the strength of EPC, which lead to internal distrust, which might eventually lead individual member states to keep traditional channels open. This, in turn, produces a wider credibility gap, which increases the record of failures.

Second parameter of the matrix. If the "management of routine consultations" and activities in "institutional frameworks" (like the UN General Assembly, CSCE/OSCE, or self-induced and self-created group-to-group dialogues like the one with the Central and European countries [CEEC]) are concerned, the record is better. This is also true if a general "policy outline" (with no, or only "soft," implications) is to be formulated. Then EPC/CFSP has been quite useful—for example, the definition of CSCE/OSCE principles, general peace initiatives, and human rights.[26] But a further precondition is important: No high policy interests must be at stake (contrary to subjects discussed within the UN Security Council) and no major divergences among member states must arise.

If the "instruments of the EC" ("first pillar") can be adopted for relations with third countries, the degree of effectiveness will be higher:

"Access" to the EC market and money (ECU [European currency unit] diplomacy) are positive incentives ("carrots"). In this case, there will be a positive spillover for EPC/CFSP.

Reasons explaining the record of EPC/CFSP in this respect are:

1. The EC procedures are generally more efficient insofar as the internal debate about the division of competences can be solved.
2. Offers of that kind are "cheap" for the foreign policy establishment.
3. The EU can demonstrate itself as a "civilian power."
4. The engagement can be fine-tuned in due course.
5. The real costs might be shifted to a later time ("promise now—pay later," if still necessary).

Academic Research—A Triple Performance Check

The "Ivory Tower" Check

In order to have a closer look at academic performance, we use a triple validity check. In the first validity check—the "ivory tower" check—we try to detect the way in which theoretical contributions in this area of analysis may explain the evolution and development of EPC toward the Maastricht stage and to look at what they could offer in terms of further projections and predictions. Following Merton's "middle range theory,"[27] we could expect a useful analysis to explain the process in the EPC since 1970. Contributions of that kind would also help us answer the increasingly relevant question of how to "digest 1989" and the Maastricht Treaty. Are the results of research from the 1970s and the 1980s also applicable in a new environment, or are we on the verge of a totally new paradigm?

A first answer to this check indicates that most generalizations about EPC and CFSP are "static," such as the one calling it a "regime"; but are there no changes from the early 1970s to the middle of the 1990s? At best, we get comparative evaluations. This approach is useful to describe two points between the original EPC and the second pillar of European Union. Even with these generalizations, there are few attempts to identify the major factors that would explain the evolution from EPC toward CFSP (or at least explain why there have been such limited changes) in real performance.

The "Committee Room" and "Public Opinion" Check

In a second validity check—the "marketplace" and "committee room" check—we test how relevant results are for the *public debate* and for *drafting constitutions,* such as the Single European Act or the Maastricht Treaty. Are researchers influencing the *political* agenda?

A first answer to this check is as follows: Political scientists show a remarkable capacity to react to ongoing events in the EU arena ("short reaction lag"). The real impact of academic research on political decisionmaking is, however, not easy to assess.

We might need to have a longer-term view. The development of European affairs, with the multiplication of meetings and the broadening of agenda points, has changed the outlook and, to a certain degree, the constituency of politicians active in this field. Strong national support for a given policy is no longer a sufficient guarantee for that policy to prevail. It also needs to find some degree of acceptance with European partners; otherwise, it is usually doomed to failure. Ensuring such acceptance has, of necessity, become part of the professional duty of European ministers. This most likely explains the considerable increase, in recent years, of the number of conferences or speeches given in foreign European capitals by political decisionmakers of most European countries. A similar increase is observable in the number of interviews given to foreign European newspapers and the number of articles published in learned publications.

In that exercise of external persuasion aimed directly at public opinion in other European countries, politicians cannot easily play on emotions or gut feelings, on national traditions or prejudices that are not theirs and that they therefore do not master. Caution and experience recommend the use of rational arguments and abstract debate, which are easier to communicate across national borders. This, of course, begins to approximate the form and atmosphere of academic debate, and it does seem that political speeches frequently seek inspiration in academic work. How else can one explain the unexpected, triumphant, and ambiguous success of so abstract and academic a concept as "subsidiarity"?

Another example of academic research influencing the political agenda involves the work of the European Parliament. The EP, waging for several years a permanent guerrilla warfare campaign for power and influence against the Council and member states, relies to a considerable degree on expertise coming from independent academic institutions. Now, the effectiveness of parliamentary contributions may be put into doubt, but it is likely to be continuous and increasing, due to changes in the institutional balance brought about by the Treaty of Maastricht.

The "Classroom" Check

Academic debate is also not indifferent to the formation of public opinion. Research spills over into teaching, and the increase in European studies in many universities across the continent, new institutes, and new degrees in Community law or European affairs ensure a wide dissemination of concepts and ideas among the younger generations. Implicit rejection and mistrust of political elites, manifest in most recent elections in Europe, consolidate the influence of the academic community. On television programs university professors are sought after, because they are supposed to have more credibility in the eyes of the average citizen (or televiewer) than politicians have—and, of course, politicians cannot afford to ignore what is said on television programs.

Altogether, academic research related to the foreign policy aspects of European integration has developed considerably over the years. Judging from the number of conferences and publications in Europe, the United States, or elsewhere, the "second pillar" of the Treaty on European Union elicits considerable interest. A small but dedicated academic community has been created, which specializes in this field. Ongoing developments are followed quite closely. Case studies concerning specific areas are numerous and the time lag is short between political decision and academic research or debate.

There is a real, albeit tenuous, link between academic research, decisionmaking, and public opinion. All three sides of this triangle influence each other. In this context, this book was conceived. Some authors come from an academic background; others are active in the foreign policy activities described herein. May their collective effort contribute to a better understanding of a process of considerable importance for the future of European integration.

Notes

1. On an EC/Twelve average 72 percent were in favor of a greater EC responsibility for resolving conflicts in the world. See *Eurobarometer 40* (Brussels: European Commission, 1993), p. 68.

2. William and Mary Lecture given by Prime Minister John Major at the University of Leiden, 7 September 1994. *Press Notice, 10 Downing Street,* p. 9.

3. As called for in the mandate for the IGC negotiations. "European Council Presidency Conclusions," Turin, 29 March 1996, *Agence Europe,* 30 March 1996.

4. See Barbara Lippert's contribution in Chapter 11 of this volume on relations of the EU with Central and Eastern European countries and Jörg Monar's contribution on the political dialogue with third countries and regional political groupings in Chapter 14.

5. For an appraisal of the EU–U.S. relationship, see Roy Ginsberg's Chapter 16 in this volume.

6. See "The Political Agenda for Europe" in the Presidency Conclusions, 15/16 December 1995, *Agence Europe,* 17 December 1995.

7. See Henry Kissinger's "Year of Europe" speech of 23 April 1973, in Heinrich Siegler, *Europäische Politische Einigung II* (Bonn: Siegler & Co., 1973), pp. 320–323.

8. "Die Europäische Union. Bericht von Leo Tindemans an den Europäischen Rat," *Bulletin der Europäischen Gemeinschaften,* Beilage 1/76, pp. 12–13.

9. See Simon Nuttall's contribution in Chapter 2 of this volume on EPC's performance since its inception in 1970 and Günter Burghardt's Chapter 17, analyzing the potential and limits of CFSP.

10. See Christopher Hill, "The Capability-Expectations Gap, or Conceptualizing Europe's International Role," *Journal of Common Market Studies* 3 (September 1993), pp. 305–328.

11. See Fraser Cameron's contribution in Chapter 6 on the European Commission's role and Thomas Grunert's Chapter 7 in this volume on the European Parliament's association with CFSP/EPC.

12. See, in particular, David Allen's contribution in Chapter 12 on the Twelve's policy toward the Soviet Union and the states of the former Soviet Union and Patrick Keatinge's contribution in Chapter 15 of this volume on the Union's role in Somalia.

13. See Siegler, *Europäische Politische Einigung II,* pp. 320–323.

14. For a detailed analysis of the Union's performance in former-Yugoslavia, see especially Geoffrey Edwards's Chapter 10 in this volume.

15. For an appraisal of the creation of the Common Foreign and Security Policy element of the Maastricht Treaty, see Philippe de Schoutheete's contribution in Chapter 3 of this book.

16. For an assessment of the institutional aspects of EPC/CFSP, see Elfriede Regelsberger's contribution in Chapter 4 in this volume.

17. Explicit reference in Art. J.4, 6 on the EU's security and defense identity as well as a general revision clause in Art. J.10.

18. See Elfriede Regelsberger's Chapter 4 in this volume.

19. As to its mandate and first deliberations on CFSP see *Agence Europe,* 30 March 1996 and 8 May 1996, as well as the intermediate report for the Florence European Council in June 1996.

20. See especially Reinhardt Rummel's Chapter 19 in this volume "CFSP and Conflict Prevention: Priorities for the Intergovernmental Conference 1996/1997" in *CFSP Forum* 1 (1996), pp. 4–5.

21. See also Mathias Jopp's Chapter 9 in this volume analyzing the role and performance of WEU.

22. Illustrative here are: *Report of the Reflection Groups,* op, cit., point C; WEU Council of Ministers, *WEU Contribution to the European Union Intergovernmental Conference of 1996,* Madrid, 14 November 1995, point 50 onward.

23. Elfriede Regelsberger and Wolfgang Wessels, "The CFSP Institutions and Procedures: A Third Way for the Second Pillar," in *European Foreign Affairs Review* 1 (1996), pp. 29–54.

24. For details see *Report of the Reflection Group,* Brussels, 5 December 1995, point B.

25. High-level expert group on the CFSP: "European Security Policy Towards 2000: Ways and Means to Establish Genuine Credibility," Brussels, 19 December 1994.

26. For an evaluation of the Twelve's involvement in the CSCE/OSCE, see Heinrich Schneider's contribution in Chapter 13 of this book.

27. See R.K. Merton, *Social Theory and Social Structure* (Glencoe, Ill.: 1949).

Part 1

History:
From EPC to CFSP

2

Two Decades of EPC Performance

Simon Nuttall

The Origins[1]

European Political Cooperation (EPC) was established on 27 October 1970, when the foreign ministers of the European Community adopted the Luxembourg Report. Twenty-three years later, on 1 November 1993, the Treaty on European Union entered into force and so brought into being the successor to EPC, the Common Foreign and Security Policy (CFSP) of the Union.

EPC began as a largely intergovernmental activity. It was part of the political deal at the Hague summit in 1969 that this should be so. France, in particular, was determined that no taint of Community or supranational procedures should sully the pure milk of national foreign policy. This had been a tenet of Gaullism and one that the then French president, Georges Pompidou, found it neither proper, nor politically advisable, to abandon. His successors two decades later took a similar view, and by then the French had been joined by other member states with similar views. Their combined efforts during the Intergovernmental Conference, which led to the signing of the Maastricht Treaty, ensured that the future CFSP, to all intents and purposes, lay firmly within the intergovernmental tradition from which it had arisen.

This intensified the contradiction that had been inherent in EPC throughout its existence but that had become more acute as the Community, and later the Union, extended its original ambitions. Thus, EPC—the victim of its own success—found that it was expected to play an international role to which it had not yet fully adapted. EPC was designed to coordinate national foreign policies; the Union, as its tenets announce, is expected to have a common foreign and security policy. This is difficult to achieve by the intergovernmental method.

Nevertheless, intergovernmentalism could not remain as pure as its hard-line proponents would have liked, and it proved to have an inner dynamism that rapidly produced more significant results than mere "lowest common denominator" positions. The early successes of EPC were considerable and surprised its participants almost as much as those successes surprised the outside world, beginning with the United States. The member states found themselves having to run when they would have preferred to walk, and rather sedately, at that. This, in itself, was a perpetual spur to institutional and practical progress.

Historical Overview[2]

EPC is to be judged on its performance. For that reason alone, giving a historical account of EPC's development and achievements—as they appeared to others no less than as they were viewed from within the system—is a useful exercise. Yet the form these developments and achievements took determined both the evolution of EPC and the shape of the CFSP, as established in the Maastricht Treaty. A knowledge of the past is therefore essential in order to understand the present, let alone to attempt to gaze into the future.

The history of EPC is diffuse,[3] and it seemed to present no recognizable pattern as it occurred. This was the inevitable result of its essentially reactive nature. For the sake of convenience, I have divided it into four broad periods, assigning clearly identifiable characteristics to each. The first one lasted from the early beginnings of EPC in 1970 until roughly halfway through the decade. During this period, EPC succeeded in forging a united position concerning the Conference on Security and Cooperation in Europe (CSCE), which had a significant influence on the way in which that Conference developed. Within a few years of its foundation, EPC was already playing a considerable role in world affairs and had enough influence to help determine how the balance would be struck in East-West relations. Not long afterward, the attempt to adopt a unified and distinctive position on "the Middle East question" had made considerable progress. EPC was never able to go as far and as fast down this road as many people would have liked, in large part because of the braking effect of U.S. political pressure, but a coordinated policy was achieved, which shielded member states from the worst effects of hard-line, pro-Arab or pro-Israeli policies and contributed to safeguarding the Community interest. During the same period, a modus vivendi was found with the United States, the first timid steps were taken in crisis management (Cyprus and "the Spanish question"), and the beginning of a policy that reflected ideals of moral responsibility in the world was seen in the adoption of a Code of Conduct regarding South Africa.

By the end of this first period, EPC had pretty well settled its structure and operating procedures. The concept of Working Groups preparing issues for the Political Committee, which itself had become a decisionmaking forum, responsible to foreign ministers meeting on a regular basis outside the Council framework, had been established. The Group of European Correspondents and the COREU network were both in place, and they played an important managerial role.

The second period lasted through the rest of the decade until 1981 or 1982. It was a dismal time for EPC. Nothing seemed to get accomplished; there were few imaginative initiatives, and, when action was called for, none was taken or it was taken too late (for example, in Afghanistan). There were a number of reasons for this: one was certainly the prevailing morosity in the Community because of the economic downturn; another, more immediately, was France's comparative lack of interest in the process, as President Giscard d'Estaing turned his attention to a wider stage. This stagnation led to two efforts at reviving EPC. The first one was launched in 1980 by Lord Carrington, who was disgusted by the Nine's failure to take decisive action about Afghanistan, which was as much attributable to deficient procedures as to lack of will. By dint of a pragmatic approach and hard negotiating, this led to the adoption of the London Report in October of the following year, which set a new basis for EPC operations for the following six years. A more ambitious attempt in 1981, by Foreign Ministers Genscher and Colombo, petered out after two years' discussions and resulted in the disappointing Stuttgart Solemn Declaration of June 1983.

While not revolutionary, the London Report was useful, in that it provided the opportunity to reaffirm the EPC institutional set-up and codify some of the practices that had come into existence since the Copenhagen Report. Most innovations reflected the Community's increasing prominence on the world stage—the "Troika" mechanism and EPC coordination by diplomatic missions in foreign countries. The peripatetic "Troika" Secretariat was an interesting, but unhappily short-lived, experiment.

The third period saw a revival of activity in EPC, mainly due to the pressure of outside events. In rapid succession, the Ten had to cope with the declaration of martial law in Poland, the invasion of the Falkland Islands, and the invasion of Lebanon by Israel. These challenges were met, at least in part, by the increased readiness of the member states to make use of Community instruments to enforce their foreign policy decisions. These could take the shape of economic sanctions, as were imposed against the Soviet Union and Argentina, or programs of economic assistance, as were created in Central America and South Africa. European Political Cooperation was beginning to have a policy that could be seen in concrete form, not just through declarations, and the interaction between EPC and the Community—which later came to be known in both the Single European Act (SEA) and the Maastricht Treaty as "consistency"—was no longer taboo.

This period was also marked by a deterioration in relations between EPC and the United States, as the Ten found it increasingly difficult to summon up any enthusiasm for the trenchant foreign policies being conducted by the Reagan administration. U.S. policymakers, on their part, regarded the Europeans as a bunch of "wimps" because of their flaccid response to the challenge of international terrorism. The result was tension in East-West relations, in Central America, and because of Libya. Whatever other failures EPC had known, it had certainly succeeded in acquiring a foreign policy personality distinctly different from that of the United States.

The Ten's inability to discuss defense questions meant that they were unable to integrate into European foreign policy making the other great question of the period—and one potentially damaging to trans-Atlantic relations—namely, the question of the installation of Euromissiles. Ireland, Denmark, and Greece were all opposed, for different reasons, to any discussion in EPC of the military aspects of security. Attempts to widen the scope of permitted debate—as, for example, by Germany in the Genscher-Colombo Initiative—failed.

The third period saw the entry into force of the Single European Act,[4] Title III of which first established political cooperation in an act recognized by international law. The provisions of this section of the SEA did little more than consolidate previous EPC practices, but it was significant that they were included in an instrument that also amended the Treaty of Rome. No conclusion had been reached in the debate over whether European foreign policy should stand within or without the European Communities, but no doors had been closed either, and the decision not to conclude a separate treaty on foreign policy cooperation was thought by some to point the way to the future.

The fourth and final period of EPC extended from the second part of 1989, when the great events in Central and Eastern Europe radically changed the features of the political map by which the world had steered its course for more than forty years, until the enactment of the Treaty on European Union. The scale and rapidity of these events proved to be too great for the machinery of EPC to master. The response to the challenge of finding a new form of relationship with other European countries, who were newly emerging from Soviet tutelage, was primarily an economic one, given by the Community and shaped by the Commission. EPC's lot was to follow breathlessly in the wake of events. The absorption of the former East Germany into the Community and the Western world was negotiated either over the heads of EPC, by the Four Powers, or beneath their notice, by the Commission. Not surprisingly, therefore, many took the view that the time had come to jolt EPC out of its intergovernmental ways and integrate it into traditional Community procedures, which included making decisions according to majority vote and providing the Commission with a greater foreign policy role. At the same time, EPC's failure to hold a united position in the later stages of the Gulf crisis—let alone play a military part in the war—combined with the fear of a U.S. withdrawal from Europe, provided a strong incentive to envisage once again an autonomous European defense capability. This formed the background of the foreign policy discussions in the intergovernmental conference that led to the Maastricht Treaty, but when the moment came for making decisions, fear of imminent peril had receded and the instinct to retain national prerogatives at all costs had regained the upper hand.

The negotiations that led up to the Maastricht Treaty and the events of the last period of EPC will be described in more detail in following chapters. The remainder of the present chapter will discuss selected themes from the first three periods of EPC's history, in order to cast light on how it developed and how that development has influenced the CFSP of today.

The CSCE: EPC's Entrance onto the World Stage

EPC was set up just about the time the West was organizing its response to the Soviet initiative, in order to attend a pan-European security conference. At first, the United States did not pay much attention to this initiative; it was preoccupied with the closing stages of the Vietnam War, and Secretary of State Henry Kissinger seemed temperamentally averse to the sort of multilateral diplomacy that such a conference required. Thus, the Europeans had a clear playing field, and they made good use of their opportunity. The work they did, during the five years leading up to the Helsinki Final Act in 1975, set the agenda for the CSCE and largely contributed to its success. This was EPC's debut onto the international stage, and it was widely remarked—the more so, as Aldo Moro, president of the Council, signed the Final Act on behalf of the Community.

The European Community member states had good reason to seize the opportunity that was offered. This course of action was consistent with the desire for détente and the twin-track approach of the Harmel Initiative of the late 1960s, and it was appropriate to the sort of international persona that the Six, and later the Nine, were trying to create. Additionally, it provided a form of insurance policy in the face of their uncertainty about how long and on what conditions the United States would be prepared to stay in Western Europe.

If they had so desired, the member states could have contented themselves with creating a loose coordination of national policies toward the CSCE, in pursuit of a shared objective. That they went further and engaged in a truly collective effort, creating in the process new mechanisms for EPC, can be attributed to two factors. On the political side, Germany was extremely anxious to avoid any suspicion that it was encouraging renewed ties with the countries of Eastern Europe at the expense of its commitment to West European integration. A collective approach toward the CSCE within the European Community was the best defense against mistrust of the *Ostpolitik*. Second, on the procedural side, the expiry at the end of 1972 of the transitional period (during which EC member states' national trade policies toward the state trading countries could be maintained) meant that the Community would, in any case, have to adopt a common policy toward the CSCE insofar as trade policy matters were concerned. The arrangements for coordinating the activities of EPC and of the Community itself were an interesting institutional by-product of the process.

The intensive work carried out in EPC enabled the Nine, in January 1973, to table a paper that, in effect, set a comprehensive draft agenda and mandate for the Conference, thus determining the course of discussions right up to the signing of the Final Act in August 1975. The Nine had achieved their objective of ensuring that the Conference would tackle issues of substance, rather than contenting itself with empty declarations, and that a political section would be balanced by both an economic initiative and a section on human liberties.

The collective nature of the work in EPC had been reinforced by the inclusion of the Commission in a de facto leading role on matters of trade policy and by the allocation of work to different member states in all the complex and technical areas of discussion. If each of the member states had to undertake this preparatory work separately, they would not have been so thoroughly prepared for the ensuing multilateral discussions. The status of the European Community, with a new, enhanced political dimension, was made evident by the number of papers that were tabled collectively and by the fact that at the Helsinki meetings, in both 1973 and 1975, the representative of the presidency announced that, in addition to his national capacity, he was acting on behalf of the Community. No one could miss the arrival of this new international actor.

The Middle East: The Limits to European Action[5]

At the first EPC ministerial meeting in Munich in 1970, the first item on the agenda was the Middle East. It had been put there at the request of France. French diplomacy, under the guidance of General de Gaulle, had been recently converted to the Arab cause. Whereas, in 1956, France had taken part in the Suez operation in support of Israel, by the time of the June War in 1967 Paris was clearly on the Arab side. The general wanted a break with past policy and wanted to be in a better position to defend France's economic interests in the region; but he also wanted a policy that was different from that of the United States.

Other members of the Community had different views. For various reasons, Germany and the Netherlands, in particular, were more inclined to support the Israeli position. This divergence, and the lack of mechanisms for consultation, meant that when the June 1967 war broke out, the Community failed to have any meaningful discussion of the situation—let alone reach a common position—even though there had been a European summit in Rome only a few days before. This failure is considered to have been one of the prime reasons for the renewed resolve of the EC member states to engage in foreign policy consultations among themselves, which led, in due course, to the Hague summit decision.

The discussions at the Munich meeting were therefore bound to be difficult—yet they led within six months to an agreed position (the Schumann Document), which marked the beginning of a distinctive collective position on the Middle East and in which Germany and the Netherlands had significantly adapted their national positions. True, the document had to be laid aside because of premature disclosure, but the principle had been established that the desired outcome of policy consultations was to produce a position (however apparently lacking in substance) upon which all could agree and to which all could commit themselves.

The contents of the Schumann Document were not, in and of themselves, earth-shattering, and they attracted less attention than, for example, the later Venice Declaration. The interest of the exercise remained overwhelmingly domestic, perhaps its most useful feature being that it allowed countries like Germany to bring about a shift in domestic policy, which it considered desirable, under the cover of Community solidarity.

Political cooperation was subjected to a much stiffer test two years later on the outbreak of the October War. The initial reaction came, not from EPC, but from the member states acting separately, the greatest divergence being between the positions of France and the Netherlands. The Arabs reacted by selectively applying their oil embargo only against certain member states. The British and French were "friends" and were treated accordingly; the Dutch, like the U.S. representatives, were "enemies"; and the rest were "neutrals." The Nine realized that this treatment had to be countered by a common action. They issued a statement that represented an advance on the Schumann Document, by referring to the legitimate rights of the Palestinians. The pace was set by the British and the French; the Dutch found it convenient to be able to present this departure from their traditional policy as a gesture to EPC discipline rather than as a bow to Arab pressure. The Arabs took a relatively favorable view of the declaration, and the Community was exempted from the cutback in oil supplies. However, the embargo on oil supplies to the Netherlands was not lifted, and although this was of little practical consequence, the failure to uphold the principle of the free movement of goods throughout the Community caused considerable offense to the Dutch. Community solidarity was not yet an overriding principle.

The relatively new machinery of European Political Cooperation had enabled the Nine to avoid the worst effects of the conflict. It even allowed them to make an initially favorable response to the approach made by the Arabs to the EC summit in Copenhagen in December, offering a cooperative dialogue. This response, however, led the Nine into immediate and serious difficulties with the United States. The United States wanted to engage the Europeans to join their own club of oil consumers and, by presenting a united front, to exert more effective pressure on the Arab producers. They feared that if the Europeans committed themselves to a cooperative dialogue with the Arabs, covering both political and economic questions, they would not only join, in effect, a club of oil producers, but they would also be drawn into policies concerning the Middle East that were incompatible with those the United States wished to pursue.

The United States won. The Euro-Arab Dialogue—which, with much difficulty and after many years, the Nine succeeded in establishing with the Arab League—had no political component and, on the economic side, was confined to relatively innocuous and therefore uninteresting areas of cooperation. The position that had been worked out in political cooperation was a compromise, as was inevitable given the procedures that were followed, and therefore did not inspire the Europeans with sufficient confidence in the rightness of their cause for them to feel able to carry their point against strong U.S. resistance. Even had they been sufficiently confident, it is unlikely that consensus would have been found to insist on maintaining their own position, whether over the Middle East or anything else, once the United States made it plain that to do so would endanger the trans-Atlantic relationship.

The same difficulties were encountered later, when the Nine were preparing the Venice Declaration. Although it was a significant move forward in European policy on the Middle East, the declaration was considerably less bold than had originally been intended, and this was the direct result of U.S. intervention. As long as there seemed to be any life in the Camp David process, EPC policy on the Middle East remained fairly quiescent, although the Europeans did not like being excluded from the process and mistrusted a policy that divided the Arab countries. Only when final disillusionment with Camp David set in did the Nine begin to consider, in the early part of 1980, an initiative of their own. In order to fill what was seen as a dangerous policy gap, they wanted to promote a new UN Security Council Resolution that would include a stronger commitment on the Palestinian issue. In the face of strong U.S. opposition, supported by the Israelis and the Egyptians, the Nine had to moderate their ambitions. The final declaration contained no reference to a new UN Security Council Resolution, and the language used for the role to be played by the Palestinians in the peace process ("association" rather than "participation") had been toned down. As a result, the effect on the Arabs, who knew the original intentions, was not what had been hoped. Once again, the

Europeans found that there were limits to their ability to frame autonomous policies, which they could not ignore without seriously endangering their overall relationship with the United States.

Relations with the United States:
The Trans-Atlantic Dilemma

The implicit trans-Atlantic bargain underlay Henry Kissinger's "Year of Europe" initiative in 1973. Kissinger's purpose was to achieve linkage. In the speech he made in April of that year, President Nixon's national security adviser said, "We will continue to support European unity. . . . We will not disengage from our solemn commitments to our allies. . . . We expect, in return, that their policies will take seriously our policies and our responsibilities." An even more difficult requirement was the U.S. request to be consulted before final positions were adopted by the Europeans. The importance of this can be seen from the example of the previously mentioned Venice Declaration: Had the United States not been informed of the contents of the declaration before final decisions were made, it would not have been able to intervene to secure changes. A further U.S. requirement was that the text in which the form of consultations was to be fixed should be concluded, on the European side, by the member states acting separately and not collectively. The United States had been alarmed by European attempts to make the presidency their sole negotiator and feared that this development would cut off their access to individual states, reducing the possibility of intervening in the EPC process.

The Europeans in EPC were reluctant to concede to U.S. demands. Negotiations were undertaken, and draft was succeeded by counter-draft throughout the year. One year after Kissinger's speech, no agreement had been reached, and meanwhile, relations had become even more difficult because of differences following the October War. The Gordian Knot was cut at the Gymnich meeting in April 1974. The idea of any formal declaration was abandoned. Instead, there was a gentleman's agreement, which was never written down, that was revealed to the public by Foreign Minister Genscher in less-than-opaque terms only two months later and that could be interpreted in a number of ways, depending on how one looked at it. In essence, the agreement was that the United States was to be kept informed by the presidency about the EPC's plans, in sufficient time for the United States to react if it had serious objections.

The vagueness of the Gymnich Agreement meant that its application was variable, but for the time being it satisfied U.S. needs. As time went by, the United States pressed for contacts with EPC at levels below that of the Political Committee, to which they had, on French insistence, long been confined. By the mid-1980s, the Europeans were also concerned about the decline of the U.S.-European relationship as a result of frequent differences in policy during the Reagan years. At the European initiative, regular Troika meetings of political directors were instituted in 1986, and other contacts were strengthened. The Twelve still hesitated, however, to agree to contacts at the Working Group level. These were not accepted until four years later, and the whole relationship was put on a formal footing, with the addition of regular summit meetings, by the Transatlantic Declaration of November 1990. The collapse of the Communist regimes in Central and Eastern Europe had succeeded where seventeen years previously, against a background of East-West tension, Kissinger had failed.

Crisis Management: From Cyprus to Poland

In the early days, political cooperation chose its own agenda. The selection of the CSCE and the Middle East as areas for cooperation among the Six was a deliberate political choice. This controlled and selective approach to foreign policy could not last. Before long, the growing international persona of EPC obliged it to react to crises. The first important test (barring the previously discussed October War) was the Cyprus coup in July 1974.

When Archbishop Makarios was overthrown in a coup mounted by Nikos Sampson with the support of the Greek Colonels, EPC immediately issued a statement of support for the independence and territorial integrity of Cyprus and their opposition to any intervention or interference that tended to put this into question. The presidency was asked to bring this position to the attention of the governments concerned. In so doing, EPC not only condemned the coup, it warned both Greece and Turkey against intervening in the situation. When, nevertheless, Turkish troops landed in Cyprus five days later, EPC diplomacy remained active and certainly contributed to bringing about a ceasefire. The Community was less successful subsequently in dealing with the situation. Part of the reason lay in its unwillingness, or its institutional inability, to throw its relationship with Greece, Turkey, and Cyprus into the balance by deploying the Association Agreements with those countries. More important was the abandonment of a neutral stance between Greece and Turkey, when Greece applied to join the Community following the collapse of the Colonels' regime. Whatever the deficiencies of this long-term viewpoint and policy, however, the Nine's immediate reaction to the crisis had been rapid, efficient, and comparatively effective.

These qualities did not distinguish EPC's handling of the condemnation and subsequent execution of five Basque terrorists by the Spanish authorities in the summer of 1975. When EPC's tardy and hesitant demarche asking Spain for a reprieve on humanitarian grounds was ignored, the Nine had great difficulty in coordinating their reaction and ended up withdrawing their ambassadors from Madrid in some disorder, which did nothing for their image as a foreign policy making body. Similar confusion was created the following year when the Nine were unable to agree on a coordinated recognition of the MPLA government in Angola.

Why did political cooperation sometimes succeed in crisis management and sometimes not? One crucial prerequisite was that the member states had to find themselves in agreement on policy before coordination started. This was the case concerning Cyprus, where the Nine had no difficulty in unanimously condemning the coup and the subsequent Turkish invasion. This was not the case with the Basque terrorists. Certain member states had been hesitant to respond to the Dutch call for a European initiative, with the result that the demarche came late and lacked conviction. A further element was whether or not EPC had a properly worked out plan. This existed in the case of Cyprus: EPC swung its weight behind the British government's policy of getting the Greeks and Turks to the negotiating table. In the case of the Basque terrorists, since the member states had not agreed upon the aims, it is not surprising that they were not in agreement on the means and that their action therefore lacked coherence. This was the drawback of a policy process whose main virtue was to paper over the cracks. Finally, procedure played its part. The French presidency, which was in office at the time of the Cyprus coup, took immediate action in order to issue a statement the following day, and when the Turks invaded Cyprus a few days later, the ambassadors of the Nine in Paris were summoned to the French Foreign Ministry to facilitate an immediate decision on the appropriate reaction. The Italian presidency at the time of the Basque affair did not follow this course. Instead, it sought consensus by COREU (the EPC telex network), which was inevitably time-consuming and devoid of the dynamism that could only be provided, in a consensus system, by face-to-face contact.

As time passed, EPC's capacity to respond to unexpected international events evolved.[6] The response was sometimes hesitant, either because the decisionmaking process was defective or because the member states preferred to put off a difficult decision, but there was a growing realization that membership in European Political Cooperation carried with it a responsibility to take a position and, preferably, to act. It was thought that failure to do this displayed weaknesses in the system. Three examples of crisis management are the Iran hostage affair, the Soviet invasion of Afghanistan, and the declaration of martial law in Poland. These demonstrate the way in which EPC's approach developed.

When U.S. embassy staff in Teheran were taken hostage in November 1979, the United States at first sought international support in order to persuade the Iranian government to release the hostages and then, when this proved to be ineffective, to impose economic sanctions. After a UN Security Council Resolution had been vetoed by the Soviet Union, the United States applied unilateral sanctions and expected their allies to do likewise.

These moves embarrassed the Nine. Although they had no difficulty in condemning the Iranian action, they were divided on the advisability of sanctions and delayed in making a decision. France and Denmark were, in any case, opposed in principle to applying Community sanctions, and in the end consensus could be reached only on the adoption of sanctions by each member state acting individually. The credibility of this position was further impaired by the failure, at first, of the U.K. Parliament to adopt the necessary measures.

Whether or not EPC's response to the Iran hostage crisis is to be considered a failure depends on the view taken of the merits of the case. The delays were caused, not by inadequate consultation procedures, but by understandable uncertainty about the extent to which it would be proper to give way to U.S. pressure. In fact, the evolving position of the Nine was followed with intense interest by other countries who were similarly subjected to U.S. diplomacy, and in many cases, it was used as a model. The Japanese foreign minister even made a pilgrimage to Luxembourg to meet European foreign ministers before solidifying the final position of his country.

The case of Afghanistan was very different. Here EPC was caught off guard. Soviet forces invaded Afghanistan on Boxing Day 1979. European Political Cooperation had practically closed down for the holidays, and the presidency was in the process of passing from Ireland to Italy. An attempt to fix a common position by COREU was unsuccessful, with the result that the member states responded separately, and with considerable differences of emphasis, to the demarches made to them between Christmas and the New Year to justify the Soviet action. The incoming Italian presidency did not act quickly, and the ministers in January did little more than condemn the invasion and adopt some housekeeping decisions that would affect the Community. It was not until February 1980 that EPC decided on a significant diplomatic initiative—a guarantee of the permanent neutrality of Afghanistan in exchange for the withdrawal of Soviet troops. Although this was turned down by the Soviet Union, as was EPC's proposal a year later for an international conference, it was favorably received by the Third World and the Islamic world and it considerably enhanced the reputation of political cooperation. The success of the initiative with the Soviet Union was never certain, but it would have had a far better chance if the Nine had struck while the iron was hot, in the days immediately after the invasion. They had been let down by the lack of a mechanism to deal with crises and the absence of institutionalized responsibility for foreseeing them and proposing an appropriate response.

The debacle of the Afghanistan affair spurred the member states into reviewing the functioning of political cooperation. The British had attempted such a move the previous year, in order to prepare for Greek enlargement, but the attempt had foundered in the face of French indifference or active opposition. Now the discussions were more successful and led to the adoption of the London Report in October 1981. This contained several provisions designed to prevent a repetition of the Afghanistan mistakes and, in particular, to put the Ten in a better position to deal with crises. These included the commissioning of studies to make possible a longer term approach, instead of reacting to world events as they occurred; the setting up of the peripatetic "Troika" Secretariat, which was later superseded by the EPC Secretariat that was established by the Single European Act, only to be subsumed into the Council Secretariat under the provisions of the Treaty on European Union; the possibility for the presidency to delegate certain tasks to its successor or to request its predecessor to complete tasks already begun (not surprisingly, this facility was never availed of); the setting up of a "crisis procedure" whereby the Political Committee or ministers could be called together within forty-eight hours; and an encouragement to Working Groups to analyze areas of potential crisis and to prepare a range of possible reactions.

The machinery for long-term planning scarcely worked at all, partly because of the apparent inability of most foreign ministry machines to succeed at this activity and partly because no permanent body was given responsibility for seeing that it was done. The crisis mechanism proved to be inadequate almost immediately, when the Ten found themselves to be in similar difficulties concerning Poland as they had been in two years earlier concerning Afghanistan.

In 1981 public support for Solidarity had reached a high level, at the same time that the economic situation was rapidly worsening. Intervention by the Soviet Union was widely feared, and, while the Community was promising a limited degree of aid and was warning the Soviet Union against engagement, NATO planning concentrated on the Western response to possible Soviet military action. As it turned out, the Polish government itself imposed martial law, a scenario for which the West was unprepared.

The timing was particularly inconvenient for political cooperation. Martial law was announced on 13 December 1981, and thousands of Solidarity supporters were arrested. The Ten had practically no time to prepare their position. The Political Committee was meeting on 14–15 December and had to prepare a declaration for ministers to issue immediately. Under the circumstances, it was not surprising that the declaration temporized. The situation was complicated in the following weeks by the strong pressure exerted by the United States toward applying sanctions. This course of action was resisted by Germany, in particular, which wished to save as much as possible of the policy of détente.

Matters came to a head during the Christmas holidays. It proved impossible to hold a special meeting of ministers, in spite of the brand-new crisis mechanism that had been adopted only two months earlier, and the meeting of political directors had to be described as "unofficial" in order to be held at all. The reluctance to meet was not procedural; since the Ten did not know which line to take, they naturally preferred not to meet.

Only at a special meeting on 4 January did ministers edge toward a line of action, and even then, a decision on imposing sanctions was postponed for further discussion in the Community. That body proved to have greater flexibility than EPC, and the urgent need to respond to the situation, and to U.S. pressure, meant that the opposition of countries such as Denmark to the Community's taking action on foreign policy issues could no longer be sustained. Sanctions were applied to the Soviet Union by Council Regulation. This proved to be an extremely important precedent. The ice was broken; the rigid separation between EPC and the Community was relaxed, and in the future, Community instruments could be employed for the implementation of foreign policy goals. This new technique was put to significant use during the Argentinian invasion of the Falkland Islands, in the case of South Africa, at the outbreak of the Gulf War, and as a response to civil war in former-Yugoslavia.

Central America: The Ten Between East and West

Latin America had not traditionally been an area of great interest for EPC. Active policy involvement only began after the election of President Mitterrand in 1981, followed by the installation of a socialist government in France. Regis Debray was an adviser in the Elysée, and Claude Cheysson, who previously, as EC commissioner, had done his best to develop the North-South dialogue, became foreign minister of France. Subsequently, German foreign minister Genscher was convinced of the need for Europe to be more active in Central America, and the combined force of France and Germany ensured that there was an active and substantial European policy, even though other member states had doubts and qualms—especially when the course driven by EPC met with objections from the United States.

The basic philosophical difference between European and U.S. approaches was the degree of tolerance for Marxism as a system. The Ten took the view that bad social and economic conditions provided fertile ground for the growth of communism and that the proper course was to tackle the root of the problem. The United States, especially in the early years of the Reagan administration, took the more simplistic view that communism was wrong and had to be rooted out wherever it appeared, by force if necessary. The two approaches were illustrated by statements made almost simultaneously in June 1983. The European Council in Stuttgart, in a definitive policy statement, declared that "the problems of Central America cannot be solved by military means, but only by a political solution springing from the region itself and respecting the principles of non-interference and inviolability of frontiers." At the same time, President Reagan said: "We must not listen to those who would disarm our friends and allow Central America to be turned into a string of anti-American Marxist dictatorships."

The Ten, caught up by the logic of their analysis, now had to decide how to translate their words into deeds. It was Genscher, with the support of Cheysson, who pushed through the idea of an agreement between the Community and the countries of Central America, along the lines of the agreement with ASEAN but with a strengthened political dialogue. It was argued that the Central American countries would have to organize themselves on a regional basis in order to have a dialogue with the Ten, and that this would, in itself, be a factor of stability. The support for regional integration was an important element in the policy of the Ten, who were inclined by experience to believe that the Community's own experiment along those lines could be beneficial if transplanted to other regions.

The first EC–Central America Conference to discuss this approach was held in San José in September 1984. It was marked by strong tension between the Europeans and the U.S. participants, who intervened heavily behind the scenes to discourage the Ten from pursuing their policy. The Community's point of view was stated most clearly by EC commissioner Pisani, who said: "It is only if this Central American solidarity asserts and organizes itself that the danger of external intervention feared by all can really be removed." To many, the external intervention referred to could equally have come from the United States as from the Soviet Union.

To conclude an agreement with the Central Americans was not enough; the Ten also had to find money to contribute toward improving the economic and social conditions of the region. Here the difficulties began; the only practicable source was the Community budget, and a tough negotiation was necessary before funds could be made available. The discussion was complicated by disagreement on "conditionality," although the term had not yet come into common usage. Should Nicaragua benefit from Community aid or not, as long as it had a Marxist regime? A compromise was reached whereby aid was effectively provided, although Nicaragua was not specifically mentioned as a beneficiary.

The amount of aid provided by the Community was probably not enough to have an appreciable impact on the political situation. Nevertheless, the effort required from the Central American countries to prepare their encounters jointly with the Community and the cover given by the Community to Latin American efforts to work out a solution without the intervention of the great powers were undeniably positive contributions. Above all, the Ten provided a respectable point of reference that enabled the countries of the region to avoid having to choose between the United States and the Soviet Union.

The Falkland Islands: Community Solidarity[7]

When Argentina invaded the Falkland Islands in April 1982, it did not immediately occur to the British authorities to seek action by the European

Community in support of their cause. Admittedly, the Ten quickly issued a statement condemning the armed intervention and calling for Argentinian withdrawal, but the request for support for trade sanctions, launched in the United Nations, was addressed to Britain's EC partners individually rather than to the Community as a whole. British action in the Community was confined to calling for measures to prevent the circumvention of national measures taken by member states under Article 224 of the Treaty.

It was the Commission, with the support of the Belgian presidency, that suggested that the Community should adopt sanctions as such, based on Article 113 of the Treaty (the common commercial policy). This would not only safeguard Community competence, it would avert the confused situation that would inevitably arise concerning the circulation of goods within the Community, if member states adopted national trade restrictive measures that were bound to differ in detail. The Commission also had in mind the requirements of Community solidarity, given that the Falkland Islands were "a British territory linked to the Community," to which the provisions of Part IV of the Treaty applied.

While there was considerable support for sanctions and a desire to display solidarity with the United Kingdom, member states differed on the propriety of using a Community instrument to achieve this aim. These differences did not appear in public, however, and when the Community imposed sanctions a fortnight after the invasion, the impact was considerable. The sanctions were not retroactive and were lifted on the termination of hostilities, so their direct effect on trade was probably small, but the psychological effect was considerable, and they are reported to have influenced the attitude of banks toward their Argentinian creditors.

The effect of the action in EPC, following so closely the imposition of sanctions on the Soviet Union, considerably strengthened the image of the Community as an effective foreign policy making body. This image was only partially impaired by the subsequent disintegration of the consensus when the sanctions, which initially had been introduced for one month, were due to be renewed. The Ten had assumed that the situation would not come to war and that the intensive diplomatic efforts that had been undertaken to reach a peaceful solution, through the mediation of the United States, would be successful. When these hopes were disappointed, and especially after the sinking of the *General Belgrano,* member states began to set less store by Community solidarity and to pay more attention to their domestic concerns. Ireland and Italy, in particular, had difficulties—Ireland because of the deteriorating relationship between Irish prime minister Charles Haughey and Margaret Thatcher over Northern Ireland, as well as genuine indignation over the sinking of the *Belgrano,* and Italy because of electoral pressure from the large community of people of Italian origin in Argentina. When these two member states withdrew from the Community sanctions, Denmark had no choice but to follow suit, given the national resistance to political action by what was seen as an exclusively economic Community.

Although it would be going too far to suggest that British intransigence over agricultural prices was a contributory factor, there was certainly a feeling that the United Kingdom was pocketing EC solidarity over the Falklands and giving precious little in return. The difficulty was compounded by a relaxation of U.K. diplomatic effort away from its EC partners, giving the impression that their support was taken for granted. This had a negative effect.

No other event, on the scale of the Falklands, that called for Community solidarity occurred in the history of EPC. EPC's reaction can therefore, with difficulty, be considered a precedent. There were, however, some lessons to be learned from the situation, the principal one being that solidarity is a two-way street and that support received has to be recompensed by support given.

South Africa: A Case of Conscience[8]

Public opinion in the Western world throughout the 1970s and 1980s condemned the system of apartheid in South Africa. It cost European Political Cooperation nothing to follow suit. Difficulties arose, however, when pressure mounted for EPC to move from words to action. The pressure came, in particular, from member states whose economic stake in the country was not so great as to provide an effective counterpressure. It was resisted by those member states who were in the reverse position—Britain, France, Germany, and Portugal. The main issue over which the member states disagreed was the question of whether to impose an embargo—first on arms and later a wider economic embargo.

The first direct action taken by EPC was triggered in 1977 by the need for the Nine to take a common position at the UN Conference on Apartheid to be held in Lagos in August of that year. The proximate cause, while not significant in itself, is noteworthy because it showed that the expectation that the success of the political cooperation process had engendered—that the Nine would take a common position in international conferences—itself served as a stimulus toward harmonizing national foreign policy positions that themselves lay far apart. On this occasion, it became obvious that the Nine would not be able to agree on an embargo. Rather than go to Lagos with a weak diplomatic position, the Nine gratefully accepted the suggestion made by the British and German foreign ministers, David Owen and Hans-Dietrich Genscher, of a Code of Conduct governing the behavior of European firms in South Africa, modeled on that which had been introduced previously, on a national basis, by the British government.

Opinions differ as to the effectiveness of the Code of Conduct in bringing about change in South Africa, whether in the conditions of employment of black workers or in the policy of the government. It is nevertheless certain that the code did make some contribution—that the overall positive effect was greater than if it had not been adopted—and that it would not have existed had it not been for the pressure exerted by the political cooperation process. It also provided a vivid demonstration of what throughout its history was a principal feature of EPC—namely, that the policies adopted were not those most adapted to the circumstances, but those on which the member states succeeded in agreeing. In other words, EPC was essentially an inward- not an outward-oriented process. This naturally gave rise to tensions and misunderstandings on the part of third country partners, who expected the European Community to produce something more like a national foreign policy but on a larger scale.

Although the Netherlands, in particular, continued to press for further restrictive measures, the Code of Conduct acted for many years as a lightning rod against the need to take additional action. It was not until 1984 that increasing violence in South Africa made a further response unavoidable, and the turning point came when the South African government declared a state of emergency in July 1985. It took over a year thereafter to put together a definitive package that combined "restrictive measures" (economic sanctions) and "positive measures" (a program of assistance managed by the European Commission to benefit the victims of apartheid).

It is even more difficult to determine the effect of this package than it was in the case of the Code of Conduct. The Ten were not alone in applying sanctions, and the changes that came about in South Africa can be attributed, if at all, only to the cumulative effect of the disapproval of the world community as a whole. In a negative sense, it may be said that if the Community had not joined in this global effort, the impact would have been considerably lessened. At the same time, the Community was a safe model for other countries, which reasoned that whatever the Community, with all its procedural difficulties, was able to agree on must be a reliable course of action for individual third countries exposed to conflicting pressures. This was certainly true in the case of Japan, which modeled its sanctions on those of the Community.

The benefits of the "positive measures" were more obvious, although paradoxically, because they were managed by the Commission without "political" interference by the member states. Again, Japan chose to use the Kagiso Trust, a body that had been established at the urging of the Commission to act as a channel for the distribution of aid, for its own aid program in South Africa.

EPC's policy in South Africa is particularly interesting because it marked the beginning of a greater receptivity to the pressure of public opinion in the field of foreign affairs, given greater resonance through the activity of one or two particularly determined member states operating within the framework of EPC. The imposition of sanctions could have been justified on realpolitik criteria only in the very long term; in the short and medium terms, it was probably against the economic interests of the member states of the

Community. They were nevertheless driven to make these decisions because of the way in which the EPC machinery operated. This marked the beginning of a policy switch toward "conditionality" and a willingness to allow human rights considerations and concern for democratic rule to play a much greater part in the councils of political cooperation.

Defense

Political cooperation traditionally did not deal with questions of security, let alone defense. There were different reasons for this. Memories of the collapse of the European Defense Community, and the reasons for it, were still alive; after the first enlargement, the United Kingdom strengthened the camp of those countries that opposed autonomous European defense arrangements in case these should be seen as being in opposition to NATO, and Ireland remained a neutral country (although for domestic rather than international reasons); after the second enlargement, the hostility between Greece and Turkey meant that discussions on security would be even more complicated.

The reality was more complex. Although the member states did not discuss security openly in EPC, they came with a baggage of positions on defense and security issues, which colored their discussions on other topics that supposedly had no defense connotations. These positions were almost invariably conditioned by the attitudes of the member states toward the superpowers and, in particular, the view they took of the East-West conflict.

Thus, whereas policy on détente was decided in NATO and was backed up by the twin-track decision, the European NATO members' position was further developed in EPC, beginning with the work done on the CSCE. This, in turn, had a negative influence on discussions in NATO. The Ten's concern about the East-West policy of the Reagan administration was reflected in the policies adopted—or not adopted—in EPC on, for example, Afghanistan, Poland, and the shooting down of a Korean airliner—not to mention the attacks on Grenada and Libya. Indeed, European Political Cooperation congratulated itself on having contributed by its actions to bringing about the resumption of disarmament negotiations between the United States and the Soviet Union in January 1985.

This greater flexibility in practice than was apparent from the official texts had its limits, however. Some member states had hoped, or feared, that building on the experience of the CSCE, EPC would be chosen as the forum for the coordination of positions for the Conference on Disarmament in Europe (CDE) beginning in 1984 in Stockholm. In fact, this had to be done in NATO. Two years later, the Ten had strong views on the outcome of the Reykjavik Summit, at which President Reagan had come within a hairsbreadth of giving away the Euromissiles over the heads of the Europeans;

however, they were institutionally prevented from giving expression to these views. The limitations appeared most clearly when it came to drafting texts that governed the objectives and scope of political cooperation. What the member states could get away with behind closed doors, and sometimes even in public declarations, they could not commit themselves to in documents that provided the quasi-legal basis for their activities.

Thus it was that the London Report of 1981 confined itself to referring to the "political aspects" of security, in order not to create difficulties for Ireland. Two years later, Foreign Minister Genscher's attempt to provide the Community with a security dimension failed; the Solemn Declaration of Stuttgart merely referred to the "political and economic aspects of security." Neither of these formulations had any noticeable influence on what was actually discussed in EPC. The failure at Stuttgart did, however, lead to the first revival of Western European Union (WEU). Again, the question of security was one of the most thorny to be discussed in preparation for the Single European Act. Because of the opposition, for different reasons, of Ireland, Denmark, and Greece, closer cooperation in the field of security had to be limited to those states that so desired it and within the framework of WEU or the Atlantic Alliance.

The inability of political cooperation to take a position consistently and openly on defense questions gave the corpus of foreign policy that it elaborated a special nonmilitary tone that distinguished it from the national foreign policies of the member states. This was seen to be either an advantage or a disadvantage, depending upon one's point of view. It was increasingly seen to be a disadvantage in the unstable period following the collapse of the Communist regimes in Central and Eastern Europe, as the Gulf War broke out, and when civil war intensified in Yugoslavia. The old taboos were finally abandoned in the Treaty on European Union.

Conclusions

After twenty years of experience, EPC stood on the threshold of the negotiations that were to lead to the Treaty on European Union. Those years of experience could not be ignored. A whole generation of European diplomats had been reared in a climate of opinion that took the European dimension of national foreign policy making as something normal and desirable. Positions were adjusted to take into account those of the European partners.[9]

Perhaps even more important, an extensive foreign policy machinery had been built up.[10] There were innumerable meetings of Working Groups and of the political directors, the ambassadors of the Twelve in foreign countries met regularly, and the number of COREU telegrams that were exchanged escalated. Participation in these activities was routine, as was the regular obligation to take on the by now extensive duties of the presidency.

The principle of consensus that governed the system had been attenuated by its practice. Increasing readiness, and indeed compulsion, to make use of Community instruments was leading to a de facto amalgam between the intergovernmental and the integrationist systems.[11] For the practitioners of EPC, this was the way European foreign policy should be run.

Since it was these same practitioners who were for the most part in charge of the Maastricht negotiations, it comes as no surprise that they endeavored to perpetuate the system with which they were familiar and that attempts to introduce a substantial revision of it were defeated. How that came about is described Chapter 3.

Notes

1. David Allen, Reinhardt Rummel, and Wolfgang Wessels, eds., *European Political Cooperation* (London: Butterworths, 1982).

2. Simon Nuttall, *European Political Co-operation* (Oxford: Clarendon Press, 1992).

3. For an insider's view see Philippe de Schoutheete, *La Cooperation politique europeenne,* 2d ed. *(*Brussels, 1986).

4. Jean De Ruyt, *L'Acte unique europeen* (Brussels: Edition de l'Université de Bruxelles, 1987).

5. Ilan Greilsammer and Joseph Weiler, *Europe's Middle East Dilemma. The Quest for a United Stance* (Boulder: Westview, 1987). Panayiotis Ifestos, *European Political Cooperation* (Aldershot: Avebury, 1987).

6. Alfred Pijpers, Elfriede Regelsberger, and Wolfgang Wessels, eds., *European Political Cooperation in the 1980s* (Dordrecht: Martinus Nijhoff Publishers, 1988). Reinhardt Rummel, ed., *The Evolution of an International Actor* (Boulder: Westview, 1990).

7. Geoffrey Edwards, "Europe and the Falklands Crisis," *Journal of Common Market Studies* 4 (June 1984), pp. 295–313.

8. Martin Holland, *The European Community and South Africa* (London: Pinter, 1988).

9. See also Christopher Hill, ed., *National Foreign Policies and European Political Co-operation* (London: Allen and Unwin, 1983).

10. Also toward third countries and groupings. See Geoffrey Edwards and Elfriede Regelsberger, eds., *Europe's Global Links* (London: Pinter, 1990).

11. Alfred Pijpers, *The Vicissitudes of European Political Cooperation* (Unpublished, 1990).

3

The Creation of the Common Foreign and Security Policy

Philippe de Schoutheete de Tervarent

Origins and Background

As it was in the negotiations leading up to the Treaty of Maastricht the wish to establish (in what was to become Title V) the principles, the method, and a draft outline of the means of a Common Foreign and Security Policy (CFSP) was a response to the collective challenges facing Europe at the end of the 1980s—or, at least, to the challenges as they were perceived by European leaders at that time. It is necessary to underline this point because, as events unfolded and, in particular, as the Community's inability to find a convincing and effective way of intervening in the Yugoslav drama became evident, certain observers were led to believe that the Twelve had pointlessly engaged themselves in a purely verbal and rhetorical description of an enterprise that was ambitious, vain, and without any real significance. For these critics, the effort quite obviously exceeded the strength and cohesion of the Twelve. I note that such a critical analysis, which to my mind is excessive, implies that the Twelve should intervene, or should be able to intervene, in any crisis within their geographical area. Without such an implied notion, the criticism would be meaningless. In fact, it was just the need to take on new international responsibilities, and therefore to be able to intervene, that induced several European governments to recommend that a common foreign and security policy be instated. With hindsight, the response manifested in the Treaty may seem inadequate, but the challenge was well perceived by member states, and the fact that an effort was made to meet it should be welcomed and not criticized.

In European circles, the psychological climate toward the end of the 1980s was distinctly optimistic. On the one hand, the internal market was becoming a reality, and its logical extension—economic and monetary union, which had always been a distant goal—was now on the verge of

41

being effectively negotiated. On the other hand, the collapse of communism was leading to the emergence of democratic governments in Central and Eastern Europe, which looked to the Community with great expectations. The institutional framework of Western Europe was seen as a model and a success story. The Twelve were the main source of aid and inspiration that would enable Central and Eastern European countries (CEEC) to manage the difficult transition to democracy and a market economy. Everything seemed to point to the Community gradually taking upon itself the role of a major regional power—even if, in fact, it quite possibly did not wish to do so. This trend was confirmed at the highest level, since, at the 1988 Paris summit of the industrialized countries (G7), the Community—that is, the European Commission—was entrusted with the coordination of the whole of Western aid to the CEEC. Of course, this basic optimism was not free from anxiety: How were the reunification of Germany and the new situation in Eastern Europe to be handled? What changes should be made to the institutional framework of the European Community in order to enable it to play the role of a major European power? How many new powers would be necessary for how many new responsibilities?[1]

Speaking at the College of Europe, in Bruges, in October 1989, President Delors said: "We can assume the international responsibilities only through an accelerated deepening of the Community approach, thus facilitating the emergence of a Grand Europe."[2] As is often the case, the president of the Commission expressed a sentiment fairly widely held in political circles in member states. Jacques Delors was not alone in thinking that the mechanisms of European Political Cooperation (EPC), pragmatically developed over twenty years, were meritorious, useful, but insufficient to meet the challenges of the 1990s. As Sir Leon Brittan put it, political cooperation currently lacks bite: "Europe talked while Bosnia burned."[3] Moreover, the traditional separation between EPC and Community activity was growing more cumbersome as the Twelve were gradually taking up a more obviously political role, especially in Eastern Europe. Examples of inconsistency in the way the two branches of European activity were operating became notorious. A case in point was when foreign ministers, meeting in New York within the format of EPC, decided to impose a trade embargo on Haiti—only to establish a few weeks later, when meeting in Council in Brussels, that such a measure was contrary to the General Agreement on Tariffs and Trade (GATT) and the Lomé Agreements.

In the development of European Political Cooperation, it has frequently been the case that external circumstances became the root cause of further and, at times, decisive progress in the established procedures. Such external pressures very often strengthen the internal logic that, in the course of the years, has tended to narrow the gap between Community affairs and EPC. When, on the basis of the Delors report, the Community was on the point of beginning a negotiation on economic and monetary union, which could ultimately lead to a common monetary policy and a single currency, there were many who called for a strengthening of Europe's political structure. A country's currency, its foreign affairs, and its security have always been considered the pillars of national sovereignty. Now that one of these pillars might perhaps be managed in common, what about the others? The German government was not the only one to ask whether economic and monetary union should not have a counterpart in the political sphere.

The Irish Presidency: The Launching of an IGC

In this general atmosphere, the Belgian government published a memorandum on 21 March 1990 calling for a new look at the Community's institutions.[4] Referring to the motivations underlying the internal development of the Community, its democratic deficit, and external challenges, the document set forth a number of practical proposals to be discussed either on the occasion of the intergovernmental conference (IGC) that was called to deal with economic and monetary union, or in a parallel conference. Foreign policy was not the only, or even the principal, subject covered by the memorandum, but it did constitute an important part. Firmly stressing the problems of Central and Eastern Europe, the Belgian government noted that "in international affairs a truly common foreign policy is required more urgently than ever before" and that "the Community should participate as a political entity in the discussion of these affairs." The paper suggested that the General Affairs Council should once again become the hub of the Community's political decisionmaking by providing a "common framework" for Community action, European Political Cooperation, and the member governments. To this end, it recommended greater cooperation between the Committee of Permanent Representatives (COREPER) and the Political Committee. Finally, it demanded "that it should be possible to discuss, without restriction, questions concerning security in the broadest sense." Several provisions in the Treaty of Maastricht were to give substance to these initial ideas.

The Belgian Memorandum, drawn up after discreet contact had been made with various capitals, was an attempt at putting into practical terms a number of ideas that were afloat in European circles. If it met with considerable initial approval, that is because it answered expectations widely shared among member states. It also served another purpose, which was to show that political initiative does not necessarily originate in the larger member states—a point that Belgian diplomacy frequently tries to make. The memorandum was immediately backed, in general terms, by the Dutch, Spanish, and Italian governments and benefited from a favorable comment on the part of President Mitterrand. The document appeared in time for the special European Council that the Irish presidency had called on 28 April

1990 in Dublin for the discussion of German reunification and the Community's relations with the other European countries.

Some days before this, on 19 April 1990, President Mitterrand and Chancellor Kohl addressed a joint message to the Irish presidency, stating their aim of speeding up the political construction of the Europe of the Twelve.[5] Their letter stressed democratic legitimation, efficiency of the institutions, unity, and coherence in common action, which also figured in the Belgian Memorandum. It further set out:

- An aim, that is, the definition and implementation of a common foreign and security policy
- A procedure, that is, the convocation of an intergovernmental conference parallel with that on European monetary union
- A timetable, that is, the entry into effect of the economic and monetary, as well as the political, union on 1 January 1993

The two documents (i.e., the Belgian Memorandum and the Mitterrand-Kohl message), which were laid before the April 1990 European Council in Dublin, were complementary and were, in fact, referred to in the Council's conclusions as the papers on which future discussion should be based. However, as the skepticism of at least one member state, the United Kingdom, had been publicly proclaimed, the European Council limited itself, at this first stage, to requesting the foreign ministers to give "most careful consideration" to the question of whether modifications to the treaty were necessary. Extreme caution did not exclude ambitious long-term perspectives since the conclusions also reaffirmed the commitment of the European Council to political union and support for a dynamic evolution of the Community.

Two months later, the European Council, meeting once again in Dublin, on 25 and 26 June 1990, decided to call an intergovernmental conference on political union for 14 December 1990, thereby catching up on the conference on economic and monetary union that was already scheduled. The European Council added that a thorough dialogue should be established with the European Parliament and that the General Affairs Council should ensure proper cohesion between the work done by the two IGCs. The decision of the European Council was based on a report submitted by the foreign ministers, prepared by the Political Committee and COREPER, which made use of various national contributions in order to complement the initial Belgian initiative and the Mitterrand-Kohl letter. The political atmosphere in the Community was under the influence of German reunification and deep changes in Eastern Europe; there seemed to be an evident need for Europe to be more proactive, more operational, in the field of foreign affairs. This idea was gaining support and credibility even in countries, such as Denmark, that were traditionally opposed to initiatives of this kind.

None of the national contributions presented in the first half of 1990 contained any explicit or detailed solutions for the problems to which the novel concept of a "common foreign and security policy" gave rise. In particular, there was no further Franco-German contribution to flesh out or elucidate the letter of 19 April 1990. The section of the foreign ministers' report that dealt with this new ambition therefore largely took the form of questions listing the problems raised by this new concept. Among these were the field of application (including the security dimension), the decisionmaking process, and the role to be played by Community institutions. These three issues were indeed to dominate the debate that, a year and a half later, was to lead to the Treaty of Maastricht.

There can be no doubt that the two European Councils held in Dublin under the Irish presidency gave a powerful impulse to the political *relance* of the Community, thereby reflecting the optimism then prevalent in European political circles. This dynamic impulse was, at the time, clearly perceived by public opinion. Flora Lewis wrote in the *Herald Tribune* of 27 June 1990: "The European Community is off and running." *Le Monde,* of the same date, stated: "For some months Europe has been carried forward on a wave of events coming from outside." The *Financial Times* carried the headline: "Motor of EC-Integration Shifts into Another Gear." The acceleration that Delors had called for, some months earlier in his Bruges speech, was obviously materializing. No criticism was heard from national parliaments or major opinion makers.

This sense of movement took the form of proposals or contributions made in the following weeks and months by almost all Community governments. With hindsight, it is significant to note that there was no national or community opposition to this development, except the traditional reluctance of the Thatcher government to follow the ambitious views of other member states. But even that reluctance was not radical: The communiqué of the Dublin European Council in June 1990 made a point of saying that the decision to call a second intergovernmental conference on political union was carried unanimously. At that time, the worry of the negotiators was clearly not the support of public opinion, which seemed guaranteed since twelve heads of state and government had twice expressed their agreement in at least apparent harmony with their public opinion, their press, and their parliaments. Their anxiety concerned the substance to be given to new concepts such as common foreign and security policy, European citizenship, or subsidiarity, which were mentioned in the conclusions of the European Council, but whose content and significance clearly had not been studied in depth by any of the participants.

The Italian Presidency: Preliminary Debates

Under the Italian presidency, the second half of 1990 was devoted to the task of clarifying these concepts. It was not the time for negotiations, since the

IGC was not to convene before 14 December 1990. It was rather a matter of preparing that conference, drawing up the points of convergence and divergence, identifying new routes to be explored, and taking note of the concerns of this or that country. This task had been entrusted to the personal representatives of the foreign ministers. These, in many cases but not always, were the permanent representatives to the Community. An idea put forward by certain ministers to entrust this preparatory work to their respective undersecretaries was quickly dropped. The decision to do so, which followed the precedent set by the Single European Act, is no doubt due to the different situations prevailing in the member states: Some ministers do not have an undersecretary; others, where there is a coalition government, may have one belonging to a different party; and some undersecretaries are in charge of other governmental tasks, which would not allow them to devote the necessary time to such an absorbing exercise as preparing an intergovernmental conference. The method adopted, which was later confirmed with regard to the negotiations proper, most likely affected the final outcome. In retrospect, it may have contributed to the widely held impression that the Treaty of Maastricht was a technocratic artifact, out of touch with political will in the member states. As a matter of fact, there is, however, every reason to believe that the foreign ministers' decision was intended to ensure that they would personally exercise the most effective possible control over the preparatory work. In order to exercise *their own* personal political control, they preferred to call on the work of officials rather than on that of fellow politicians. This should not come as a surprise.

The months before the first meeting of the intergovernmental conference certainly were of seminal importance to what was to become Title V of the Treaty of Maastricht. During that period, many contributions nourished the debate on a common foreign and security policy. They came from member states (notably Greece, Spain, and the Netherlands) or from institutions (opinion of the Commission of 22 October 1990, European Parliament resolutions of 11 July and 22 November 1990, declaration by the Inter-Parliamentary Conference of the Community of 30 November 1990),[6] or from the Italian presidency, which, throughout these six months and with a particular view to the two European Councils in Rome, endeavored to move the discussion forward on this point of essential significance for the coming conference. Gianni De Michelis, the Italian foreign minister, was particularly active in this field. The debate was marked by one rather surprising phenomenon: silence on the part of the French and German authorities. Despite recurrent press rumors and some discreet utterances, no new document approved by Paris and Bonn appeared before December 1990 to elucidate the views of these two capitals on the subject matter of the letter of 19 April of that year. Inevitably, the other member states tended to conclude therefrom that the main purpose of the letter had been to proclaim a common purpose but that there was, in fact, no political concept agreed upon between

Paris and Bonn as to what a common foreign and security policy should be. This gave all the more importance to the conceptual exercises in which the other member states indulged on this issue, as did a number of institutions, especially the European Parliament with its various versions of the Martin Report.

This intellectual effervescence, channeled by the work of the personal representatives, enabled the presidency to identify some points of convergence, which were then drafted into the communiqué issued by the Rome European Council of 14 and 15 December 1990. This was to set out the framework within which the intergovernmental conference would operate:

1. First, there was general agreement on the aim. Both the Commission and those member states that expressed a view supported the objective formulated in the Franco-German letter. The Parliament put forward the consideration that a common foreign policy covering matters of peace and security is a fundamental element of political union. In October 1990 a conference of representatives of all the parliamentary assemblies of the Community (a forum that was meeting for the first time) declared that a political union, including a common foreign and security policy on matters of common interest, should be put in place. In December 1990, therefore, the European Council was able to note broad agreement that the Union should be called upon to deal with issues of this nature.

2. Second, it was understood that the new common policy should apply only to certain issues. The Commission's opinion states clearly that what is under discussion is a common, not a single, policy. It introduces the notion of "vital common interest." This formulation had been used beforehand by President Delors. Speaking to the European Parliament in January 1990 (i.e., well before the question of a new conference had arisen), he alluded to the Tindemans Report of 1975 and proposed to set the following aim: "We identify essential joint interests and open the way, not to an identical external policy, but to actions in pursuit of those essential interests."[7] This wording was approved and adopted by the European Parliament. It can be presented as an application of the principle of subsidiarity to the field of foreign affairs; the Union should act in this field only where a vital common interest makes intervention at that level more effective.

3. It was agreed that, as has always been the practice in political cooperation, progress must be gradual. The Commission speaks in its opinion of "stepping up the process" by means of a flexible and pragmatic approach. For the Parliament, it is a matter of "tending toward" common policies. The Spanish paper refers to a stage "in the gradual development of the European Union." This is what the Rome European Council implies in its conclusions when it speaks of a "continuous evolutionary process."

4. Finally, everyone approved the need for more coherence in the way

problems were dealt with. This implied that Community matters and those that so far had come under the heading of "political cooperation" must be pulled closer together. This point, mentioned in the Belgian Memorandum, was taken up in the Commission's opinion and firmly stressed in the documents emanating from Parliament and in the declaration of the Interparliamentary Conference ("political co-operation must become an integral part of the treaty and of the Community's structure"). Some consequences of this trend were already apparent and fairly generally accepted: a single decisionmaking center, a stronger COREPER, a joint secretariat, a certain right of initiative for the Commission, consultation and information of Parliament, and a shared responsibility of the presidency and the Commission in matters of external representation.

Without pretending to put forward substantive draft provisions before the conference had even met, the Rome European Council did, in December 1990, refer to the above-mentioned elements and express its satisfaction at the broad agreement on the basic principles of a common foreign and security policy, which should result from a "continuous evolutionary and unified process." We should not underestimate the contribution of the Italian presidency: Starting from a vague and undefined concept, it managed in a few months to establish some fundamental points of possible agreement. To a certain extent, the conclusions of the Rome European Council already contain in a fairly precise outline the essence of the Maastricht Treaty, as far as foreign policy and security are concerned.

Two external events came indirectly to the aid of the presidency in these pre-negotiations: Saddam Hussein's invasion of Kuwait in August 1990, which very clearly highlighted the question of the military role Europe might be called upon to play in its geographical environment, and the internal crisis of the British Conservative Party, resulting in the departure of Margaret Thatcher and her replacement by a prime minister who was perceived as being less fundamentally opposed to the aspirations of Great Britain's principal continental partners.

But the Rome conclusions left open a crucial issue that, in the course of the discussions, had proved to be delicate and controversial: What, at the end of the day, should be the essential difference, the qualitative leap, marking the passage from EPC to CFSP? On 6 December 1990, a few days before the Council met, President Mitterrand and Chancellor Kohl addressed a letter to the presidency in which they set out certain principles that, they felt, should guide the negotiations on a common foreign and security policy. This text was kept in general terms and left many questions open, especially with regard to the institutional framework of the treaty and the scope of the proposed new commitments. In an article published in the journal *Foreign Policy* in the autumn of 1990, at a moment when everywhere in Europe new concepts were being tested, President Delors put forward the following questions: "What is the extent of our economic, social, and political ambition within the Community framework? . . . Does the Community have the political will to act in a coherent and unified way on these vital foreign policy issues?"[8]

January 1991: The State of Play

The preliminary debates that took up the second half of 1990 made it possible, if not to solve, then at least to identify the issues that would have to be addressed if an answer was to be found to these vast problems. Subsequent to the points of convergence identified above, the issues that were to dominate the discussions throughout 1991 may be summed up as follows:

Security. What is the term "common security policy" meant to convey? Does it include defense? Should it, as the Commission proposed in its opinion of October 1990, include a commitment to reciprocal defense, as set out in Article V of the Treaty on Western European Union (WEU)? What is to be the relationship between the Union, WEU, and NATO?

Vital common interests. How should they be identified? Should an attempt be made a priori to draw up a list? Foreign ministers meeting informally at Asolo in October 1990 tried their hand at this and the so-called Asolo list, lengthened at times and shortened at others, had a long but not very fruitful career in the course of a number of meetings at the ministerial and official level. Should some authority (the European Council?) define these "vital common interests" in the light of any given situation? If foreign affairs and security are to be the subject of a common, but not of a single, policy, how are we to ensure that national foreign and security policies will conform to that laid down in common? What level of constraint is acceptable? Can sanctions be envisaged in case of nonobservance?

Graduality. How should it be achieved? In quantitative terms, by a gradual increase in the number of issues dealt with (on the basis of the "Asolo list")? In qualitative terms, by arrangements beginning at a modest level of common action but developing progressively with the help of a revision clause? In temporal terms, on the basis of a fixed timetable?

Institutional structure. How integrated should the working framework of the Union be? Should concern for coherent decisionmaking be taken to the point of total fusion between former European Political Cooperation and Community activities? Including the respective powers, rights, and competences of Community institutions? Or should the continuation (or perhaps strengthening) of an intergovernmental structure be accepted? Can a common foreign and security policy be managed solely by consensus? Should we envisage, as indeed the Commission proposes, to vote in some case by qualified (or possibly "reinforced qualified") majority? If so, in what circumstances?

The conclusions of the Rome European Council certainly mark some progress, but it must be considered that many fundamental questions were left open for discussion by the IGC, which opened on 14 December 1990.

The First Months of the Luxembourg Presidency

During the preparatory stages, the differences of view between the member states on these various issues had remained more or less implicit. They were to be more formally and more explicitly stated during the first months of the Luxembourg presidency and centered on two main themes:

- The question of security and defense, including the role of WEU and its relationship with the Union and NATO
- The structure of the Union, including the role of the European Council, Community institutions, and majority voting

In the matter of security, Franco-German thinking was somewhat elucidated by a joint document distributed in February 1991:[9] It proposes to set up a common European defense system that will not cast doubt upon any NATO commitment and that could be based upon the integration of WEU in the European unification process by making that organization subject to directives issued by the European Council. These ideas were supported by countries such as Italy, Spain, and Belgium (especially the latter), which, however, insisted on the links that such a structure must have with the Community (and not exclusively with the European Council). In particular, they insisted on the role to be played by Community institutions (which are not mentioned in the Franco-German paper). Other countries—like the United Kingdom, supported by the Netherlands and Portugal—considered such a scheme to be unrealistic and dangerous, inasmuch as it could put trans-Atlantic solidarity and the functioning of NATO at risk. Sir Douglas Hurd said in February 1991: "I do not believe that there is a case for including defence within the common foreign and security policy."[10] At the same time, the United Kingdom was putting forward some "draft Treaty provisions," which, in fact, went no further than limiting operational adjustments of the provisions of Chapter III of the Single European Act. The British draft does not even mention the word "defense."

The debate on security and defense was, of course, not taking place in a political vacuum; the United States initially followed the debate with some apprehension and made its concern known in every nation's capital through a memorandum, known in diplomatic circles as the Bartholomew-Dobbins Memorandum. Washington was particularly alarmed by the idea of subordinating WEU to directives issued by the European Council. It feared the emergence of a monolithic bloc within the Alliance and the danger of the latter becoming marginalized. There was even concern that Irish neutrality, eventually strengthened by the accession of new member states with a similar tradition, might, through the European Council, influence WEU and thereby, indirectly, NATO. U.S. fears were gradually set to rest by careful explanations and assurances given by various European governments. In May 1991 Secretary of State James Baker accepted in principle the idea that a common foreign and security policy developed by the European Union could have a defense dimension if certain conditions linked to NATO were respected. By the end of the negotiation, Washington saw positive advantages in including defense in the European treaty framework, but in the initial stages these fears did further complicate a debate that was already quite confusing.[11]

The second debate concerning the structure of the European Union was, in many ways, the remake of an old, never settled, discussion whose main elements go back to the negotiations on the Fouchet proposals in 1961. The importance of this debate, both in 1961 and in 1991, should not be underestimated. It divides those in favor of an intergovernmental Europe from those wishing to see a *communautaire* Europe, with the ultimate goal being a quasi-federal structure. The solution is fundamental to any conceptual approach to what has been happening in Western European political structures since the 1950s.

Thanks to a good deal of pragmatism and a number of implicit compromises, it had been possible over a period of twenty years to eschew any theoretical debate on this issue during the gradual evolution of political cooperation. However, the new Franco-German initiatives in the field of foreign and security policy, the envisaged move from "Community" to "Union," and silence or equivocation on the role of the classical treaty institutions (Commission and Parliament) in these new policies gave rise to the fear that a fragile balance might be upset, which, since the Davignon Report in 1970, had made it possible to sidestep old controversies. Such fears were soon voiced by the Netherlands. Two days before the first meeting of the Intergovernmental Conference, a letter, dated 12 December 1991, from Prime Minister Lubbers and Foreign Minister Van den Broek drew the attention of the European Council to the fact that the "Political Union" must develop on the basis of Community structures and, in any case, should not accentuate the intergovernmental element in the European construction. This was to remain a leitmotif in the Dutch position, but the concern was, of course, shared by the Commission and also by other delegations from small or medium-sized countries who have always regarded Community institutions as their best defense against any attempt at domination by larger member states. However, this logic had its limits. When asked by the presidency whether they saw a role for the Court of Justice in common foreign policy, nearly all member states (with the exception of the Netherlands) answered negatively in the very first stages of the negotiation.[12] This, of course, implied that the new policy could never be completely identical to other common policies of the Community. It might be called a "common policy," but it would not be a "community policy" because community policies are by nature subject to community institutions, including the Court. The implications of this early decision were more far-reaching than was perhaps realized at the time; much of the subsequent debate on the structure of the Union has been influenced by it.

Negotiations were certainly not made easier by the fact that the line-up of member states differed on the two basic issues of security and structure. The Benelux countries and Italy, for instance, could welcome the ambitious goals put forward by France and Germany in the field of foreign affairs, but they had serious difficulties with the marginalization of Community institutions in the proposed procedures. Others, such as Great Britain and Denmark, saw positive advantages in the proposed procedures but were skeptical about the goals.

In an intergovernmental conference, the presidency shoulders responsibility for the difficult and frequently lonely task of bringing together the strands of the negotiation while searching for agreement and compromise. For this task, Luxembourg had to take into account not only the disparate views of the member states, but also the contributions coming from the European Parliament and the Commission, both of which had tabled draft articles concerning foreign and security policy. In formal legal terms, neither Commission nor Parliament are participants in the intergovernmental conference but, in reality, their contributions could not be ignored.

Before the formal opening of the conference in Rome in December 1990, the European Parliament had already adopted the third version of a report on political union presented by David Martin, British Labour MEP (Member of the European Parliament). This report contains draft articles that are the first specific proposals for treaty amendments on foreign and security policy.[13] The proposed text of Article 130.u makes a distinction between the external aspects of Community competence (trade, currency, etc.), which must be handled in accordance with Community procedures, and the political aspects of foreign policy that are dealt with by other procedures. It is worth noting that a similar approach had already been taken by the European Parliament in 1984 when approving the draft treaty presented by Altiero Spinelli. In the Martin Report, when dealing with external issues of a political nature, the Commission and member states share the right of initiative, the Council decides by qualified majority, member states may be authorized to "opt out" from the policies agreed upon, and these policies are conducted by the Council, the Commission, or the member states, as the case may require. These were undoubtedly ambitious proposals, especially as far as the voting mechanism was concerned. It is not easy to judge their influence on the negotiating position of the various member states. Nevertheless, they were the first to be tabled, they were agreed upon in Parliament, and at least one member state—namely, Italy—had formally stated that it would not ratify the treaty without the previous approval of the European Parliament. The position of that institution was something the presidency therefore had to take into account.

For its part, in March 1991 the Commission tabled proposals concerning foreign policy. These took the form of treaty articles (numbered from Y.0 to Y.32) covering foreign and security policy, as well as policy on foreign trade and development aid.[14] This text interprets and tries to put into treaty language the conclusions of the Rome European Council with regard to cohesion, progressive development, and subsidiarity. It distinguishes between:

- Matters that the European Council has declared to be of vital common interest (Article Y.3). These are dealt with by common policy, decisions are taken by qualified majority with at least eight member states voting in favor, and, in exceptional cases, a member state may be dispensed from the obligations flowing from the common policy.
- Other issues of foreign policy (Article Y.4). They continue to be governed by a form of political cooperation that, in practice, hardly differs from the type set out in the relevant articles of the Single European Act.

On security, the Commission text takes up (Article Y.12) the mutual defense commitment contained in Article V of the WEU Treaty, envisages the gradual integration of that body into the Union (Article Y.15), joint meetings of foreign and defense ministers (Article Y.14), and the possibility that a member state may, for cogent reasons, be dispensed from certain obligations under the common policy (Article Y.13). "The Community must acknowledge the deficits of the past and play its part with regard to the political and military responsibilities which are traditionally incumbent upon our nations," said President Delors.[15]

It is interesting to note that, contrary to what some delegations stated at the time, the Commission was not advocating a full assimilation of foreign policy issues to traditional Community procedures. Article Y.3, which is the innovative article, implies that it is on the basis of consensus that matters of vital common interest are recognized by the European Council. The Commission's right of initiative is shared with the presidency and/or with a simple majority of member states (Article Y.3). Parliament's role is purely consultative (Article Y.5). The Court has no jurisdiction (Article Y.10). While putting foreign policy, external trade policy, and development cooperation under the same heading, obviously in order to stress coherence, the

Commission was, in fact, accepting that Community procedures as such could not be transposed to the foreign policy field.

The Luxembourg Non-Paper: April 1991

Taking all this into account, the presidency submitted a "non-paper" on 12 April 1991 that is an embryonic version of what was to become the Treaty of Maastricht.[16] What are the main features of that interesting document?

1. A clear separation between the "European Communities" (Article B.1 of the common provisions) on one side, foreign policy and justice (Article B.2) on the other. The presidency compromise does cover all these matters in one treaty and places them within the same "Union" (whereas some negotiators were still thinking, explicitly or implicitly, in terms of separate treaties and different "Unions"). Yet it sets them beside each other (see Article B.2: "The Union shall also be based . . . ") without much indication of the institutional relationship between them or, indeed, on the nature of the "Union" itself.
2. The presentation in treaty terms of a number of practical provisions on which the Rome European Council had established that member states were close to agreement, such as the respective roles in foreign and security policy of the European Council, the Council, the Commission, Parliament, COREPER, the Political Committee, and the Secretariat.
3. Differences in procedures between cooperation (Articles G, H, and I) and common actions that are to be gradually implemented in all fields in which the member states have vital and common interests (Articles J and K). In this latter case, the Council can provide that the modalities of implementation shall be adopted by majority (the *type* of majority is left open).
4. The possibility of using WEU for decisions, with implications in the field of defense, and the possibility of reviewing these provisions in 1996 with a view to a common defense policy in the long term.

The Luxembourg "non-paper" was hotly discussed in public from the moment it made its appearance. The main points at issue were the general structure of the treaty (rapidly known as the "pillar system") and the security dimension. Belgium, the Netherlands, and Italy saw in the "pillars" a confirmation of the intergovernmental approach that they wished to avoid. Others considered the text to be a realistic basis for negotiation since it more or less reflected, in their view, the points on which the member states might in the end be able to agree. On the basis of any objective analysis and with knowledge of the final outcome, it must be admitted that in the field of foreign policy, this paper already contained several key elements of the Treaty of Maastricht.

The Commission was critical because it considered that the proposals put forward by the presidency affected not only its proper institutional role but also the unity of the European integration process. Of course, Article B.1 provided for a single institutional framework, but the juxtaposition of the pillars in Article A appeared to consolidate the intergovernmental nature of the new fields of action. The Commission was not alone on this point. In *Le Figaro* of 7 June Mark Eyskens, the Belgian minister, wrote: "We must at all cost maintain the unity of the European Community and avoid the establishment of a Political Union with its own mechanisms, some of which would be intergovernmental, alongside the existing Communities."

The institutional structure retained for the Union, of course, has consequences in a variety of issues: the decisionmaking process, majority voting, the maintenance of the Commission's right of initiative, and recourse to the Court of Justice. This is what the Parliament implied when, on 14 June, it adopted a resolution calling for the "unity of the legal and institutional system within the four institutions, the decisionmaking procedure, executive, jurisdictional action, and control." In April 1991, the report introduced by the German MEP Hans-Gert Poettering demanded that "an end be put to the intergovernmental nature of political co-operation."[17] This was going in a direction exactly opposite to that of the presidency paper.

As to security, the proposals in the Luxembourg "non-paper" were going too far for strict "Atlanticists," such as Britain and the Netherlands, in that it envisaged the Union providing itself with a common defense policy in the long term (Article L.3). France, Spain, and others considered that such a vague prospect was falling well short of what was needed and ought to be the ambition of the Twelve. Confusion was increased by the fact that a parallel in-depth exercise was going on in NATO about the future of the Alliance, whereas the future of WEU also seemed a subject for discussion. In February a Franco-German paper had called for close association between WEU and the Union. Secretary of State Baker drew attention to U.S. concern about the relations between the Union and NATO. He asked that discussions begin regarding a common foreign and security policy between the Community and those NATO countries that were not members of the Community. The plan to organize future European security seemed to be floating on a sea of uncertainty between various forums. Nicole Gnessoto wrote: "In fact, perplexity is the only thing the European countries have in common. The strategic upheaval is so universal and so rapid, in view of the fluidity of what is happening in Europe and beyond, that no one wishes to close firmly this door or that, or to opt in advance for one security structure or another."[18]

The Luxembourg European Council: June 1991

Taking both criticism and general atmosphere into account, the presidency presented a new document on 18 June 1991 in the form of a draft treaty.[19] In foreign policy, this text differs significantly from its predecessor, without changing the essentials.

1. The preeminence of the Community in the structure of the Union is now clearly underlined (Article A). It is the Community that forms the basis of the Union and other policies or "pillars" (such as the common foreign and security policy) have only a complementary role. The new treaty is no more than a stage in a gradual process leading toward a Union with a federal character.
2. The single institutional framework of the Union is now clearly referred to in the general provisions of the treaty (Article C) whereas before it appeared only, as a side issue, in the provisions concerning common foreign and security policy.
3. The Union states as one of its objectives (Article B) the definition of a common foreign and security policy that, in the long term, will include the definition of a defense policy, a point that the April "nonpaper" did not clearly express.
4. Article J.2 introduces, optionally, voting by qualified majority on the implementation of a common foreign and security policy (this had been left open in the April text), and Article K confirms that common action, once defined, shall be binding on the member states in the conduct of their policies with, however, an "opting-out" provision whenever a member state faces a major difficulty. Similar provisions did not apply to political cooperation as it then existed, so that progress was apparent.
5. A new intergovernmental conference was to be called in 1996 to review the provisions concerning security (Article L.5) and other aspects of foreign policy (Article N).

Obviously, the Luxembourg presidency's new draft was not acceptable to many member states as it stood. Great Britain and Denmark rejected the federal objective assigned to the Union. Most of the modifications introduced in the new draft went in the direction of the more *communautaire* member states; nevertheless, the Netherlands and Belgium continued to criticize the structure in pillars that the new draft maintained. Most people wondered whether a common defense policy was conceivable without a formal defense commitment, that is, an alliance. This was Delors's point of view: "This common defense policy only makes sense if it expresses a double solidarity: unity in the analysis and action in the area of foreign policy and mutual engagement to assist a member state whose integrity is threatened."[20]

Yet, all agreed that the presidency had manifested skill and imagination. The European Council conclusions of 28 and 29 June 1991 state that this text "constitutes a basis for further negotiations." These were to be finalized in Maastricht at the end of the year. As far as the common foreign and security policy is concerned, the European Council notes that the decisionmaking process (majority voting) for its implementation needs to be further examined. The question of "strengthening the Union's defense identity" (a strange formulation—at the time, there was neither a Union nor a defense identity) was postponed to the end of the negotiations.

The Dutch Draft Treaty

At the end of Luxembourg's presidency, the road toward Maastricht seemed to be mapped out in a relatively straightforward way. Much still needed to be straightened out, but the general direction was clear and the final result could be guessed. And yet, the draft treaty was to meet with a further major obstacle. On 4 June 1991, Foreign Minister Genscher, wishing to impress his colleagues with the historic significance of German reunification, invited them to Dresden for an informal ministerial meeting. In the course of this meeting, much of the discussion turned on the future political union and on the Luxembourg draft treaty, whose main elements were common knowledge. The incoming president, Foreign Minister van den Broek, unhappy with the general approach of the existing draft, came away convinced that another, more orthodox and more "unitarian," draft treaty (with no "pillars"!) had a real chance of success, since eight member states had seemed to indicate that they could accept such a proposal. In August 1991 a new text was drawn up in the Ministry for Foreign Affairs in The Hague. The first versions of this began to circulate unofficially in early September 1991. The official text was tabled on 23 September of the same year. The treaty, conceived in The Hague and oddly entitled "Treaty for a European Union," did away with the "pillar" structure.[21] Common foreign and security policy became Chapter 1 of the fourth part of the treaty, which also covered commercial policy and development aid, as had been suggested by the Commission in March 1991. There was, of course, a price to be paid: The whole concept of a defense policy (on which the Netherlands had never been very keen) was put in brackets, and the points on majority voting and on the constraints of common actions that had been introduced in the June draft treaty text disappeared, as did also the review clauses. Basically, the procedures envisaged for the common foreign policy were the same as those already practiced in political cooperation (Article B.1), except for particular

cases in which the member states were to decide unanimously to do otherwise (Article B.2). On the general issues of principle concerning European
integration, there is much to be said in favor of the Dutch draft treaty text.
It is certainly consistent with views long held and always vigorously
defended by that country in its approach to European affairs. In the specific
field of foreign and security policy, however, the practical consequences of
such an approach are on the negative side. Since such a policy does not easily fit into the Community procedural framework, which was not conceived
with that sort of policy in mind, and since the Dutch approach had as its
main objective excluding a separate procedural framework within the
Union, little more could be done than to maintain the informal consensual
rules that have governed political cooperation in the course of the years. In
the Dutch approach, there was no question of a real breakthrough in common foreign and security policy.

The personal representatives, who had been negotiating for over a year
and thought they had the areas of possible agreement clearly mapped out,
gave the new draft treaty text a very reserved welcome. So, apparently, did
the various capitals in the course of bilateral contacts with Dutch diplomacy. Belgium, of course, clearly concurred with the general approach, but
elsewhere, strong reservations or anxious criticisms were voiced concerning
either the federal undertone of the text or the risk of delay that a controversial paper could entail. France and Britain showed clear disapproval,
Germany and Italy had doubts, at the very least. Nevertheless, the presidency persisted in its course and did not seem to realize that it was heading for
failure. When, on 30 September, ten member states meeting in the Council
showed, for different reasons, their clear preference for the draft that had
been on the table in June 1991, the matter was closed. Diplomatic circles in
The Hague spoke of "Black Monday" and the *NRC Handelsblad* of 2
October 1991 carried the headline "Suicide in The Hague" (*"De Haagse
Zelfmoord"*) and spoke of unsure priorities, lack of leadership, insufficient
consultation, and faulty appreciation. The net result, after this strange
episode, was that the Luxembourg draft was the only one left in the running.
What had been, in July 1991, only a basis for negotiation acquired increased
authority and credibility.[22]

The End Game

The rejection of the Dutch alternative text created a vacuum. There were
only two months left to meet the deadline of the Maastricht European
Council, and some essential negotiating elements, such as security, were still
in limbo. This explains why October and November 1991 brought forth
many proposals for discussion at special ministerial meetings at Haarzuylen

(5 and 6 October), Noordwijk (12 and 13 November), and Brussels (2 December). On 4 October 1991, the presidency produced a revised version of the Luxembourg text that had been on the table in July. An Anglo-Italian document on defense and, on the 11th, a Spanish-French-German paper were also presented.[23] Belgium put forward a number of suggestions, especially on the decisionmaking process. Many important issues were still open in other parts of the treaty, but on the foreign policy side this intensive debate concentrated on four points:

1. *Security:* The Anglo-Italian document spoke of a European defense identity with a long-term perspective going in the direction of a common defense policy. The Spanish-French-German communiqué referred to a policy covering all matters of security and defense, with a long-term perspective of common defense. The distinction between "defense" and "defense policy" is not merely semantic; it involves the relationship with NATO, and the question of whether, in time, the Union should assume a defense commitment and thereby become an alliance.

2. *Western European Union:* Should this institution be equidistant from the Union and NATO, or should it be an integral part of the European construction? This debate was, of course, not unrelated to the preceding one.

3. *Majority voting:* The Spanish-French-German communiqué pleads for qualified majority voting to implement measures under the common foreign and security policy; Belgium, Italy, and Greece expressed similar views, but the United Kingdom, Denmark, and Ireland would not agree. Portugal considered that if majority voting on foreign policy were to be adopted, it could only operate on the basis of one country equals one vote, and not on the weighted majority system that had been operating in the Community since the 1950s. The Netherlands maintained that majority voting could only be envisaged on the basis of Community procedures, that is, the Council should only vote when a proposal of the Commission was on the table.

4. *The "passageways"* (*passerelles* in French): Since the "pillar" structure was now seen as inevitable, several countries considered that the possibility of transferring some matters from intergovernmental to Community procedure should at least be provided. A similar problem was arising in the third "pillar" (on matters of police and justice) and was to be partly solved by Article 100c of the new treaty.

The October 1991 meeting at Haarzuylen concentrated mainly on foreign and security policy and made considerable progress. As a result of debates within NATO and WEU, consensus was beginning to appear on both sides of the Atlantic as to what the future security framework could look like. Some role would clearly be given to the European Union in connection with WEU. The Franco-German determination to do something concrete in the defense field was illustrated by the announcement on 11 October 1991 of the creation of a common army corps. The United Kingdom remained reluctant, but it was becoming obvious that the treaty would include some mention of defense. Similarly, the concept of "common action" in the foreign policy field, already mentioned in the July draft, was gaining credibility. Two questions remained disputed to the end: the choice between "defense policy" or "defense," and the introduction of majority voting.[24]

On all these issues, including the concept of common action, Britain remained unconvinced, and, in several cases, it had the explicit support of one or more member states. Nevertheless, the choice of options was narrowing and it was becoming clear that the formulation of the articles on common foreign and security policy would probably not, at the last minute, block the conclusion of the treaty.

The presidency's new draft treaty,[25] which was on the table at the opening of the European Council, speaks of "defense policy" and not of "defense" (Articles A and D.5), provides no organic link with WEU (Article D.2), introduces qualified majority voting for the implementation of the common foreign and security policy (Article C.1), and contains a *pro memoria* with regard to the evolutionary clause (Article J), in other words, the "passageways."

Such was the position on the eve of the final meeting. It was at Maastricht itself that the negotiations brought agreement, after a relatively short debate, on the disputed points in the form of words that are now known to us:

- Confirmation that defense policy could, in time, lead to a common defense (Article J.4.1)
- Confirmation that WEU is an integral part of the development of the European Union (Article J.4.2)
- Limitation of qualified majority voting to cases in which the Council had previously so decided to vote (Article J.3.2)
- Finally, the general "passageway" (Article B, par. 5), which, on the insistence of the Belgian delegation, will enable a shift to be made from intergovernmental cooperation to Community procedures[26]

The introduction of the concepts of common defense and of majority voting in the foreign policy field were undoubtedly concessions made by the British government, which had long opposed such proposals. Both concessions are, however, qualified. Common defense is postponed to an uncertain future, and majority voting is limited to a degree that casts doubts on its practical applicability. Nevertheless, the point of principle was settled, and given the long history of the underlying debate, it is not a small achievement.

Conclusion

The negotiations on Common Foreign and Security Policy that led up to the Maastricht Treaty were certainly not easy. Officials and ministers spent a considerable amount of time arguing on issues such as the "Asolo list," majority voting, or the role of WEU. Nevertheless, with hindsight, it seems obvious that the Treaty, while innovative in many other fields, such as Monetary Union or legislative co-decision, brings few changes to the field of foreign policy. This is the conclusion that most observers and many participants would draw from the first few months of experience in the application of Title V of the Treaty.

Analysis of the negotiating process itself enables us to identify some reasons for this limited success. The fact is that the concept, initially formulated by Kohl and Mitterrand, of a Common Foreign and Security Policy was duly written down in the Treaty but without any in-depth discussion of its meaning and its implications. As shown above, no debate at all took place in 1990, and in 1991 it was limited to a few points, undoubtedly important, but which clearly did not cover all the issues. If we compare this to the treatment of a similarly complex and important objective—namely Economic and Monetary Union (EMU)—the contrast is obvious. A group of central bankers and experts, chaired by Delors, had debated for more than a year and drafted a detailed report of EMU even before the intergovernmental conference was called. Nothing similar was ever attempted for foreign and security policy.

Ministers and officials, working under time pressure and without a previously agreed upon framework similar to Delors's report on EMU, were confronted with politically charged and potentially conflictual issues. They did what most people do in such circumstances. They put the objective down in writing and postponed the implementation to a future date—namely, the 1996 Intergovernmental Conference. This, of course, meant that the Twelve had failed to agree, or even seriously to debate, a number of important issues linked to the Common Foreign and Security Policy, such as:

- The decisionmaking process, including majority voting
- The means of implementation, including finance and the role of Community institutions
- The implications of a common defense policy

Those weaknesses were soon to become apparent, once Maastricht was ratified.

Notes

1. For a contemporary analysis of the motivations in the foreign and security field, see Philippe de Schoutheete, "Gemeinsame Aussen- und Sicherheitspolitik in der Politischen Union: Machtzuwachs und Politische Verantwortung," *Integration* 1 (1991), pp. 3–9.

2. Jacques Delors, *Le Nouveau Concert Européen* (Paris: Editions Odile Jacob, 1992), pp. 335–336, unofficial translation.

3. Sir Leon Brittan, *Europe: The Europe We Need* (London: Hamish Hamilton, 1994), p. 168.

4. The Belgian Memorandum was published by *Agence Europe: Europe Documents* no. 1608, 29 March 1990. See also an analysis by Peter Ludlow in *The Annual Review of Community Affairs 1991* (London: Brassey's, 1992), pp. 404–406, and Franco Algieri, "Setting the Options: The Proposals Concerning Foreign and Security Policy," in Wolfgang Wessels and Christian Engel, eds., *The European Union in the 1990s—Ever Closer and Larger?* (Europäische Schriften no. 70) (Bonn: Europa Union Verlag, 1993), pp. 207–208. Y. Doutriaux, *Le Traité sur l'Union Européenne* (Paris: Armand Colin, 1992), p. 28, and J. Cloos et al., *Le Traité de Maastricht* (Brussels: Bruylant, 1993), pp. 51–52 also deal with it.

5. The Kohl-Mitterrand letter was published by *Agence Europe* no. 5238, 20 April 1990. See Doutriaux, *Le Traité sur l'Union Européenne,* pp. 28–30, and Cloos, *Le Traité de Maastricht,* pp. 53–55.

6. A brochure issued by the Publications Office of the Communities in Luxembourg, entitled "1993: Les Nouveaux Traités," presents the main texts adopted by the European Parliament in the course of the negotiations and the final declaration by the Inter-Parliamentary Conference of the Community of 30 November 1990.

7. Delors, *Le Nouveau Concert Européen,* p. 209.

8. Jacques Delors, "Europe's Ambitions," *Foreign Policy* 80 (Fall 1990), pp. 14–27.

9. *Agence Europe: Europe Documents* no. 1690, 21 February 1991.

10. Douglas Hurd, *Churchill Memorial Lecture,* Luxembourg, 19 February 1991.

11. With regard to the evolution of the U.S. attitude concerning European ideas on defense in the spring of 1991, see David Buchan, *Europe: The Strange Superpower* (Rennes: Editions Apogée, 1993), pp. 53–54.

12. Cloos et al., "Le Traité de Maastricht," p. 466. This book coauthored by Ambassador Weyland, the Luxembourg personal representative, gives interesting insights into the negotiation, particularly under his country's presidency.

13. Parliamentary brochure, "1993: Les Nouveaux Traités," pp. 139–143.

14. *Agence Europe: Europe Documents* no. 1697–1698, 7 March 1991.

15. Jacques Delors, speech at the International Institute for Strategic Studies, London, 7 March 1991. *Le Nouveau Concert Européen,* p. 291, unofficial translation.

16. *Agence Europe: Europe Documents* no. 1706, 16 April 1991.

17. Document European Parliament, no. 146.269, point 2.

18. Nicole Gnessoto, "Défense européenne: Pourquoi les Douze?" *Cahiers de Chaillot* 1 (Paris: Institut d'Etudes et de Sécurité de l'UEO, 1991).

19. *Agence Europe: Europe Documents* no. 1722/1723, 5 July 1991.

20. Delors, *Le Nouveau Concert Européen,* p. 303, unofficial translation.

21. *Agence Europe: Europe Documents* no. 1733/1734, 3 October 1991.

22. This point is made by the Luxembourg negotiators themselves: Cloos et al., "Le Traité de Maastricht," p. 90. "What the European Council in Luxembourg failed to do was done by the Dutch Presidency by conferring a new authority to the Luxembourg text."

23. *Agence Europe: Europe Documents* no. 1737, 17 October 1991.

24. During the course of the negotiation, the Institute for European Studies, Université Libre de Bruxelles, organized at regular intervals one-day seminars on the state of the negotiation. One was held on 8 November 1991 and the proceedings, published by the Institute, give a sense of the atmosphere a month before the Maastricht meeting.

25. *Agence Europe: Europe Documents* no. 1746/1747, 20 November 1991.

26. "I am referring specifically to a key sentence in the common provisions, that is Article B, introduced as the result of a proposal made by Belgium. It should be recognized that this country has always fought to establish such links." President Jacques Delors speaking to the European Parliament on 12 December 1991. Delors, *Le Nouveau Concert Européen,* p. 187.

Part 2

Institutions:
The Stage and the Players

4

The Institutional Setup and Functioning of EPC/CFSP

Elfriede Regelsberger

To assess the Common Foreign and Security Policy (CFSP) provisions of the Treaty on European Union (TEU) shortly after their coming into force on 1 November 1993 bears certain risks. Much of the analysis has to be based on the text (Title V, Article J, TEU) and the objectives and interests that led the contracting parties to accept the results of the Intergovernmental Conference of 1990–1991, because the first "test phase" of the CFSP implementation has covered only a short period of time. In order to compensate for this, a recourse to the fundamentals of the old European Political Cooperation (EPC) at the end of the 1980s might be helpful. A recollection of the criteria set by the heads of state and government of the EC member states themselves in April 1990, needed for the creation of a European Union,[1] could also serve as a yardstick. Since the focus of this chapter is on institutions and procedural arrangements, the then Twelve's first criterion—that is, the capacity to respond efficiently and effectively to external challenges—is of particular relevance here.[2]

Whether or not the transition from EPC to CFSP will constitute a qualitative leap or not "will depend on the future choices of the participants,"[3] to a large degree. The first months of implementation seem to reflect a series of "paralyzing uncertainties,"[4] caused mainly by the first negative Danish Referendum in 1992, the meager results of the Referendum in France, and the long ratification procedures in both the United Kingdom and Germany. Furthermore, the well-known "retarding forces" among the Twelve and a lessening of the participants' enthusiasm to tackle the open questions produced a business-as-usual style. The old habits and principles were obviously kept even beyond 1 November 1993, the date EPC officially expired. Some argue that the next rounds of enlargement of the Union will require at least another streamlining of CFSP's internal structures, if not another comprehensive revision. Others preclude substantial changes and an actual reorientation in the perception of the participating governments except in extreme cases, such as massive international crises and war—a somewhat realistic, though unsatisfying, assessment.

Recent EPC History (1985–1993): Growth Factors and Limits of the Old System

Compared to the early days of EPC when participants were skeptical as to whether the attempt to harmonize national foreign policies would materialize at all,[5] EPC in the late 1980s and early 1990s appeared to be an extraordinarily stable structure. Despite considerable changes in its composition (such as increasing the number of participants from the original six to fifteen, with plans to include more governments by the end of the century), in its personnel (rotation of national diplomatic services) and new external conditions (détente, East-West divide, new European architecture, German unification, etc.), EPC never suffered an institutional crisis. None of the participating governments ever questioned their belonging to the "club." Instead, EPC was increasingly appreciated as "a central element in the foreign policies of all member states."[6] The attractiveness of EPC stemmed largely from its intergovernmental character, which gave participating governments the final say, based on the consensus of all. EPC was not designed to absorb national diplomacy; it allowed for the pursuit of both collective and individual national foreign policies. Neither did EPC produce a shift in loyalties from the national to the European level; it left foreign policy untouched, as one of the key domains of the nation state. According to certain political science theories on international cooperation,[7] the Twelve's interest in EPC was based on the conviction that collective foreign policy making should have a greater say in international politics than "going it alone." This pooling of national sovereignties could even be enhanced by the existence of specific rules[8] that could take the form of a confidential *coutûmier,* politically binding reports of the foreign ministers (1970, 1973, 1981) but also legally binding texts, as illustrated by the Single European Act (Article 30, SEA) and later by the Union Treaty.

Frequent Use and Extension of the EPC/CFSP Infrastructure: Some Data

According to practitioners involved in the EPC/CFSP business, the past years have been marked by a considerable increase in internal consultation activities. This positive trend applies to both the gatherings of the foreign ministers and to the various administrative levels (political directors, European correspondents, and experts), as well as to the meetings among the member states' embassies in third countries and at international organizations.

Table 4.1 signals that the numbers exceed by far the minimum standard of consultations indicated in the legal provisions.[9] Normally, political directors met every month (except for August) and if necessary—for example, in certain crisis situations—even more often. The same applies to the ministerial level in which the calendar of the EC General Council offered a semipermanent exchange of views on EPC-related issues, in addition to the "proper" EPC gatherings. The provisions for "emergency meetings," on the contrary, have been rather rarely applied—not because of disagreement, but because the present existing opportunities to meet are believed to be sufficient. It seems as if recourse to the crisis procedure launched with the London Report in 1981 is necessary only in exceptional cases of the highest political relevance. As a general rule, one could say that since a well-defined *acquis politique* already exists, no additional meetings are needed. Then the EPC telex network (COREU) is used as the most efficient means to reach a rapid decision—that is, within forty-eight hours or less.

Table 4.1   Frequency of EPC Meetings

Institution	1990	1991	1992
Expert Groups	93	105	109
European Correspondents	12	18	22
Political Committee	12	18	22
Foreign Ministers / General Council	15	27[a]	16
European Council	2	2	3

Note: a. Obviously due to IGC negotiations.

As Table 4.2 illustrates, the most significant growth took place between 1985 and 1986 (80 percent). This explosion is only partly, and to a lesser degree, due to the entry of Portugal and Spain into the EPC in 1986. The large number of messages since that time reflects the increased interest of the Twelve to hear their partners' views on specific issues and on a semipermanent basis.

Table 4.2   Number of COREUs

1985	1986	1990	1991	1992	1993	1994
5,400	9,800	7,548	10,184	11,394	11,714	12,699[a]

Source: Institut für Europäische Politik: *CFSP Forum* 1 (1995), p. 8.
Note: a. From 1 July 1994 onward, four applicants (Austria, Finland, Norway, and Sweden) participated in the network.

This extensive use of the internal communication network is also particularly apparent at the expert level, where the passing years are marked both by an intensification of cooperation in the already existing expert groups and the creation of new ones (mainly as a response to the international environment—e.g., the production of chemical and biological weapons, illegal arms exports, and drug trafficking). Table 4.3 indicates a consistently high interest among the member states in exchanging views on standard EPC items such as the Middle East, developments in Latin America, the Conference on Security and Cooperation in Europe (CSCE), et cetera, as well as on efforts to improve and intensify the EPC system of communication itself. The frequency of meetings and the setting up of new ones also depended on the individual presidencies and diplomats involved (e.g., the interest of the Dutch in human rights issues led to the creation of such an expert group in the second half of the 1980s).

Table 4.3   The Frequency of EPC Expert Meetings Between 1985 and 1992

Working Groups	1985	1986	1987	1988	1989	1990	1991	1992
Administrative Affairs	4	1	2	2	2	3	3	4
Africa	7	7	9	6	6	6	6	7
Asia	5	5	4	6	6	6	7	7
CSCE	7	6	11	7	7	9	10	7
Communications (Heads)	2	2	2	1	2	2	2	2
Communications (Experts)	—	—	—	—	1	2	2	2
Consular Affairs	3	3	2	2	3	2	4	4
Cooperation to Combat International Terrorism	4	6	6	7	4	5	4	4
Conventional Arms Export	—	—	—	—	—	—	—	1
Drugs	—	—	—	—	—	2	4	4
Eastern Europe	9	8	9	8	8	7	8	7
Euro-Arab Dialogue	6	2	—	1	3	4	3	3
Exports of Illegal Arms (Ad Hoc Group)	—	—	2	—	2	—	—	—
Human Rights	—	—	—	3	5	3	4	5
Judicial Cooperation (Civil and Criminal Law)	6	3	7	4	5	6	9	8
Latin America	6	7	5	7	6	6	8	10
Medical Affairs	—	—	1	—	—	—	—	—
Middle East	10	10	11	10	9	8	7	8
Mediterranean	—	—	—	—	—	—	—	—
Non-Proliferation (Nuclear)	3	4	4	4	3	5	6	6
Policy Planning	5	2	2	4	4	4	4	4
Precursors of Chemical and Biological Weapons	—	—	—	1	3	2	4	4
Protocol	1	1	3	2	3	2	2	2
United Nations	6	6	7	6	7	5	5	5
UN Disarmament	3	3	4	6	5	4	3	5
Total Meetings	87	76	91	87	94	93	105	109

Source: Author's calculation according to EPC data.

Presidential Overload: The Limits of Procedural Adaptations

Due to the increase in the Twelve's internal and external activity, the presidencies' workload—including their responsibility for the smooth running of the EPC business (organizational duties, internal negotiation, and mediation) and outside representation—grew considerably over the past years. With the creation of a secretariat as an auxiliary body, through the Single European Act,[10] at least the administrative burdens of the presidency could be alleviated. However, the key role of the presidency remained untouched. Certain procedural novelties introduced by the ministerial decision and passed in the course of the Single European Act[11] were born out of the fundamental need to secure efficient consultation mechanisms among a steadily extended and geographically distant group of participants. The rule to convene Working Group meetings in the rooms of the EPC secretariat in Brussels was generally accepted since 1987, even though it took EPC participants some time to familiarize themselves with the EC business atmosphere in Brussels. This atmosphere was obviously very different from those of meetings held in the various capital cities of each presidency, where meetings were conducted with individualistic flair. Some expert groups—for example, those dealing with communication matters, the European correspondents, and the planning group—continued to follow the old practices since these better facilitated their specific tasks.

At the level of the political directors, the preference was still for the "traveling circus" of former EPC days, despite all the physical and organizational efforts linked herewith and burdening those directly involved. The main argument put forward by EPC representatives was this: For its decisions, the Political Committee relied on extensive reporting by the Working Groups, whose chairmen belonged to the staff of the presidency and who were therefore easily accessible to the foreign ministry of the presidency. This argument was not necessarily convincing, because the number of participants traveling to a Political Committee meeting was considerable since it also involved the political directors' closest staff, not merely one representative from each member state. The "peripheral" location of certain capitals, insufficient traveling connections, and the requirement of reliable participation and representation of member states in EPC and Community business[12] made Brussels the obvious choice as a central location. This preference was to gain ground in the 1990s.

Not only did the web of contacts at a directorial and ministerial level put considerable strain on the personalities involved among the twelve EPC countries themselves but their attractiveness as dialogue partners for nonmember states also brought about considerable involvement from foreign ministers, diplomats, and, particularly, the presidency. Given their traditional responsibilities to act in the name of their home countries, the foreign ministers and their high-ranking advisers were occasionally forced to delegate tasks to lower levels. Internally, this meant another dispersion of the EPC staff and required additional coordination efforts. It could also imply a loss of maneuverability, given the political profile or weak authority of these other personnel. More than once, however, certain political figures—particularly from the big EC member states—showed a lessening degree of interest in EPC's contacts with the outside world, especially in those cases in which full representation at a ministerial level was required because of political commitments the Twelve had taken over (e.g., in most of the group-to-group dialogues)[13] but also in cases in which the Troika format was applied. These participants sometimes felt themselves to be low-ranking compared to the "real" spokesman of the Twelve, the presidency, and they therefore preferred to stay at home. Attempts to overcome the discrepancy that had emerged between the Twelve's obligations toward their dialogue partners and the practical fulfillment of the political dialogues were only a partial remedy. These attempts focused on practical measures of how to "economize" EPC's international posture—for example, by linking political dialogues with the calendar of normal EPC meetings and by reducing the traveling obligations for the EPC staff in the home capitals by entrusting certain dialogue functions to the resident diplomats. More than once, however, the Twelve had to realize that what might be justified from an EPC management viewpoint was not well received on the part of the dialogue partners. Observed from outside, the composition of the Twelve and their level of representation were perceived as an expression of Europe's expectation of privileged, individual treatment as a dialogue partner. As such, EPC performance had to be understood as a political signal that had direct impact on Europe's credibility as an interlocutor.

As it did in previous years, recent EPC history revealed time and again the general flaw in the practice of rotating presidencies. Even though one may argue that the practice helps to compensate for negative effects that might be created by weak and unskilled personalities among the Twelve, the question of continuity and identity in external performance is of greater relevance. The potential value of a six-month presidential term to promote confidence and mutual understanding in a turbulent international environment is obvious. An extended use of the Troika formula, as practiced in the past, could only partly compensate for the limits of the rotation system—not to mention organizational problems, personal rivalries, et cetera.

In addition, the EPC's external profile seems to be hampered by the fact that small member states maintain only limited diplomatic services and are not necessarily represented in all parts of the world. Thus, when it comes time to issue the EPC *acquis* toward the addressees, the acting presidency might be forced to entrust certain tasks to the preceding, or incoming, official. It seems as if this sort of "burden sharing" is widely accepted in normal—that is, organizational—business. Another variant of this principle that was already foreseen in the London Report of 1981 has rarely been applied in the 1990s: entrusting one of the Troika members with tasks that the acting presidency is unable to fulfill. Such a far-reaching distribution of presidential responsibilities is perceived as being counterproductive to the general understanding that each country wishes to conduct "its" presidency alone and make maximum profit from it.

In retrospect, the real novelty in the EPC decisionmaking process since the Single European Act—the creation of a secretariat[14]—also assisted in reducing presidential burdens to a certain degree. Although designed to function in a minimalist fashion—that is, to "assist" the presidency in the daily management of EPC and, in particular, to organize the meetings, make the room reservations, secure the distribution of documents, draw up the minutes of the meetings, and so on—the secretariat successfully exploited these functions fully and even enlarged its activities in the area of conceptual work. Of course, to a varying degree and depending upon the understanding of the individual member states in the chair, the secretariat was allowed to draft texts to be submitted to the Political Committee, the foreign ministers, and even the European Council. Moreover, the preparation of the speeches of the president-in-office for the UN General Assembly and for his interventions in the European Parliament, as well as the drafting of the responses to parliamentary questions, were acknowledged as an extremely valuable alleviation of the presidency's duties. Regarding the possibility that the secretariat might be tempted to present itself as an interlocutor for the outside world,[15] concern among the member states was difficult to overcome. The simple fact of being placed in Brussels, where the majority of third countries had established diplomatic bonds with the EC and where the international press was present, made, however, certain activities indispensable. The secretariat inevitably became a source from which to request information on EPC. With considerable skill, the secretariat, and particularly its respective "head," entered this domain over the years, being also closely associated with the European Parliament, as agreed upon in the SEA.[16] It seems as if the limited capacities of the secretariat—particularly its focus on EPC "domestic" affairs—helped to overcome the existing reservations among the Twelve. The secretariat[17] was increasingly perceived as a valuable means to compensate for the discontinuities inherent in the system of rotating presidencies, which also found its expression in the Twelve's decision (in the 1990–1991 Intergovernmental Conference) to enlarge its staff considerably and also to accept its closeness to Community institutions.

Increasingly aware of the limitations of a strictly diplomatic approach to international problems and conscious of their failure to present themselves as a unified actor, the European Community made considerable efforts over the years to come closer to their goal of a more consistent policy.[18] In procedural terms, the provisions of the Single European Act (Article 30[3a], SEA)—that is, to hold EPC meetings on the fringe of the Council—were used intensively. Initially, these gatherings took the form of informal luncheons before Council sessions, without formal agenda and without the presence of the EPC staff, but beginning in 1989, preference was given to a more institutionalized format. Thus, ministers met in the same conference room to discuss first the Council's agenda and then that of EPC or vice versa, the two sessions being interrupted by a break, in order to allow for a change-over of experts from Community to EPC business. This was particularly welcomed by the EPC officials, as they were able to be present during negotiations and, consequently, did not depend only on the information and assessment they received from the political top. According to EPC sources, one of the earliest and most successful examples of this joint approach was the EC/Twelve's policy toward the countries in Eastern Europe. Notwithstanding the importance of such a pragmatic procedure compared to the rigidity and orthodoxy of earlier EPC days, the approach remained ad hoc. Attempts were also made to familiarize the EPC staff with Community business and vice versa—for example, through joint meetings of political directors and permanent representatives. However, no clear-cut plans emerged for a sensible division of labor or a fusion of tasks, which would serve as a starting point for the deliberations during the Intergovernmental Conference.

CFSP Provisions and Reality: A Mixed Balance

Roughly fifteen months after getting the CFSP under way, the experience so far revealed both success and failure. While the Council's view put emphasis on significant progress in quantative and qualitative terms,[19] the Commission document more openly describes the first months of application as a "laborious process," without substantial improvement.[20] Concern and dissatisfaction are expressed particularly with regard to the following provisions and their application in practice.

The Member States' Obligation to Support the CFSP Actively and Unreservedly in a Spirit of Loyalty and Mutual Solidarity (Article J.1[4])

It is true: Member states' governments continue to attach considerable importance to belonging to the CFSP framework. Participants underline the strategic significance of the system in terms of having greater access to information and analysis, compared to unilateral diplomatic practice. None of them has therefore questioned the value of the gatherings and their joint endeavors "to speak with one voice" to the outside world. While insiders occasionally espouse a "qualitative belief in the awareness of the need to act together,"[21] from the outside traditional patterns of behavior seem to prevail. As the former EPC, CFSP is seen as an extremely useful instrument for national foreign policy making. In contrast, the emergence of shared convictions among the member states progresses slowly. In line with such an

understanding is the frequent use of well-known intergovernmental procedures, while the possibility of majority voting is ignored.[22] The Union's
enlargement from January 1995 onward seems to confirm this trend despite
the declared openness of representatives of the European Free Trade Association (EFTA) toward the TEU objectives and the next reform. The new
member states also prefer traditional diplomatic procedures to get acquainted with the CFSP system. Reliance on coordination and unanimity produce,
on the output side, a huge number of declarations—again, a key feature of
the old EPC.

Some rightly argue that a common CFSP identity can be better promoted by strengthening existing procedural arrangements and, in particular, by
the application of majority voting. Even though the view is widely shared
that sticking to unanimity decisions will lead to paralysis, particularly in a
Union of more than fifteen members, neither the various governments nor
outside observers are ready to draw the following conclusion: Community
experience suggests that the possibility of a majority vote changes the negotiation style—that is, instead of claiming a veto position, a more constructive position is adopted, thus accelerating the entire negotiation process and
leading to concrete results. The introduction of the majority vote as a general principle would, however, also require opt-out clauses. A supposed
"coalition of the able and willing" must not be blocked by a minority group.
Member states might find themselves in a situation in which vital national
interests, but also disinterest, prevent them from joining the others. If one
follows the argument that the theoretical existence of the majority voting
plan already changes the mode of negotiations without yet being applied,
then a debate on opt-out models and their consequences or on the external
profile of the Union becomes less important. Moreover, if majority voting
would become a reality, criteria would have to be established as to who is
charged with supervision of a given opt-out situation and what conclusions
should be drawn regarding implementation of such a decision (i.e., who carries the financial burdens—only those who are in favor, the Community
budget, or . . . ?).

Given the British government's massive obstruction of progress in this
direction, others therefore favor the more moderate approach toward positive abstention. Although, as a principle, it existed previously in former EPC
tenets, the member states' intention not to veto a decision when a qualified
majority of member states were in favor of it was formulated during the
TEU negotiations. Due to certain reservations, however, this formula did not
become part of CFSP provisions. It should rather be understood to be a political commitment and was therefore only annexed to the Treaty in a declaration. To give its existing application an even greater weight, the next
Intergovernmental Conference (IGC) could decide whether to integrate the
principle into the CFSP part of the Treaty, which, in substance, would be
equivalent to Article 148(3), EC Treaty.

Even if one does not share the view that the EU's declaratory diplomacy is rather useless, its value becomes more limited at a time when both external challenges and expectations about the Union's capacity to act and the Union's willingness to do so have grown immensely. Shortly after the first experiences, it became obvious that the existing structures, even in their revised version, did not suffice. The requirement for an early and continued analysis of external developments and the definition of the Union's common interests are a focal point of today's debate. Institutionally speaking, the Political Committee, the central organ of EPC, is increasingly unable to fulfill this guiding function, due to several factors. The overall responsibility the political directors carry for the foreign policy of their countries at the national level does not allow them to devote enough energy and time to CFSP; their professional background is traditionally outside the Community business—a factor that emphasizes the problem of the pillarization of the Union's external relations instead of fostering consistency. Furthermore, the Political Committee's work on the substance of the Union's foreign policies suffered from an unclear division of labor between the political directors and the Committee of Permanent Representatives (COREPER). Once the Twelve had decided to entrust the Council with the responsibility for CFSP, COREPER, the central body in charge of preparing and implementing the Council work, entered the former exclusive domain of the political directors.[23] Since it was left to the post-IGC period to clarify the division of labor between the two bodies,[24] competition was strong and controversial negotiations began. The formula agreed upon acknowledged a continued key role for the Political Committee concerning the established items of the CFSP agenda and the respective implementation of CFSP policies. The permanent representatives are principally entrusted with the technical preparatory work of Council sessions. They can, however, also add comments to the work done by the political directors and, as practice has shown, can accentuate the debate on agenda items, particularly when matters of "high politics" are interrelated with Community business. As the controversial debate about the financing of CFSP demonstrated, COREPER's role has been decisive in this respect when, in 1993–1994, their expertise was sought to enable the CFSP to benefit from the Community budget.[25]

Figure 4.1 may help illustrate the institutional turbulence referred to, which also extended to the expert level. The ministerial decision to "simply" transform the existing EPC Working Groups into the usual Council structure, that is, the Working Parties (see Table 4.4), produced immense controversies on how to respond to the fusion trend and enormous bureaucratic infighting. They were most obvious in those cases in which expert groups already existed, both in the EPC field and the Community's external relations. A merger of these two "lineages" raised such sensitive questions as who could or should replace whom, who should be in charge of taking the floor in the name of the national delegation, and which kind of division of

Figure 4.1 Institutional Adaptations

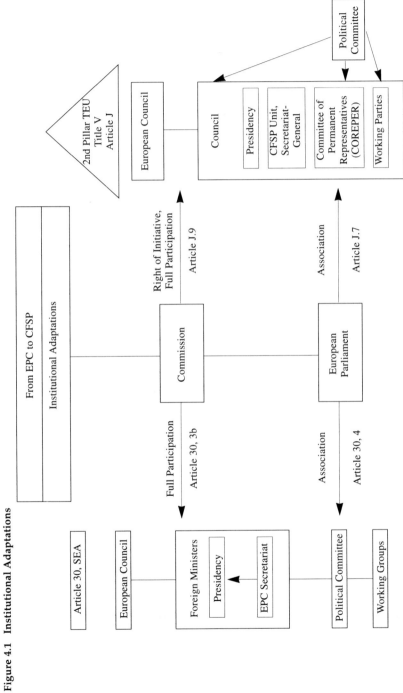

Table 4.4   Transformation of EPC Working Groups into Council Structure

Standing Working Parties	Merged of
Asia	• Asia Group (EPS) • Working Group on Asia (EC)
Central and Eastern Europe (deals with relations to Poland, Hungary, Czech Republic, Slovak Republic, Romania, Bulgaria, Estonia, Latvia, Lithuania, Slovenia [envisaged])	• Eastern Europe Group (EPC) • Working Group on Eastern Europe (EC)
CIS (deals with relations to Belarus, Ukraine, Moldova, Russia, Armenia, Azerbaijan, Georgia, Kazakhstan, Turkmenistan, Uzbekistan, Tajikistan, Kyrgyzstan)	• Eastern Europe Working Group (EPC) • Working Group on the former USSR (EC)
CSCE	• CSCE Group (EPC) • Ad Hoc Working Group on CSCE (EC)
Latin America	• Latin America Group (EPC) • Working Group on Latin America (EC)
Mashreq/Maghreb (deals with relations to Algeria, Morocco, Tunisia, Libya, Mauritania, Egypt, Lebanon, Israel, Jordan, Syria)	• Euro-Arab Dialogue Group (EPC) • Mediterranean Working Group (EC) • Working Group on Euro-Arab Dialogue
Middle East/Gulf (deals with relations to Iran, Iraq, Yemen, Gulf States, Saudi Arabia, Oman, the Emirates, Bahrain, Qatar, Kuwait)	• Middle East/Maghreb Group (EPC) • Mediterranean Working Group (EC) • Working Group on Gulf States (EC)
Middle East Peace Process (all issues related to the peace process)	• Replaces the Special Coordinating Group on Middle East Peace Process (EPC)
South Africa (discussions related to the implementation of joint action)	• Takes over activities of Africa Group (EPC) • The Development Working Group (EC)
Ad Hoc Former-Yugoslavia (deals with the countries of former-Yugoslavia, including Slovenia, and will be reviewed after end of the conflict)	
Other Standing Working Parties	• Administration affairs • Africa • Communication • Consular affairs • Drugs • Human rights • Nonproliferation of chemical and biological weapons • Nuclear nonproliferation • Policy planning • Protocol
South-East Europe (deals with relations to Albania, Cyprus, Turkey, Malta, Andorra, San Marino)	• Telecommunication • Terrorism • United Nations • UN disarmament • Conventional arms exports • Public international law • Security

labor corresponded best to the matter being treated. The fusion was less strained in those areas where no Council Working Party had previously existed. In areas such as human rights, conventional arms exports, nonproliferation, or planning staffs, the old EPC circles did not have to fear immediate competition from Community counterparts. However, even the simple fact that the EPC groups became part of the Council infrastructure did not remain without influence. Participants noted a withering away of the old "club" atmosphere, caused by an increased number of participants—for example, from the Council's legal services, the national administrations, and a more output-oriented debate.

Among the institutional novelties, the least controversial one is the secretariat. Intentionally set up as an auxiliary to the presidency, its influence on the substance of the CFSP policies remains limited. Though better staffed than during the EPC period, the new CFSP unit inside the secretariat-general of the Council of the European Union[26] cannot compensate for the discontinuities caused by the rotation of presidencies and the presidential overload, which, for example, is visible in the numerous dialogue commitments with third countries (see Table 4.5) and in the occasional temporary deadlock at other CFSP levels. Even in an upgraded format or as part of a new central force that will be created to supply common background analysis, greater continuity in action, and even a clearer representation of the Union,[27] the secretariat's role will remain limited. Any such new body must create a strengthened political will in order to take the CFSP objectives seriously.

*Confusion over the Instruments
and the Weaknesses of the Pillar Structure*

To go beyond the often criticized declaratory diplomacy of EPC Article J.3 (TEU) introduces the instrument of joint actions. Based on general guidelines by the European Council, through which CFSP is to receive greater political authority,[28] it is the Council's responsibility to decide upon joint actions that offer a very concrete and visible policy toward a given international problem. With the coming into force of the Maastricht Treaty, the Twelve were able to present the first areas for these new instruments based on the existence of "essential common interests."[29] Though designed as a very clear-cut, precise, and visible exercise, "on the spot" CFSP reality tells a different story. Since the final outcome of a joint action has to be based on a general assessment of the given problem and has to correspond to the Union's intention to choose a global approach, occasional overlapping of the agenda items formally attributed to the different pillars of the Union are but natural.

The same "phenomenon" occurred with regard to the other created instrument, that is, common positions, through which the Union wishes to explain, in a somewhat more solemn way,[30] their external posture toward

Table 4.5   Overview of Political Dialogue Commitments (as of 31 December 1994)

Countries/Groups	Basis
Albania	Joint Declaration, 11/5/1992
Australia	Council Decision, 7/5/1990
ASEAN	Various EC/ASEAN Decisions, 11/9/1978–8/1/1993
Baltics	Joint Declarations, 11/5/1992
Canada	Declaration on EU/Canada Relations, 22/11/1992
CEEC (countries of Central and Eastern Europe)	Copenhagen European Council, 22/6/1993 & Council Decision, 8/3/1994
Central America	Final Act of Luxembourg Conference, 12/11/1985
China	Exchange of Letters, 5/1994
Cyprus	Council Decision, 18/7/1988 & Decision of Association Council, 21/12/1992
Gulf Cooperation Council	—
India	EU/India Political Statement, 20/12/1993
Japan	EU/Japan Joint Declaration 18/7/1991
Malta	Exchange of Letters, 29/4/1988
New Zealand	Political Committee Decision, 6/9/1990
Non-Aligned Countries	Political Committee Decision, 5/9/1990
Pakistan	Political Committee Decision, 12/2/1992
Rio Group	Declaration, 20/12/1990
Russia	Partnership and Cooperation Agreement, 24/6/1994
South Korea	Political Committee Decision, 6/6/1989
Sri Lanka	EU/Sri Lanka Statement, 16/5/1994
Turkey	Decision of Association Council, 9/11/1992
Ukraine	EU/Ukraine Cooperation Agreement, 14/6/1994
United States	EU/U.S. Declaration, 23/11/1990

Note: In principle, Association/Cooperation Councils with Egypt, Israel, Lebanon, Morocco, Syria, and Tunisia also cover political dialogue issues.

another country or region. CFSP circles tend to interpret such tendencies as an almost natural part of the logic of an issue, thus giving, at least from their point of view, the "right" guidance to follow-up decisions to be made in the first pillar—similar to the immediate interrelationship foreseen in Article 228a (EC Treaty) in the case of economic sanctions. Community circles and, in particular, the Commission wish to see this as an overstepping of CFSP competences—not only on an individual, case-by-case basis, but on the contrary, as a fundamental problem of intergovernmentalism invading the Community's sphere. More than once,[31] the Union got bogged down in institutional quarrels.

Although they are not always noticed immediately by those outside the Union, these internal constraints of the pillar structure are detrimental to the Union's efficiency and need to be clarified at the IGC.

In day-to-day operations, another problem arose regarding the instruments. The Treaty provisions do not specify in great detail the nature of common positions compared to joint actions. As the latter were perceived as the key instruments of CFSP, they should be reserved for very special and detailed issues, while common positions can cover the broad range of day-to-day matters and perhaps express in a more formal way the Union's *acquis politique* on international issues.[32] As the Commission's report on the functioning of the TEU states:[33] "The net result is confusion about the role of the different instruments." Joint actions were both punctual and broad, specifically the one to dispatch a team of observers for the parliamentary elections in Russia in November 1993, or the December 1993 Council decision on a joint action concerning support for the transition toward a democratic and multiracial South Africa.

Inextricably linked to a more effective and more visible CFSP is the question of money. Without being fully aware of the consequences and practical implications, the TEU signatories defined the guiding principles in Article J.11.2. Based on the early experiences of EPC—in other words, that its expenditure was covered by the member states—it was natural that CFSP would be made operational through national financial contributions. As a second, however unlikely, possibility, financing from the Community budget for operational expenditures was also foreseen. Economic recession and national budgetary restrictions, however, made frequent recourse to the Union's budget more necessary than initially envisaged. Making the joint actions operational via Community money meant, however, another battle-field—this time between the Council and the European Parliament, due to the latter's competences as part of the budgetary authority. Members of the European Parliament (MEPs) were thus able to impose their views on the structure of CFSP operational expenditure against the will of the most "enthusiastic" intergovernmentalists among the member states. In line with the majority of member states and supported also by the Commission, operational expenditure from the Community budget for CFSP actions will be attributed to the Commission section and will thus be subject to the Community's financial regulations.[34]

The first cases of application suggest greater efficiency and a quicker availability of the means.[35] This explicit interconnectedness between the first and second pillar and the institutions concerned carries certain risks for the institutional balance and the roles of the different bodies thus far in the area of EPC/CFSP. Even those integrationists among the Twelve/Fifteen who are ready to accept the EP's access to CFSP via the budgetary procedure have become strong opponents of an EP strategy that attempts to establish a direct link between an agreement on the CFSP expenditure and an extension of parliamentary rights in the overall CFSP decisionmaking. CFSP insiders massively criticized the EP's strategy as absurd and too excessive when it escalated into a dispute over Parliament's greater political control in the second pillar. The EP's struggle for a very broad interpretation of Article J.7 and, in particular, its understanding of a preconsultation in situations in which common positions and joint actions have to be decided is in clear contrast to the policy of information and ex-post consultation that member states wish to see. Because of this theological dispute and the basic fear of setting precedents, an interinstitutional agreement between the EP and the Council on the modalities of financing the CFSP could not be concluded, even eighteen months after the Maastricht Treaty came into force.[36]

To conclude, the transition from EPC to CFSP, in institutional and procedural terms, has been long and laborious. The setting up of a single institutional framework questioned well-established practices and prerogatives. The interference caused by discussion of multitudinous subject matters opened an unexpected range of conflicts that obscured legitimate political debate on the substance of a true CFSP. Given the limited political will of the member states to take their commitments seriously, the potential for a reform will be meager. It could well be that an "alibi" debate on a minor issue will overshadow a serious discussion on the real defects of CFSP and possible remedies.

Notes

1. *Bulletin of the EC* (4-1990), point 1.12 of the conclusions of the presidency.

2. The other elements—unity and coherence in international actions and the lack of democratic legitimacy—are dealt with particularly in the chapters by Fraser Cameron, Thomas Grunert, and Horst-Günther Krenzler/Henning C. Schneider in this volume.

3. Simon J. Nuttall, "The Foreign and Security Policy Provisions of the Maastricht Treaty: Their Potential for the Future," in Jörg Monar, Werner Ungerer, and Wolfgang Wessels, eds., *The Maastricht Treaty on European Union. Legal Complexity and Political Dynamic* (Brussels: European Interuniversity Press, 1993), p. 135.

4. Philippe de Schoutheete de Tervarent, "L'introduction d'une politique extérieure et de sécurité commune: Motivations et résultats," in Monar, Ungerer, and Wessels, *The Maastricht Treaty on European Union,* p. 132.

5. As to the history of EPC, see, among others, Alfred Pijpers, Elfriede Regelsberger, and Wolfgang Wessels, eds., *European Political Cooperation in the 1980s. A Common Foreign Policy for Western Europe?* (Dordrecht: Martinus Nijhoff Publishers, 1988); and the contribution of Simon Nuttall in Chapter 2 of this volume. Regular analysis on EPC/CFSP is also to be found in Werner Weidenfeld and Wolfgang Wessels, eds., *Jahrbuch der Europäischen Integration* (Bonn: Europa Union Verlag) (published every year from 1980 onward).

6. Affirmed as early as 1981 in the "London Report" of the foreign ministers (13 October 1981).

7. Wolfgang Wessels and Joseph Weiler, "EPC and the Challenge of Theory," in Pijpers, Regelsberger, and Wessels, eds., *European Politcal Cooperation,* pp. 229–258.

8. Heins-Jürgen Axt, "Kooperation unter Konkurrenten. Das Regime als Theorie der außenpolitischen Zusammenarbeit der EG-Staaten," in *Zeitschrift für Politik* 3 (1993), pp. 241–259.

9. Article 30(3a), SEA.

10. Article 30(10g), SEA.

11. See, particularly, Point IV of the decision of the foreign ministers adopted on 28 February 1986: "European Political Cooperation meetings shall normally be held at the seat of the Secretariat. Ministerial level and Political Committee meetings take place in the Capital city of the Presidency."

12. Explicitly referred to in Article 30(5), SEA, and reaffirmed in the Common Provisions of the TEU (Article C).

13. See the contribution of Jörg Monar in Chapter 14 of this volume.

14. Article 30(10g), SEA.

15. As rather vaguely defined in the ministerial decision of February 1986, the last item on the list of the secretariat's functions.

16. For example, by presenting the *acquis politique* in the Political Commission of the EP (renamed as "Committee on Foreign Affairs, Security, and Defense Policy" after the Maastricht Treaty). As for the role of the EP, in general, and EPC/CFSP, see the contribution of Thomas Grunert in Chapter 7 of this volume.

17. For an insider's assessment of the secretariat's work, see Wilhelm Späth, "Die Arbeit des EPZ-Sekretariats. Eine Bilanz," in *Europa Archiv* 6 (1990), pp. 213–220.

18. As explicitly required in Article 30(5), SEA.

19. See the respective report on the functioning of the Treaty on European Union, prepared for the work of the Reflection Group, March 1995.

20. See the respective report on the functioning of the Treaty on European Union, prepared for the work of the Reflection Group, April 1995.

21. Council president Alain Lamassoure in the EP plenary session of 26 April 1995, *Agence Europe,* 27 April 1995.

22. As a typical approach, see Douglas Hurd, "Developing the Common Foreign and Security Policy," *International Affairs* 3 (1994), pp. 421–428.

23. Article J.8(5), TEU, and Article 151, EC Treaty.

24. See the relevant "Declaration on the Practical Arrangements in the Area of CFSP," annexed to the Treaty on European Union.

25. See *Agence Europe,* 28–29 December 1993 and 7–8 March 1994.

26. See also the preliminary organizational chart in *CFSP Forum* 3 (1994), p. 2.

27. See the various proposals presently under discussion, i.e., Groupe d'experts à haute niveau sur la PESC: La Politique de Sécurité de l'Europe à l'horizon 2000: Les voies et moyens d'une véritable credibilité, Brussels, 19 December 1994; Günter Burghardt: "Ein ständiges GASP-Gremium in Brüsssel," May 1995.

28. See Barbara-Christine Ryba (who goes further and attributes a decisive role to the heads of state and government for the substance of CFSP). "La politique étrangère et sécurité commune (PESC). Mode d'emploi et bilan d'une année d'application (fin 1993/1994)," *Revue du Marché commun et de l'Union européenne* 384 (1995), p. 22.

29. Essential common interests are meant to exist on the following pre-conditions: (1) The region or a country concerned is geographically close to the EC; (2) the Union has specific interests in the political and economic stability of the region or a country; and (3) there is a threat to the security interests of the Union. See the "Report of the Foreign Ministers to the European Council," Annex I to the conclusions of the presidency of the European Council, 26–27 June 1992, Lisbon.

30. Thus is the understanding of Ryba, "La politique étrangère," p. 17.

31. As concrete examples, the Union's policy toward Rwanda and the Ukraine are cited. See ibid., p. 22.

32. For this interpretation, see the "Council Report to the European Council," 29 October 1993, Chapter 4.

33. See the Commission's report on the functioning of the TEU, p. 66. A similar judgment is also given in the Council's report on the functioning of the TEU and the need for further clarifications emphasized, p. 52.

34. For further details, see Thomas Hagleitner, "Financing the Common Foreign and Security Policy (CFSP)—A Step Towards Communitarization or Institutional Deadlock?" in *CFSP Forum* 2 (1995), p. 6.

35. As the financing of the administration of the town of Mostar has demonstrated so far, where both Community money and national contributions were used. See Miguel Levy, "L'administration de la ville de Mostar par l'Union Européenne," Bruges, 1995.

36. For details on the subject also with regard to the distinction between administrative and operational expenditure, which again constitutes a source of conflict between Parliament and Council, see Ryba, "La politique étrangère," p. 19, and the contribution of Thomas Grunert in Chapter 7 of this volume.

5

The Actors Involved: National Perspectives

Christopher Hill

The last ten years have been paradoxical in terms of the national foreign policies that have been coordinated in European Political Cooperation (EPC), now become the Common Foreign and Security Policy (CFSP) of the European Union (EU). On the one hand, these national traditions and sets of interests have appeared to become ever less distinctive from each other; and the governments of the twelve member states* have been content to allow a persistent if gradualist trend toward strengthening the collective elements at the expense of the particular, through the Single Act and the Treaty of Maastricht. On the other hand, a succession of dramatic events, centered around the two major military conflicts in the Gulf and the Balkans, have demonstrated the difficulty of achieving joint actions, and have reinforced the public perception of Europe as a broken-backed international actor, with national interests more to the fore even than in the 1980s. Partly in consequence and partly in parallel, the realist and neo-realist theorists have returned, without any disabling sense of anachronism, to the explanation of the European Community. In particular, realism has been given a new lease on life with respect to the analysis of European diplomacy.[1] As for practitioners, they are as divided as citizens and commentators on whether national foreign policy is now simply a variation on the European theme or still the heart of international politics in the region. Views vary according to country, to place in the bureaucratic machine, to posting abroad (the further from Europe, generally the more skeptical a diplomat will be about EPC), to generation, and simply according to personal temperament and worldview.

---

*For the most part this essay will use the terms "the Twelve" and "EPC," rather than "the Fifteen" and "CFSP," simply because most of the available evidence about European foreign policy cooperation refers to the period before the Maastricht Treaty and therefore, by definition, before the 1995 round of enlargement.

85

The paradox of realism's increased relevance in a time of the institutional advancement of the Community needs deconstructing, so as to reach a judgment as to whether the apparent resurgence of national foreign policy is merely a temporary interruption of a longer-term trend toward diplomatic integration, or *per contra,* a demonstration of the fragility and superficiality of the convergence that the Europeans thought they had achieved over two decades of EPC. As I have argued elsewhere,[2] it may be more plausible, in fact, to present a picture of a continuing dialectical relationship between centripetal and centrifugal forces in the making of foreign policy in Europe, where assuming a victory for either side would be to commit the crassest of teleological errors.

Deconstructing the Paradox

In order to make sense of the above paradox, it is necessary to show how it breaks down into three subordinate issues.

1. The first sub-issue is the extent to which genuinely *collective* interests and perceptions have emerged to underpin CFSP. Conversely, how much diplomacy of significance is now left outside the joint process? The term "interests and perceptions" suggests that the objective and subjective elements should be placed in contradistinction, and, indeed, even if we recognize the inevitably contested nature of "interests," it is worth looking at those things that the (now) Fifteen might have a stake in, qua Fifteen (interests arising out of areas in which one's life is affected, like it or not, by any changes, as opposed to values, which may apply to anything), before outlining how far they *see* themselves as needing to act in common.

The EU member states have, by definition, a major interest in protecting the existence and prosperity of the Union itself. This is a truism about national foreign policy, but it is rarely pointed out at the collective level. A common foreign policy must aim to ensure that the community out of which it arises does not suffer as a result of external threats, whether military or otherwise. In the case of the EU as it has historically developed, this largely means a threat to the effective workings of its institutions and of the single market. Only the member states plus the Commission hold this particular brief, although the United States and the rest of NATO have held the major responsibility for defending the geographical entity of Western Europe as a whole from armed attack. How EPC was supposed to carry out this task was always unspecified and, in part, accounts for the uneasy relationship between EPC and the Community proper. Much of what actually went on in EPC seemed only tangentially concerned with protecting European economic interests in the outside world, even in the general sense of encouraging the free movement of peoples, goods, information, and money on which the European export drive depended, because that was the province of the Community institutions and of national governments. EPC seemed, for much of the time, to have a reflexive purpose, that of protecting and promoting itself.[3]

On the other hand, EPC was very active in sponsoring the values that underpinned the whole EC project—namely, democracy, soft-edge capitalism, a zone of peace between member states, and diplomatic mediation between third parties designed to undercut the causes of major conflicts whose conflagration might, in time, draw Europe in more directly and damagingly. Moreover, the very creation of the CFSP is intended as an acknowledgment of the need for economic relations with third states in order to have a diplomatic arm. Finally, as the United States has, since 1990, come steadily to reduce its own military presence in Western Europe, so the Community-become-a-Union has turned more explicitly to thinking about taking responsibility for its own physical defense. The EC states always had a vital interest in the defense of Western Europe; now they also have an increasing stake in the arrangements for so doing, via the buckles that connect the EU to the Western European Union (WEU) and WEU to NATO. In other words, they have agreed to such progress partly as they have emerged from under the shadow of U.S. dominance, and they have only done so in the most carefully circumscribed way, still preserving the principle of national freedom of action in foreign policy through the intergovernmental nature of Pillar Two of the Maastricht Treaty.

In terms of perceptions, there can be no doubt that the way in which national foreign policy makers within the Twelve (it is too soon to speak for the three newcomers) think about their states' roles in the world has been affected by ten, fifteen, or twenty-five years of working within EPC (depending upon when a country entered the EC). But they also still tend to see solidarity as serving, rather than replacing, national independence. This part of our paradox has four aspects:

- Member states accept that there can now be no turning back to the pre-EPC condition. Coordination with partners is now an established part, even the fulcrum, of national foreign policies. Furthermore, on the basis of the bicycle theory—staying on means staying in motion—the CFSP must continue to go forward if it is to survive (but the destination must not be specified).

- Even the biggest member states now have a strong sense of the weakness of unilateralism. Neither Paris nor London labor under any romantic illusion about what could be achieved through a strategy of no entanglements. On the other hand, following Isaiah Berlin, "freedom to" is not "freedom from," and the benefits of collective action

bring with them restrictions on the ability to opt out—or should do
so, in theory. In practice, not surprisingly, most states want it both
ways.

- The smaller member states now have a more heightened sense of
their involvement in and responsibility for the international system
than they had during the Cold War. Yet if their sense of their own profile is heightened, they also have a sharp awareness of their reliance
on the peculiar form of collective security provided by the EC.

- Outside observers of European foreign policy, rarely naive in their
expectations these days, have accepted the EPC process as a working diplomatic caucus. Indeed, for a variety of different reasons,
most of them quite concrete, many of them seek to establish a political dialogue with the EU, *as well as* healthy bilateral relations.

Thus, there are good reasons for supposing that individual member
states now have both practical stakes in and a perceptual attachment to the
evolving CFSP. However, they tend to regard it as an add-on to national foreign policy rather than as a substitute for it, and there is still not a substantial amount of foreign policy left outside the estate of EPC, as we shall see
below when discussing the practice of foreign policy. The purpose, for the
present, is to show how the common project has continued to advance,
despite and sometimes because of the difficulty of reconciling it with national diplomacy.

2. The second element of the current paradox in which the CFSP is
enmeshed is the need to emphasize collectivity in order to ensure that new
entrants are impressed with the force of the *acquis politique*. In other words,
solidarity becomes an instrumental value rather than something sought in its
own right. The candidate countries—Austria, Finland, and Sweden in the
early 1990s, the Visegrád states for the next decade—must not be allowed to
have the impression that they can pick and choose which parts of common
foreign policy to adopt. Indeed, it was made clear to them that the price of
entry would be the surrender of neutrality. That the three states have managed so far to achieve entry without turning their foreign policy traditions
upside-down is either a sign of the light constraints imposed by the CFSP, or
a confirmation of the need to stress the *acquis politique*. Without this
emphasis, the new entrants would presumably have made even less of a
move toward the median position represented by CFSP. The consequence of
the enlargement dimension is, however, that the existing members of the EU
are driven to play up their unity more than is justified by the record of their
own actual preferences.

3. The last leg of the paradox we have been examining refers to the way
in which member states like to use EPC as a platform for their national self-
projection, only to find that when they pursue the instrumental approach to

the point of insouciance about detachment from the group, then their position can soon seem very exposed. This is true for all three of the subgroups that we can observe among the twelve member states. The first of these includes only Britain and France, the two states that have most often seen EPC as a vehicle for sustaining their own evanescent world power role, and therefore the most reluctant to see procedures introduced that would genuinely commit them to majority decisions in foreign policy. In particular, they have shown themselves unwilling even to consider the gamble involved in abandoning their privileged Security Council roles in favor of a collective European seat, at the same time that they have promoted the UN as the basic source of legitimacy for European interventions outside the EC's borders, and, in France's case at least, at the same time that their rhetoric has gone along with German visions of a fully developed EC foreign policy. As permanent members of the Security Council, the two countries have kept their ten partners at arm's length, resisting any implication that they might be acting at the behest of the Union. On the other hand, they have hardly proved able to live up to the status of independent great powers that joint membership of the P5 (Permanent Five) group bestows on them.

The second group of states that we can identify within EPC also strikes an uneasy balance between national concerns and collective aspirations. Italy, Germany, and Spain are all middle-range powers committed to CFSP but limited in their ability to assert themselves by their history in the middle part of this century. Their modern leaders are often keen to claim domestic advantage from the rehabilitation of their national diplomacy, which EPC has made possible, but they have also generally been intelligent (and responsible) enough to see that this must be done subtly. They have seen the value of the "alibi" function of collective action and the dangers of careless opt-outs of the kind that came naturally to Giscard d'Estaing or Margaret Thatcher. On the other hand, there is no doubt that as fascism recedes into history, both external and internal constraints on distinctive national positions for this group of countries will diminish. If the system remains purely intergovernmental, then it is perfectly possible either that these three states could start to emulate British and French semidetachment from CFSP or engage in more assertive struggles over the leadership and direction of the whole business.

Finally, we have already alluded to how the "smaller states" have, in large part, owed their greater activism in world politics in recent decades to EPC, and that some of them have consequently been its most enthusiastic supporters. Even Greece, which remains geopolitically peripheral to the collective enterprise (even if more by its own definition than by that of its partners), has came round quite quickly to accept the value of EPC as a process, as Françoise de La Serre pointed out.[4] More recently, although it has quarreled with its partners over the recognition of the former-Yugoslav Republic of Macedonia, its main complaint is that it has not had the support that a member state has the right to expect from its partners on a matter of vital interest.

In general, the smaller states' contribution to the paradox of a developing CFSP alongside national divergences is that they are eager to contribute their own *particular* perspective to any common positions or joint actions—and this will often lead them to oppose what, at least, their domestic populations may perceive as the realpolitik of the bigger member states—while, at the same time, recognizing their dependence on their larger partners for political and military "cover." In forsaking quietism in international relations, states like Belgium or Denmark are, in fact, risking the costs that all forms of interventionism can incur—namely, antagonizing other, non-like-minded, states and drawing attention to themselves. In these circumstances, they may wish to retain the freedom to dissociate themselves from a high-profile "European" policy, as Greece did in the early 1980s over the Soviet Union, Belgium and others seemed anxious to do during the Gulf War, and Ireland and Denmark continue to do over WEU.

The Practice of Foreign Policy

Having attempted to disentangle the different national and collective elements of European foreign policy, it is now time to turn more directly to the question, heralded above, of what content still remains in national diplomacy. The best way to do this in a limited space is to contrast what states can do, or can be expected to do, reasonably well; what they cannot do; and what it is unreasonable to expect of either national or European diplomacy, given the inherent intractability of so much of international relations.

What Can National Foreign Policies Still Do?

There are at least four categories of action that nation-states can and do still undertake on the international scene with a fair chance of success:

1. The first is the protection of particular historical interests and the promotion of associated bilateral relationships. The extent and importance of these ties, which are both extra-EU and intra-EU, will vary from state to state, but all have them. Luxembourg has special relationships with all its neighbors, which must be managed so as to ensure support but not suffocation. At the other extreme, the bigger states all cultivate their own dialogues with major countries like China, Russia, and the United States. Nor is this any longer a question of slowly dying colonial ties; France places importance on its relations with India and Nigeria, while Britain has had preoccupying problems with both Libya and Syria. In the middling group of mem-

ber states, Denmark is not about to abandon its bilateral dealings with Norway, while Portugal and the Netherlands are particularly embroiled with Indonesia over East Timor. To be sure, they wish to strengthen their position by harnessing the CFSP to the cause, but they have had only limited success, given the commercial disincentives for their partners to antagonize Jakarta.

2. The second surviving purpose of national foreign policy is to exert checks and balances on and within a European foreign policy, to the extent that it might take on a life of its own. It is still difficult to imagine a collective process that would operate on the basis of extensive majority voting on matters of more than trivial significance in foreign policy, and part of the reason is that the units of the system still wish to have the capacity to put a brake on what might be seen as risky, expensive, dangerous, or simply immoral initiatives. If one state were able to set in motion European foreign policy, over and above the reservations of a minority, it is conceivable that instances of adventurism (largely diplomatic future military actions cannot be ruled out) could create Europe's own "quagmires," with the concomitant backwash of internal recriminations. Bosnia springs readily to mind in this context, as do the Kurdish "safe havens." The current consensus method of decisionmaking in the CFSP may lead to what is, at times, a stultifying paralysis and conservatism, but, by the same token, it also produces a caution and a pacific approach that have been all too rare in the history of European diplomacy. Not only do all the major states have to adhere to a position for it to be carried forward, but even the opposition of a single small state can be enough to damage the credibility of a common policy and to rob it of much forward momentum.

3. The third function still left to national foreign policy is to express the differing perceptions of different types of state, large and small, weak and strong, *within* an intensive foreign policy making process, as opposed to the routine exchanges between wholly separate and self-consciously sovereign nation-states in more normal, and less effective, international organizations, such as the UN General Assembly or the Conference on Security and Cooperation in Europe (CSCE), which bind states so loosely that communication between the different classes of states is highly ritualized and inconsequential, when not actually antagonistic. Within the CFSP, whatever its defects, member states have no choice but to become closely acquainted with each others' positions and outlooks, when the presidency is taken by all in turn and when more than twelve thousand messages via COREU, the EPC telex network, are exchanged per year between the Twelve.[5] The big states will often become impatient with their smaller colleagues' views and sometimes ignore them. Accordingly, the minnows will not always bother even to express a divergent opinion. But if, in international relations, small states are to find an inside track through which to influence the more important players, then CFSP surely provides the best available.

4. The fourth and last thing that national foreign policies still do is to act as a manageable reference point for democratic accountability, something noticeably difficult to achieve in relation to foreign policy inside giant states like the United States, the former Soviet Union, or China, and not easy even in medium powers. The current arrangements for the European Parliament to hold the CFSP accountable are not adequate, although it is accurate both that the same is true in many member states and that since direct elections, the Parliament has definitely stimulated debate on Europe's external relations. However, the practices and the theory behind the CFSP are as remote from most European citizens as are their MEPs (members of the European Parliament), and short of a radical transformation of the very constitutional base of the Union, they will remain so. In this context, political debate about issues such as Macedonia or Algeria is much more likely to have bite when focused on governments in Athens and Paris than on the irregular and peripatetic sessions of the European Parliament. There are, at times, encounters over foreign policy issues in the Strasbourg Chamber that are nearly as passionate as that in the emergency session of the House of Commons on 3 April 1982 over the invasion of the Falkland Islands. The trouble is that hardly anyone notices.

What Can National Foreign Policies Not Do Very Well?

It is also important to turn over the coin from the functions of national foreign policy within the CFSP. What can states not now do very well in the sphere of foreign policy?

The answer is twofold (although there may be more minor functions that could be added to the list). First, it is difficult to be self-sufficient in defense, and all the pressures are toward collective defense in the form of alliances, burden sharing, and forward defense. It is not absolutely inconceivable to go it alone, as Israel and Serbia have both shown. However, states like the Western European ones are not in a position to receive the kinds of blank checks that Israel has enjoyed from the United States in the past, and would not wish to accept the costs that have attached to Serbia's display of ruthless egoism. In every area of defense policy, the CFSP states display the desire to cooperate (if not integrate) and a recognition that they simply cannot afford the expensive insurance policies provided by modern weapon systems and efforts at mobilization. Even where they withdraw from the common effort, as during the Gulf crisis, they demonstrate national weakness more than strength. Those Western states that joined the anti-Saddam coalition came out of the war, on the whole, with their image as significant powers enhanced. Those, like Belgium or Germany, that would or could do little, drew the conclusion even more strongly that they should push on with the European defense project. Of course, the Gulf War illustrated another fundamental truth for all the Europeans: That cooperation on defense does not necessarily mean cooperation through the EU or even WEU. NATO's significance as the provider of command systems and military infrastructures was all too evident in 1991, and the Balkan War has only reinforced that impression.

The second thing that even strong EC member states can no longer do alone is to pursue an independent global role. Britain more or less lost confidence in its ability to be a global power after African decolonization and the Suez/Skybolt/Polaris humiliations at the hands of the United States. The decision to withdraw military bases from "east of Suez," made in late 1967, confirmed the tendency to limit the scope of foreign policy largely to what the Duncan Report of 1969 called "the area of concentration"—that is, Western Europe and the northern Atlantic. Since then, Britain's extra-European activities have all been embarrassments, with only incidental gains: Rhodesia, the Falklands, and Hong Kong. Even the Gulf War produced no illusions in London about returning to global activism. Defense expenditure has continued to decline.

The same is broadly true for France, although the tendency to blur the distinction between the destiny of France and of Europe as a whole, together with the confidence with which the elite in Paris still look on the *rayonnement* of French culture and influence worldwide, from the base of the DOMTOMs and the French African Community, disguises the extent to which ambitions have been reined in. But since the Suez fiasco of 1956, France has increasingly accepted, some rhetoric notwithstanding, that it cannot compete with the superpowers and has usually behaved with caution in areas like Lebanon, Chad, Bosnia, or Algeria, where it could easily have been drawn into a damaging conflict. The French "lessons of Vietnam" were learned earlier, and perhaps better, than the United States' lessons. And if globalism is no longer a realistic option for France and Britain, then it is no kind of option at all for the other states of the EU.

Security.   What is the term "common security policy" meant to convey? Does it include defense? Should it, as the Commission proposed in its opinion of October 1990, include a commitment to reciprocal defense as set out in Article V of the Treaty on Western European Union? What is to be the relationship between the Union, WEU, and NATO?

Vital common interests.   How should they be identified? Should an attempt be made a priori to draw up a list? Foreign ministers meeting informally at Asolo in October 1990 tried their hand at this and the so-called Asolo list, lengthened at times and shortened at others, had a long but not very fruitful career in the course of a number of meetings at the ministerial and official level. Should a certain authority (the European Council?) define these "vital common interests" in the light of any given situation? If foreign affairs and security are to be the subject of a common, but not of a single, policy, how are we to ensure that national foreign and security policies will conform to that laid down in common? What level of constraint is acceptable? Can sanctions be envisaged in case of nonobservance?

Graduality.   How should it be achieved? In quantitative terms, by a gradual increase in the number of issues dealt with (on the basis of the "Asolo list")? In qualitative terms, by arrangements beginning at a modest level of common action but developing progressively with the help of a revision clause? In temporal terms, on the basis of a fixed timetable?

Europe cannot, either together or severally, be expected to provide an alternative source of "leadership" in the international system to the United States and the defunct Soviet superpower. Too many states are historically tired of having to take their cues from Europe in the colonial and neocolonial eras, and Europeans are not insensitive to the fact. They only wish to envisage significant interventions outside their own region as a last resort. Such apparently clear-cut issues as Iraq's attack on Kuwait occur only once in a political generation and should not be regarded as typical. Nor is it feasible to expect Europe to become one of the "poles" of a multipolar world, at least without a constitutional self-transformation and a dramatic upgrading of its military capability.

Lastly, although the national versus collective issue in foreign policy is part of the general dilemma of how far Europe should galvanize itself into further integration, it should not be expected to carry the weight of providing an answer. Although it is not unreasonable to argue that if a federal union is to come about, then foreign and defense policy should be the first and most important area to be handed over to the center, it is also true that we are not talking here about small, developing societies facing an obvious external threat. Rather, the EU consists of fifteen well-established states, not particularly threatened from the outside, for each of whom foreign policy is a key symbol of identity and sovereignty. For them, settling the constitutional issue over foreign policy is likely to follow on from, and not precede, institutional change of a more general character. In itself, foreign policy can create and sustain a sense of common purpose among a people(s) only up to a limited point, as the experiences of the Grand Alliance between 1941–1945, of NATO and of the Arab League amply demonstrate. It is thus somewhat unreal to conduct the debate about sovereignty and integration first and foremost in terms of the CFSP, which will itself have to wait for wider events. Foreign policy still leans more toward the nation-state than toward the European Union.

The Structure of Foreign Policy

Let us now try to draw together the threads of this discussion of the role of national foreign policies in the changing world of European external relations. The main argument is that it would be foolish to assume that the national element is becoming marginalized in CFSP, and, in summary, we can identify five main reasons for this view:

1. *The weight of history*—in terms of the state, the experience of war, and national identity. Long-established states and those who have had to fight for their survival will be understandably reluctant to relinquish the ultimate right to opt out for the notional benefit of collectivism. Conversely, newer or reborn states actually welcome the chance to develop their own policies under the shelter of collective support. When the point of final choice arrives, they may prove surprisingly reluctant to surrender a hard-won distinctiveness.

2. *Nationalism*—If nationalism is not a universal phenomenon, it is certainly not one to be underestimated, even in stable states, as the unpredicted developments of the last ten years show. The persistence of recession and of sharper international economic competition can only heighten domestic pressures to protect "us" and forget about "them" (even when "they" are friendly). And nationalism at the social and economic levels is never going to go hand-in-hand with a willingness to surrender autonomy in the foreign policy area—rather, the reverse. It should not be forgotten that although the single market and the operation of transnational enterprises rule out mercantilist responses within the EU, member states are still fiercely competitive with each other in third country export markets. This spills over from time to time into foreign policy, as we have seen in relation to South Africa and to China.

3. *Constitutional dispositions*—Foreign policy is usually an executive prerogative, and its exercise is closely tied up with the general powers and status of the executive. Since executives are rarely interested in hara-kiri, it follows that they will drag their feet in agreeing to the creation of a new center of decisionmaking. This is true both of diplomats, who have a trade union interest in preserving the national network of job opportunities, and of politicians, who realize that the international prominence to be achieved as prime minister of Portugal within an intergovernmental system may not be available in a more federal structure. On the other hand, some small countries, like Belgium and Luxembourg, do tend to be enthusiastic supporters of a unified European diplomacy, which promises to concentrate resources around the physical heart of the Union.

4. *Distinctive national interests*—By definition, separate states have separate commercial, political, strategic, and cultural interests. The key questions relate to how far, within a grouping like the EU, these diverge seriously, and how far they may be converging and fading over time. There are good reasons to suppose that convergence and the common diagnosis of problems is occurring, but the key word here is "time." How long does genuine community building, let alone Euro-state building, take—especially given the voluntary basis of constitutional change within the Union, and

(thankfully) the lack of the kind of traumas that welded the U.S. union together in the last century?

5. *Bureaucratic politics*—Even in a system of formal decisionmaking like CFSP, with its mixture of intergovernmental and integrationist elements, there will still be a formidable amount of national and institutional game playing, as the history of the Commission, of the presidency, and of the Committee of Permanent Representatives (COREPER) shows. This will not end with the new, more integrated, and more Brussels-centered mechanisms for making external policy. Indeed, in the short and medium terms, it may well increase. It would, of course, continue under a federal system, as we can see in Washington, but the point here is that such patterns of competition only play into the hands of the nationalist opponents of further progress in foreign policy integration.

But even if the national dimension must remain central for all those who wish to understand the realities of current European diplomacy, it is equally true that the process is dynamic. Actors are shaped and constrained by structures over time, and the structure as well as the context of European foreign policy has changed considerably in the last decade, increasing both the actual centripetal pressures and the expectations of progress. If Western European diplomacy in general has had to break and reform in the aftermath of the Cold War, it is clear that the CFSP has become even more attractive for outsiders, that member states cling to it for psychological and physical security, and that it is in effect the core of a new loose European subsystem, with various other groupings orbiting at varying degrees of proximity. In this light problems like that of Greek isolation over the former-Yugoslav Republic of Macedonia become exceptions that prove the rule; Greece was in fact desperately anxious to have the support of its EC partners and offended that the diplomatic alliance did not seem to extend as far as solidarity toward a partner over a perceived vital (national) interest. It is true that the majority were perhaps less than sympathetic to a state with a long history of disruption within EPC, but they must also have realized that Greece could not abandon such a core value in the interests of the majority principle, let alone merely to preserve the appearance of unity (as the Declaration on Voting in the field of the CFSP, attached to the Maastricht Treaty, requests of states[6]). On the other hand, Greece would be even less likely to envisage life outside the CFSP system, and has been careful not to marginalize itself in general. Indeed it has joined both the WEU and the Schengen Group in the last year.

CFSP should thus be seen as a collaborative framework of increasing solidity whose strength partly derives from the very fact that it permits national policies to continue in parallel. In the long run, by virtue of the fact that there are few rivals to its structuration capability, it may lead to those national positions being so redefined in common terms that they fade almost to nothing. For the present, the national and collective tendencies exist in a condition of more or less dynamic equilibrium.

Notes

1. In the relatively small world of writing about European Political Cooperation, there has always been a strain of realist thought alongside the dominant integrationist school. Alfred Pijpers has been the most explicit representative of realism, but the work of Christopher Hill and others on national foreign policies also has obvious realist characteristics. See Alfred Pijpers, "European Political Cooperation and the Realist Paradigm," in Martin Holland, ed., *The Future of European Political Cooperation: Essays on Theory and Practice* (London: Macmillan, 1991), pp. 8–35; and Christopher Hill, ed., (1) *National Foreign Policies and European Political Cooperation* (London: Allen & Unwin, 1983); (2) *The Actors in Europe's Foreign Policy* (London: Routledge, 1996 forthcoming). There has been regrettably little writing from other traditions on the national dimension. For a view from a reflectivist perspective, see Knud-Erik Jorgensen, "Analyzing Informal Links Between National and European Levels of Foreign Policy-Making," paper prepared for the conference "The External Role of the European Union: Dynamics, Predictions, and Policy Needs," Utrikespolitiska Institutet, Stockholm, 9–10 December 1994.

2. Christopher Hill, (1) "The Foreign Policy of the European Community," in Roy Macridis, ed., *Foreign Policy and World Politics,* 8th ed. (New York: Prentice Hall, 1991); (2) "The Capability-Expectations Gap, or Conceptualizing Europe's International Role," in *Journal of Common Market Studies* 3 (September 1993), pp. 305–328.

3. This is part of what Roy H. Ginsberg has called the "self-styled logic" of European foreign policy cooperation. See his *The Foreign Policy Actions of the European Community* (Boulder: Lynne Rienner Publishers, 1989).

4. Françoise de La Serre, "The Scope of National Adaptation to EPC," in Alfred Pijpers, Elfriede Regelsberger, and Wolfgang Wessels, eds., *European Political Cooperation in the 1980s: A Common Foreign Policy for Western Europe* (Dordrecht: Martinus Nijhoff, 1988), pp. 196–197.

5. In 1994, 12,699 messages were transmitted on the COREU network, including 3,041 sent by the two presidencies of that year. This compares with figures of 7,548 and 1,349 for 1990. The data are taken from *CFSP Forum* 1/95 (Bonn: Institut fur Europaische Politik), p. 8.

6. The "Declaration on Voting in the Field of the Common Foreign and Security Policy" stated that "the Conference agrees that, with regard to Council decisions requiring unanimity, Member States will, to the extent possible, avoid preventing a unanimous decision where a qualified majority exists in favour of that decision."

6

Where the European Commission Comes In: From the Single European Act to Maastricht

Fraser Cameron

> The Commission shall be fully associated with the proceedings of Political Cooperation
>
> *Article 30.3(b) (SEA).*

This sentence in the 1987 Single European Act (SEA) provided the legal basis for the growing involvement of the Commission in political cooperation. The SEA also gave the Commission (together with the presidency) responsibility for ensuring consistency in the external policies of the Community. The Commission's external delegations were also drawn into the European Political Cooperation (EPC) framework by the commitment to intensify cooperation between member states, diplomatic missions to third countries, and international organizations.[1]

The Commission's role in EPC remained limited as long as the agenda was dominated by traditional foreign and security policy issues. However, with the collapse of communism in Central and Eastern Europe, the emphasis turned more to financial and economic diplomacy. Technical and even humanitarian assistance grew in importance. This trend was confirmed at the 1989 Arch G7 summit, which gave the Commission the task of coordinating assistance to, initially, Poland and Hungary and later all countries of Central and Eastern Europe. The PHARE program for economic reconstruction led to the TACIS (Technical Assistance to the Commonwealth of Independent States) program for the countries of the former Soviet Union. The Commission also gained a prominent role by negotiating the Europe, or association, Agreements with the countries of the region.

These practical tasks given to the Commission increased its authority and standing when it came to negotiating the CFSP chapter of the Maastricht Treaty; but the Intergovernmental Conference (IGC) required unanimity and there was no EC-wide agreement on including Common Foreign and

Security Policy (CFSP) in the Community framework nor on granting the Commission substantially increased powers in this sensitive area.

Nevertheless, the Commission emerged from the IGC with its position strengthened by a number of articles in Title V of the Maastricht Treaty. Article J.9 (Treaty on European Union, or TEU) states clearly that "the Commission shall be fully associated with the work carried out in the CFSP field." The Commission secured a shared right of initiative to bring forward proposals; it was given the task, together with the presidency, of regularly informing the European Parliament about CFSP developments; its delegations were tasked, along with member states, missions to intensify cooperation in third countries; and its permanent place in the Troika was confirmed. Together with the Council, the Commission was tasked with preserving the overall coherence of the Union's external relations (Article C, TEU).

Increasingly, foreign policy is inextricably linked to economic, trade, development, and interior policy. In this sense, the Commission plays a powerful role in ensuring coherence between the different pillars of the Treaty on European Union. The Commission already possesses significant powers with respect to trade policy and negotiates for the Community as a whole, for example, in the General Agreement on Tariffs and Trade (GATT). The Commission also plays an important role in monitoring the Single Market and moves towards Economic and Monetary Union, both of which impact substantially on external relations. The Commission also plays an important role in implementing and monitoring sanctions, for example, regarding South Africa, Iraq, and Bosnia; and its development aid policy is not without political overtones.

The Commission's Role and Structure

The Commission plays a number of different roles in the external relations of the Union—as a participant, an initiator, an executor, a negotiator, and an arbitrator—and it shares representational responsibilities through the *bicephalous* presidency/Commission and Troika formulas.

As a participant, the Commission is represented at all levels in the CFSP structures. The president of the Commission attends European Councils, and the commissioner for External Political Affairs (sometimes accompanied by his colleagues for External Economic and Trade Relations and Cooperation and Development) attends the General Affairs Council and the special "Gymnich" and other ad hoc meetings. The political director plays a full role in the Political Committee while the European correspondent and his small team ensure that the necessary coordination is accomplished within the Commission, including Commission representation on all Working Groups.

As an initiator, the Commission has played an increasingly important role in shaping EU policy through its communications to Council. In 1994 these covered such diverse areas as Central and Eastern Europe, the Ukraine, the Baltic states, the Mediterranean, South Africa, and Asia.

To manage the Commission's growing role in CFSP, the decision was made in the spring of 1993 to create a new directorate-general (DG) responsible for external political affairs. The first commissioner to hold this portfolio was the former Dutch foreign minister, Hans van den Broek, and the first director-general was the political director, Günter Burghardt.

The latter had previously been based with a small team covering EPC inside the secretariat-general, which reported directly to the president. The reorganization provided for five directorates, covering: (1) Multilateral Issues; (2) Europe, including the Community of Independent States (CIS); (3) North America/Asia; (4) Africa/Middle East/Latin America; and (5) Management of External Missions. A number of units, such as Planning, Parliamentary Relations, and Inspection of Delegations, report directly to the director-general. When the staffing freeze in the Commission coincided with the creation of the new DG, it was not possible to fill all posts in the early phase. The number of Brussels-based staff in DG IA totaled 260 in the summer of 1994.

The establishment of DG IA, however, was certainly not trouble-free. In the early months, there were skirmishes with DG I and DG VIII over staffing and disputes on areas of competence and external representation. Yet with van den Broek and Sir Leon Brittan sharing the same political philosophy, these disputes, inevitable in a sizable bureaucracy, were not allowed to get out of hand. The running of the Commission's external delegations was put under a joint committee representing DG IA, DG I, and DG VIII, with DG IA in the chair and responsible for making proposals. In the beginning, there were also problems with a lack of coordination between the new and older, established DGs, but after a session with President Delors in late 1993 the situation improved, and by the summer of 1994 there were few problems with coordination of policies. There were regular meetings between the cabinets and senior management of DG I and DG IA. It was clear that van den Broek engaged in political dialogue with third countries and Brittan covered trade issues.

There were critics of the Commission's decision to split external political and economic issues, but one of the problems Delors faced was dividing suitable portfolios between seventeen commissioners—a problem that was further acerbated following enlargement of the Union. Overall, it is fair to say that the creation of the new DG will strengthen the Commission's capacity to play a full role in CFSP, particularly in exercising its shared right of initiative. DG IA, of course, has a wider role than just CFSP; it also includes the political aspects of Community procedures, for example, in human rights and relations with international organizations such as the UN, Conference on Security and Cooperation in Europe (CSCE), and the Council of Europe.

The advent of the Santer Commission brought further changes to the organization of external relations in the Commission. Jacques Santer made the decision to reunite the political and economic divisions and establish four directorate-generals, with mainly geographical responsibilities. He established a committee, presided over by himself, to coordinate external policy. Van den Broek maintained his responsibilities for the day-to-day running of CFSP and gained control of Central and Eastern Europe plus Russia and the CIS. Sir Leon Brittan saw his portfolio reduced to the industrialized world. Manuel Marin continued to cover Latin America, the Mediterranean, the Middle East, and developing Asia, while João de Deus Pinheiro assumed responsibility for the ACP (sixty-nine countries in Africa, the Caribbean, and the Pacific area), including Lomé.

It remains to be seen how these changes will operate in practice, because there are still a number of potential problem areas, in terms of competence. For example, security or human rights questions in North Africa would involve van den Broek as well as Marin. Trade issues in Eastern Europe would involve van den Broek and Brittan.

During the first months of the operation of CFSP, the Commission, like the member states, was ultra-cautious about using its right of initiative. Sensitive to political feelings, the Commission preferred to make its input into CFSP through supporting the initial five joint actions and tabling papers and contributing its expertise to missions of major political interest—for example, to South Africa, the Ukraine, and Rwanda. There was a general welcome for the Commission papers and recognition that the Commission, with its considerable experience and lack of any national axes to grind, was in a unique position to put them forward.

Relations with the Council and Parliament

The Commission also had to establish a working relationship with the newly created CFSP Unit in the Council Secretariat headed by the British diplomat Brian Crowe, and his Belgian deputy Pierre Champenois. The unit, some twenty strong, had as its principal tasks support for the presidency, preparation of meetings, and briefing of political dialogue partners. In fact, there is little overlap in the functions of the CFSP Unit and DG IA. Officials from both bodies meet regularly, and the Commission has even seconded one of its staff to serve in the secretariat. It is difficult to imagine the Council playing a much bigger role than at present, given its limited staff resources.

Commissioners have taken their new responsibilities to inform and consult with the European Parliament on CFSP issues very seriously. Van den Broek has been a regular attender at sessions of the Committee dealing with external political relations and has won the respect of all parties for his responses.

Case Studies

Central and Eastern Europe

It has been noted above how the Commission's role was strengthened as a result of its coordinating G24 assistance to the Central and Eastern European Countries (CEEC). The increasing experience of dealing with the CEEC, combined with the traditional economic and technical expertise of the Commission, was to stand in good stead as attention focused increasingly on how to promote reforms in the region.

The Commission opened delegations in all the CEEC and established teams of experts to administer the PHARE and TACIS programs, the largest technical assistance programs in the world. The Commission also negotiated the Europe, or association, Agreements with the CEEC and produced the background papers for both the Edinburgh and Copenhagen European Councils, which made the historic decisions regarding the principle of future membership of the EU for the CEEC.

In both the negotiations for the Europe Agreements and the preparation of the papers for the European Councils, the Commission played a key role—first, in securing a flexible mandate from member states, and second, in producing some imaginative proposals to strengthen EU-CEEC relations, which were agreed upon by the member states and the CEEC. For example, it was the Commission that came up with the idea of a structured, institutionalized relationship with all CEEC. This is intended to bring the CEEC closer to the institutions of the Union and involves a dialogue at all levels and on all matters of common concern within the three pillars. A secondary element was the promotion of cooperation among the CEEC.

The Commission is also playing a major role in the follow-up work as a result of the decisions made at the Corfu and Essen European Councils involving acceleration of agreed upon joint programs and the establishment of new areas of cooperation. EU policy toward the CEEC is thus a good example of the Commission consistently being in the driver's seat as the EU train seeks to catch up with the breathtaking developments in Central and Eastern Europe.

With the Baltic states, Slovenia, and Albania the Commission has performed a similar role. It has negotiated on behalf of the EU Trade and Cooperation Agreements. The task ahead for the Commission is twofold: to ensure the successful implementation of these agreements and to monitor developments with a view to proposing moving to association agreements in due course.

Free trade agreements with the Baltic states have been completed prior to the entry of the Nordic countries (who have free trade agreements with the Baltic states) into the Union. Negotiations with the Baltic states and Slovenia on a Europe Agreement were expected to to be concluded in 1995.

Regarding the CIS, the Commission began negotiations for a Partnership and Cooperation Agreement (PCA) with Russia, the Ukraine, Belarus, and Kazhakstan in the first instance. These negotiations proved to be problematical, partly because of the confused situation in these countries and partly because of different interpretations of trade issues such as dumping, and problems over acceptance of human rights clauses. After much hard bargaining, the PCA with Ukraine was signed in the spring of 1994 and that with Russia on the eve of the Corfu summit in June 1994.

Preventive Diplomacy

Two issues, one general and one specific, are worth mentioning in terms of the Commission's role in preventive diplomacy. The general concerns the Balladur Proposal for a Pact of Stability in Europe. The Commission was fully involved from the beginning in the discussions and development of the pact proposals, making a substantive political input and establishing possible economic "carrots," mainly through imaginative use of the PHARE program. The specific case was the Commission's role in the dispute between Slovakia and Hungary over the Gabcikovo-Nagymaros Dam, in which the Commission took the lead in arbitrating between the parties and succeeded in getting the two governments to submit the case to the International Court of Justice.

Enlargement

The Commission's role in enlargement of the Union is crucial. First, it has to give an opinion on the candidate's suitability for membership. Second, once negotiations begin, the Commission plays a central role in ensuring coherence of Union policies, seeking compromise solutions, and preparing the accession treaty. Third, it has to give its approval on the outcome.

With regard to the enlargement negotiations with Austria, Sweden, Finland, and Norway, the Commission was involved with all four countries since 1990 in negotiations over the European Economic Area (EEA). These difficult negotiations, resulting in the four countries accepting some 60 percent of the *acquis communautaire* (circa fourteen thousand pages of legislation!) provided a dry run for the actual EU membership negotiations, which opened on 1 February 1993 and which were completed in the spring of 1994. Hans van den Broek was the commissioner responsible for the enlargement negotiations and his special task force included officials seconded from DG IA.

Human Rights

The Commission has become increasingly active over the past few years in the field of human rights. In this, it has been guided by the various declarations of the Council, most notably the resolution of 28 November 1991 on Human Rights, Democracy, and Development. Most of the financial resources available to the Commission have been devoted to supporting the democratic process, including free elections, strengthening public administration, and judicial systems. It is interesting to note that two of the Union's first joint actions were support for the electoral process in Russia and South Africa.

In 1992, the Commission disposed of 26.4 million ECU (European currency units) directly and 46 million ECU indirectly, funding operations as diverse as support of the street children in Brazil to training lawyers in Africa. As regards CEEC/CIS, it has allocated special funds under the PHARE and TACIS programs to promote human rights and democracy. Perhaps most important, it has made all third party agreements conditional on respect for human rights—often to the annoyance of the third parties.

Furthermore, the Commission plays an active role in the UN Commission on Human Rights and was an active participant at the UN World Human Rights Conference in June 1993, where new emphasis was placed on strengthening the rights of women, minorities, and deprived persons. The Commission has also made numerous contributions to the CSCE, including the Warsaw Conference on the Human Dimension.

Lomé

The Lomé Convention is the largest single aid program in the world and one of the EC's principal instruments in overseas development. Negotiated by the Commission, the Lomé Convention establishes a special relationship between the Community and the ACP group, which includes the majority of the world's poorest countries.

The terms of the Lomé Convention are negotiated by the two parties and updated at regular intervals. The current Lomé Convention, the fourth, runs from 1990–2000—twice the duration of its predecessors—thus providing for increased stability in EC-ACP relations. It provides for 12 billion ECU of aid in the form of grants, soft loans, and interest-rate subsidies in the first five-year period. The Commission plays a key role in monitoring Lomé and implementing the policies agreed upon, principally through its delegations in the ACP countries.

ECHO

The European Community Humanitarian Office (ECHO) is a service of the Commission under the direct responsibility of the commissioner for Development, Cooperation, and Humanitarian Affairs (changed under the Santer Commission), with the task of managing humanitarian aid to all countries in the world outside the EC.

The EC is the largest donor of humanitarian aid in the world, with ECHO dispensing over 600 million ECU in 1993. It is financed from the Community budget, the Lomé Conventions, and the Emergency Reserve. That year it made over nine hundred decisions on humanitarian aid, working closely with UN agencies, nongovernmental organizations (NGOs), and national governments. Over sixty NGOs have signed framework partnership agreements with ECHO. One significant area of emphasis is former-Yugoslavia (63 percent), where ECHO manages the EC aid program. No less than thirty-five countries received humanitarian assistance from ECHO in 1993.

ECHO has sought to improve coordination in member states' contributions to humanitarian aid and has also established regular links with UN agencies and the U.S. government.

Security Issues

Mindful of the sensitivity of some member states, the Commission has tended to adopt a low profile in security issues. Nevertheless, the Commission contributes actively in the Group on Security, which seeks to define the Union's strategic interests and the ways to further them. It plays a full role in other Working Groups of the Council dealing with security issues, such as proliferation, arms transfers, and embargoes. Its services cooperate closely on the industrial aspects of armaments policy (the Commission has consistently proposed the abolition of Article 223 of the Rome Treaty, which prevents an open market in this sector). The Commission is also actively involved in a number of other security initiatives, including dual use export controls, the Pact for Stability, the Middle East Peace Process, and the economic aspects of security.

Following ratification of the TEU, a formal working relationship has been established with WEU (made easier by WEU's move to Brussels in January 1993). It involves regular consultations, exchange of documents, and participation (in the presidency delegation) in WEU meetings. The Commission has also established an informal working relationship with NATO, involving meetings at all levels.

CSCE

Although the CSCE was based on the principles of sovereignty and equality among the participating states, the EC indicated at an early stage that it would act as a group and be bound by CSCE commitments. The Community's identity was most forcefully expressed through Basket II and, to a lesser extent, in Basket III. There was never an EC delegation in CSCE and the Community as such cannot make proposals; but the negotiations in the second basket, for example, were conducted by Commission officials, who are included in the national delegation of the country holding the presidency of the Council. The Helsinki Final Act and other CSCE acts and declarations are not only adopted by individual EC countries but also on behalf of the Community by the Council presidency. Initially, some CSCE participating states, for example, the former Soviet Union, opposed this collective EC behavior, but gradually the opposition lapsed, partly as a result of perestroika and partly as a result of the Commission's close involvement in the Bonn conference on economic cooperation.

The Bonn Document, in which participating states committed themselves to multiparty democracy, the rule of law, respect for human rights, and the introduction of market economies, was based almost entirely on a Commission draft. Participants also noted that international economic cooperation and domestic reform were interdependent and acknowledged that more competitive conditions would enable reforming countries to participate to a greater extent in the international economic and financial system. The Bonn conclusions were a reflection of the Commission's interest in promoting the transformation of centrally planned states to market economies and established criteria for giving assistance. The conclusions covered most of the essential Basket II issues: business conditions, economic information, property rights, economic policies, energy, environment, investment, and monetary and financial questions.

At the Paris summit in November 1990, President Delors signed the Paris Charter, along with other heads of state and government, thus confirming the Commission's increased status in CSCE. The Commission continued to make a substantial input, within its area of competence and interest, into the Helsinki, Berlin, and Budapest Review Conferences.

Conclusion

The Commission's role under CFSP remains to be fully defined. The term "fully associated" is slightly ambiguous and can be interpreted in different ways. Nevertheless, the Commission has some strong cards in terms of its permanent membership of the Troika, its involvement in presidency/Commission summitry, its worldwide network of delegations, and its responsibilities under the Treaty of Rome for Community policies and budgets. The creation of DG IA should further strengthen the Commission's role in CFSP, which, in the final analysis, will be judged by the quality of its contributions to policy formulations and implementation.

In terms of personalities, the Commission has been fortunate in having van den Broek as the first occupant of the external political affairs portfolio. His vast experience and standing in the world have been of considerable benefit in combating some of the ideological challenges to the Commission's role in CFSP from certain member states. As a result of these challenges, the Commission has been cautious, and some would argue too cautious, in carving out a role for itself since the TEU entered into force in November 1993. Most of its initial inhibitions have been overcome, yet there remain some doubts and hesitations, for example, concerning how far to go in defending the purity of the Community pillar.

Outside the formal structures of CFSP, the Commission plays an influential role in terms of promoting the debate on ensuring an effective role for the Union in external relations. Its planning staffs, for example, maintain regular contact with think tanks and researchers throughout the Union, ensuring that problem areas are identified and possible solutions considered. Commission staff are widely sought for conferences and seminars, in order to provide the "European" perspective, while hardly a diplomatic dinner or reception takes place in Brussels without the Commission being present.

In reintegrating the political and economic aspects of external relations, the Commission was signalling its view that the artificial division made little sense in terms of priorities vis-à-vis the outside world. This debate will be resumed with the member states in 1996.

Note

1. See Simon Nuttall, "The Commission and Foreign Policy Making," in Geoffrey Edwards and David Spence, eds., *The European Commission* (London: Harlow, 1994), pp. 287–302. Nuttall's contribution provides a good historical review of the Commission's struggle to gain acceptance in EPC.

7

The Association of the European Parliament: No Longer the Underdog in EPC?

Thomas Grunert

The Common Foreign and
Security Policy After Maastricht

At present, the provisions of the Union Treaty concerning the Common Foreign and Security Policy (CFSP) are based on an intergovernmental approach entailing the following procedures:

- Unanimity in decisionmaking
- A right of initiative shared by the member states and the Commission (Article J.8 [3], Treaty on European Union, or TEU)
- Provisions on the competence of the European Court of Justice are not applicable (Article L, TEU)
- The European Parliament (EP)'s involvement is confined to a mere right to be consulted and informed (Article J.7, TEU)

There are thus clear limits to the development of an efficient and democratically legitimized common security and defense policy.

In the European Parliament's view, its role regarding common foreign and security policy is less than satisfactory, for its involvement is largely nonbinding and it has scarcely any supervisory powers. The corresponding Article (J.7, TEU) reads:

> The Presidency shall consult the European Parliament on the main aspects and the basic choices of the common foreign and security policy and shall ensure that the views of the European Parliament are duly taken into consideration. The European Parliament shall be kept regularly informed by the Presidency and the Commission of the development of the Union's foreign and security policy. The European Parliament may ask questions of the Council or make recommendations to it. It shall hold an annual debate on progress in implementing the common foreign and security policy.

Since Parliament has always been a vocal advocate of developing a common foreign and security policy, it takes a critical view of the "pillar structure" of the Treaty of Maastricht through which the common foreign and security policy is kept outside the structure of the Community (cf. A3-0123/92 of 7 April 1992). Furthermore, the European Parliament has expressed the view that the present division of responsibilities between the institutions of the Union in the field of foreign policy can only be accepted insofar as the present phase is regarded as a transition phase eventually leading to a comprehensive democratization of the processes of planning and implementing the common foreign policy (A3-0322/92 of 18 December 1992). The decisionmaking process of the common foreign and security policy should be democratized through the due involvement of the European Parliament. This should be achieved through the transfer of co-decision and supervisory powers and through the use of consultation procedures and approval procedures on fundamental decisions (see inter alia: A3-107/91 of 10 June 1991).

The European Parliament has also adopted a number of resolutions advocating the gradual and full incorporation of the Western European Union (WEU) and its institutions into the European Union (see, for example, A3-0189/92, 20 January 1993). Behind the position adopted by Parliament on each occasion lies the conviction that the development of a European Union is inconceivable without a common foreign, security, and defense policy.

Main Features of CFSP

In the context of the various systems added, modified, or confirmed in the Maastricht Agreement, the common foreign and security policy and the policy on justice and home affairs are, as far as procedures and approach are concerned, the same kind of institutional, decisionmaking, and operational structure. The main features making up this structure are as follows:

1. Each of these two policies comprises a Community section and—which is more important—an intergovernmental cooperation section.

   - The Community has responsibilities in foreign policy (commercial policy, development, etc.).
   - The common foreign and security policy, administered by the new structure deriving from European Political Cooperation (EPC), may extend to all spheres.

2. Action in the two spheres is twofold:

   - Exclusively intergovernmental cooperation; thus common positions; the obligation for the member states to abide by them; implementation by the member states and, within its field of com-

petence, by the Community. The matters dealt with in this way are
still the responsibility of each state.

- Joint measures: hence setting of joint objectives; the obligation
  for the member states to abide by them; implementation by the
  member states or the Community or by specific administrative
  structures such as Europol or departments of WEU. In principle,
  the matters dealt with in this way are no longer the responsibility
  of the individual states.

3. Decisions in these two fields are prepared by committees of high-
   level national officials, who do not belong to the Committee of
   Permanent Representatives (COREPER).
4. The European Council plays a general guiding role in the decisionmaking process for the common foreign and security policy.

   - As regards exclusively intergovernmental cooperation, the princi-
     ple is acting in concert and consultation within the Council. The
     latter may draw up common positions. The behavior of the Union
     and its member states in international organizations are also dealt
     with in this context.
   - As regards common measures, the Council decides unanimously
     whether a matter is to be the subject of joint action and deter-
     mines its scope, objectives, et cetera. In the field of justice and
     home affairs, there is specific reference to the principle of sub-
     sidiarity. The Council may decide that implementation is to be
     achieved by a qualified majority.
   - The Commission is to be fully involved and has a nonexclusive
     right of initiative, except for police and customs cooperation.
   - The European Parliament must be consulted on the main aspects
     of the two policies, is regularly informed, and may put questions
     to the Council.
   - The Court of Justice has no role (except, probably, in defining the
     limits of Community competence).

5. The annex to the Treaty contains the following, as far as the common
   foreign and security policy is concerned: a list of the fields covered
   by joint action from the beginning (Conference on Security and
   Cooperation in Europe [CSCE], disarmament and arms control, nonproliferation of nuclear weapons, and the economic aspects of security); a kind of agreement with WEU, which strengthens its military
   structure, envisages its full integration into the Union, and raises the
   issue of cooperation between Parliament and WEU Assembly; an
   invitation to all the member states to join WEU.
6. As regards the European Economic Community (EEC) Treaty, it
   should be noted that an amendment to Article 228 empowers
   Parliament to give its assent (by a simple majority) on international
   treaties that are already (Article 238, EEC Treaty) subject to assent,

cooperation treaties (containing special institutional provisions), and treaties having important budgetary implications and entailing amendments to decisions taken under the co-decision procedure.

The Role of the Institutions

Before examining the subject more closely, we should establish some basic points: On the one hand, the Union is given responsibility for foreign and security policy, while on the other, the democratic deficit seems to be accentuated in this area. As an example, we could quote the new Article 228a of the EEC Treaty, according to which the Council may decide to interrupt in part or completely economic relations with a third country without having to consult the European Parliament.

Furthermore, the creation of a common foreign policy with mechanisms and procedures of its own must not under any circumstances undermine the Commission's powers in the implementation of the external aspects of Community policies.

However, the developing Community has to define the role of each of the institutions in the implementation of the common foreign and security policy. In this, as in the other common policies, the principle of the separation of powers is not applied fully.

In the individual states, foreign and security policy is traditionally the exclusive competence of governments. This is because of the very nature of the policy, the legislative nature of which is fairly limited. Parliaments can monitor government action in the field of foreign policy using the usual instruments—questions, motions of no-confidence, the adoption or rejection of international treaties, and by means of ratification procedures. However, the often confidential and secret nature of foreign and security policy limits the traditional activities of parliaments.

Under the Community system, the chief legislative body, the Council, is also given the role of originating and managing foreign policy while the executive, the Commission, is only given a right of initiative. Parliament's role is even more marginal since it has limited powers to propose legislation (by means of recommendations) and is not able to sanction the activities of the Council.

The development of European integration might ultimately lead to the creation of a two-chamber system consisting of Parliament and the Council, in which the executive, the Commission, will be responsible for administering foreign policy and will be subject to parliamentary control, including censure. The Maastricht system will operate in the short and medium term, and hence, quite apart from institutional considerations, the question arises as to which organizational procedures will ensure the effective operation of the system.

It is not Parliament's role to implement foreign policy, although it must have the powers needed to influence the Council, monitor its activities, and ensure that these activities are in the interests of the peoples of the Union.

In view of this, the Commission and the Council should ensure that a constant flow of information reaches Parliament. The Commission should also undertake to submit to Parliament the names of its delegates and representatives outside the Community. It is up to Parliament to exploit the budgetary procedure as an instrument for exerting control and influence in order to ensure that its opinions are taken into account. However, the lasting struggle on interinstitutional agreement with regard to Article J.11 (TEU) (provisions concerning the financing of CFSP) has shown that this is not easy. Finally, the creation of a genuine common foreign policy would be assisted by the creation of joint embassies wherever possible.

A New Interinstitutional Balance?

It is too early to assess the functioning of interaction between the Union's institutions in the CFSP area. We are still in a test phase and the Treaty dispositions leave a large space for maneuver and interpretation. This holds true as much for the consultation procedure, the taking into consideration of Parliament's recommendations by the Council, and the budgetary procedures applicable to administrative and operational expenditures in CFSP (Article J.11, TEU).

As has been said before, the Treaty on European Union confers the main powers in the field of foreign and security policy upon the Council. It is for the European Council to decide that a matter may be the subject of joint action, and the presidency is responsible for carrying out such action. Once the European Council has established the principles and general guidelines, the Council implements its decisions. Decisions are made unanimously, except in cases where it has been (unanimously) decided to vote by a majority.

The Commission is involved in foreign and security policy and has a right of initiative. The Court of Justice is completely excluded from the system. Parliament is consulted about the main aspects of the policy and fundamental decisions concerning it. It has the right to put questions or submit recommendations to the Council. Finally, it holds an annual debate on developments in foreign and security policy.

As Parliament has advocated on several occasions,[1] the Council should accept the obligation to consult Parliament beforehand and regularly on foreign policy decisions.

This means that proposals for decisions and joint action on foreign and security policy should be promptly forwarded to Parliament, even unofficially in certain cases, so as to enable the relevant parliamentary bodies to state their views. This has not been the case so far.

Special channels must therefore be set up for the forwarding of information from the Council to Parliament. Parliament should have access not only to the decisions that the Council intends to adopt, but also to all the necessary information. The cases in which the Council adopts joint action without requesting the prior opinion of Parliament must be restricted to a minimum, and, in any case, the Council should consult Parliament as soon as possible.[2]

In order to make the Council's activities clearer and more transparent, the respective competencies of COREPER and the Political Committee must be defined. Parliament must have specific and responsible interlocutors and no longer tolerate the existence of gray areas in the administration of foreign and security policy.

As noted above, the "nonlegislative" and confidential nature of foreign policy is not conducive to the traditional forms of consultation. While it is perfectly feasible for the general guidelines of the policy—such as the biannual work program or the presidency's report—to be presented in plenary, it seems difficult to apply these procedures to individual measures or declarations. Parliament would not be able to deliver its opinion with the necessary promptness and would not be able to ensure the degree of confidentiality that the Council might wish.

In fact, often the international situation leads the member states to take up positions at short notice that do not fit in with the breaks in parliamentary sessions and the separation between the various places of work. Consequently, a fast channel must be set up via the competent parliamentary bodies, in particular, the Committee on Foreign Affairs, Security, and Defense, to act as the Council's special interlocutor.

The following procedures could be established: proposals for decisions to be forwarded immediately to Parliament via the Committee on Foreign Affairs, Security, and Defense; in urgent cases, Council representatives and the committee bureau could meet, for example, at the end of certain Councils in which foreign policy measures are on the agenda; in addition, the Council presidency (or even representatives of the Troika, to make the system more flexible) should attend committee meetings at least once a month; there should also be a "question time" in the committee on subjects agreed on beforehand with the Council presidency. Finally, in cases of relative urgency, the committee could hold extraordinary meetings not included in the usual calendar of meetings.

The above proposals apply *mutatis* to relations between the Commission and Parliament. The Commission also should undertake to inform the committee of what it intends to put forward, accompanying such proposals with an assessment of the budgetary implications of the proposals.

Furthermore, the Commission should ensure that it forwards to Parliament relevant information it receives from its delegations of the offices representing it. The necessary steps to ensure confidentiality should, of course, be taken. This would allow Parliament to monitor the activity of offices abroad and obtain information on the preventive diplomatic measures that the Community intends to adopt.

As far as relations between the Commission and the Council are concerned, the presidency should preserve the role of the Commission as representative of the Community and the Union in international relations.

The Council Decision of 26 October 1993

In October 1993 the Council decided to establish closer relations with the European Parliament in the CFSP area. The following guidelines were adopted:

1. In addition to the existing arrangements, the presidency will attribute the utmost importance to the obligation to inform, in concert with the Commission, and consult Parliament, as provided for in Article J.7 (TEU). The presidency and the Commission will acquit themselves of these tasks as regularly as possible and in a manner compatible with the sensitive nature of certain information and discussions.

The presidency will be in constant contact with Parliament in the areas covered by CFSP:

- By attending, in addition to the two colloquia, whenever this is useful or necessary, the meetings of Parliament's Committee on Foreign Affairs, Security, and Defense Policy
- By participating, if need be, in Parliament's debates in plenary session
- By continuing the practice of the general-secretariat of the Council attending the start of each meeting of the Committee on Foreign Affairs, Security, and Defense Policy
- By having recourse to the practice of written information

2. At each Council meeting, the presidency will inform the Council of Parliament's reactions, communications, questions, recommendations, or resolutions concerning CFSP.

3. The presidency will organize consultation of Parliament on the major aspects and fundamental options of CFSP:

- When there is any organized oral or written information as provided for above
- During the annual debate provided for by the Treaty on European Union
- When the European Council approves general guidelines for joint action

The Council decision was welcomed by the European Parliament, although it was obvious that the guidelines would not clarify all the questions the Maastricht Treaty had left open. Moreover, the political practice still has to prove to what extent the guidelines will be implemented.

New Powers for the European Parliament?

The Recommendation Procedure

The Maastricht Agreement provides for a specific procedure in addition to the consultation procedure—the power to make recommendations.[3] The recommendation is a political, rather than a legal, instrument; it is not legally binding, but it is a political act addressed primarily to the Council, and its value is enhanced if specific majorities are required for its adoption (e.g., an absolute majority of members).

It is up to Parliament to exploit to the full this opportunity offered by the Maastricht Treaty. The power to issue recommendations on foreign policy has been transferred to the relevant committee if time is particularly short. The committee is a specialized forum for the discussion of foreign policy, especially insofar as it maintains continuous links with the Council presidency and with the Commission. To assign this power to the committee, subject to possible referral back to plenary, in accordance with procedures and specific forms, helps to prevent increasing the burden on plenary sittings.[4]

Recommendations are to be addressed to the Commission and/or the Council and are also to be sent to inform the other institutions. They should outline the background to the issue in question and indicate succinctly (in two or three paragraphs) what kind of action Parliament considers the Council should opt for. The recommendation achieves two aims: to ask the Council to adopt a specific approach and to confer legitimacy on its action.

In urgent cases, Rule 46 is superseded by Rule 92. This latter rule sets out an urgent procedure under which the Committee on Foreign Affairs, Security, and Defense Policy may submit a "recommendation" to the Council in the field of the common foreign and security policy without a report having to be drawn up on the basis described above.

This procedure may be initiated by the committee itself, subject to authorization by the Conference of Presidents (or by the president of Parliament when this is not possible), of following a proposal for a recommendation under Rule 46 (either because the text of the proposal calls for application of the urgent procedure by the committee, or because the committee considers this necessary following receipt of the proposal).

Judicious use of this instrument would enhance the powers at Parliament's disposal. In fact, it is difficult to imagine that the Council would wish to deviate systematically from Parliament's position. It is more likely that it would, as at present in the cooperation procedure, tend to accept—at least in part—the suggestions put forward by Parliament.

Control Functions

The question then arises as to how Parliament can exercise control over the work of the Council and, to a lesser extent, over that of the Commission. When joint action is adopted, Parliament must be able to approve or reject what the Council decides. This is what generally happens in a normal institutional relationship, in which the parliamentary body approves or rejects the government's policy. Although under the Community system the European Parliament cannot censure what Council does, it is in the latter's interest to ensure that Parliament agrees with its policy.

Parliamentary control will be carried out once a year in the debate on development in foreign policy provided for in the Treaty on European Union, but also in individual cases, depending on the importance of the subject under discussion. Effective use of this "discharge" instrument in the sphere of foreign policy would make the Council extremely receptive to Parliament's opinion. There would be substantial negative repercussions if Parliament did not approve of the Council's approach on particularly serious matters, and this danger would induce the Council to try to obtain Parliament's prior approval in order not to find itself in conflict with it at a later stage.

Another effective instrument for control is the motion of no-confidence, or censure, against the Commission. In the relationship between the Community institutions and Parliament, the latter could use this instrument, not only when the Commission is the direct target, but also and above all when the intention is to affect the Council. It is an imperfect and indirect institutional instrument, but Parliament should nevertheless have recourse to it in cases where there is a particularly serious clash with the Council on foreign policy.

In the absence of other powers such as the possibility of blocking the execution of joint action or the adoption of a common position, the only instrument it has at its disposal is to censure the Commission, which will ultimately damage the Council and the member states that, in the final analysis, appointed it. On the other hand, Parliament's strategy should make the Commission endeavor to submit to Parliament beforehand the initiatives that it intends to submit to the Council, and to withdraw such proposals when they do not meet with Parliament's approval. Obviously, persistent refusal on the part of the Commission to comply with Parliament's opinion should lead to the tabling and adoption of a motion of censure.

The Consultation Procedure

As in European Political Cooperation (Article 30[4], Single European Act [SEA]), the European Parliament is to be regularly informed by the presidency of the Council, and now also by the Commission, about the development of the Union's foreign and security policy (Article J.7, TEU). It is a new feature that the presidency is to consult the European Parliament "on the main aspects and the basic choices of the common foreign and security policy" and ensure that its views are duly taken into consideration (the latter requirement was also laid down in Article 30[4], SEA). The European Parliament may ask questions of the Council or make recommendations to it, and "shall hold an annual debate on progress in implementing the common foreign and security policy" (Article J.7, TEU).

Article 91 of the EP's rules of procedure sets out Parliament's rights to be consulted and informed on CFSP matters. Article 91(1) makes the Committee on Foreign Affairs, Security, and Defense Policy responsible for ensuring that Parliament is consulted in this area and that its opinions are taken into account. This task is carried out when the Council and Commission appear at the meetings of the committee (in principle at all meetings); via oral questions in plenary to those institutions; and via the committee's dialogue with the presidency.

On all these occasions, it is important that the committee, and, in particular, its *rapporteurs,* should be enabled to keep close a check on the development of the CFSP in order to monitor the extent to which its opinions and proposals for recommendations have been acted on. No official consultation of Parliament has taken place yet. The only case offering a certain interest here is a letter from the Belgian presidency (corresponding to the second half of 1993) to President Klepsch, informing him of the first five common policy decisions by the Council and stating that the Council had taken account of the comments of the Committee on Foreign Affairs and Security. This letter obviously does not amount to a full consultation, as any consultation must be prior to the event if it is to be meaningful.

Once there is an official consultation of Parliament, the committee will be in a position to draw up a report and submit it to Parliament. This report may contain a proposal for a recommendation. Should it be necessary, there will be nothing to prevent recourse to the urgent procedure under Rule 92.

According to mainstream opinion, consultation should be seen as an obligation upon the Council to ask Parliament's opinion on certain problems before making a decision.

Nonetheless, consultation is to some extent arbitrary, as the "main aspects" and "basic choices" are not defined. If the consultation mechanism is to be meaningful, it must apply to common positions and joint actions. With reference to the practice of consultation, the president-in-office proposed that intentions be announced at the beginning of each presidency and a report submitted at the end of it. More frequent meetings with the Committee on Foreign Affairs and Security are also planned, to discuss the implementation of the policies adopted.

In order to exploit the consultation procedure fully, the European Parliament could establish a "procedure for matters of urgency," so as to be able to bring its influence to bear on decisions that need to be taken quickly.

In spite of all this, it remains unclear how it can be ensured that the opinions expressed by the European Parliament, when it is consulted, are not disregarded at the implementation stage of CFSP. As has been said before, consultation does not provide a legal guarantee that Parliament's views will be taken into account. Thus, there is a new democratic deficit in CFSP. However, hardly any national parliament in the the world has a constitutional guarantee that its foreign policy proposals are followed by its government.

Security and Defense Issues[5]

Most of the observations made above should also apply, by analogy, to security policy. As a result of the Maastricht Treaty, the Western European Union has become part of the development of the Union and is responsible for security matters. Parliamentary control over the activities of the WEU Council must be carried out by Parliament, the only democratically elected body. This means, according to various texts adopted by the European Parliament, that to all intents and purposes the European Parliament must replace the WEU Parliamentary Assembly, which consists of members who, according to the statutes, must be members of the national parliaments and of the Parliamentary Assembly of the Council of Europe. In view of this, the European Parliament should enjoy the same rights of initiatives and control that it has vis-à-vis the Council and the Commission—questions, recommendations, et cetera.

It is therefore essential that in the course of the integration of WEU into the Union's institutional system, the WEU Council should formally commit itself to answering questions and presenting its activities during the EP plenary or in the committee—in other words, applying the procedures governing the foreign policy sphere.

Alongside joint action, the common security policy represents the essential updating of EPC by the Maastricht Treaty. The common security policy should, in the long term, lead to a common defense policy (Article J.4, TEU) and even a common defense. These would naturally be dependent on a pledge to provide mutual aid in the event of a military attack (see Article 5 of the modified WEU Treaty).

WEU is being used as a defense component of the Union and as the European pillar of the Atlantic Alliance. In accordance with the security preferences of the EC member states, it is thus subject to a *géométrie variable*. The link with the European Union seems closer, however, so that the integration of WEU into the Union on expiry of the Brussels Treaty seems likely.

Integration of WEU into the Union could help resolve the problems of nonidentical membership, potential conflicts of competence in arms cooperation, and the lack of (parliamentary) monitoring of WEU activities. On the basis of experience of defense bureaucracies at the national level, it should be made a condition of further defense policy integration that the European Parliament be given adequate powers of supervision.

The move toward the institutionalization of WEU as a defense structure in parallel with the European Union raises three main problems: the fact that their membership is not identical, potential conflicts of competence between the Union and WEU, and, in particular, the lack of control over WEU activities.

WEU's lack of accountability to the Union is the central problem of cooperation between the two organizations. The fact that WEU is to elaborate and implement the Union's decisions and actions at the latter's request does not mean that WEU is accountable to the Union.

The demands of the European Parliament go even further. In particular, it demands that the creation of a military component in the EU should be subject to its approval (B3-1703/91).[6] It also wishes to be able to oppose (and thus prevent) the use of military force if a majority of its members are against it (B3-1639/91).[7] Moreover, the EP advocates that the conference, held to review the CFSP provisions, should decide that military missions to be undertaken by WEU require the approval of the European Parliament acting on a majority of its members, and the approval of the parliaments of the member states participating in such missions.[8]

The general lesson to be drawn from experience at the national level is that parliamentary control over CFSP is indispensable. The Turkey affair at the German defense ministry, which resulted in the resignation of Defense Minister Stoltenberg, serves as an example to demonstrate that the lack of control over the defense bureaucracy is clearly very great. The way in which this bureaucracy's thinking is dictated by external constraints prevents it from considering alternatives, at a time when defense needs to be thought about primarily in political, rather than military, terms. A distinguished academic body, the Oxford Research Group, comes to the following conclusion:

> Management of defence decisions, procurement and military forces in the absence of proper systems of accountability and democratic control has proved to be costly, wasteful and dangerous. Therefore, if the EC decides to take on a defence role, the European Parliament must have the recognised basic powers of accountability and democratic control in place before this becomes a reality.[9]

Bearing in mind the revision of the Treaty in 1996, the European Parliament is therefore reluctant to advocate further integration in the security and defense field until genuine parliamentary control is guaranteed.

Other Instruments

Besides the procedures provided for in the CFSP framework, there are certain other Community procedures that the European Parliament can use to influence foreign policy decisions:

1. The EP can decide general foreign policy guidelines for development cooperation, to which the cooperation procedure applies. The same is true for the foreign policy aspects of other Community policies.
2. Pursuant to Article 228 of the EEC Treaty as amended, the assent of the European Parliament is now required for association agreements with third countries and international organizations if:

- They establish a specific institutional framework, or
- They have important budgetary implications, or
- They entail amendment of an act adopted under the co-decision procedure

The European Parliament's right of assent is reduced in value, however, by the fact that according to Article 228a (EEC Treaty) the Council may suspend agreements to which Parliament has assented, without consulting it.

Moreover, the proposals of the Commission and the European Parliament themselves included provisions for a right of assent for Parliament for other kinds of agreement or for all agreements between the EC and third countries and international organizations (Article 27, SEC[91] 500; par. 16, A3-0107/91).

3. As regards administrative expenditures and operational expenditure on CFSP that are charged to the EC budget, the European Parliament can exercise its powers under the budget procedure (Articles 203 and 206b, EEC Treaty).[10]

4. It is sometimes argued that national parliaments, too, have only very limited powers of co-decision over foreign and security policy, because this policy area has no legislative character. However, unlike the European Parliament, national parliaments can exercise control over the executive by means of a vote of no-confidence. The European Parliament possesses a similar power only vis-à-vis the Commission, but not vis-à-vis the Council, which is primarily responsible for CFSP. Apart from this, it should be obvious that, in a climate of general disillusionment with politics, multinational diplomacy requires not less but more transparency and parliamentary co-decision.

Summary

Taken as a whole, the European Parliament's involvement in CFSP is felt to be inadequate and falls short of its expectations. Among other things, Parliament had called for the right of assent for all basic decisions on CFSP (par. 16, A3-0107/91). The intergovernmental conference to be convened in 1996 will therefore be called upon by Parliament to remedy the new democratic deficit in CFSP.

The special problem of parliamentary control over Community security policy will be discussed in conjunction with its institutional aspects.

Article J.7 (TEU) describes the role assigned by the Treaty of Maastricht to the EP in the field of foreign and security policy. This description must be interpreted in such a way that it approaches as closely as possible the EP's call in its resolution of 10 October 1991,[11] which states that the European Parliament "shall be associated with the formulation of foreign policy and shall monitor its implementation." To this end, the EP calls on the European Council to "define the essential common interests which shall be submitted to the European Parliament for approval."

Under Article D of the Maastricht Treaty, the European Council is to report regularly to the European Parliament. Should any of these reports fail to be sufficiently prompt or precise, the EP must, at all times, be in a position to respond on its own initiative. For this reason, continuous monitoring of foreign policy by the committee responsible is necessary. Therefore, the presidency has declared its willingness to notify the committee at every meeting of the current state of affairs. This is part of the institutional *acquis,* which from the EP's vantage point was supposed to be promoted through changes to the Rules of Procedure. With the implementation of the Maastricht Treaty, every committee meeting will—if necessary—be a colloquy in the sense of Rule 57 of the Rules of Procedure, or—to put it another way—there will no longer be any specific quarterly colloquies. Consideration might also be given to enabling committee meetings to receive and discuss confidential information more easily than before.

The European Parliament—and that means every Member of the European Parliament (MEP)—can also use questions to exercise Parliament's monitoring and initiative function. In the future, these will all be addressed to the Commission or Council and no longer to EPC.

The European Parliament has been granted a special instrument in the form of "recommendations" to the Council. The European Parliament has no right to propose legislation in the field of foreign and security policy, though it can seek the cooperation of the Commission, which is dependent on it. But it can employ recommendations in such a manner as to give them considerable political weight. This entails making spare use of this instrument and employing an efficient internal filter when recommendations are drawn up, in order to fully exploit its special political status and importance. One might consider reserving draft resolutions to contain recommendations for the committee responsible. This would avoid every resolution adopted under the urgent procedure being elevated to this rank, thus devaluing the recommendation as a weapon.

The European Parliament insists on permanent and intensive information from the Council and Commission. It could exercise its rights of control above all through questions, debates, resolutions, and through its budgetary powers. Through its recommendations, it might play an important part in shaping the European Community's common foreign policy. The activation of all the instruments described earlier and their ability to affect the work of the Council, the European Council, and the Commission will form one of the key tasks of the Committee on Foreign Affairs, Security, and Defense over the parliamentary term that started in July 1994. Their full exercise will obviously depend on the interinstitutional agreements to be concluded in this area with the Council.

Positions Taken by the European Parliament

Since the preparatory phase of the Maastricht Intergovernmental Conference, the European Parliament has adopted a number of reports dealing with its role in the foreign and security policy field. The following reports can be considered to represent the key positions Parliament has taken so far.

Hänsch Report[12]

According to the report "on the Structure and Strategy of the European Union with regard to its Enlargement and the Creation of a Europe-wide Order," the European Parliament must have a considerably enhanced control over foreign and security policy, in particular with regard to the role of the European Union and its decisions in the "system of confederative cooperation in Europe" and the further development of the European Union, as it shall be given the right of assent with respect to all fundamental common foreign and security policy decisions, the conclusion of international treaties, and all decisions adopted unanimously by the Council in the framework of the European Union.

Verde Report[13]

This report "on the Establishment of the European Community's Common Foreign Policy" is one of the foreign policy manifestos of the EP. It considers that, at present, Parliament does not have the powers and instruments it needs to play an appropriate role in a common foreign and security policy and therefore requests that the relevant powers be broadened. Moreover, the report confirms the opinion it expressed in its resolution of 10 October 1991 on the Intergovernmental Conference on Political Union that it should participate in formulating foreign policy and monitoring its implementation and considers that Parliament must make maximum use of the instruments at its disposal under the Maastricht Treaty.

According to the report, the selection of areas for the implementation of joint action, as adopted at the European Council meeting in Lisbon, is merely illustrative and may be supplemented in the light of changes in the international situation. It is also assumed that when the European Council identifies common interests leading to joint action, it will first take into consideration the priorities and initiatives of Parliament.

Furthermore, it is noted that, according to the conclusions of the European Council in Lisbon, questions with implications for defense, within the meaning of Article J.4 of the Maastricht Treaty, are not subject to the process involved in common action, but the EP reaffirms its right to be consulted in order to ensure democratic control over this important sphere of action of the governments of the member states.

The text expresses the belief that, given the specific nature of foreign policy, provision must be made for special procedures to guarantee the confidentiality of proceedings; otherwise, the Union's activities in this sector will be seriously undermined.

Importance is given to the financial side of foreign policy activities. In this context, Parliament reserves the right to take action under the budgetary procedure to ensure that due account is taken of its opinions.

Another key paragraph considers that, in the event of a serious prolonged dispute with the Council and/or the Commission on foreign policy issues, the EP must resort to a motion of censure on the Commission, this being the only effective means of pressure at its disposal when supervising the executive and the member states that appointed it.

Resolution A3-0040/93 (European Council)[14]

The European Parliament considers, in this resolution on the conclusions of the European Council held in Edinburgh in December 1992, that the objectives of the common foreign and security policy set out in the Maastricht Treaty may form the basis of a policy in line with the interests of the citizens of the Union, if implemented democratically and fully integrated into the Community system.

Moreover, Parliament underlines the advisability of including foreign and security policy in the Community's terms of reference, making it subject to fully democratic and controllable decisionmaking procedures.

On top of that, Parliament insists in this resolution that the provisions concerning a common foreign and security policy should under no circumstances call into question the existing mechanisms dealing with the external aspects of Community policies, which must be implemented normally and in compliance with the prerogatives of the European Parliament.

De Gucht Report[15]

In recent years, the European Parliament has repeatedly taken a position on the structuring of future relations between the European Community, on the one side, and the Atlantic Alliance and WEU, on the other.

As regards the Maastricht Treaty on European Union and the annexed Declaration on WEU, the report "on future relations between the European Union, the WEU, and the Atlantic Alliance" concentrates on relations between the Community institutions and WEU bodies.

The report stresses that the EC has consistently endeavored to develop a CFSP since 1987, whereas it cannot become a genuine Community policy until the member states abandon the intergovernmental approach and make decisions that can be democratically controlled.

The report emphasizes the importance of a coherent single institutional framework in view of, first, the coherence required by the Treaty on European Union; second, the demands of the new security situation, which call for coherence between all aspects (military and nonmilitary) of security policy; and, third, the transparency and clarity of institutional structures necessary for public understanding and democratic control. It is implicit in the report that this coherent single institutional framework also means that majority voting should be more widely used in the field of foreign security and defense policy, that a single uniform administrative structure should be established, that Parliament should acquire the authority to exert democratic control over all aspects of this policy, and that the Commission should have a larger role.

The establishment of a coherent single institutional framework requires a gradual approach in several stages:

- In the first stage, the Union should reorganize its own institutional structure, bearing in mind that WEU is from now on part of the Union.
- In the next stage, the institutions of both the Union and WEU should define precisely their integrated relationship and merge at a practical level.
- In the final stage, as a result of a new intergovernmental conference and at the end of the period of fifty years mentioned in Article XII of the Modified Treaty of Brussels, in 1998, the Union should fully incorporate WEU, taking full responsibility for foreign, security, and defense policy, as well as for the relations with the Atlantic Alliance.

The report proposes that the involvement of the EP in the CFSP procedures should be developed on the basis of the following principles:

- The EP should draw up its own proposals on security and defense
  policy and scrutinize the relevant decisions of the WEU Council.
- Representatives of the WEU Council should be regularly invited to
  report on its activities to the committee of the European Parliament
  responsible for security and defense matters.
- The directly elected EP should scrupulously monitor decisions and
  actions taken under CFSP, not only by the Council, in the context of
  Article J.7 (TEU) but also by the Commission, and should use all the
  instruments conferred on it by the treaties.
- Parliament's Committee on Foreign Affairs and Security and the
  WEU committees should intensify their cooperation, and Parliament
  should establish a full committee on security and defense.
- In line with intentions expressed in the Declaration on Western
  European Union annexed to the Treaty on European Union, the
  European Parliament should strive to establish close cooperation
  with WEU bodies, particularly its parliamentary assembly.
- In the second stage, Parliament and the WEU Assembly should hold
  joint sessions, with their competent committees holding simultaneous meetings.
- Parliament's rights of supervision should be further developed and
  become comparable to those available to national parliaments with
  respect to national security policy.
- Parliament should adopt procedures to allow the Committee on
  Security and Defense, or its bureau, to meet without delay in the
  event of a sudden international crisis, to have consultations with representatives of the Council and Commission, and to make recommendations to the Council.
- The provisions of the Treaty on European Union on the assent of the
  European Parliament for international agreements should be broadly
  interpreted.
- In the third stage, the European Parliament should replace the WEU
  Assembly in its entirety at the plenary and committee level, the powers and voting conditions of the Parliament being defined by the
  intergovermental conference.
- Assent by an absolute majority of Parliament's component members
  should be required for fundamental decisions on foreign policy,
  security, and defense (and especially on military intervention) and
  should be extended to the conclusion of agreements between the
  Union and third countries or international organizations on disarmament and arms control, as well as to defense agreements in which the
  Union is involved.

- Given that security and defense will continue to grow in importance as a subject to which the European Union must address itself, Parliament should be equipped with adequate administrative support to deal with these matters.

Other Resolutions

Looking back on the positions adopted hitherto by the European Parliament on this pattern of relations, it can clearly be seen that the conclusions of the De Gucht report continue the logic of the positions previously adopted:

1. Parliament's resolution on the Helsinki II Conference (9 October 1990) notes that the Treaty of Rome may not stand in the way of transferring unrestricted powers in security and defense matters to the European Union, and that, far from being revived, the Western European Union should be integrated into the European Union.

2. In its resolution of 10 June 1991 on the prospects for a European security policy, highlighting the significance of a European security policy and its impact on European Political Union, the European Parliament advocates close cooperation and the coordination of the Community's activities and those of the future European Union in the area of foreign and security policy with the institutions of the North Atlantic Treaty Organization and calls for the commitments entered into by the member states under the WEU Treaty to be taken into account in drawing up a common foreign and security policy of the European Community and to be adjusted according to Community policy.

3. In its resolution on the Intergovernmental Conference on Political Union (B3-1639/91), the European Parliament calls for:

- The phased implementation of security and defense policy with a precise and binding timetable, taking into account the time limits laid down in the WEU Treaty.
- The possibility of certain executive powers over Community decisions to be conferred on WEU until 1996.
- The powers of WEU to be transferred to the Community after that date.
- The formulation of security and defense policy to be regarded as falling within the Community's sphere of competence, taking due account of the various member states' international commitments, particularly within NATO.

4. In its resolution of 7 April 1992 on the results of the Intergovernmental Conferences, the European Parliament complains that the "pillar" structure of the Maastricht Treaty "leaves the common foreign and security

policy outside the European Community Treaty" and "provides for defence matters to be delegated to WEU without providing for appropriate parliamentary control of the activities of this organisation."

5. The same criticism is repeated in the resolution on the establishment of the European Community's common foreign policy of 18 December 1992, in which the European Parliament takes the view that arrangements for implementing the mechanisms laid down in the Maastricht Treaty for interaction between Parliament, Commission, and Council in the area of security policy must be developed. In that connection, rules must be drawn up with the other participating institutions—in particular, the WEU Council—that are compatible with an efficient discharge of the duties of representation and democratic supervision incumbent upon the European Parliament.

6. And in the resolution on the structure and strategy of the European Union, of 20 January 1993, looking ahead to its extension and the creation of a pan-European order, the European Parliament takes a position on the structuring of relations with WEU and NATO. In particular, it calls for WEU, as a mechanism of common defense policy, to be more closely linked with the institutions of the European Union during a transitional period and to be integrated into the Union in 1996. It also welcomes the WEU decisions of 19 June 1992 on institutionalizing and structuring the dialogue, consultation, and cooperation with the states of Central and Eastern Europe.

In relation to NATO, Parliament takes the view that this organization is going through a process of organizational and material redefinition from which it can be expected to emerge as a mechanism guaranteeing security for the whole of Europe and maintaining close ties between Europe, on the one hand, and the United States and Canada, on the other. It expresses the hope that NATO will become the central element in a comprehensive non-aggression and mutual assistance pact to be concluded by all its member states with all other European states, including Russia and possibly other states in the territory of the former USSR.

7. The European Parliament again comments on cooperation between WEU, the European Union, NATO, CSCE, and the United Nations in its resolution of 27 May 1993 on developments in East-West relations in Europe and their impact on European security, calling inter alia upon the European Community to commit itself at all levels to building up a common, concordant, pan-European security system involving the existing security organizations (NATO, WEU, NACC [North Atlantic Cooperation Council], etc.) within the framework of the CSCE (par. 19). EPC and the member states are similarly asked to take initiatives along these lines within NATO and WEU (par. 20). Parliament also calls for a policy of convergence and burden sharing between the various European and Euro-Atlantic institutions (par. 37) and expresses the wish that organizations such as NATO and WEU should act, as far as possible, only within the framework of the Charter of the

United Nations and that an effort would be made toward the further development of the United Nations as a peacemaking organization (par. 36.).

Conclusions and Outlook

It is important to recognize from the outset that images of how a European political union is to develop vary radically, both across and within member states. Nowhere is this variety more obvious than in the field of a common foreign and security policy. This is understandable given the nature of the subject: Foreign policy is the definition and pursuit of national values, whereas security policy is the defense of those values from exterior challenges.

Therefore, a European foreign and security policy can only be established insofar as Europeans share the same values in relations to the outside world. In the establishment of a series of cooperation and coordination measures, we can thus hope both to reflect existing shared interests and to work toward the removal of obstacles to greater union. When referring to obstacles, two distinct types can be identified: "differences of form" and "differences of substance." "Differences of form" are essentially those differences that occur through a lack of communication between the member states. They can be partially removed through the coordination of meetings, better information, efficient feedback techniques, and so forth. Through regular meetings and frank exchanges of views, better relationships will develop between the foreign policy elites of member states. This is, of course, desirable but the gap between elite opinion and public opinion should not be allowed to widen.

"Differences of substance" are more serious and are based on the historical interests of member states. The transition from a national to a European identity will be a gradual one, particularly given the violent history of intra-European relations and the heavy involvement in colonial affairs. In the medium term, recognition must be given to members' differing interests in foreign affairs.

The Maastricht Treaty creates several possibilities for the increase of the European Parliament's influence in the field of foreign and security policy, both through explicit articles and through a broad interpretation of some general provisions. The present interinstitutional discussions concerning the revision of the CFSP dispositions in the framework of the 1996 Intergovermental Conference (IGC) may pave the way to reach a less ambiguous and more satisfactory role for the European Parliament as a co-player in the shaping of common foreign, security, and defense policies, as well as a body to legitimize the decisions made in this area.

It is obvious, on the other hand, that the EP's ideas and demands concerning parliamentary scrutiny in the CFSP area exceed by far the role national parliaments play in this area in our parliamentary democracies. Hence, it is not very likely that most of the requests put forward by the EP will find a positive response in the framework of the 1996 IGC. This will probably be true with regard to the claim to "communitarize" the second pillar of the Maastricht Treaty, as well as to the general demands for a greater role in shaping and controlling the policy in this area.

Moreover, first experiences have proven that it is extremely difficult to reach interinstitutional agreements on CFSP that are acceptable to both the EP and the governments of the member states. Obviously, the governments do not want to commit themselves by formalized and binding accords in this area, which would enhance Parliament's influence. However, there is some reason to believe that with regard to the consultation procedure, progress could be made.

The European Parliament certainly will remain an underdog in CFSP, as it has been an underdog in EPC, compared to the influence of the European Council, the Council, and also the Commission. On the other hand, Parliament will be less of an underdog than is the case for the House of Commons or the *Assemblée Nationale,* to mention only two examples.

One thing can be taken for granted: The EP will use the influence it has gained since the Single European Act as much as possible. Its budgetary powers, its ability to block most of the agreements the European Union may wish to conclude with third countries, and its power to impede the accession of new members to the Union provide it with enough leverage to make its voice heard.

Notes

1. See Cassanmagnano Cerretti's opinion on the outcome of the Intergovernmental Conferences (Doc. A-0123/92, Part II).

2. In order to make the forwarding of documents easier, a telematic network could be set up, linking the two institutions in real time and enabling documents to be transmitted through data processing circuits. This would speed up the whole procedure.

3. See European Parliament, *Rules of Procedure,* June 1994. Rule 46 concerns Parliament's power to make recommendations to the Council.

4. The mechanism is straightforward: To initiate the procedure, twenty-six members or a political group must table a proposal for recommendation to the Council on a subject falling within the field of CFSP; this proposal is referred to the Committee on Foreign Affairs, Security, and Defense Policy, which decides whether or not a report should be drawn up. Should the committee decide to draw up a report, it takes the form of a proposal for a recommendation, a brief explanatory statement, and, where appropriate, the opinions of the committees consulted. This report is submitted to Parliament following adoption in the committee.

5. On further aspects of the EU-WEU relationship, see also the contribution of Mathias Jopp in Chapter 9 of this volume.

6. See the resolution on the Intergovernmental Conference on a Common

Foreign and Security Policy, adopted on 24 October 1991, OJ C 305, 25 November 1991, p. 98.

7. See the resolution on the Intergovernmental Conference on Political Union, adopted on 10 October 1991, OJ C 280, 28 October 1991, p. 148.

8. See the resolution (A3-0109/94) on the Development of a Common Security and Defense Policy for the European Union—objectives, instruments, and procedures, adopted on 24 March 1994.

9. See "Institutional Consequences of a European Security Policy" with particular reference to parliamentary accountability; Oxford Research Group; Study submitted to the European Parliament on 21 June 1991.

10. An interinstitutional agreement in this area is still under negotiation in 1996!

11. Resolution B3-1639/91 on the Intergovernmental Conference on Political Union, adopted on 10 October 1991, OJ C 280, 28 October 1991, p. 148.

12. Resolution A3-0189/92, adopted on 20 January 1993, OJ C 42, 15 February 1993, p. 129.

13. Resolution A3-0322/92, adopted on 18 December 1992, OJ C 21, 25 January 1993, p. 503.

14. Resolution on the European Council Report on Progress Towards European Union, adopted on 11 March 1993, OJ C 115, 26 April 1993, p. 175.

15. See Resolution A3-0041/94, adopted on 24 February 1994.

8

The Question of Consistency

Horst-Günter Krenzler and Henning C. Schneider

> Common foreign and security policy is the framework which must enable the Union to fulfil the hopes born at the end of the Cold War and the new challenges generated by the upheavals on the international scene, with the resultant instability in areas bordering the Union. The aim of common foreign and security policy is to enable the Union to speak with a *single voice* and to act effectively in the service of its interests and those of the international community in general.[1]

In these conclusions of 29 October 1993, the European Council fixed clear objectives for the Common Foreign and Security Policy (CFSP). Article J of the Treaty on European Union (TEU), entered into force on 1 November 1993, establishes a "common foreign and security policy." This drafting seems to suggest that there would be one action in Common Foreign and Security Policy and one actor. In reality, this is not the case—hence the importance of the "question of consistency." Consistency is a twofold concept: on the one hand, between the Union and its member states (vertical consistency), and, on the other hand, between the European Community's external relations and CFSP (horizontal consistency).

That the Community should be seen to be consistent in its external economic and political relations has always been a priority of European policy. Safeguarding Europe's interests and fundamental values through effective foreign policy methods calls for the definition of common interests, uniform positions, and the development of consistent activities like preventive diplomacy. The failure of preventive diplomacy calls for uniform action and homogeneous image (e.g., voting at the United Nations). The Union must speak with a single voice *and* act consistently—"going it alone" cannot be too vehemently rejected. The pressing need for this is underscored by recent political demands on the Community and the member states (in Iraq, former-Yugoslavia, former–Soviet Union, Haiti, and Rwanda).

It is therefore necessary to ask to what extent the Treaty on European Union provides satisfactory mechanisms facilitating the elaboration of a common foreign and security policy, increasing its cohesive effect on the member states, and bridging the traditional division between the Community's external relations and the member states' intergovernmental cooperation. Does Title V of the Treaty, in particular, with its provisions on a common foreign and security policy, permit consistent positions to be reached and adhered to? Is the burning "question of consistency" being answered satisfactorily? The question of what innovations the Maastricht Treaty has brought and whether they can be expected to produce a qualitative leap forward in consistency can only be answered by comparison with the previous state of provisions on consistency and efforts to achieve it.

The Term "Consistency" and Its Expression in Law

A word's everyday meaning is of only limited value when attempting to define its political usage. The dictionary gives "density," "firmness," and "agreement" as synonyms for "consistency." Physics could be of further assistance in the question of terminology, where coherent beams of light are defined as light-bundles that have the same wavelength and form of oscillation. In terms of European policy, consistency can be defined as coordinated, coherent behavior based on agreement among the Union and its member states, where comparable and compatible methods are used in pursuit of a single objective and result in an uncontradictory (foreign) policy.[2] Do the Treaty's dispositions live up to this definition?

The Maastricht Treaty did not invent the concept of consistency. It had already found its way into law via the Single European Act, the preamble of which stresses the need for Europe "to aim at speaking ever increasingly with one voice and to act with consistency and solidarity in order more effectively to protect its common interests."[3] Still more relevant, however, to the issue of consistency is Article 30 (5) of the act, which provides that "external policies of the European Community and the policies agreed in European Political Cooperation (EPC) must be consistent." For the very first time, two previously unconnected areas—the external policy of the Community and foreign policy cooperation between the member states—were brought together and subjected, with unusual clarity, to the need for consistency. The Single European Act owes to this attempt—binding in international law—to "unify" the two areas of activity the first of the three words in its title.[4] The Single European Act can therefore be viewed overall not only as a *Vorgründungsgesellschaft*[5] of the European Union, but also—as attested by the many similarities and parallels in the wording—as a pioneer of the need for consistency in the context of CFSP.

The development of a more uniform stance by the Union in its external relations was also one of the main reasons for the negotiation of the Maastricht Treaty. At the Dublin summit of April 1990, the leaders of the twelve member states identified unity and consistency as one of the chief objectives for the future.[6] In the Treaty itself, consistency is explicitly mentioned in Title I ("Common provisions"). At the very beginning of the Treaty, in Article A (TEU), the Union is required "to organize, in a manner demonstrating consistency and solidarity, relations between the member states and between their peoples." Article C (TEU) adds to this requirement of internal consistency the need to "ensure the consistency of its external activities as a whole in the context of its external relations, security, economic, and development policies." The aim of internal and external consistency shall be served by a single institutional framework (Article C, TEU).

This objective is defined more precisely in terms of CFSP in Article J.1 (TEU). It specifies CFSP's general objectives and provides that the Union shall develop into a cohesive force in international relations. The aim is not only to ensure the coordination of all resources available to the Union with a view to consistency, but also to impose the obligation to avoid contradictory behavior that is implicit in consistency. Like its forerunner, Article 30 (2) (d) of the Single European Act, Article J.1 (4) explicitly calls upon the member states to refrain from certain actions in the interests of consistency: "They (the member states) shall refrain from any action which is contrary to the interests of the Union or likely to impair its effectiveness as a cohesive force in international relations." The general obligation laid down by the second paragraph of Article 5 of the EC (European Community) Treaty—namely, to abstain from any measure that could jeopardize the attainment of that Treaty's objectives—has been hereby specified in the field of CFSP.

The reference to the Union's interests means that the first step toward consistency must be the definition of Europe's common foreign policy interests, and then, agreement on common positions and joint actions. A typical example of this process, which also illustrates the interaction between the European Union and the Community, is the codification of earlier practice in the EC Treaty's newly inserted Article 228a, which requires the Council—once a consensus has been reached on common foreign policy—to impose, by a qualified majority, economic sanctions proposed by the Commission with a view to ensuring consistency with common positions or joint actions adopted unanimously under CFSP.[7]

Who Is Responsible for Consistency?

Whereas Article 30 (5) of the Single European Act made the presidency of European Political Cooperation and the Commission equally responsible for ensuring consistency,[8] CFSP has brought a shift of the responsibility for consistency.

CFSP sees the Union, in the person of the presidency, take center stage as a protagonist with responsibilities of its own. This is the result of a notable difference in wording between the Union Treaty and the Single European Act. Where Article 30 (5) of the Single European Act refers to "policies agreed" within the cooperation framework, Articles J.1 (4) and J.4 (4) (TEU) refer throughout to an independent "policy of the Union." Article J.5 (TEU) invests the presidency of the Council with extensive responsibility in the implementation of the common foreign and security policy.

The onus of consistency shifts according to whether it is a question of consistency between the policies of the Union and the Community or the Union and the member states. While Article C (TEU) makes the Council and the Commission responsible for the consistency of foreign- and external-policy measures taken in the various policy areas (horizontal consistency), Article J.1 (4) (TEU) understandably gives the Council a special role in ensuring consistency between the Union and the member states (vertical consistency). The mechanisms to achieve the horizontal consistency in the field of policy are much more elaborate than those established to achieve vertical consistency between the Union and the member states. The Commission's right of initiative in the domain of CFSP, which is now enshrined in the Treaty of European Union, is an additional instrument to ensure horizontal consistency.

However, notwithstanding the reinforced institutional connection between the Common Foreign and Security Policy and the external activities of the Community, responsibility for maintaining consistency in the Union's policy matters continues to be shared by two bodies, Commission and Council, with the Council additionally acquiring responsibility for ensuring greater consistency between the Union and the member states. The dual structure of foreign and security policy, on the one hand, and Community policy, on the other, coupled with the tension between Union and member states, is not an ideal basis for conducting a more consistent policy. It remains to be seen to what extent the Council, as a body, is able to attain the requisite consistency between the stance of the Union and that of the member states.

The Substance of Consistency

The Practical Scope of the Need to Be Consistent

The objective scope of the need to be consistent is extended by the Union Treaty. Previously limited to foreign policy and the economic and political aspects of security policy in the context of European Political Cooperation (see Article 30 [6] [a] of the Single European Act),[9] it has now been significantly widened by Article J.1 (TEU) to encompass all aspects of security policy. European security policy now has political, economic, and military dimensions, with the latter being delegated to the Western European Union (see Article J.4, TEU). In view of the strictly theoretical divisibility of foreign and security policy issues, this innovation of the Maastricht Treaty may become of great practical significance.

Procedures and Instruments for Achieving Consistency

Procedures—the Single Institutional Framework. Effectively ensuring consistency requires suitable procedures. The Single European Act drew a clear distinction between the structures of European Political Cooperation and those of the Community, opting for a duopolistic procedure. This led to EPC and the Community handling the same areas of activity in parallel.

The Maastricht Treaty attempts to mitigate this duopolistic structure— which, in fact, continues to exist—with the Single Institutional Framework. The general provisions of the Union Treaty introduce, in the first sentence of Article C (TEU), the framework "which shall ensure the consistency and continuity of the activities" carried out in pursuit of the Union's objectives. With regard to this procedure, the "Declaration on practical arrangements in the field of the common foreign and security policy" annexed to the Union Treaty identifies three areas in which ad hoc organizational arrangements are to enhance consistency in matters of foreign policy: the first is cooperation between the Political Committee and the Committee of Permanent Representatives (COREPER), the second is the merger of the Political Cooperation secretariat and the general-secretariat of the Council, and the third is cooperation between the latter body and the Commission.

As noted in particular in the Council's report of 21 October 1993,[10] which was adopted by the European Council on 29 October,[11] there has been some progress in all three areas.

Consistency should be enhanced by detailed arrangements for cooperation between the Political Committee, which is responsible for CFSP, and the Committee of Permanent Representatives, which has a general responsibility for the preparation of Council meetings and a specific responsibility for Community policy. The Political Committee will, in principle, now meet at the Council headquarters (it used to meet in the capital of the country occupying the presidency) the week before the Council itself meets. The presidency will inform the Political Committee of the preliminary draft agenda for the Council meeting. The Council may ask the Political Committee to hold its meeting at the same time as the Council's and provide appropriate opinions on the latest political developments.

Under Article 151 of the EC Treaty, the Committee of Permanent Representatives remains in charge of preparing the work of the Council. Noting this competition between institutions, the Council's report of 21

October 1993 states that the opinions of the Political Committee intended for the Council should figure on the agenda for the Committee of Permanent Representatives as a way of guaranteeing the required consistency with the Community contributions handled by that committee. The opinions of the Political Committee intended for the Council are to be forwarded as quickly as possible. It remains to be seen whether this problematic dualism does not, in practice, create tension between the Committee of Permanent Representatives and the Political Committee.

A key factor in optimizing consistency is the merger of a series of Working Parties, which currently report to the Political Committee (within the EPC structure) or the Permanent Representatives (within the Community structure). With the entry into force of the Maastricht Treaty, all Working Parties became Council Working Parties. They can be divided into two categories: corresponding Working Parties with the same geographical area will be unified and have a single title. The Working Parties thus merged deal with all issues, be they in the province of the Community or CFSP;[12] the agenda will have to be carefully coordinated. The second category comprises Working Parties that will continue to exist separately; consistency between their activities in different parts of the world will be ensured by the organization of joint meetings whenever subjects of wider interest are to be discussed.[13]

The merger of the EPC secretariat with the Council's general-secretariat was heralded by the Council's decision of 11 May 1992.[14] This has now been implemented.

The Council's report of 21 October 1993 stresses the desire of the Council and the Commission to reach agreement on the practical arrangements in a third area, namely, cooperation between the Council's general-secretariat and the Commission. The presidency, assisted by the general-secretariat of the Council, was therefore instructed to open discussions on the matter with the Commission.

The Treaty on European Union represents a new stage in the development of a Union identity in matters connected with CFSP. However, notwithstanding all the innovations and procedural improvements observed since their unification within a single institutional framework, which should not be underestimated, the Maastricht Treaty confirms the Single European Act's structural duality between the Community's external relations and intergovernmental cooperation between the member states in CFSP. The old twin-track approach will continue to mark foreign policy in the future. This approach may have negative affects on the Union's position on the international scene. The practical worth of the advances obtained by procedural improvements has yet to be proven.

Instruments.   The instruments introduced by the Maastricht Treaty, the "common position" and the "joint action," which go beyond the concerted and convergent action of member states on a matter of foreign and security policy of general interest (J.2 [1], TEU), are of particular importance in increasing consistency. They should make it more stringent for the individual member states to align their foreign policies with the decisions of the Union.

• Common Position. Aside from the concerted and convergent action as first step (J.2 [1], TEU), the second step toward consistency is provided by Article J.2 (2) (TEU), which introduces the notion of the "common position." Common positions are defined by the Council and constitute guidelines for the member states, which "shall ensure that their national policies conform to the common positions."

As with the Single European Act, there is no obligation for the member states to take the second step and to reach a common position. However, in contrast to the Single European Act, once reached, a common position is now binding. Whereas the Single European Act, in Article 30 (2) (c), described common positions as constituting only a "point of reference" for the member states' policies, the member states must now "ensure" that their foreign policies conform to "common positions."

• Joint Action. Article J.3 (TEU) provides an even more significant instrument to ensure consistency in the shape of "joint action," which can be described as a third step of the consistency procedure.

The report of the ministers of foreign affairs to the Lisbon European Council of June 1992 describes joint actions as "an additional instrument which implies a strict discipline among member states and enables the Union to make full use of the means at its disposal."[15] Joint action has been designed as the key instrument in the field of vertical consistency between the Union and its member states. What exactly is meant by "joint action" is, however, debatable, since there are differing interpretations of the relationship between intergovernmental and Community contributions to a joint action.

Joint action is first and foremost a joint action between the Union and the member states (vertical consistency), as Article J.3 (4) (TEU) prescribes: "Joint actions shall commit the member states in the positions they adopt and in the conduct of their activity." The joint action can be supported by a Community action.

The relationship between a joint action (CFSP), which primarily commits the member states to combine their foreign policy activities, and Community measures (EC) is not one of subordination. They remain separate but should be mutually complementary to ensure the consistency of external activities.[16] There is a danger that an extensive interpretation of joint action, subordinating member states and Community actions, would cause Community contributions in the area of foreign policy to lose their specification, resulting in the transfer of Community powers in external affairs to the province of CFSP. This could have as a consequence the extension of CFSP's intergovernmental procedure to the Community contribution (e.g., unanimity rather than qualified-majority voting). Such an approach would denature the Community contribution, reduce its effectiveness as a contribution to a global common foreign-policy action, and would over time inevitably reduce the Community to an executive branch of CFSP. This would be contrary to the EC Treaty and the three pillar approach.

The European Council has identified several priority areas in which joint actions might be considered.[17] They are linked to the strengthening of the security of the Union and its member states. Most are geographically neighboring areas that can be considered to form part of the Union's direct sphere of interest: Central and Eastern Europe, Russia, and former-Yugoslavia. More traditional areas of the Community's external relations are South Africa and the Middle East. The Council also identified the main multilateral domains in which joint action may be taken. Security matters, such as the Conference on Security and Cooperation in Europe (CSCE) process or the pact of stability, are in the forefront.[18]

According to the Council report of 21 October 1993, the procedure for joint action also breaks down into three stages.[19] First, the European Council defines general guidelines as a framework for joint action, deciding at regular intervals whether new guidelines are needed. The next step, which actually opens the procedure for a joint action, is when the Council unanimously decides on the basis of the above guidelines that a matter should be a subject of joint action (Article J.3 [1], TEU). Whenever the Council decides on the principle of joint action in this way, it is acting on a proposal from the presidency, the member states, or the Commission. It must, at the same time, lay down the ground rules for the joint action and decide whether—and, if so, in what areas—decisions are to be made by a qualified majority. The final third step is to determine the exact scope of the joint action and the measures required for its implementation. In order to guarantee the full effectiveness of the measures adopted, the Council takes account of any proposals that the Commission thinks necessary for the implementation of the joint action, together with the positions of the member states, which indicate what measures they intend to adopt pursuant to the joint action.

At the same time, the Council also considers whether the member states should be invited to commit their national resources to the implementation of the joint action and whether the joint action is to be pursued in concert with nonmember countries and international organizations. The Council must furthermore ensure that the joint action is specific and generally visible. The purpose of the joint action (its precise scope, general and specific objectives, conditions, and possible duration) and the means to be used (procedures, possible recourse to a qualified majority, funding, and cooperation with nonmember countries) must be set out in every single case. Once the president and the general-secretary of the Council have signed a decision concerning joint action, it has to be published in the *Official Journal of the European Communities.*

Financing. The question of financing is, of course, also relevant to the implementation of joint actions and common positions within CFSP. In the past, the Council determined the financial parameters on a purely ad hoc basis. In the future, however, such decisions are to be based on specially drawn-up principles and budget provisions.

In the first step, the Council in its consultations agreed (21 February and 7–8 March 1994) on the following three principles: First, there should be a strict separation between CFSP actions and supporting Community measures, to avoid an overlap of the first pillar by the second pillar. Second, the character of the foreign policy calls for a rapid mobilization of the needed means. And finally, deciding a common action, the Council has to define the financial means. As basis for its decision, the Council needs a financial plan, which shows the exact purpose of use and the exact amount of costs affecting the Union.

The point of reference in the Treaty is Article J.11 (2) (TEU), which separates administrative expenditure and operational expenditure. Pursuant to this article, the administrative expenditure on CFSP is basically charged to the budget of the European Communities, and there exists a common agreement that the institution that caused the expenditure also has to pay for it. There is now also an agreement on the subject matter of administrative expenditure (salaries, traveling and staff costs, and expenses for preparing a common action or an international conference concerning CFSP items).

Operational expenditure, however, may be charged by the Council to either the budget of the European Communities or to the member states. Considering the Community financing, two options are possible: financing within the framework of the budget "Council" (Single Budget II) or within the budget "Commission" (Single Budget III, Part B).

The first option is clearly at a disadvantage. It raises the need for a new administrative structure (with the risk of overlaps) and the problem of finding a modus vivendi with the European Parliament and its role as a budgetary authority (Article 203, TEU). Parliament, for its part, is demanding that its rights in the budget procedure will be respected with regard to budgetary aspects of joint actions and common positions and that it will be consulted before expenditure in every single case. In his final conclusions on 17 February 1994, the *rapporteur* of the foreign affairs committee of the European Parliament, Member of the European Parliament (MEP) McMillan-Scott, stressed the importance of allocating the operational expenditure not within the Council line, otherwise the Parliament should declare not to apply the existing Gentlemen's Agreement on this budget line. According to this agreement, the Parliament will exercise its right of control only on operational expenditures of the Commission, but not on operational expenditures within the budget line of the Council. Having this possibility of change in mind, all national delegations, except for the delegation of France and the United Kingdom, have drawn attention to this Gentlemen's Agreement, which the Parliament could annul, if the Council budget also includes operational expenditure in the future. For these reasons, the second approach, the allocation within the budget "Commission," should be preferred. It also respects the competence of the Commission for executing the budget.

The operational expenditure to be charged to the budget of the member states is also explicitly mentioned in Article J.11 (2) (TEU), but in practice it should be limited to a small number of cases. The basis for allocation is the gross national product (GNP), with the possibility for the Council to agree unanimously in exceptional cases upon another basis for allocation. As the framework of Community provisions is not automatically applicable to the cases in which the Council charges the operational expenditure to the budget of the member states, it is necessary to draft specific provisions for an effective administrative and control structure on the national contributions. As prototype for this structure, one could take the provision of the European Development Fund (EDF) or of the European Cooperation on Scientific and Technical Research (COST).

The unanimity role.   Joint actions under the Maastricht Treaty offer the Union new scope for a consistent foreign and security policy. The possibility of recourse to qualified-majority voting when implementing a joint action could create new opportunities for effective action. There are, however, grounds to doubt the practical usefulness of this option, since the member states still have to vote unanimously in favor of deciding certain questions of implementation by a qualified majority. There is reason to suspect that unanimity will generally remain a prerequisite not only for the European Council's guidelines or the decision that a matter is a subject for a joint action, but for the implementation of the joint action, too (see the final sentence of Article J.8 [2], TEU). The declaration annexed to the Union Treaty on voting in the field of CFSP is not enough to dispel this suspicion, even though it expresses, with regard to Council decisions requiring unanimity, the readiness of the member states to avoid, as far as possible, preventing a unanimous decision where a qualified majority exists in favor of that decision. This declaration is, however, simply a nonbinding statement of intent.

The need for unanimity on all the essential elements of the joint action constitutes a threat to consistent action by the Union and the member states that should not be underestimated. What must be avoided at all costs is that a measure that would otherwise have been implemented by a qualified majority in the Community framework is now defined as part of a joint action requiring a unanimous decision. The relevance of this misgiving was illustrated by the difficulty of lifting economic sanctions against South Africa and of imposing economic sanctions against Haiti in the face of different points of view of the member states; in both cases, two member states succeeded with the requirement of a unanimous decision by the Council.

Practical Examples

An example of the successful implementation of consistency between Union and member states, on the one hand, and CFSP and Community, on the other, is provided by the first joint action, which involved the dispatch to Russia of observers to monitor the parliamentary elections of 12 December 1993 and the referendum on a draft constitution. The Council's decision of 9 November 1993 was made in the light of the general guidelines of the European Council and referred expressly to Article J.3 (TEU).[20] In addition to the decision to send election observers from the member states and the Commission, the Council decided that the Union would coordinate its efforts in conjunction with the international organizations concerned and, in particular, the Council of Europe and the CSCE. Particularly worthy of note is the short-term setting-up of a special European Union monitoring unit in Russia, placed under the authority of the presidency, to which the Commission was closely associated. Within only five weeks, this unit, which was coordinated with the help of the Community delegation in Moscow, managed to carry out in full its allotted task of effectively coordinating the observers. The cost of the operation was borne by the Community budget.

In the second joint action, which concerned Bosnia-Herzegovina, the Council decided, on 8 November 1993, to cooperate more closely with other international organizations and, in particular, the UNHCR and UNPROFOR, in order to fulfill the UN Security Council's resolutions regarding humanitarian aid.[21] The presidency and the Commission were to seek to cooperate with the UN High Commissioner of Refugees (UNHCR) and UN Protective Force (UNPROFOR) on a short-term basis, with a view to drawing up a report on aid-convoying requirements. The presidency was also authorized to contact the relevant institutions in order to study the conditions for, and ways and means of, reopening the airports of Tuzla and Mostar and to approach nonmember countries to find out what they could contribute to relief operations. Provision was lastly made for the presidency to contact the UN Secretary-General regarding the involvement of nonmember countries and UNPROFOR.

The decision on 8 November 1993 was followed by other decisions of the Council that completed joint actions, especially with the financial aid for the administration of the city of Mostar.[22] It was also ruled that half of the needed support (24 million ECU [European currency units]) would be charged to the budget of the European Communities; concerning the rest, which would be charged to the member states, the Council would decide later.

Notwithstanding the many detailed arrangements, considerable scope is left for initiatives by the member states. The Council decision states that the member states of the Union will do everything possible to strengthen their participation in UNPROFOR.[23]

Another joint action was carried out to support the democratization process in South Africa.[24] A coordinated program of assistance was developed for the preparation and monitoring of the elections. At the same time, a cooperation framework was set up to consolidate the economic and social foundations for the transition. The work connected with this joint action was delegated to a new "South Africa" Working Party.

One month later, another example of a joint action was given as the European Council confirmed, in the context of the Union's decision to support the Middle East process by joint action, that it would "mobilise political, financial and economic means" for this purpose, through a joint action and relevant Commission proposals.[25] The complementary character of the Community action appears clearly in this decision.

The instrument of the joint action was also chosen for the initiative of the Stability Pact in December 1993 concerning the question of minorities, the inviolability of frontiers, and the cooperation in Central and Eastern Europe.[26] This action can be described as a "classical" example of the joint action because of its concrete objectives.[27] It is interesting to mention that the costs for the rounds of talks were charged as administrative expenditure to the Community budget; in addition, the decision declared in Article 5 that there would be no operational expenditure.

The first joint action in the area of security policy was decided by the Council on 25 July 1994, concerning the preparation for the 1995 conference for the participating states of the treaty on the nonproliferation of nuclear weapons.[28] This decision was based on the general guidelines of the Corfu European Council and intended to strengthen the international system of nonproliferation of nuclear weapons by supporting the objectives of the Treaty, especially the principle of universality and its unlimited and unconditional prolongation. The joint action included démarches of the presidency to extend the consensus of the European Union in the area of nonproliferation and stressed explicitly, as in the case of the Stability Pact, that it had no operational expenditure as a consequence.

Also of increasing importance for the realization of consistency in practice are the common positions. With the first common position in March 1994, the Union defined its guidelines for imposing an embargo against the Sudan.[29] The second common position at the end of May 1994 was taken to restrict the economic relations with Haiti;[30] with the decision on 14 October 1994, this embargo was lifted.[31]

In the declaration that was part of the common position on 24 October 1994 concerning Rwanda, the Council expressly stated the priority of the return of all refugees to Rwanda.[32] Therefore, the European Union declared as its objectives to continue the humanitarian aid for the refugees, to install an economic reconstruction program, to resume the development cooperation, and to initiate measures to support the neighboring countries. In spite of this comprehensive declaration, it must be emphasized that in the case of Rwanda, there was not a real political will to speak with one voice. Two countries, France and Belgium, had taken national initiative, before the Union was able to find a common position. The common position concerning Rwanda also raised the question about the institutional balance between the first (Community) and the second (CFSP) pillar: Covering objectives both from the field of economic aid and cooperation, this common position affected measures that fell under the competence of the Community, in which the Commission had the exclusive right of initiative. In the view of the Council, it seems to be quite difficult to reduce CFSP and its common positions to "purely political" scopes when the real substance of its actions are the result of Community policies. More and more member states believe that a common position expressed by a single decision based solely on Article J.2 (TEU) can and should englobe all external activities of the Union, including Community aspects, albeit in "general terms."[33] Other member states, as well as the Commission, believe that a multiview approach, in line with the three-pillar approach, should be followed.

The two schools of thought confronted each other again, when it came to the next example of a common position: the European Union policy toward the Ukraine. The Council common position mentions the development of a strong political relationship with the Ukraine, the support of the Ukraine's efforts regarding nuclear disarmament[34] and its participation in the Stability Pact. Also, a number of practical steps shall be taken, for example, a visit by the Troika at foreign minister level to present a coherent EU policy to the Ukrainian government. This text does not contain any specific mention of actions to be undertaken in the Community framework, which was the case in the common position concerning Rwanda. The discussion on a consistent model for future Council decisions continues in view of a compromise, setting out in one comprehensive document the objectives and priorities of an EU policy correctly reflecting the actual structure of the EU Treaty—for instance, the separation of the pillars. A decision based on Article J.2 (TEU) only, would be of no value regarding aspects of Community policy included in the operative part of the common position, especially since the wording of Article J.2 (2) (TEU) only binds member states and not the Community. The discussion shows the difficulty of translating the three-pillar approach into practice.

Joint Representation on the International Stage

Another spin-off of consistency is a united front in dealings with nonmember countries and international organizations. When putting across the Union's point of view, there is, however, a risk that third parties will be irritated by its multitude of spokesmen and will fail to see it as an independent actor.[35] Article J.5 (TEU) endeavors to counter that by reinforcing, compared with the Single European Act (see Article 30 [7] and [10]), the presidency's role in putting across the Union's interests. It is clearly stipulated that the presidency represents the Union in matters coming within CFSP. The presidency is also responsible for the implementation of joint action and, in principle, expresses the position of the Union in international organizations and international conferences. It has, however, to be said that third parties can only really acknowledge the Union's identity in foreign and security policy if the member states largely renounce independent action on the international scene.

As another contribution of consistency, Article J.6 (TEU) requires the diplomatic and consular missions of the member states and the Commission Delegations in third countries, and their representations to international organizations, to cooperate in ensuring compliance with common positions and common measures adopted by the Council. A special case is the UN Security Council. Member states that are also permanent members of the UN Security Council are to step up their cooperation so that they can articulate coherently and defend the positions and interests of the Union and the other member states. A consistent approach to nonmember countries is, last but not least, also significant in terms of the Union citizenship that is dealt with in the Union Treaty.

Legal Character of the Consistency Requirement

The rules of CFSP—like those of EPC before them—are not part of Community law. Though CFSP is the subject of cooperation within the Union, it was deliberately not incorporated by the signatories into the supranational domain of the European Communities.[36] The foreign and security policy brought in by the Union Treaty is therefore not a "common" policy in the sense of, for instance, the "common commercial policy." The need for consistency imposed on the member states by Title V of the Union Treaty has therefore only a binding legal character in the area of public international law.

Nevertheless, the question has to be asked whether the consistency requirement cannot also be binding in Community law. The Council is denied recourse to the instruments of Community law (Regulations) for the conduct of the common foreign and security policy, since Article J.11 (1) (TEU) does not make CFSP subject to Article 189 of the EC Treaty, which enumerates the legal instruments. Consideration must, however, be given to whether the principle of Community loyalty (Article 5 of the EC Treaty) cannot, in some cases, provide a basis for obliging member states to conduct consistent foreign policy activities not only in international law, but in Community law as well.

Article 5 of the EC Treaty extends to the member states' actions abroad: They must abstain from any measure that could jeopardize the effectiveness and the implementation of Community external policy measures.[37] Pursuant to Article 5 of the EC Treaty, Community law prohibits activities by a member state that might undermine the effectiveness of actions within the province of the Community, such as commercial policy measures under Article 113 of the EC Treaty. As it now stands, Community law requires consistency for matters within the province of the Community.

Since the Maastricht Treaty is now trying to reinforce the link between Community action (EC) and joint action (CFSP) and this is leading to a strong interaction between Community measures and resources and those of CFSP, it is doubtful whether the CFSP consistency obligation can still be seen as binding only under international law. When CFSP joint actions are combined with Community measures in an operation by the Union as a whole, the Community obligation imposed by Article 5 of the EC Treaty spreads into the domain of CFSP, meaning that consistency could be considered obligatory under Community law as well as international law.

The conclusion that consistency is an obligation under international law, and possibly under Community law, too, leads to the question of the extent to which sanctions are available to enforce consistency.

Consistency cannot be directly supervised by the European Court of Justice, since Article L in the final provisions of the Union Treaty does not extend the Court's jurisdiction to CFSP. If, however, one shares the above understanding of Community loyalty and the obligation under Community law to be consistent, failure to comply with the consistency requirement could, at least in certain cases of joint action, be seen as a breach of Article 5 of the EC Treaty, constituting grounds for the justiciability of consistency.[38] The door of a Court review could also be opened by Article M (TEU), which points out that "nothing in this Treaty shall affect the Treaties establishing the European Communities": Even if the powers of the Court do not directly cover Title V, they extend to Article M (TEU). When matters of Title V of the TEU affect the EC Treaty, a review of the Court, including CFSP matters, should be possible in view of the legal systematic.

Even if one recognizes a weak, indirect, partial justiciability, the weapon is a blunt one. Like European Political Cooperation before it, CFSP lacks effective legal means of enforcing horizontal policy consistency and vertical consistency among the signatories to the Treaty. It seems inconsistent to identify in very clear terms the responsible parties and the legal obligation, while neglecting the requisite control by a suitable neutral body. This will require decisive instrumental improvements in the future and, in particular, the extension of the Court of Justice's direct powers of control.

Assessment and Prospects

The world underwent fundamental change in the period from the entry into force of the Single European Act in 1987 and the Maastricht Treaty, which entered into force in November 1993. The end of the conflict between East and West, symbolized by the fall of the Berlin Wall, German reunification, and the democratic revolutions in Central and Eastern Europe, has opened up entirely new opportunities for foreign and security policy. At the same time, however, it has brought considerable foreign policy challenges in the form of political instability at the Union's frontiers. It is uncertain just how apt the Union Treaty's second pillar is to confront these historic challenges; the text of the Treaty has, to a certain extent, been overtaken by the rapid course of events.

Though certain long-winded formulas in the Single European Act have been replaced by clearer and more transparent rules, with the possibility of adding legally binding but not enforceable common positions and actions, the Maastricht Treaty perpetuates the dualism of the Community's external relations and the intergovernmental structure of the foreign and security policy.[39] While joint action in the context of CFSP can basically be considered a step forward, the fundamental requirement, including the possibility of deciding whether subsequent decisions may be settled by qualified majority vote (thus far never used), does not facilitate action and the rapid implementation of policy.

The duplication of work in a duopolistic structure could weaken the Union's potential strength in international affairs. The Union also lacks a genuine foreign policy mandate, remaining dependent on the political will of the member states. This gives continued scope for national reservations, sensitivities, and constitutional problems, which could, in the future, incite individual member states to go it alone, undermining the Union's credibility by inconsistent behavior. The changes made in relation to the Single European Act are altogether too timid and do not adequately serve the European Union's need to assert itself on the international scene.

As early as 1696, the philosopher Gottfried Wilhelm Leibniz (1646–1716) coined the term "pre-established harmony" ("*prästabilisierte Harmonie*") to describe the innate harmony of body and soul. Some three hundred years later, this concept should serve as a model for CFSP of the future. Even here, true harmony is no distant utopia. The review conference scheduled for 1996 opens the way for changes to the provisions on CFSP (Article N [2], TEU, in conjunction with Article J.10, TEU). The ultimate goal remains the overcoming of all national objections to the establishment, under the democratic control of the European Parliament, of a true Community mandate in the domain of CFSP, which would finally make discussion of consistency irrelevant.

Notes

Horst G. Krenzler writes in a personal capacity and his views do not necessarily reflect those of the European Commission.

1. "Conclusions of the European Council, 29 October 1993" (Doc. SN 288/93), p. 2 (emphasis added).

2. Cited here and on consistency in European foreign policy in general: Veerle Coignez, "A Test Case of Consistency: The San José Dialogue," in Reinhardt Rummel, ed., *Toward Political Union,* (Baden-Baden: Nomos Verlagsgesellschaft, 1992), pp. 105–118; Jochen Frowein, "Die vertragliche Grundlage der Europäischen Politischen Zusammenarbeit (EPZ) in der Einheitlichen Europäischen Akte," in Francesco Capotorti et al., eds., *Du droit international au droit de l'integration* (Baden-Baden: Nomos Verlagsgesellschaft, 1987), p. 254.; Meinhard Hilf and Eckhard Pache, "SEA Article 1, sidenote 15," in Hans von der Groeben et al., eds., *Kommentar zum EWG-Vertrag* (4th ed.) (Baden-Baden: Nomos Verlagsgesellschaft, 1991); Horst G. Krenzler, "Die Einheitliche Europäische Akte als Schritt auf dem Weg zu einer gemeinsamen Außenpolitik," *Europarecht* (1986), p. 384 et seq.; Jörg Monar, "The Foreign Affairs System of the Maastricht Treaty: A Combined Assessment of the CFSP and EC External Relations Elements," in Jörg Monar, Werner Ungerer, and Wolfgang Wessels, eds., *The Maastricht Treaty on European Union* (Brussels: European Interuniversity Press, 1993), p. 144; Peter Christian Müller-Graff, "Europäische Politische Zusammenarbeit und Gemeinsame Außen- und Sicherheitspolitik: Kohärenzgebot aus rechtlicher Sicht," *Integration* 3 (1993), pp. 147–157.

3. Fifth recital in the Preamble.

4. Hilf and Pache, "SEA Article 1, sidenote 1," in von der Groeben et al., eds., *Kommentar zum EWG-Vertrag.*

5. Müller-Graff, "Europäische Politische Zusammenarbeit," p. 149.

6. *Bulletin of the EC* 4-1990, point 1.12.

7. Some editions of the Treaty explicitly refer to consistency in the (unofficial) title to Article 228a of the EC Treaty as amended by the Maastricht Treaty; one example is that of the German government's *Presse- und Informationsamt (1992).* On consistency within Article 228a in general, see Geiger, *EG-Vertrag,* 1st ed., 1993, Article 228a, sidenote 3.

8. Krenzler, "Die Einheitliche Europäische Akte," p. 389.

9. Elfriede Regelsberger, "Gemeinsame Außen- und Sicherheitspolitik nach Maastricht—Minimalreformen in neuer Entwicklungsperspektive," *Integration* 2 (1992), p. 87; Müller-Graff, "Europäische Politische Zusammenarbeit," p. 153.

10. "Presidency Report, Council of the European Communities, 21 October 1993," (Doc. 9252/93), pp. 26–28, Annex II. *The Bodies of the CFSP.*

11. "Conclusions of the European Council, 29 October 1993" (Doc. SN 288/93), p. 1.

12. The Working Parties in question are: ad hoc Yugoslavia (EPC) + ad hoc Yugoslavia (EC); Latin America (EPC) + Latin America (EC); Asia (EPC) + Asia (EC); CSCE (EPC) + ad hoc CSCE (EC); Middle East–Maghreb/Middle East Coordination (EPC) + Mediterranean (EC); Euro-Arab Dialogue (EPC) + Euro-Arab Dialogue (EC); Eastern Europe (EPC) + Eastern Europe/former-USSR (EC). See Presidency Report, 21 October 1993, p. 27.

13. The Working Parties in question are: Africa (EPC)—ACP (EC); Latin America (merged)—Africa (EC); Asia (merged)—Africa (EC); Human Rights (EPC)—Development (EC); United Nations (EPC)—External Relations (EC).

14. "Conclusions of the Council, 11 May 1992" (Doc. SI 92/348), p. 17 et seq.

15. Report to the European Council in Lisbon on the likely development of the common foreign and security policy with a view to identifying areas open to joint action vis-à-vis particular countries or groups of countries, *Bulletin of the EC* 6-1992, point I.31.

16. Cited from second sentence of Article C of the Maastricht Treaty and the annexed diagram.

17. "Conclusions of the European Council, 29 October 1993" (Doc. SN 288/93), p. 3.

18. Cf. "Conclusions of the European Council, 26–27 June (1992)" (Doc. SN 3321/1/92), p. 34 et seq. The fields mentioned are: restoring peace or ensuring political stability; the CSCE process; disarmament and controlling arms exports; nonproliferation of nuclear and chemical weapons; respect for international borders, minority rights, and human rights in general; justice and internal affairs (e.g., the drug trade).

19. "Presidency Report, Council of the European Communities, 21 October 1993" (Doc. 9252/93), pp. 24–25, Annex I: *The Instruments of the CFSP/Joint Action.*

20. "Council Decision of 8 November 1993 concerning the joint action decided on by the Council on the basis of Article J.3 of the Treaty on European Union concerning the dispatch of a team of observers for the parliamentary elections in the Russian Federation," OJ L 286, 20 November 1993, p. 3.

21. "Council Decision of 8 November 1993 concerning the joint action decided on by the Council on the basis of Article J.3 of the Treaty on European Union on support for the convoying of humanitarian aid in Bosnia-Herzegovina," OJ L 286, 20 November 1993, p. 1 (93/603/CFSP).

22. OJ L 339, 31 December 1993, p. 3 (93/729/CFSP); OJ L 70, 12 March 1994, p. 1 (94/158/CFSP); OJ L 134, 30 May 1994, p. 1 (94/308/CFSP); OJ L 205, 27 July 1994, p. 3 (94/510/CFSP). See also the new common positions in this area: OJ L 266, 15 October 1994, p. 10 (94/672/CFSP), and OJ L 266, 15 October 1994, p. 11 (94/673/CFSP).

23. "Council Decision of 8 November 1993."

24. Decision of 8 November 1993 concerning South Africa (Doc. 9622/93), pp. 10–11.

25. "Conclusions of the European Council, 10 and 11 December 1993" (Doc. SN 373/93), p. 29.

26. "Council Decision of 20 December concerning the joint action decided on by the Council on the basis of Article J.3 of the Treaty on European Union on the inaugural conference on the Stability Pact" (93/728/CFSP), OJ L 339, 31 December 1993, p. 1.

27. See Brian Crowe, director-general of the CFSP, on the CFSP, *Agence Europe* no. 6343, 24–25 October 1994, p. 3.

28. "Council Decision of 25 July 1994 concerning the joint action adopted by the Council on the basis of Article J.3 of the Treaty on European Union regarding preparations for the 1995 Conference of the States parties to the Treaty on the Non-Proliferation of Nuclear Weapons" (94/509/CFSP), OJ L 205, 8 August 1994, p. 1.

29. "Council Decision of 15 March 1994 on the common position defined on the basis of Article J.2 of the Treaty on European Union concerning the imposition of an embargo on arms, munitions, and military equipment against Sudan" (94/165/CFSP), OJ L 75, 17 March 1994, p. 1.

30. "Council Decision of 30 May 1994 concerning the common position defined on the basis of Article J.2 of the Treaty on European Union regarding the

reduction of economic relations with Haiti" (94/315/CFSP), OJ L 139, 2 June 1994, p. 10.

31. "Council Decision of 14 October 1994 concerning the common position defined on the basis of Article J.2 of the Treaty on European Union regarding the termination of the reduction of economic relations with Haiti" (94/681/CFSP), OJ L 271, 21 October 1994, p. 3.

32. "Council Decision of 24 October 1994 concerning the common position adopted by the Council on the basis of Article J.2 of the Treaty on European Union on the objectives and priorities of the European Union vis-à-vis Rwanda" (94/697/CFSP), OJ L 283, 29 October 1994, p. 1.

33. See *Agence Europe* no. 6351, 5 November 1994, p. 4.

34. "Common position of 28 November 1994 defined by the Council on the basis of Article J.2 of the Treaty on European Union on the objectives and priorities of the European Union towards Ukraine" (94/779/CFSP), OJ L 313, 6 December 1994, p. 1. On 16 November 1994 the Ukrainian Parliament had ratified the Non-Proliferation Treaty with a reservation.

35. Simon J. Nuttall, "The Foreign and Security Policy Provisions of the Maastricht Treaty: Their Potential for the Future," in Monar, Ungerer, and Wessels, eds., *The Maastricht Treaty on European Union,* p. 137.

36. The third paragraph of Article A (TEU) provides that "the Union shall be founded on the European Communities supplemented by the policies and forms of cooperation established by this Treaty." This division is confirmed by Article E (TEU), which refers to the different legal bases for the institutions' powers.

37. European Court of Justice, *Commission v. Council* (AETR), Case 22/70, *European Court Reports,* 1971, p. 275. Manfred Zuleeg, "Article 5, sidenote 6," in von der Groeben et al., eds., *Kommentar zum EWG-Vertrag.*

38. It seems also, according to the jurisprudence of the Court of Justice on the significance inside the Community of international agreements, not entirely precluded, that consistency (as a legal concept drawn primarily from international law) should be used to interpret Community law. See Pierre Pescatore, "Die Rechtsprechung des Europäischen Gerichtshofs zur innergemeinschaftlichen Wirkung völkerrechtlicher Abkommen," Völkerrecht als Rechtsordnung— Internationale Gerichtsbarkeit—Menschenrechte, Festschrift for H. Moser, p. 661 et seq. Frowein, ibid., p. 254; Peter Gilsdorf, "Die sicherheitspolitischen Schutzklauseln, insbesondere die Artikel 223–225 EWGV in der Perspektive der Europäischen Union," *Aussen- und sicherheitspolitische Aspekte des Vertrages von Maastricht und seine Konsequenzen für neutrale Beitrittswerber,* Glaesner/Gilsdorf/Thürer/Hafner, pp. 56–57.

39. See, to this and to the connected problems and claims, also the resolution adopted by the European Parliament from 24 February 1994 concerning the future relations between the European Union, the WEU, and the Atlantic Alliance, par. I.6, II., and III.; text in *Europe Documents,* no. 1873, 4 March 1994, p. 1.

9

The Defense Dimension of the European Union: The Role and Performance of the WEU

Mathias Jopp

This article analyzes the role and performance of Western European Union (WEU) as the defense component of European integration—in particular, the interinstitutional relationship between WEU and the European Union (EU) and the way in which the stipulations of the Treaty on European Union (TEU) have been and could be used to bring WEU into play. The analysis would lack clarity if WEU's relations with NATO were not included, since these have implications for the development of a European military security policy. Naturally, WEU's contribution for reducing the security vacuum in Central Europe is also discussed and, finally, some critical points are made regarding the further development of a European security and defense policy, including proposals for improving its effectiveness.

The Historical Context

Security and defense had already played an important role at the beginning of European integration. In the early 1950s, the project of a European Defense Community (EDC) was launched for three reasons: first, to establish after two world wars a lasting peace structure through military integration among West European states; second, to defend Western Europe against the Soviet threat; and third, to build up Western Europe to become a "third power," able to play an active role in preventing the cementing of a bipolar world.

After the failure of EDC in 1954, European integration became primarily an economic affair in the framework of the European Economic Community (EEC), established in 1956–1957. Security and defense were organized within NATO, and WEU, founded in 1954 on the basis of the Brussels Treaty of 1948, guaranteed control over

Germany's rearmament and enabled it to become a member of the Atlantic Alliance.

After three decades as a so-called Sleeping Beauty, WEU gained new impetus in the first half of the 1980s. The reason for this development had to do with the impossibility of creating a security and defense identity within the framework of the European Community (EC) and European Political Cooperation (EPC). In particular, it was Greece, Ireland, and Denmark that resisted such a move. Hence, in the 1984 Rome Declaration, the intention was expressed to use WEU as a forum of coordination on Alliance affairs and wider security issues for the foreign and defense ministers of its—at that time—seven member states (out of ten EC countries).[1] Yet WEU remained in the shadow of NATO, and most WEU member states showed only occasional interest in their institution. Although Western Europe had some influence on East-West relations through the developing EPC outside of the Rome Treaty, this was only related to political aspects of security. Throughout the Cold War, the willingness of EC members to expand integration beyond the economic and diplomatic fields was rather restrained in comparison to the role that NATO and the United States played as guarantors of Western Europe's security.

This situation changed with the end of the Cold War and the revolutions in Central and Eastern Europe in 1989–1990, which radically altered the parameters of security and integration in Europe.[2] With the breakdown of the Soviet empire, the long-standing direct threat to the security of Western Europe disappeared. West Europeans felt more secure and less dependent on U.S. protection. Under these new conditions, it seemed easier than ever before to bring security and defense policies into the sphere of European integration. The old dream of Western Europe achieving more of an equal partner status with the United States appeared more realistic, given the redistribution of political weights at the end of the Cold War. The long-standing U.S. interests in a more equitable sharing of the security and defense burdens of the West, with Western Europe assuming a greater responsibility in the security domain, pointed in the same direction. Predominantly, the wish to integrate unified Germany more tightly into West European structures and prevent a process of post–Cold War renationalization worked as a basic catalyst for deepening integration. Together, these resulted in the aim of creating a European Union with a Common Foreign and Security Policy (CFSP), with the objective of the "eventual framing of a Common Defence Policy (CDP) which might, in time, lead to a Common Defence."[3]

WEU and European Union: An Ever Closer Relationship?

The Maastricht Treaty on European Union—as concluded by the heads of state and government in December 1991 and as it came into force on 1

November 1993, after a long period of uncertainty over its successful ratification—gives WEU a very particular role in the process of European integration. This resulted from the fact that member states could not agree on the Union having a direct defense responsibility. They therefore decided that the question of a CDP should be renegotiated in 1996, and they accepted that until then, WEU, in accordance with a declaration by its member states, should play the role of the defense arm of the Union, as well as that of the European pillar of the Atlantic Alliance.[4] Thus, WEU forms the nucleus of a compromise solution between countries such as Great Britain, the Netherlands, Portugal, and Denmark, which feared anything that could weaken NATO, and other countries such as France, Germany, Belgium, and Spain, which wanted to introduce responsibility for defense policies into the framework of the European Union.[5]

According to the Maastricht Treaty, the CFSP of the Union covers all aspects relevant to the security of the Union. This can include military aspects as well. However, the Union itself does not deal with defense issues as such and may, therefore, request WEU "to elaborate and implement decisions and actions of the Union which have defence implications."[6] This does not prevent WEU from developing its own policies and priorities in the area of defense, since it remains an autonomous institution; but, in practice, as has been shown by the second Gulf War and the Yugoslav crisis, the interplay between WEU and the EC/EU is rather close, a relationship that was brought, ex post facto, into legal terms with the Maastricht Treaty.

The present WEU operation in Mostar, Bosnia-Herzegovina, is an example of how the stipulations of Article J.4 of the Union Treaty can be used. WEU, on the basis of a formal request by the EU, provides a police element to help restore public order and security in this city, in which police officers from WEU countries are directly responsible to the EU administrator, Hans Koschnick. Another example is worth mentioning, even if it is related to a period prior to the conclusion of the negotiations on the Maastricht Treaty. In August 1991, on the basis of a Franco-German initiative, the twelve EC foreign ministers meeting in the framework of EPC decided to ask WEU to look into the possibilities of deploying an interposition force in Eastern Croatia. WEU subsequently developed different options without, however, a practical consequence, since there was no agreement among the Twelve on any of the proposals made by WEU.[7] Great Britain, in particular, was among the most reluctant countries, for various reasons (including its experience with the difficulties of keeping peace in Northern Ireland) but also because, at that time, it did not wish to see the establishment of a precedent with regard to WEU's role before the completion of the Maastricht Treaty negotiations. Germany, realizing that it would, in any case, be unable to contribute militarily, quickly withdrew from the proposal. As far as today's management of the Yugoslav crisis is concerned, WEU is (apart from the Mostar operation) directly involved in the monitoring and enforcement of the UN embargo in the Adriatic and on the Danube.

In these cases, WEU does not act on behalf of the Twelve but in accordance with relevant UN Security Council resolutions that had been supported by EPC.

Other areas in which WEU could act on the basis of Article J.4 (TEU) are disaster relief operations and humanitarian and rescue tasks—for example, the evacuation of EU citizens from a crisis region. Peacekeeping could also be a task for WEU, even without UN authorization in the event of a request to the EU, or WEU directly, emanating from all parties involved in a conflict. In practice, however, WEU/EU members prefer to carry out peacekeeping and humanitarian tasks under a UN mandate. The Petersberg Declaration of WEU (June 1992) mentions, in addition to these possible operations and in addition to WEU's contribution to Allied defense, the use of "combat forces in crisis management, including peacemaking."[8] This can only be considered in two cases: Either there would be a UN Security Council authorization for the use of force, or WEU would act on its own or on behalf of the EU, on the basis of Article 51 of the UN Charter (Collective Self-Defense), in order to support a country that was attacked, even if it did not belong to an alliance. In such a case, however, problems of consensus within the EU and WEU could be very great, given the difficulty of defining a situation as being clearly an attack of one state against another and in view of the growing relevance of intrastate and cross-border ethnic conflicts in today's conflict scenarios.

The arrival of the UN as an important actor in European security had a constraining effect on West European autonomy in crisis management because of the provisions of the UN Charter and the decisionmaking procedures in relation to UN Security Council resolutions.[9] The difficulty of EU and WEU members reaching an agreement on when and how to react also has to be taken into account. However, apart from these problems, it is nevertheless true that WEU is on its way to structuring its capacities and that it has undertaken the first steps to fulfill its function as an integral part of the development of the European Union (even if it remains an institution on its own).

One interesting aspect in that regard is that the length of WEU presidencies has now been reduced from a one-year to a half-year term, in order to better synchronize WEU and Union procedures. Whether it will be possible to harmonize the presidencies of both institutions, which would create a strong link between WEU and the European Union, is more than an open question, since the enlargement of WEU to include other EC/EU countries has led so far to only Greece becoming a new member of WEU, whereas Ireland and Denmark chose the option of becoming observers. Denmark could create some difficulties for the EU, if decisions need to be made in the CFSP, during its presidency, that would have defense implications.[10] Denmark may not insist on its defense opt-out indefinitely but, for the near future, the problem will be magnified when the neutral European Free Trade

Association (EFTA) countries are full members of the European Union—even if they have already reduced or modified their traditional security concepts. It could, however, be argued that countries like Finland and Austria, which feel more exposed than the other EU states to risks deriving from instability in the Balkans or in Russia, may eventually become enthusiastic about security and defense integration.

Since the Maastricht Treaty came into force, working relations have been established between WEU and the European Union that function quite well at both the level of the presidencies and that of the secretariats-general. However, for nearly a year, there was confusion over the extent to which the European Commission should be involved in WEU meetings and should be able to obtain information and documents from WEU. Countries such as Britain and France were reluctant to grant the Commission relevant access to WEU since they view this EU body as a symbol of the Community's mechanisms of integration. Nevertheless, in early October 1994, a consensus was reached, due primarily to German insistence, that the Commission may obtain information from WEU and participate in WEU meetings as part of the delegation of the country holding the EU presidency and insofar as the Commission's competencies under the TEU are concerned. This can include meetings of Working Groups dealing with Mediterranean issues, humanitarian or rescue tasks, and requests of the EU.

The intergovernmental sub-bodies of CFSP and WEU work largely separated from each other, due to the specificity of their work on either political or military issues. The only exemption exists when deputy political directors or their representatives are involved in meetings of both organizations (the WEU Special Working Group and the Security Group of the EU) so that some paralleling between WEU and the EU is assured in the conceptual work for Europe's security policy. On the whole, relations of WEU with the EU are developing slowly but steadily with, however, less reciprocity than in the case of relations with NATO (as shown in the following subsection). The problems that existed in WEU with respect to the question of the EU Commission's involvement in the defense component of European integration and the fact that there is no WEU element present at, for example, EU General Affairs Council meetings, sheds light on the future difficulty of creating stronger links between the two organizations or even integrating WEU into the EU framework.

WEU Relations with NATO: Competition and Cooperation

Traditionally, WEU has had a special relationship with NATO ever since member states transferred a degree of practical authority to the latter when they decided, in Article IV of the modified Brussels Treaty, not to duplicate structures of NATO that were relevant to Allied defense. In their declaration, annexed to the Maastricht Treaty, WEU member states also agreed on developing WEU as the European pillar of the Atlantic Alliance and doing so in a way that would complement the activity of NATO. These fundamental aspects of the WEU-NATO relationship have not prevented strained relations between both organizations in recent years.[11] These were particularly tense throughout 1992 because, inter alia, of the duplicate assignments of WEU and NATO ships in the Adriatic to monitor the UN embargo. There was also rivalry over which of the two organizations should support peacekeeping and crisis management activities of the UN and the Conference for Security and Cooperation in Europe (CSCE). Whereas countries such as the Netherlands and Britain preferred that NATO be given this task, other countries, notably France, favored WEU. Finally, both organizations received a mandate from their member states to support measures that were decided by the two above-mentioned collective security organizations.[12]

In the course of 1993, the WEU-NATO relationship began to improve. First, there was the fact that with the move of WEU's headquarters in January 1993 from London to Brussels, both institutions began to establish working relations with each other. Second, the shift from competition to greater cooperation was, in part, influenced by the changes in governments in France and the United States. France became less obstinate about WEU's role and more flexible and pragmatic vis-à-vis NATO.[13] The United States, under the new Clinton administration, appeared much more relaxed than the Bush administration toward the development of a European defense identity. Under these new conditions, cooperation between the two organizations has been facilitated and has also become more visible: A joint NATO/WEU command has been formed for the Adriatic operation, with NATO's Military Committee accepting responsibility to the WEU Council in connection with this operation. Joint Council meetings have taken place (five such meetings so far) and both secretaries-general participate regularly in ministerial meetings of each other's organization.[14]

Improved relations between WEU and NATO can also be attributed to the acknowledgment by WEU member states, on the background of the Yugoslav experience, that NATO has comparative advantages in the domain of complex military operations requiring solid command structures and certain military assets. Because of this fact, most WEU states were in favor of NATO managing the control and enforcement of the "no fly" ban over Bosnia-Herzegovina and providing air cover for the UN forces in the security zones (including air strikes wherever necessary). NATO's military expertise will be directing the implementation of a peace agreement in Bosnia, should it be reached, and is the reason why it is seen to be the appropriate organization to be in charge of the eventual withdrawal of the UN Protective Force (UNPROFOR). The awareness of WEU's deficiencies led to the WEU Ministerial Council's proposal in November 1993 that WEU should be able, in principle, to use NATO headquarters, command structures, and communications lines in certain crisis situations.[15] The details of this proposal were then discussed in consultation with the North Atlantic Council, representing the first important joint input from WEU members to the Allied decisionmaking process, which undoubtedly contributed to the success of the NATO summit on 10 and 11 January 1994.

The conclusions of the Alliance's January 1994 summit were important for three reasons: NATO Allies, including the United States, fully appreciated the development of a European defense identity, which would put an end to most of the open ideological disputes over the role of WEU and NATO in European security policies. Second, the NATO Council accepted that collective assets of the Alliance could be used by WEU, and, third, it decided to develop the concept of Combined Joint Task Forces (CJTF) as a means of strengthening cooperation between WEU and NATO and facilitating contingency operations.[16]

The question is, however, whether the CJTF concept can be successfully implemented and whether it will work in practice. The development of this concept has not, up to now, made enough progress—due, in part, to the problems that France still encounters when it encounters questions about its relationship with NATO in military crisis management (notably, with a view to the role of Supreme Allied Commander Europe [SACEUR]). In addition, no basic decisions can be expected from France until a new president has been elected. Another reason for the CJTF concept's slow progress is that, above all, it is WEU that wants something from NATO, and—although WEU has already introduced into NATO a joint position on principles for the possible use of CJTF elements by WEU, as developed by its Political-Military Working Group—within NATO work has not advanced far.

Other problems are related to the implications of a successful implementation of the CJTF concept. The use of NATO headquarters and other assets by WEU would, of course, require a consensus with the U.S. representatives in the North Atlantic Council. This could be delicate if the United States held a different view or feared that a particular European operation could drag it into some sort of involvement that it precisely wished to avoid. It would also imply a very close operational link between WEU and NATO. With this in mind, many in NATO think that WEU is merely a suborganization of the Alliance, and U.S. analysts have already characterized WEU's role as a "gap-filler" for Western crisis management in all those cases where the United States and NATO, as such, do not wish to become engaged.[17] It is this perspective, in particular, that worries some Europeans, notably French decisionmakers.[18] Alternatively, it can be argued that the use of NATO assets under the auspices of WEU would, in fact, equip the EU (via a request to WEU) with instruments of a common defense policy before the Maastricht process arrived at this stage or, at least, would parallel efforts at strengthening the European defense cooperation.

WEU's Performance and Institutional Build-up

Looking at WEU's performance up to the present, it can be seen that one of the basic difficulties stems from member states' attitudes on whether, when, and how to react through WEU. In the case of the crisis in Somalia, WEU played no role. In the case of the crisis in Rwanda, after weeks of delays, the Council agreed on WEU supporting member states' efforts to contribute to crisis management measures.[19] The Planning Cell was tasked to serve as a coordination and contact point. However, those member states that gave support to the French humanitarian mission in Rwanda, Operation Turquoise, did so in coordination with Paris directly and not through the Planning Cell in Brussels. In the case of the Yugoslav crisis, WEU has, from the outset, focused on creating plans for peacekeeping, the protection of humanitarian convoys, and the possibilities of establishing security zones; but since member states did not wish to see WEU becoming directly engaged in these operations, most of these plans were given to the UN.

Apart from the previously mentioned operation in Mostar, WEU's activities became more visible in the Adriatic and on the Danube. In the Adriatic, WEU first operated independently, but on a cooperative basis, with NATO. It did so by building upon its experience, gained during the two Gulf Wars, in which ships of WEU member states were successfully engaged in embargo controls and minesweeping.[20] However, the situation in the Adriatic changed when the UN Security Council enlarged the mandate from monitoring to enforcing the embargo. From that point onward, a joint command was formed between NATO and WEU, the latter relying on the former's command facilities.

On the Danube, WEU runs a rather atypical operation for a defense organization (similar to the Mostar case). It supports the Riparian states—Hungary, Romania, and Bulgaria—with police and customs officers from its member countries, in order to make the embargo against Serbia and Montenegro more effective. The Danube mission was strongly favored by Germany since, until recently, it had felt constitutionally constrained in its participation in WEU, NATO, or UN crisis management operations. Other countries, notably Britain and France—which are, because of their military abilities and status as permanent members of the UN Security Council, the leading countries in WEU in all questions relating to military crisis management—raised doubts on whether WEU should continue to carry out atypical tasks. However, in view of the UN and NATO's involvement in former-Yugoslavia, the question about appropriate niches for WEU's activities is a real one. As long as most of its member states show a preference for the UN or NATO being in charge when it comes to ground and air operations, WEU will only play a role in certain special cases.

WEU is still a military organization in the early stages of its operational development. It is true, however, that, up to now, it has implemented the

Maastricht decisions with relative success. The Council has been strengthened since the appointment of special permanent representatives to WEU in January 1993. The ambassadors meet now on a weekly basis and have the support of military advisers. The Planning Cell, which came into operation in April 1993, has approximately thirty military officers and deals, inter alia, with generic and contingency planning. It is located at WEU headquarters in Brussels and is directly responsible to the Council. It also has links with the Chiefs of Defense Staff (who meet twice a year) through the military delegates to WEU. A WEU Satellite Center has been established in Torrejón (Spain) to train experts in the interpretation of satellite images. It already has some operational capacity, and member states intend to develop it to be the ground component of a space-based observation system. After the absorption of the former Independent European Programmes Group (IEPG), in connection with WEU's enlargement to include other EC/EU countries and European NATO allies, a West European Armaments Group (WEAG) has been set up within WEU that can help develop a European armaments agency. Forces answerable to WEU have been defined, including multinational formations such as the Eurocorps, NATO's Multinational Division Central (in which Germany, Britain, Belgium, and the Netherlands participate), and the Anglo-Dutch Amphibious Force.[21] These forces may be used, apart from contributing to Allied defense, for certain missions, as defined in WEU's Petersberg Declaration (humanitarian and rescue tasks, peacekeeping, and peace enforcement operations). Furthermore, a paper on WEU's policy in peacekeeping, drawn up by the previous Luxembourg presidency, has been approved by the Council; the Planning Cell is working on the possibilities of how humanitarian and rescue tasks could be carried out; and a document on WEU's procedures in times of crisis has been concluded. More forces answerable to WEU may be defined and exercises will be held in cooperation with NATO or on a separate basis, and WEU will certainly continue to develop its procedures and structures.

Notwithstanding these actual or planned improvements, there still remain a variety of problems. The Planning Cell lacks sufficient support for its work by the member states. The Satellite Center is not yet a permanent body (its experimental phase ends in 1995/1996), and it needs more resources to develop its operational capacity further for the verification of arms control agreements and crisis monitoring. It will also be difficult to create, within a few years, a "system" of space-based observation satellites to be used for military purposes, particularly at a time when member states face serious budgetary constraints. The armaments agency, which could rationalize and combine member states' resources, does not even exist as a detailed plan on paper, and most countries still tend to prefer national solutions for adapting their defense industries to the post–Cold War situation.[22] Finally, some of the multinational forces answerable to WEU, like the Eurocorps, are not yet fully operational, and there is also a lack of appropriate structures for politico-military management at WEU's headquarters in Brussels—not to mention the lack of real-time intelligence capacities and some problems that still exist when it comes to operations at a greater distance.

Partly for these reasons, only a limited number of types of operation can, at present, be carried out by WEU alone. This implies that apart from the lack of political will to use WEU for crisis management tasks, Europeans have to improve their military capabilities, in order to enhance WEU's capacity to act as the military wing of the EU.

Relations with Central and Eastern Europe

Notwithstanding the difficulties that WEU is still facing in order to be able to function properly as the military arm of the EU and the European pillar of NATO, it plays a very useful role in projecting stability eastward. WEU has tried, as did NATO, to react appropriately to the growing pressure from Central and East European countries regarding the question of membership or security guarantees of Western security institutions. NATO created the Partnership for Peace (PFP) and WEU introduced the status of associate partner for the nine Central European states that had previously participated in WEU's Forum of Consultation and that have Europe Agreements with the EC/EU (or may soon have such agreements, such as Bulgaria, the Czech Republic, Estonia, Hungary, Latvia, Lithuania, Poland, Romania, and Slovakia).

Their special status in WEU gives the nine Central European countries the opportunity to become more acquainted with the security and defense dimension of the European Union, and they may also profit from certain advantages linked to this formalized relationship. Associate partners participate regularly in WEU Council meetings (every two weeks), they can be invited to intergovernmental Working Groups, they have a liaison arrangement with the Planning Cell, and they can associate themselves with activities or operations of WEU by, for example, offering forces for specific missions.[23] Even if they cannot participate in the Council's work, as much as it is related to internal WEU affairs or to WEU's relations with the EU and NATO, WEU has opened up parts of its own organization to Central European countries that come close to their interests.

Compared to NATO, which offered cooperation outside of its ordinary procedures, WEU could go much further for a variety of reasons: First, most WEU members participate in NATO's integrated military structures and, therefore, collective defense issues are not discussed very much within WEU. Second, it was possible to achieve a consensus after introducing a special status for Central European countries within WEU. Third, WEU has already had some experience with the concept of variable participation in its activities, as is shown by the existence of the status of observer (Denmark and Ireland and, in the future, probably Austria, Finland, and Sweden) and the status of associate members (Iceland, Norway, and Turkey).

The status of being an associate partner is not linked to any formal security guarantee, but the fact that Central European countries now sit regularly at WEU's Council table signals to other countries, including Russia or Serbia, that associate partners are seen as belonging to a priority area of Western Europe's security interests.[24] What that might imply in a situation of conflict or crisis is an open question, but it is hoped that WEU's association policy will have some preventive effects. Another important side effect should be mentioned: By granting a special status to Central European countries, including the Baltic states, WEU has, to some extent, anticipated the drawing of lines on a West-East axis for future rounds of an Eastern enlargement of the EU. It is this effect, in particular, that caused critical echoes within the EU since it happened before the EU itself had decided on negotiating Europe Agreements with the Baltic states.

The initiative for introducing the status of associate partner was launched by Germany and France, with Britain joining in somewhat later. Without these three important countries pulling at the same end of the rope, although for different reasons, it would have been difficult to overcome the reluctance on the part of southern WEU member states, such as Italy, due to these countries' general skepticism regarding the perspective of an eastern enlargement of the EU and WEU. Another problem was the appropriate definition of associate partner status, in order to make a clear distinction between them and associate members of WEU, which are full members of NATO. In particular, the problem was related to Turkey, which wishes to become a full member of the EU and WEU and which has had an association agreement with the EU since 1964. The problem could be resolved temporarily by upgrading the status of associate members, giving them the possibility of defining forces answerable to WEU and of nominating officers for the Planning Cell, and by connecting them to WEU's communications system (WEUCOM).[25]

WEU now encompasses a total of twenty-four countries that are represented within its framework, which implies a great challenge to manage internal coordination efficiently in order to meet the objective of developing a common identity among all countries concerned, in matters of security and defense policies. This also applies to a few simple, practical problems. Who can participate in the various meetings? Who has access to which kind of documents? The experiences gained by WEU, with its concept of variable participation, may also be of future value in the possibility of using more flexible concepts of integration by the EU.

Apart from the importance of an intensified security dialogue with Central European countries and the related potential structural security effects, the new status of Central European countries in WEU must be given a practical dimension. Possibilities for closer cooperation with associate partners lie in the areas of peacekeeping and crisis management (the Danube Operation may serve as an example in this respect), verification of arms control agreements (the CFE [Conventional Forces in Europe] Treaty and Open Skies), and the development of joint positions and initiatives with regard to the CSCE. The latter may be seen by the EU as an attempt by WEU to interfere in the performance of the CFSP. On the other hand, it could be argued that it would be a missed opportunity if WEU did not use its framework of twenty-four countries to formulate common positions on the CSCE or to support respective positions of the EU if they were so developed within the CFSP.

Prospects

Looking at the prospects of European integration in the field of security and defense policies, a number of unanswered questions need to be tackled in the coming years. First, there is the problem of WEU's operational weaknesses, which implies that WEU will depend for some time on the use of NATO mechanisms and the support of the United States, at least as far as sophisticated or larger military operations are concerned. If the Europeans really wish to become more independent in their security policies, they have to build up WEU's capacities, a matter that can only be achieved step-by-step and over a longer period, in view of the budgetary constraints that all member states are facing.

WEU's limited operational ability is not only a handicap with regard to crisis management. Once the European Union is enlarged to include countries from the North and, later, from the East, the question arises as to how the security of new Union members can be guaranteed.[26] The problem may not be so pressing in the case of the accession of neutral EFTA countries to the EU (even if it also exists here in principle) since these countries wish to maintain, for a certain length of time, their independent defense. However, their attitude may change, and once Poland, the Baltic states, and other Central European countries enter the Union, the problem will become even more acute, considering their definite interest in security guarantees. If WEU is unable to provide these guarantees, NATO would have to be enlarged concurrently with the widening of the EU in order to establish a homogeneous strategic area within an enlarged European Union. Will the United States be prepared, in the end, to extend their security guarantees correspondingly? Would France be prepared to accept a broadened NATO that would, in a certain way, overarch the European Union?

If WEU is not developed into an autonomous collective defense organization or NATO is not broadened, no formal security guarantees can be given to new members of the EU. It could be argued, however, that some sort of de facto security guarantee exists, in any case, for new Union members that have a common border with Russia and the CIS, since it is difficult to imagine that both WEU and NATO would simply stand back if a new, peripheral member state were subjected to a serious external threat or even an attack. A response in that case, however, would not involve any automatism. It would not be clear cut and, as a consequence, different zones of security would exist within the EU, with two classes of members: members with an Article V guarantee and members without it.

The existence of second-class members would not be acceptable from the viewpoint of the political cohesion of an enlarged EU and with respect to the development of an effective CFSP, notably insofar as questions of West-East relations are concerned. It will therefore be of overriding importance to find appropriate solutions for the security implications of an enlarged Union in terms of European defense capabilities, the institutional links and arrangements between WEU and the EU, and, above all, the development of a viable relationship between the EU and NATO.

Another basic problem is the lack of a European strategy or security doctrine. Current moves in security integration are based on a system of increments: One starts with building structures and creating instruments, then consideration is given to possible responses in certain crisis situations and, later on, perhaps to strategies. So, the horse is saddled from behind without knowing much about the race course. What remains unanswered is the question of where to go—that is, the basic orientation of Europe's security policy. Shall the EU remain primarily a civil power? Shall it become a regional or a global power, able to carry the related responsibility and possessing the necessary military means? Many member states have no clear positions themselves in this respect, nor is there a common view on this matter. The lack of a strategic vision is, to a great extent, due to the difficulties in reaching a common assessment of certain external developments because of the differences in interests and perceptions that have grown since the disappearance of a common massive threat. Perhaps Western Europe is presently moving from being a civil power to a regional one. Yet even here, doubts can be raised in view of Western Europe's weak performance in handling the Yugoslav crisis.

This problem has its impact on the work currently being undertaken in WEU on the development of a Common European Defense Policy,[27] in the wider sense of a common military security policy—an issue that will also be on the agenda when the review conference on the Maastricht Treaty is opened in 1996. As long as there is no basic agreement on the role that Europe should assume in international security, it is very difficult to define Europe's needs in military terms[28] and to agree on the necessary military capacities to be developed in order to fulfill a certain role. This includes the appropriate institutional mechanisms and decisionmaking procedures for both arriving at a yet-to-be-defined Common Defense Policy in stages and putting it into practice as efficiently as possible.

A further problem results from the shift, in relevant aspects of responsibility for European security, from the United States to Europe.[29] Western Europe is confronted with the task of exercising a leadership role in certain circumstances. It is doubtful whether this can be done successfully with policies that rely purely on intergovernmental procedures and, in principle, on the basis of consensus. Greater efficiency in decisionmaking would require applying majority voting in CFSP matters[30] and considering appropriate voting modalities for defense aspects in order to avoid blockades, at least in cases where a majority of EU/WEU states were in favor of taking a certain action. Better capacities for security policy planning and common risk analysis could also help prepare the ground for delicate decisions on security and defense matters should it become necessary. Yet that alone would not be enough, as long as a more common structure for security policy making is lacking, in the sense of being a forward-oriented driving force in Brussels, because governments tend to react rather than to plan for future eventualities.

Moreover, there is the problem of the departmentalization of security policy making in the forms of WEU, CFSP (with its dual structure—COREPER and Political Directors), the Commission (with its DG 1A and Department for Security Aspects), and the EC itself (with its external economic relations and their implications for Western Europe's security interests). This situation requires an enormous amount of coordination and leads to time-consuming procedures and even twice the amount of work, which is, on the whole, disadvantageous for developing a cohesive and efficient defense policy. Improving working relations between the institutions involved may be one way to try to solve this problem. Integrating WEU into the framework of the EU would probably be better, but the preconditions for such a step are not very promising. Instead of converging trends between WEU and the EU, there is, at present, a tendency favoring variable geometry. WEU's association policies vis-à-vis countries that are not members of the EU, or countries that are neither members of the EU nor of NATO, make it difficult to envisage a merger of the EU and WEU. The EU, on the other hand, with its enlargement policies toward neutral EFTA countries, produces, in effect, a greater number of observers in WEU, which creates, at least temporarily, obstacles to achieving an identity of membership between both organizations.

Finally, the more WEU develops its own structures and institutional identity, the more difficult it may be to integrate it into the EU framework—not to mention reluctance on the part of the governments of some member states, notably Britain, to develop the EU significantly. Certain members of WEU feel that WEU's own problems could become worse if it were integrated into the confusion of the EU's security policy. In addition, it has to be taken into consideration that WEU, as a defense organization, has its specificity, in terms of internal security regulations, which does not make it any easier to incorporate it into the structure of a traditionally civil organization.

Even if there were a consensus about integrating WEU into the EU, it would pose, because of the above-mentioned factors, institutional problems that would be very difficult to resolve. However, elements from the model of Monetary Union could be used, in the sense of creating a fourth pillar within the EU. The Council of Ministers of the defense pillar and its sub-bodies would then constitute a special institution within the EU. Meetings would have to be held either in a different composition from that of the CFSP pillar and other policy areas of the Union or, at least, in a form that allowed variable participation depending on the items on the agenda. This would imply accepting the opting-out of EU countries and applying strict rules for locking out member states that do not meet certain criteria. Only countries that are parties to the modified Brussels Treaty and the Washington Treaty would have the right to vote. Additionally, the other EU members could not be present when Article V matters or relations with NATO were discussed.

Whether agreement on such a model can be reached in the 1996 Intergovernmental Conference on the revision of the Union Treaty is questionable, since there is resistance on the part of many member states to the acceleration of foreign and security policy integration. Yet, if some institutional adaptations and changes in the set of rules are not made, it will certainly remain difficult to formulate and exercise an effective security policy. In the end, common institutions may, at best, serve a back-up function for ad hoc coalitions of larger member states. This may not be the worst situation as long as it would serve common interests, even if it would be difficult to call it a true common policy. However, apart from this, there is even a risk that common institutions will lose relevance; the development and fate of the International Contact Group on the former Yugoslavia serves as quite a challenging example.

It is, however, not so much the institutions, as such, that are responsible for weaknesses in Europe's security and defense policies; it is the governments that are reluctant either to make full use of these policies or to give them the necessary powers. However, without stronger common institutions, there would be danger of disintegration and renationalization, if not a revival of thinking in terms of balance of power politics, with some of the negative implications that have been witnessed throughout Europe's history. With the partial retreat of the United States and the variety of challenges and risks confronting the European Union and WEU in the East and the South— from the Baltics to the Balkans, from the Black Sea to the Mediterranean— and on top of that, with the perspective of enlargement, there is a desperate need for governments to agree on the next steps of European integration. Decisions on that will have to be made soon, for Western Europe's security and for the sake of the stability of the entire continent.

Notes

1. See "Rome Declaration of 27 October 1984," reprinted in *The Reactivation of WEU. Statements and Communiqués 1984–1987* (London: Secretariat-General of Western European Union, 1988), pp. 5–15.

2. See Dieter Mahncke, "Parameters of European Security," *Chaillot Papers* 10 (Paris: WEU Institute for Security Studies, September 1993).

3. *Treaty on European Union,* Title V, Article J.4 (1).

4. See "Declaration of WEU member states on the role of WEU and its relations with the European Union and with the Atlantic Alliance," annexed to the *Treaty on European Union.*

5. See Anand Menon, Anthony Forster, and William Wallace, "A Common European Defence?" *Survival* 3 (Autumn 1992), pp. 98–118.

6. *Treaty on European Union,* Article J.4 (2).

7. See Mathias Jopp, "The Strategic Implications of European Integration," *Adelphi Paper* 290 (London: IISS, Brassey's, 1994), p. 43.

8. "Petersberg Declaration of the WEU Ministerial Council, 19 June 1992," Part II, par. 4, *Europe Documents* no. 1787, 23 June 1992.

9. See, in this connection, Luisa Vierucci, "WEU—A Regional Partner of the United Nations?" *Chaillot Papers* 12 (Paris: WEU Institute for Security Studies, December 1993).

10. See "Conclusions of the Presidency, European Council of Edinburgh, 11–12 December 1992," *Agence Europe* (special ed.), 13 December 1992, pp. 9–11.

11. See François Heisbourg, "The European-U.S. Alliance: Valedictory Reflections on Continental Drift in the Post–Cold War Era," *International Affairs* 4 (1992), pp. 665–678.

12. See "Petersberg Declaration," Part I, par. 2, and the communiqués of the North Atlantic Council in Oslo and Brussels (June and December 1992).

13. See Peter Schmidt, "French Security Ambitions," *Aussenpolitik* (English ed.) 4 (1993), pp. 335–343.

14. See Jopp, "The Strategic Implications," p. 31.

15. See "Luxembourg Declaration of the WEU Council of Ministers," Luxembourg, 22 November 1993, par. 3.

16. See the "Declaration of the Heads of State and Government at the North Atlantic Council meeting, Brussels, 10–11 January 1994," *Atlantic Document* no. 83, 12 January 1994, par. 6, 9.

17. As an example, see F. Stephen Larrabee, "Implications for Transatlantic Relations," in Mathias Jopp, ed., *The Implications of the Yugoslav Crisis for Western Europe's Foreign Relations, Chaillot Papers* 17 (Paris: WEU Institute for Security Studies, 1994), p. 31.

18. See *Le Débat stratégique,* no. 12 (1994), p. 1.

19. For WEU's reaction in the case of Rwanda, see *WEU Press Guidelines,* Brussels, 21 June 1994.

20. See, in this connection, Nicole Gnesotto and John Roper, eds., *Western Europe and the Gulf* (Paris: WEU Institute for Security Studies, 1992).

21. See WEU's Luxembourg Declaration, par. 4.

22. See, in this connection, William Walker and Philip Gummet, "Nationalism, Internationalism, and the European Defence Market," *Chaillot Papers* 9 (Paris: WEU Institute for Security Studies, 1993).

23. See "Kirchberg Declaration of the WEU Council of Ministers, Luxembourg, 9 May 1994," Part II (document on status of associate partner).

24. See Mathias Jopp, "Langer Weg—Kühnes Ziel: Gemeinsame Verteidigungspolitik," *Europa-Archiv* 13/14 (1994), pp. 397–404.

25. See "Kirchberg Declaration," Part III (Declaration on upgrading associate members).

26. See, for the following, Jopp, "The Strategic Implications," Chap. 3 and Conclusions.

27. See "Preliminary Conclusions on the Formulation of a Common European Defence Policy," WEU Council of Ministers, Noordwijk, 14 November 1994.

28. For an attempt to do so, from a U.S. point of view, see M. E. Berman and G. M. Carter, *The Independent European Force. Costs of Independence* (Santa Monica: RAND Corporation, 1993).

29. See, in this connection, Nanette Gantz and John Roper, eds., *Towards a New Partnership. U.S.-European Relations in the Post–Cold War Era* (Paris: WEU Institute for Security Studies, 1993).

30. This argument carries an even greater weight in view of the growing number of EU members. See also Josef Janning, "Am Ende der Regierbarkeit? Gefährliche Folgen der Erweiterung der Europäischen Union," *Europa Archiv* 22 (1993), pp. 645–653.

Part 3

To Act or Not to Act?

10

The Potential and Limits of the CFSP: The Yugoslav Example

Geoffrey Edwards[1]

The conflict in the former Yugoslavia has tested the European Union[2] to its utmost, without (at least, by the end of 1994) bringing about peace. Indeed, it is arguable that its contribution has had the effect of continuing the war in Bosnia, even if it has—again, so far—also contributed to the containment of the war within Bosnia and Croatia. The Union's efforts, like those of the EC/Twelve before it, have run the gamut from preventive diplomacy, crisis management and diplomatic initiatives to facilitate settlement, sanctions against perceived aggressors and recusants and aid to those left starving and helpless, and the threat, often repeated but not implemented before the limited air strike at Gorazde in April 1994, of the use of force to make and keep peace. Few of these efforts have, in themselves, proved compelling, innovative as some of them may have been, heroic and costly others, whether in human or budgetary terms. The lessons that the Union's policies may suggest may be varied but what the policies have revealed are the limits of European Political Cooperation/Common Foreign and Security Policy EPC/CFSP and the central institutions of the Union in times of crisis, and the continued divergence of approaches, principles, and interests among the member states (as well as sometimes within them). The EU's policies have also revealed the continued dependence on the involvement of other institutions and actors, not least the United Nations, the United States, and Russia.

The Original Aims and Expectations of the EC/Twelve[3]

The Community and a number of its member states looked at the Yugoslav crisis not simply from the perspective of its implications for European security, but also, and as tellingly, from the point of view of the lessons of the Gulf War. The inability of the EC/Twelve to maintain a joint approach even before the use of force to oust the Iraqi troops may have suggested to the British that the Twelve were not ready for a common foreign and security policy, but to others, including the French and German leaders, it signaled just such a need if the EC/Twelve were to be taken at all seriously as an international actor. The fact that during the early period of the Yugoslav crisis, the Twelve were preoccupied with negotiating a CFSP within the Intergovernmental Conference (IGC) and later were concerned about the Maastricht Treaty's ratification was inevitably a complicating factor. It was one, perhaps surprisingly, that did not always work in the interests of united, positive leadership. If the immediate overall aim was clear, to maintain the status quo ante, in the sense, as President Mitterrand put it in June 1991, that the EC "must not be accused of trivialising the territorial integrity of Yugoslavia,"[4] the deepening crisis, and then continuing conflict, found unity wanting.

The threatened breakup and conflict in Yugoslavia highlighted the tensions that had lain beneath much of the surface of Soviet-dominated Eastern Europe. Initially, the ethnic/nationalist dimension, in general, was played down by the EC/Twelve in the interests of encouraging democratization and liberalization within the territorial status quo. There was little immediate support for allowing the issue of minorities to take a center stage, with all the uncertainties and complications that might then ensue, given the frequent mismatch and overlap of ethnic identities and state boundaries. If the former Yugoslav republics were the first to declare their wish to break away, they were not considered likely to be the last. The manner in which the EC/Union responded to the conflict in Yugoslavia was therefore seen as likely to provide precedents in other cases—even if that possibility rarely led member states to clarify their aims and the means of pursuing them. It was perhaps symptomatic of the EC/Union's muddle.

Nonetheless, the situation in the Balkans was particularly sensitive. As Edward Mortimer put it: "Almost all the states bordering Yugoslavia have some reason to fear being dragged into the conflict there, given that ethnic communities and semi-dormant irredentist claims cut across the existing frontiers in all directions."[5] He might also have added that two of those states bordering Yugoslavia were members of the EC. There was, therefore, a strong sense that the EC/Twelve could not simply stand aside and allow the situation to deteriorate but had, at some point, to step in to contain and neutralize the conflict as much as possible. At the outset, the EC welcomed the primary responsibility assigned to it by other institutions, notably the Conference on Security and Cooperation in Europe (CSCE) and NATO, for, as Hans-Dietrich Genscher put it, if the CSCE offered the framework of stability within which to establish a peaceful order in Europe: "The European Community is the anchorage point for the stability of that peaceful view."[6] And there was, initially at least, sufficient optimism—with hindsight, serious overconfidence—that the instruments and resources available to the EC/Twelve would be enough to provide such anchorage, even if, to begin with, those resources were moral persuasion backed by economic instruments of policy. And there was, too, initially, a belief that the coincidence of the IGC on Political Union was likely to reinforce the Union's influence since the assumption of a greater security identity was a core concern.

In addition, there were the lessons of the Gulf to be taken into account, if not learned. President Mitterrand, for one, saw Europe's dependence on U.S. leadership as demanding a reconsideration of "Europe's role in all areas" at the highest level.[7] But whatever the involvement of heads of state and of government, at least two of the lessons of the Gulf proved difficult to deal with: that boundaries could not be redrawn by force; and that the threat of force to regain the status quo ante needs to be plausible, if it is to have any chance of success, and may need to be put into practice in order to secure success.[8]

The immediate response of the EC/Twelve to the threat of Slovene and Croatian declarations of independence (they actually came in June 1991) was, of course, diplomatic support for negotiations that would allow for the maintenance of Yugoslav territorial integrity, backed up with the prospect of better, closer economic relations, including loans for infrastructure projects and the enlargement of the PHARE program. The hope was that this would suffice and that the Serbs would then re-establish the rotating presidency of a federal Yugoslavia (the Croatians were meant to be next in line) and establish a dialogue with the leaders of the republics on economic and political reforms, including improvements in the area of minority rights. As the Luxembourg foreign minister, then president of the Council, put it, Yugoslavia "could have expectations with respect of its association with the Community if its territorial unity and integrity are safeguarded. Any other attitude could jeopardize internal frontiers in Europe."[9] And, as the Italian foreign minister further suggested, any Croatian or Slovenian ideas of possible EC membership would receive a cold welcome by the EC if they went ahead with their plans for independence.[10]

Once the two republics had declared independence, Gianni de Michelis notwithstanding, and the Yugoslav army began its countermeasures, the EC/Twelve were obliged to adopt a new position. The European Council, which met on 28/29 June 1991, agreed on a number of options, including: the dispatch to Belgrade of the foreign ministers of the Troika (then comprising Luxembourg, Italy, and the Netherlands); the suspension of Community aid if the Troika's mission failed to bring about a ceasefire; and a decision to invoke the CSCE's emergency consultations procedure. The use of the ministerial Troika was considered important, in part because it meant the inclusion of the Italian foreign minister, which lent the visit greater political weight, expertise, and a certain sense of sympathy for the Yugoslav government, given their past close relations (via, inter alia, the "Pentagonale" as well as through bilateral relations[11]); but also, as the Italian prime minister was reported as saying: "A simple appeal was not enough. The world . . . is full of appeals which are ignored and what is happening on our doorstep requires more than a 'bureaucratic diplomatic' approach."[12]

Although an agreement took rather more ministerial to-ing and fro-ing than had been initially envisaged (the Troika went three times, changing its composition after 1 July to include Portugal in place of Italy), the Brioni Agreement of 8 July 1991 did seem to mark the basis for an accord between the republics and the federal authorities, at least as far as Slovenia was concerned. Under that agreement, the EC/Twelve undertook a new common responsibility, that of providing observers to monitor the ceasefire in Slovenia and "if need be" in Croatia, made up of civilian and (unarmed) military personnel.[13] The Brioni Agreement was greeted as "proof of the European Community's ability to act" by Genscher,[14] seemingly endorsing the claim made two weeks before by the Luxembourg foreign minister, Jacques Poos, that it was "the hour of Europe, not the hour of the Americans." Whether intended or not, it seemed that the EC/Twelve had taken the Yugoslav crisis on as a test case. It was perhaps not surprising that the almost immediate collapse of that and the many EC-brokered ceasefires that followed gave a hollow ring to the claim.

Conference Diplomacy and the Question of Recognition

Even if the situation in Slovenia was resolved, the position in Croatia was not, and there were growing pressures for equivalent treatment by the Bosnian and Macedonian republics. The primary hope remained that the EC/Twelve, whether through the threat or use of sanctions if promises of increased aid proved unavailing, as well as through the use of monitoring missions, could bring all the parties together to restore peace before the conflict spilled over into other areas. As exasperation grew over the failure of ceasefires to hold and the intransigence of the Serbian federal leadership, two new initiatives were launched: the Dutch with a proposal for a peace conference and the French with their proposal for arbitration.

The Dutch became increasingly concerned with the idea of a peace conference, not simply as a means of bringing pressure to bear on the seemingly intransigent Serbs to settle, but also to parry growing German pressure to recognize Slovenia and Croatia. It was one of the preconditions for the conference that "none of the six republics would be recognised as independent and sovereign states except as part of an overall settlement agreeable to all six republics."[15] But prospects for the peace conference were undermined from the beginning, in that the precondition of a verified ceasefire proved impossible to achieve. Nonetheless, it was agreed at the EPC meeting of 3 September 1991 to launch the conference under the chairmanship of Lord Carrington (former British foreign secretary and secretary-general of NATO), in the hope that the conference might itself inspire a ceasefire.

Three Working Groups were also set up under Commission chairmanship, on the constitutional future of Yugoslavia, the question of minorities, and on economic relations among the republics, together with an arbitration committee that included three eminent Community judges led by Robert Badinter of France. The conference opened on 12 September 1991 on the basis of a third precondition, that "there should be no change of borders except by peaceful means and by agreement."[16]

In October 1991, the basis of a peace plan was proposed, which posited a confederal model for Yugoslavia on existing borders with minority rights guaranteed. The confederal element was not to be territorially based since, as Lord Carrington put it: "The mosaic of Serb, Muslim, and Croat communities dictated this." The proposal proved insufficient to win support.

But if the member states appeared relieved, albeit temporarily, to be able to off-load the peace initiative onto Lord Carrington and his small team, the situation in Yugoslavia so worsened that alternative and supplementary policies had to be considered. These included the formal recognition of the republics and the possible use of force, to make as well as keep the peace. The question of force is dealt with below; the more immediate issue was that of recognition, with all the symbolic importance and political leverage it entailed. It created not just particular problems among the member states but also threatened to unravel the peace conference and undermine any credibility that the EC/Twelve had managed to create.

The pace on recognition was forced by Germany. German leaders sought to rationalize their pressure for recognition and their later unilateral recognition of Slovenia and Croatia through their own recent exercise in self-determination. If they did not recognize the right of self-determination in Slovenia and Croatia, then, as Volker Rühe, the CDU secretary general, declared, "we have no moral or political credibility."[17]

German policy both created division among the Twelve and, according to Lord Carrington, Lord Owen, and others, completely undermined the conference initiative. At times, the division, especially within France and Germany, appeared to reflect more profound concerns, with French suspicions of long-term German aims in Central and Southeastern Europe being deeply resented in Germany.[18] However, the German stance, while clearly one that sought to balance strong domestic opinion against the desirability of a common EPC position, proceeded to make a mockery both of aspirations to a common policy and the principles on which it was meant to be based. As Lord Owen remarked: "The European Community . . . recognized those republics against the judgement of France and Britain in the mistaken belief that the hallmark of a future Maastricht-type European foreign policy was simultaneous recognition."[19]

Nevertheless, the rest of the Twelve, including France, had already been gradually swinging round to the idea of eventual recognition of the breakup of Yugoslavia. Discrimination against Serbia in favor of the breakaway republics, for example, was introduced in December 1991 in the EC's economic restrictions. A compromise was then reached on 16 December whereby the Arbitration Commission was to report on the guidelines to be adopted on recognition. Croatia was held not to have met the human rights criteria set out by the Commission, but Germany nonetheless went ahead unilaterally, the others following on 15 January 1992. Despite the clear use of force and intimidation and the boycott of the independence referendum by the Bosnian Serbs, Bosnia was recognized in April 1992, arguably making an intensification of the conflict inevitable. Macedonia, on the other hand, despite meeting the criteria set by the Badinter Commission, was refused EC recognition, the Greek government claiming that the new republic had irredentist claims. It was a position maintained until April 1993 when—as the former-Yugoslav Republic of Macedonia—most of the Twelve recognized it, although diplomatic relations were not established by the majority until the end of 1993, with Greece still dissenting. Even at the diplomatic level, the Twelve seemed incapable of sustained coordinated action.

Yet even if recognition of the breakaway republics had undermined the EC's peace conference, Lord Carrington (and Ambassador Cutileiro, representing the Portuguese presidency from 1 January until 30 June 1992) continued, encouraged "to soldier on, not because anyone had any clear conception of what he should do, but more because nobody knew what else could be done."[20] They undertook continued meetings and visits to Belgrade, Zaghreb, and Sarajevo, in the hope of establishing ceasefires and further negotiations. The EC's recognition of Bosnia, for example, was based on an agreement by the Serb, Muslim, and Croatian communities on a declaration of constitutional principles brokered largely by Cutileiro in March 1992; but already the failure to make any agreements or ceasefires stick,[21] as well as the conflict in Krajina and the possible spread of fighting to Kosovo, had led to an increased involvement on the part of the United Nations. In November 1991, the UN Security Council decided to embark on a peacekeeping mission to Croatia, and the UN Secretary-General appointed Cyrus Vance as his special envoy, to try to bring about a ceasefire in Croatia. His success in brokering such a ceasefire in January 1992 resulted largely from the fact that:

> For Serbia, EC-brokered ceasefires, achieved through EC coercion, could be seen as capitulation to Germany. A UN-arranged deal, however, offered Serbs thinking in these terms an escape from Germany's embrace. Acceptance of the Vance Plan was an alternative to capitulation to the Germans.[22]

The UN Secretary-General, Boutros-Ghali, sought to exploit further the greater willingness of the Serbs to negotiate with the UN by co-hosting, with the British EC presidency, a further international conference in August 1992 in London.

The outcome of the London conference was the appointment of Lord Owen as a replacement for Lord Carrington as the EC's representative alongside Vance, as co-chairmen of the steering committee of the conference. It meant that the conference moved to Geneva with full-time co-chairmen, creating additional opportunities for more concerted efforts to be made, and with a more dominant role for the United Nations. This allowed the EC/Twelve to take rather more of a back seat while they sought to pull the Maastricht Treaty back on track after its rejection by the Danish electorate in June 1992 and its near-rejection by the French in September 1992.

The Vance-Owen negotiations, carried out over a five-month period, resulted in the peace plan of January 1993. The plan contained three elements: a declaration on constitutional principles; the division of Bosnia into ten provinces, somewhat along the lines of Swiss cantons but with international legal identity remaining exclusively with the limited central government—three of the provinces were to be governed by Bosnian Serbs, three by Muslims, two by Croats, and two mixed; and proposals relating to the cessation of hostilities and other military matters. It was a solution reached with reluctance but which, in the EC's view, reflected what was practical.

If the European Union maintained its support for the Vance-Owen Plan and its de facto successor, the Owen-Stoltenberg Plan, throughout 1993 without achieving agreement, it was, in the words of the Belgian foreign minister, Willy Claes, who had presided over the EU Council during the second part of 1993, "not for lack of trying."[23] Several times it seemed to provide at least renewed hope for a negotiated peace, as at the beginning of May 1993, when the Greek government sought to use its closer relations with Serbia by inviting the warring factions to Athens, or in late August of the same year, although by then the plan was being modified to recognize what had become inevitable, the division of Bosnia into three very largely autonomous states. By the end of September, any optimism was seen to have been misplaced, and in the absence of success the member states became somewhat fractious. Douglas Hurd, for example, was critical of the press for its coverage, especially for its adverse comments on Britain's ultra-cautiousness over the question of the use of force. Alain Juppé, the French foreign minister appointed in March 1993, on the other hand, was convinced that new, public initiatives were necessary and appeared impatient of the tendency for the EU to try to put the question of Bosnia into a sort of limbo and leave it up to Vance and Owen, or Owen and Stoltenberg, to win support for their peace plan.[24] In seeking to launch a new initiative, he found ready support in Germany, whose leadership had tended toward a lower profile after the recognition episode, it having been suggested that after that and the constitutional problem over participation in peacekeeping exercises, Germany could only "make loud noises very quietly."[25]

The new Franco-German Initiative in early November 1993 sought to break the stalemate by presenting a plan based on the proposals discussed on

HMS Invincible in September 1993, which allowed for the establishment of
a loose confederation and a military and a territorial agreement.[26] In
essence, it called on the Bosnian Serbs to concede some of the land they had
taken by force (though only some 3–4 percent more than they had already
agreed to give up, allowing the Bosnian Muslims 33.3 percent and the
Croatians 17.5) and to adopt various confidence-building measures in
Krajina in return for which sanctions would gradually be lifted against
Serbia. The initiative was formally adopted by the EU at a special meeting
of the General Affairs Council on 22 November 1993. Although it did not
lead to a second London conference to settle all the issues of the former
Yugoslavia, including Krajina and Kosovo as well as Bosnia, there were at
least further meetings in Geneva, with representatives from all sides, including UN military commanders and observers from both the United States and
Russia. The talks broke down before the end of December 1993, with Juppé
being clear as to why they did so:

> Because the Russians, on the one hand, and the Americans, on the other,
> were refusing to get involved in the process. The Serbs felt themselves
> backed by the Russians and the Moslems considered that, by holding off,
> the Americans were giving them some sort of encouragement to carry on
> the war. That's why it didn't work.[27]

It was only with the marketplace massacre in Sarajevo on 5 February
1994 that renewed efforts were made by the EU *and* the United States and
Russia to attempt to get the peace process moving again. The focus
inevitably became Sarajevo, with the Serb forces being delivered an ultimatum to lift the siege and withdraw or risk air strikes against their positions.
On the one hand, it saw a rapprochement between the French and the United
States over the role of NATO. On the other hand, it saw a Russian initiative
that allowed some cover for the Serbs to withdraw. The policy was sufficiently credible and successful that it was regarded as a model for the relief
of other designated safe areas, though without the same success.

Juppé's comments on the United States were echoed by others, including Owen himself.[28] The Yugoslav conflict has indeed caused some
extremely bitter Europe–United States recriminations. In his summing up of
the Belgian presidency, Willy Claes saw the EU's achievements during his
period in office not only in the mobilization of the humanitarian effort in
Bosnia, or the implementation of sanctions, but also in the fact that "we
avoided any serious transatlantic rift over the appropriate strategy to follow."[29] The importance of such a claim, apart, that is, from highlighting the
West's impotence, was not so surprising, given the range and depth of the
differences. As Owen suggested, the danger was: "The Europeans thinking
of the Americans as cowboys and Americans thinking of the Europeans as
wimps."[30]

Others, in the United States, held that the plan failed because it was beyond the EC/Twelve's capacity to implement it,[31] and that it was an imposed solution that further underlined the need for a credible enforcement mechanism.[32] It was also regarded as rewarding aggression and setting a bad precedent for the rest of the Balkans, especially for Kosovo, and perhaps even further afield. The Clinton administration tended, therefore, to welcome the peace process rather than the plan itself, refusing to endorse a plan that did not emerge from the warring factions themselves or one that put pressure on the aggrieved party, the Muslims. Until a "fully consensual" plan had been accepted, the United States refused to commit any troops to assist in its implementation.[33]

For the EU, the Vance-Owen Plan, whatever its defects, was the best offer, and the alternative put forward by the Clinton administration of "lift and strike" (i.e., lift the embargo on arms to the Bosnian Muslims and make punitive strikes against the Serbs) was seen as failing to provide any answer to the basic problem of Bosnia. It was regarded, too, as inconsistent and fraught with even greater dangers and difficulties, not least the dangers to the UN forces—mostly West European—already on the ground. Given the competition between the EU, the United States, the UN, and NATO to take the lead, it was clear that: "In diplomacy towards Bosnia, the old military principle of unity of command was ostentatiously absent."[34]

Novelty and Tradition in EU Diplomacy

Support for the Vance-Owen and Owen-Stoltenberg peace process was far from being the only policy undertaken by the Union. Several other initiatives were undertaken, some novel, some reverting to provisions under the Treaties. Reports of the systematic rape of Bosnian Muslim women by Serb forces caused a growing outcry in Western Europe during the second half of 1992 and led the European Council at Edinburgh in December to set up a formal investigation. This was carried out by a former British diplomat, Dame Anne Warburton, who reported in January and February 1993. Together with the reports of "ethnic cleansing," concentration camps, and other atrocities, the report led the EC/Twelve to press hard at the United Nations for the establishment first of a Committee of Experts to examine such breaches of human rights and then, largely on a French initiative, to the setting up of an international war crimes tribunal. The UN Security Council adopted the proposal in February 1993. The tribunal, the first since those of Nuremberg and Tokyo, opened in The Hague on 17 November 1993, though with little likelihood that any of those who had committed the crimes would appear before it.[35] In October 1993, the European Council also announced its decision in principle to take responsibility for protecting and rebuilding the city of Mostar—the UN being given responsibility for the protection of Sarajevo itself (see below).

Despite such attempts at innovative policy, continued conflict led the EC/Twelve also to pursue more traditional and restrictive measures to bring pressure to bear to bring it to an end. An arms embargo had been agreed upon early, in July 1991, though it was only too obvious that all sides were plentifully armed. In November 1991, after the breakdown of the peace conference, some restrictive trade and aid measures were imposed, initially on Yugoslavia as a whole but then, in December, only on Serbia, with countermeasures introduced so that Slovenia, Croatia, Bosnia, and later Macedonia would not be adversely affected—it was, in effect, a de facto recognition of these republics, well before the formal recognition of 15 January 1992. More comprehensive economic sanctions were introduced against Serbia after UN Security Council Resolution 757 of 30 May 1992. There were those, of course, who were doubtful about the efficacy of sanctions, for, as Lawrence Freedman put it:

> The economy was in a ruinous state before the fighting and will be in an even more wretched condition now. Sanctions are unlikely to be persuasive when the fundamentals of national identity are believed to be at stake.[36]

And, despite their impact on the Serb economy, sanctions were not particularly effective. But neither the EC's nor the UN's credibility was much enhanced when the threat of a further tightening of sanctions was used so often against Serbia to try to force it to exercise greater influence over the Bosnian Serbs. This was especially so when it had become clear that Serbian influence over the Bosnian Serbs was limited and sometimes only tenuous.[37] And the EC's firmness of purpose was again weakened when, largely through German intervention, the Croat government was given only a warning not to continue to use Croat forces in Bosnia or to pursue "ethnic cleansing" rather than face the introduction of sanctions.

There was, though, some innovative action in terms of policing the sanctions. The EC, with CSCE cooperation, sought to make sanctions as effective as possible by setting up a number of sanctions assistance missions to help local customs officials in Romania, Bulgaria, and Hungary, and later in Macedonia, to implement them. The EC/Twelve also welcomed the decisions by the Western European Union (WEU) and NATO to monitor and enforce implementation. In July 1992, in the margins of the CSCE summit, foreign ministers of WEU decided to make air and naval deployments available in the Adriatic and in the following month offered to make the blockade on the Danube more effective. Operations were finally decided upon for the Adriatic in November 1992 and became operational in June 1993, while they got underway with patrol boats, and so forth, on the Danube in the spring of 1993, the WEU Forum meeting in May to discuss them.[38] The WEU-coordinated naval force was far from being alone in the Adriatic, there also being nationally controlled forces from Britain, France, and the United States and officially designated NATO forces. This duplication, almost competition, was a primary issue at the first meeting of the WEU and NATO Councils in June when operational command of their forces was agreed upon, with NATO's COMNAVSOUTH officially responsible; in the Adriatic itself, coordination was undertaken on an informal basis without an official commander.

The Franco-German Initiative of November 1993 proposed the gradual lifting of sanctions against Serbia if the latter influenced the Bosnian Serbs to agree to concede territory and undertake confidence-building measures in Krajina. As we have seen, the initiative received little support from the United States, although it later received some endorsement from the Atlantic summit of January 1994. The United States, for its part, preferred a policy of "lift, lift"—lifting economic sanctions against Serbia but also lifting the arms embargo against Bosnia. By the latter means, at least, it was argued, the Bosnian Muslims would be able to win back land and would then be better able to make a peace with the Serbs that the local parties themselves could enforce. This would eliminate the need for any UN forces on the scale envisaged under the Vance-Owen Plan and its successors (some fifty thousand troops).[39] The U.S. proposal was looked on with considerable alarm by many European governments, with the partial exception of Germany, though German foreign minister Kinkel declared that there would be "no lone action by Germany."[40] The majority continued to adopt the line put forward by the *Economist* that the purpose of the embargo was primarily to limit casualties, for although light weaponry was continuing to find its way through the blockade, it was nothing compared to the heavier, more sophisticated weaponry that would doubtless flood Bosnia if the embargo was lifted, since all sides had ready outside suppliers. Second, with such weaponry at the factions' disposal, it would be even more difficult to prevent the war from spreading—to Croatia again, Kosovo, and Macedonia and perhaps beyond the former Yugoslavia. Third, in such circumstances it would be extremely difficult for the EU, the United States, and Russia not to get dragged in.[41] It would also, of course, have necessitated the withdrawal of the UN Protective Force (UNPROFOR) and the humanitarian aid agencies, multiplying the number of war casualties. However, as the United States and Russia (which reportedly supported the "lift, lift" strategy)[42] became more involved, so the absence of any settlement meant that the possibility of lifting the arms embargo became greater.

For the most part, however, the member states were able to maintain an overall unity among themselves in pursuing these diplomatic and economic initiatives, costly though the embargoes were to some of them. Nor did moves to provide humanitarian assistance create dissension, though they drew the member states inexorably into a more complicated interaction with the different sides in Bosnia. In the absence of any sustainable ceasefire, the need for humanitarian aid became ever more urgent, not least in response to the reports of widespread atrocities committed against those caught in the conflict. Moreover, assistance was also required for those able to flee from the conflict, becoming refugees either elsewhere in Bosnia or in Croatia and other neighboring states, few of whom had either the facilities or the resources easily to accommodate them.[43] The Birmingham European Council in October 1992 agreed on a four-point plan to assist the UN High Commissioner for Refugees (UNHCR), which took the lead role in Bosnia, including an EC task force to help distribute aid, and this began to operate in December 1992. Interestingly, despite the concern over Macedonia as a potential source of conflict, it was only at the Edinburgh European Council in December 1992 that Community aid was unblocked and assistance agreed upon to help stabilize the situation there. But such was the consensus on the need to continue the aid, especially in view of the difficulties and hazards of distributing it, that the European Council of October 1993 agreed to make support for convoying aid one of the first joint actions of the European Union. A subsequent decision in December 1993 set the budget at 48 million ECU (European currency units), half of which was to be borne on the EC's budget, the other half by the member states.[44]

Civil and Military Intervention

The inability to make ceasefires stick has been a perennial problem. However, the initial reaction of the Twelve was highly innovative, if ultimately limited—that is, to offer a monitoring mission (ECMM). The monitors' task was to monitor those ceasefires that were agreed upon between the various factions, initially in Slovenia, then somewhat more problematically in Croatia, and finally in Bosnia. Their responsibilities were later further extended to cover the former Yugoslavia's borders with Bulgaria, Hungary, and Albania in the effort to prevent any escalation of the conflict. At the local level, they were not wholly unsuccessful in negotiating ceasefires, but they were clearly a minimal response that reflected the absence of any consensus among the EC/Twelve to pursue any larger-scale, military intervention. Once the United Nations became more involved, the nature of the ECMM's task changed and during 1992–1993 they began to coordinate some of their activities with those of UNPROFOR, deployed in the spring of 1992, and with the UN's and the EC's humanitarian activities. The ECMM cooperated with UNPROFOR, for example, in monitoring the withdrawal of Serb forces from the Dubrovnik area and with the International Committee of the Red Cross and the UN High Commissioner for Refugees in evacuating the sick and wounded from, for example, Vukovar, and in monitoring exchanges of prisoners.

The concept of civil intervention was taken further with the decision of October 1993 to take over the administration of Mostar. The decision proved valuable in its own right, in bringing about an increasing semblance of stability as well as reconstruction, but it was also significant in terms of the EU's foreign and security policy. Although the decision was made in October 1993, it was not until after the U.S.-brokered agreement between the Bosnian Muslims and Croats that a fact-finding mission was dispatched in March 1994. The aim was to restore a basic infrastructure, to include not only economic reconstruction and rebuilding but also the restoration of public order. For the last, the use of WEU experts was envisaged in order to organize and train a joint Bosnian/Croat police force. It was the first time the WEU had been involved in a fully integrated EU joint action. Hans Koschnick was confirmed as the EU's administrator in April 1994 with a two-year mandate, together with an EU ombudsman to deal with any complaints.

The Mostar Policy was novel in two further respects: its legal base and its funding. The fact that the EU did not have a legal personality but wished to enter into a legally binding agreement caused some serious head-scratching in Brussels. The result was a long-winded formula that involved the member states of the European Union acting within the framework of the Union and with the Commission. The Memorandum of Understanding (MOU) with the two local communities (who also had no international legal standing) was signed by the president of the Council and the other members of the Troika on their own behalf in Geneva in July 1994. It raises interesting questions about the role of the European and national parliaments in any ratification process. Financially, too, Mostar suggested a new departure for the EU. Reference has already been made to the joint action that committed the Union to extend humanitarian aid, paid for in part by the member states and in part out of the Community's budget. Once the MOU was signed, the Council diverted the unspent portion of this to Mostar, raising further the prospect of the involvement of the European Parliament as the co-authority over the EC's budget.

If the Mostar decision had been made as a joint action, the issue of a more traditional peacekeeping force remained deeply divisive. The French had raised the possibility in July 1991, recognizing that it would be an important innovation but that "it is not forbidden to imagine that the Community could go much further."[45] Several other governments appeared sympathetic, or prepared at least to consider the possibility, even if only for tactical reasons. Dutch foreign minister Van den Broek, for example, in one of the Troika missions to Yugoslavia, used it as a threat—that if there was no end to the violence "then probably further appeals will be launched in favor of sending something like a peace force to the country, probably through WEU." And, indeed, when that Troika initiative failed, the French urged an emergency meeting of WEU to consider such a force, a move less surprising perhaps in view of the place WEU had in their proposals for a common foreign and security policy. But the French also pursued the possibility of a peacekeeping force through the UN Security Council. The latter, on a joint French, British, and Belgian proposal of September 1991, gave its full support to the various collective peace efforts being made and also its support for measures to assist and support the monitors of the ceasefire. Germany, for its part, raised the issue in a CSCE framework, proposing that the CSCE should authorize a defense force.[46]

The discussions that took place in WEU did so amid some acrimony. The Dutch (if only to prevent the Germans from recognizing Slovenia and Croatia), French, Italians, and Belgians were regarded as being in favor of a peacekeeping force—if a general and sustainable ceasefire could be negotiated. So, too, was Germany. However, the restrictive interpretation placed on the Basic Law by the German government during the Gulf War seemed to disbar the use of any German troops in an intervention force in Yugoslavia, since, strictly speaking, it was out of the NATO area in which German forces could operate. But even if German forces were made available—and the chancellor, the foreign minister, and the defense minister had given strong support to the idea, even if any decision would have necessitated the approval of the German Constitutional Court—others raised the question of whether German participation was actually desirable. It was, for example, suggested of Germany's call for a tougher stand against Serbia and for EC recognition of Slovenia and Croatia that it "rekindles memories of when Croatians and Germans fought side-by-side in the Nazi cause. This debars Germany from participating in any armed intervention, and thus irritates those European partners who would be obliged to implement the policy."[47] Nevertheless, Germany continued to be more favorable than most of the Twelve to a tougher intervention, the defense minister in 1993, for example, declaring that "the concentration camps in Germany were stopped by soldiers and not by demonstrations in another country."[48]

The British were particularly reluctant to envisage the idea of a European or any intervention force, in 1991 and subsequently.[49] The example of Northern Ireland was often used to illustrate how easy it was to introduce troops and how difficult it was to get them out. The British—with memories, perhaps, of wartime links with Tito—also stressed the likely numbers of troops that would be required, given the size and sophistication of much of the Yugoslav armory. As Foreign Secretary Hurd put it in September 1991: "I am very anxious that we should not exaggerate what we can do, or pretend that we in Western Europe can substitute for the lack of will for peace in Yugoslavia."[50]

When, on the initiative of the French, WEU was given the task of examining possible options, it was on the basis, first, of how to support the activities of monitors so as to make their contribution more effective, but second, that military intervention was not being contemplated. WEU examined four options: logistic support for EC/Twelve monitors, which might require some 2,000–3,000 personnel; escort and protection of monitors by armed military forces, some 5,000–6,000 personnel; a lightly armed peacekeeping force of military personnel and additional monitors to police the ceasefire, some 7,500–10,000 in all; and, finally, a full-scale peacekeeping exercise requiring between 20,000–30,000 personnel. These were discussed at a WEU meeting on 30 September 1991 that followed almost indistinguishably from that of the EC foreign ministers and to which non-WEU, EC, and NATO members had been invited. The only result, though, was that the member states agreed to be ready to give practical support to a peacekeeping force if one was created. However, the details of the contingency plans were sent on to the United Nations.[51]

Divisions over the use of force continued, even though it became increasingly a matter discussed in NATO and in the UN Security Council, rather than any specifically European forums. It had become clear that, in Croatia, the small, unarmed ECMM was unable to ensure compliance. It was, however, only after the fifteenth ceasefire between the Yugoslav National Army (JNA) and the Croatian authorities that the UN accepted involvement.[52] In Bosnia, the situation was even more difficult. For most, it was clearly the Serbs who were largely responsible for the war and for many of the atrocities carried out (though no side has been adjudged guiltless). Public statements, such as that of Hans-Dietrich Genscher in early August 1991, that "the Serbian government has clearly taken over responsibility for developments in Yugoslavia . . . [and] has destroyed the basis for negotiations and for peacefully settling the future of Yugoslavia's people,"[53] made the position of the ECMM in acting as brokers as well as monitors difficult, if not impossible. As Lord Owen remarked, the UN's concept of neutral peacekeeping had developed "painfully" over some considerable time and yet, "we put people into white uniforms and called them EC monitors, and some even thought Europe could replace the UN in the peace-keeping role."[54]

But in Bosnia, even traditional peacekeeping was also impossible, at least until there was a ceasefire to keep. Indeed, public and moral pressures, as well as considerations of realpolitik, obliged the UN to become involved *because* there was no ceasefire and led to the UN Secretary-General's recommendation for a second UNPROFOR of six thousand troops, not to maintain a ceasefire, as UNPROFOR I was attempting to do in Croatia, but to protect the delivery of aid and humanitarian supplies. At the time, it represented a qualitatively new kind of UN mission. Belgian, British, Dutch, French, Portuguese, and Spanish troops formed part of UNPROFOR II, the French followed by the British in providing the largest contingents.[55]

It has been suggested that the Bosnian operation reflects a lack of political will on the part of the major powers to tackle the more deep-seated causes of the conflict.[56] But the lack of political will also meant that it became increasingly difficult to formulate realizable objectives. In some respects, for example, a difficult situation was made even worse by moves at the UN (often led by France with support from most of the EC/Twelve, albeit sometimes with reluctance) to create a "no fly zone" over Bosnia (UN Security Council Resolution [UNSCR] 781 of October 1992) to prevent aircraft or helicopters ferrying munitions and supplies to the different armies, and the declaration of Sarajevo and five other towns as "safe areas" (UNSCR 824 of May 1993). By January 1994, it had been calculated that some 1,397 violations of the airspace had occurred.[57] Significantly, German AWACs participated in the surveillance operation, the German Constitutional Court holding such participation compatible with the constitution in April 1993. Perhaps, though of even greater significance, authorization to enforce the "no fly zone" using all necessary measures—that is, air power—was provided only in March 1993 (UNSCR 816) and the first actual engagement was not until a year later. It was only after continued attacks on Sarajevo that, again on a French initiative, UNSCR 836 was agreed upon in May 1993, which authorized UNPROFOR to take the necessary measures of self-defense against bombardment, including the use of air power.[58]

The reluctance to use such measures as air strikes was shown both in the antipathy toward the Clinton administration's advocacy of a "lift and strike" strategy and in the delays in gaining UN authorization. That, of course, did not prevent the use by member states, the European Council, NATO, and so on, of the threat of retaliation, even though they lost credibility each time they did so without any subsequent action. The major problem, as the United States somewhat belatedly came to realize, was that air strikes might cause the assailants to pause, but by themselves they were unlikely to resolve the problem. No one, however, was prepared to commit ground forces required on the scale that WEU had suggested was likely. Even after the Sarajevo ceasefire in February, the appeal from UNPROFOR for reinforcements to monitor the situation saw most EU member states (as well as others) reluctantly and belatedly assigning contingents in the hundreds, rather than in the thousands asked for. Indeed, at times—as in January 1994—the British seemed keener on using the threat of the withdrawal of their forces in the absence of any signs of peace than they were on reinforcing their contingent, though they later did so, with nine hundred additional troops.

In the meantime, the troops that had been committed by the member states for the humanitarian effort had, in effect, become hostages—and in areas such as Gorazde, it was not simply in effect. The British, especially, as well as the UNHCR and the UN's special envoy, Yasushi Akashi, on whom Boutros-Ghali ultimately delegated authority for air strikes, laid particular stress on the need to protect the humanitarian effort. Their dilemma over the U.S. proposal in February 1993 to air-drop aid to Muslim areas cut off by Serb and Croat control of the land routes was acute, insofar as there was considerable concern that such sorties would be regarded as hostile and lead to further Serb or Croat aggression. The French, on the other hand, had become persuaded of the need for stronger and swifter responses.[59] Largely at French insistence—they threatened to withdraw their forces in Bosnia if it were not agreed—the NATO summit in January 1994 moved closer to supporting the use of air strikes, especially against the further strangulation of Sarajevo, the refusal of the Serbs to reopen Tuzla airport, and their refusal to allow the rotation of UN forces in Srebrenica. Greece disassociated itself from the decision. But it was perhaps only the combination of the Sarajevo massacre, the media, and the role of the British UN commander in Sarajevo, General Rose, that finally brought the British around to supporting the tougher line. Foreign ministers meeting in the EU Council on 7 February were thus able to call for the use of all means necessary by NATO and the UN to lift the siege in Sarajevo, which, for the first time, included an ultimatum.

If the EU had perforce to rely on NATO for any military measures, so it increasingly appeared dependent on the United States, Russia, and individual member states to pursue diplomatic means of bringing an end to the conflict. The growing involvement of the United States has already been noted and that of Russia was epitomized by President Yeltsin's call for a summit of the parties involved. Neither they, nor the British and French, looked on the presidency of the Council, especially when held by one of the smaller member states (in this case, Greece—itself a complicating factor, given its position in the Balkans) as an interlocutor with the necessary weight. The prospective presidency of Germany in the second half of 1994 seemed to provide the opportunity to include Germany within the proposed Contact Group (especially when it indicated its displeasure at being excluded,[60] though Italy's efforts in a similar vein were to no avail). In any event, a formula that urged Lord Owen to enhance the EU's role in the peace process through the involvement of representatives of the international conference was agreed upon at the Foreign Affairs Council of 18 August 1994. The involvement of officials from only three member states of the Union within a permanent group was hardly in line with the spirit of the commitments entered into at Maastricht, but there was a recognition that the inclusion of the United States and Russia was vital; the "hour of Europe" had long since passed.

The Lessons of Yugoslavia

"The international community is still quite helpless as far as the causes of conflicts are concerned. . . . There is preventative diplomacy but in practice we often see too little too late."[61] Klaus Kinkel could easily have focused his remarks on the European Union, rather than on the international community. He could also perhaps have added that there is little consensus on what should follow when preventative diplomacy fails, the gap between diplomatic methods and military intervention being one that few Western governments are willing quickly to cross. That is not to suggest that the role of the EC/Twelve and the EU has been wholly negative in the Yugoslav conflict but, as Nicole Gnesotto put it: "Having been unduly virtuous at the out-set of the conflict—refusing to back the national redrawing of frontiers which were previously internal—the democracies now run the risk of an ultimate moral indignity, by accepting the *fait accompli* achieved by violent means."[62]

It is frequently held that once the threat posed by the Soviet Union dis-appeared, there was movement toward "re-nationalizing" defense and secu-rity policies. Individual states could more closely examine their own partic-ular interests and concerns in any conflict that did not appear to entail a direct threat. To some extent, that would appear to run counter to the move on the part of the twelve member states of the EC that undertook to commit themselves to a common foreign and security policy, which, ultimately, might lead to a common defense.[63] Moreover, neither NATO nor WEU dis-appeared, and, indeed, the latter was designated the European Union's future defense arm. There were, in other words, institutions and forums in which security and defense concerns continued to be discussed, command struc-tures (even if under review) remained to be employed, common exercises remained to be undertaken, and so on. Against the profound changes brought about by the collapse of communism, there were both familiar landmarks and, in the case of the Twelve, new undertakings to be implemented, even if somewhat later than anticipated because of the problems of ratifying Maastricht. They did not, however, create a system readily able to meet non-traditional security challenges. Perhaps a system built on nation-states, even one where voluntary integration appeared increasingly to be the norm, could not be expected to meet the challenge of ethnicity and nationalism and the disintegration of states, though—at least so far—the conflict has been con-tained and many thousands of individuals who may have suffered appalling atrocities, remain—again, at least so far—alive.

What the conflict in Yugoslavia revealed, therefore, was both the oppor-tunities for innovative policies in a changed European system and the limits to common action. In challenging the member states to commit themselves to common action, it brought to the fore their own particular concerns and revealed clearly that there was no overall coherent, relevant political analy-sis at the European level that encapsulated the "European" interest. Even if few had predicted the collapse of the Soviet system or even the Soviet Union itself, pundits have been predicting the collapse of Yugoslavia since the death of Tito in 1980. Few among the EC/Twelve may have sought or wished for its demise, but the policies pursued—of moral suasion and threats of economic sanction—were scarcely those that students of foreign policy could claim had been successful in the past. The threat of sanctions might be a necessary prelude to the introduction of other policies—and, in terms of public relations, is a good deal better than mere public hand-wring-ing—but, by themselves, sanctions were known to have minimal impact. As Jacques Delors has suggested: "The lesson to be learned here is that a strategic planning and analysis capability is needed at the European level."[64] Significantly, such a capability was specifically rejected by the member states for the Common Foreign and Security Policy. The wish to be driven separately by the "CNN factor" among others (and Douglas Hurd was not alone in ruing the intrusion of the media into foreign policy making), outweighed the will to be driven together. An EU planning cell hardly guarantees a rational response, given the nature of Western pluralist democracy and, indeed, the character of the EU, and the unexpected—such as the speed of German unification—can always blow even the best laid plans off course, but such a capability might provide for a more informed reaction to events.

What the Yugoslav conflict revealed, too, was that the institutional structure of the Union remained uncertain. The burden on the presidency was considerable, expertise within any one foreign ministry was variable, and the willingness or the capacity to act was changeable. Nor was the use of the Troika always an asset, even if, at the outset, it lent a certain weight to negotiations. There was, perhaps, relief on the part of some of the smaller member states that much of the negotiation could be left to the Vance-Owen or the Owen-Stoltenberg teams, or relief on the part of others that negotiations moved slowly toward the establishment of a contact group, even if it included only some of the member states and however contrary it might be to the rhetoric of Maastricht. Not all member states, of course, felt such relief; Germany, for example, was hostile until it was included, and Italy tended to remain so when not preoccupied with its internal political problems.

Nicole Gnesotto points to a certain paradox in the situation. With the agreement on CFSP, there was a stronger commitment on the part of the member states to act together. If, however, that action entailed going beyond the political and economic instruments of policy to involve the possibility of intervention, then international agreement was seen as necessary, not least to ensure public legitimation, and not just from the CSCE but from the United Nations. By seeking authorization from the UN Security Council, the EU both reduced the autonomy of the Twelve, insofar as policy then became dependent on the agreement of the United States, Russia, and China, and emphasized the inequality of the member states by highlighting the role of Britain and France as permanent members of the Security Council.[65] Such a shift toward British and French "leadership" may have been inevitable once UNPROFOR was introduced into the conflict and the Vance-Owen Plan began to be sidelined. The growing German presence in UN peacekeeping forces elsewhere may counteract the tendency, as well as strengthen Germany's claims to a permanent seat in the Security Council.

That does not solve the more general problem of inequality or ineffectiveness in decisionmaking. The question remains of whether the presidency, with or without its Troika colleagues, should continue to be the primary interlocutor for the EU or whether, as to a limited extent took place before the December 1993 Geneva peace talks, particular governments should be deputed to lead in capitals where they had particular links or close relations. Since these change over time or according to issues, it would necessarily have to be on an ad hoc basis. That, however, raises the question about the role of the Commission, which since Maastricht has legal guarantee via TEU to fully participate in all the EU's activities. Unless other changes were introduced, it would also re-emphasize the presidency's ability to coordinate member states' activities adequately and—of increasing importance, given its increased powers under Maastricht and the budgetary implications of much of CFSP—its ability to liaise adequately with the European Parliament.

Yet EU action beyond political and economic diplomacy also raised the issue of the preferred vehicle for any intervention. NATO, in many ways, gradually assumed the dominant role—as was perhaps expected, given its structure and resources—but not without some interesting twists. German involvement in the various commands had to be removed, given its constitutional predicament, while French officers had to be more closely integrated. At the political level, too, there were odd shifts and changes. There was initially a strong reaction to the Clinton administration's strategy, which may have led not just France but also Britain—not normally regarded as anything but a NATO and United States supporter—to look to forums other than NATO. And while the UN may have looked to NATO as the appropriate regional agency to implement policy under Chapter VIII, there were signs, too, that WEU sought such a role, in going ahead with its surveillance of the UN's embargo both on the Danube and in the Adriatic. And after supporting the establishment of UNPROFOR, the WEU set up an ad hoc group of representatives from foreign and defense ministries to examine ways in which it could contribute to the operation. These and other activities, such as its role in the Mostar administration, led the French foreign minister to declare that it had intervened as an organization "over and above the actions of its members."[66] Whereas the contact between WEU and the EU Council and its secretariat was regarded as random, there was a more consistent effort to establish closer relations with NATO and its secretariat. WEU's growing experience in coordinating its members activities, particularly maritime activities, may not make it a serious competitor to NATO, but it may well have become an additional factor in future discussions of preventative diplomacy.

In viewing their inability to bring an end to the Yugoslav conflict, it is easy to be scornful of the EC/Twelve's initial overestimation of the potential impact they could make. It is easy, too, with hindsight, to be critical of the mistakes made by the member states in relying on a buildup of economic sanctions or indulging in threats of intervention they had no intention or ability to fulfill. And yet, tragic though the conflict has been, it is difficult to be certain that a speedier and more forceful intervention at the beginning would have been sanctioned either by the international community or by Europe's own public, or would even necessarily have been successful. If individual Western democracies are constrained in what they can do, it is unlikely that the European Union will be less so.

Notes

1. The author is grateful to Charles Reed, Trinity Hall, Cambridge, for collecting research material for this chapter.
2. The European Union (EU) and EC/Twelve are used interchangeably throughout the chapter.
3. Geoffrey Edwards, "European Responses to the Yugoslav Crisis: An Interim Assessment," in Reinhardt Rummel, ed., *Toward Political Union* (Baden-Baden: Nomos Verlagsgesellschaft, 1992), pp. 165–190.
4. The *Independent,* 1 July 1991.
5. Edward Mortimer, "European Security After the Cold War," *Adelphi Paper* 271 (London: IISS, Brassey's, 1992).
6. Quoted by Stanley R. Sloane, "NATO's Future in a New Europe: An American Perspective," *International Affairs* 3 (1990), p. 502.
7. *Agence Europe,* 11–12 March 1991.
8. Points made, inter alia, by Jacques Delors. See Jacques Delors, "European Unification and European Security," in *Conference Papers: European Security After the Cold War* (London: IISS Adelphi Paper, Brassey's, 1992).
9. *Agence Europe,* 10 April 1991.
10. Christopher Cviic, *Remaking the Balkans* (London: Royal Institute for International Affairs, Pinter, 1991), p. 95.
11. Ibid., p. 44.
12. *Agence Europe,* 29 June 1991.
13. *Agence Europe,* 15 July 1991.
14. *Agence Europe,* 11 July 1991.
15. Lord Carrington, "Turmoil in the Balkans: Developments and Prospects," *RUSI Journal* 5 (October 1992), p. 1.
16. Ibid.
17. *Financial Times,* 4 July 1991.
18. The depths to which the argument sometimes descended can be glimpsed in Edwards, "European Responses to the Yugoslav Crisis."
19. J. Gow and J. Smith, *Peace-making, Peace-keeping: European Security and the Yugoslav Wars* (London: Brassey's).
20. Jonathan Eyal, "Europe and Yugoslavia: Lessons from a Failure," *Whitehall Paper* 19 (London: RUSI, 1993), p. 38.
21. Jonathan Eyal has suggested that by the beginning of 12 November, cease-fire agreements had been concluded and four peace plans accepted and all had broken down. Ibid., p. 43.
22. Gow and Smith, *Peace-making, Peace-keeping,* p. 36.
23. Willy Claes, "Europe as an Unfinished Symphony," *The World Today* 3 (March 1994), p. 45.
24. Alain Juppé, RFI interview, 9 November 1993, Sp.St/LON/152/93.
25. The *Independent,* 8 February 1994, quoted there from *Süddeutsche Zeitung,* 7 February 1994.
26. Referred to Juppé, 25 January 1994, SS/94/15.

27. Alain Juppé in RTL, 21 February 1994. Issued by the French Embassy, SS/94/34.

28. See the *Financial Times,* 26 November 1993.

29. Willy Claes, "Europe as an Unfinished Symphony," p. 45.

30. Lord Owen, after Secretary of State Warren Christopher's visit to Europe, *The Independent,* 10 May 1993.

31. Paul R. S. Gebhard, "The United States and European Security," *Adelphi Papers* 286 (London: IISS, Brassey's, 1994), p. 27.

32. The points made, inter alia, by Zalmay Zhalilzad, another (former) Pentagon official, in the *Wall Street Journal,* 3 December 1993.

33. Warren Christopher, USIS Eur505 11/29/93.

34. *Strategic Survey 1993–94* (London: IISS, Brassey's, 1994), pp. 6–7.

35. The United States Representative to the UN, Madeleine Albright, countered this by asserting: "The tribunal will issue indictments whether or not suspects can be taken into custody. They will become international pariahs. While these individuals may be able to hide within the borders of Serbia or parts of Bosnia or Croatia, they will be imprisoned for the rest of their lives within their own country." Quoted by Hazel Fox, "An International Tribunal for War Crimes: Will the UN Succeed Where Nuremberg Failed?" *The World Today* 10 (October 1993): 197.

36. The *Independent,* 12 September 1991.

37. Alain Juppé, for example, had declared in May 1993 that the tightening of sanctions was because: "The Belgrade authorities must be put on the spot and forced to do what they said they were going to do: blockade the border between Serbia and Bosnia," *Le Figaro,* 18 May 1993, Sp.St LON/70/93.

38. See Luisa Vierucci, "WEU: A Regional Partner of the United Nations?" *Chaillot Papers* 12 (Paris: WEU Institute for Security Studies, 1993).

39. Zhalilzad, the *Wall Street Journal.*

40. The *Independent,* 3 February 1994.

41. The *Economist,* 4 December 1993.

42. Zhalilzhad, the *Wall Street Journal.*

43. UNHCR estimated at the end of 1993 that some 4.3 million people were in need of relief in the region, 3.5 million of whom were classified as refugees and displaced persons.

44. Council Decision (93/729/CFSP), 20 December 1993, OJ L 339/3.

45. *Agence Europe,* 29–30 July 1991.

46. The *Independent,* 12 September 1991.

47. Lawrence Freedman, the *Independent,* 12 September 1991.

48. The *Independent,* 3 February 1993.

49. For a particularly strong critique of the British position, see Jane Sharp, "Intervention in Bosnia—the Case For," *The World Today* 2 (February 1993), pp. 29–32.

50. The *Times* (London), 21 September 1991.

51. Vierucci, "WEU: A Regional Partner of the United Nations?"

52. Mats Berdal, "Peacekeeping in Europe," *Conference Papers: European Security after the Cold War* (London: IISS, Brassey's, 1994), p. 62.

53. *International Herald Tribune,* 6 August 1991.

54. "The Future of the Balkans: An Interview with David Owen," *Foreign Affairs* 2 (Spring 1993), pp. 1–9.

55. See *Liberation,* 7 January 1994. Out of a total UNPROFOR of 25,000 in Croatia and Bosnia, France provided 6,000 troops, the U.K. 2,400, Denmark 1,200, the Netherlands 1,030, Spain 1,000, and Belgium 800.

56. Berdal, "Peacekeeping in Europe," p. 65.

57. *Financial Times,* 1 March 1994.

58. Alain Juppé, in a radio broadcast on RTL on 3 August 1993, was at pains to point out the French rather than the U.S. role in gaining UN agreement to the use of air strikes, Sp.St/LON/96/93.

59. UNPROFOR II was initially commanded by the French general, Philippe Morillon. General Jean Cot, the overall UNPROFOR commander in Bosnia, whose criticisms of the command structure led to his recall by the UN Secretary-General, described his troops as being fed up with being humiliated "like goats tied to a stake." The *Times* (London), 6 January 1994.

60. Germany had resented being omitted from the discussions in New York on the decision to enforce the "no fly zone" in May 1993, and Chancellor Kohl had to be mollified by the French at their next summit meeting—at least, according to Alain Juppé in his press briefing on 2 March 1994, SS.94/40, 7 March 1994.

61. Klaus Kinkel, *International Herald Tribune,* 2 December 1993.

62. Nicole Gnesotto, "Lessons of Yugoslavia," *Chaillot Papers* 14 (Paris: WEU Institute for Security Studies, 1994), p. 11.

63. See also Chapters 2 and 3 by Nuttall and de Schoutheete, respectively, in this volume.

64. Delors, "European Unification and European Security," p. 5.

65. Gnesotto, "Lessons of Yugoslavia," pp. 18–19.

66. Vierucci, "WEU: A Regional Partner of the United Nations?" p. 29.

11

Relations with Central and Eastern European Countries: The Anchor Role of the European Union

Barbara Lippert

After the political "turning of the tide" in 1989, relations between the European Union (EU) and the Central and Eastern European countries (CEEC)[1] show a strong and dynamic CFSP dimension. Crucial requirements of the Common Foreign and Security Policy (CFSP)—a solid *acquis politique,* consistency, the shaping of events in international politics, and the taking of joint actions, as well as capacities for conflict prevention and crisis management—are challenged in the wake of the re-orientation of the CEEC toward Western political and security structures, including the EU. The demise of the antagonistic East-West conflict provided a new context for EPC (European Political Cooperation)/CFSP. This new context for cooperation, partnership, and also enlargement of the EU is giving the complex issue of relations with the CEEC a high priority. However, the anticlimax after the negotiations on the Maastricht Treaty on European Union showed the difficulties for the EU in coming to terms with post-Communist Europe and its new interdependencies, even though the EU realized that "the integration of these new democracies into the European family presents a historic opportunity."[2] The shaping of foreign and security relations with the CEEC is essential for the wider-Europe strategy[3] and part of preparing those European states that want to join the EU for accession or, at least, association. Some CFSP-aspects of this strategy are treated in this contribution.

Interest Patterns: Anchoring the CEEC in the "West"

The CFSP dimension in relations with the CEEC is often metaphorically indicated, when calling the EU the anchor or center of gravity in the new Europe.[4] "The other countries of Europe are looking to us for guarantees of stability, peace and prosperity, and for the opportunity to play their part with us in the integration of Europe."[5] Notions such as "anchorage point" raise questions as to whether and how the EU is capable of living up to the huge expectations of the CEEC, both with regard to the EU's internal process of integration and its strategy for the wider Europe.

The pivotal interest of the EU in relations with the CEEC is to achieve security in its neighborhood and to limit potential risks of economic, social, and political destabilization that could spill over to the integrated Western Europe. The Union wants to cooperate with these countries for the sake of a stable and peaceful development in Europe on the lines of democracy, social market economy, and partnership. This paramount interest is mirrored by the EU's recourse to nearly all instruments at its disposal for the shaping of external relations and CFSP—trade liberalization, economic and financial cooperation, political dialogue, and joint action. The main vehicle for assisting the process of economic and political rapprochement is a tight and expanding web of bilateral treaties. From 1988 onward, the EC has signed agreements of cooperation and free trade, or the more substantial association agreements, with eleven out of the current fifteen CEEC,[6] which introduce a membership perspective for the associated country. However, to only fill a gap in the EC/Twelve's "global links"[7] with third countries was too little a contribution in the light of the dramatically changed external context in which the Community is operating after 1989. "The Community . . . cannot now refuse the historic challenge to assume its continental responsibilities and contribute to the development of a political and economic order for the whole of Europe."[8] Challenge and ambition of the Community coincided in developing from an environment taker to an environment maker. This was also due to the initial disengagement of the United States from continental European affairs and Russia-centeredness. The coordination function of the Commission for the group of twenty-four industrialized countries for technical and economic assistance signaled this new division of labor and responsibilities. Also, the program for economic reconstruction set out in 1989 and labeled with the acronym PHARE, which means "lighthouse," alluded to the capacity of the EU to be a pole for orientation and guidance. Moreover, the EC/EU reaffirmed the fair principle of also being open for the new democracies.

Most of the CEEC accept the twofold order-building function of the EU. It concerns (1) the transformation toward market economies converging with the rules and principles of the internal market and related policies in the CEEC, and (2) the shaping of a comprehensive and working security structure in Europe. Obviously, the CEEC appealed to the political founding motives of the European Community, going beyond an economic community when emphasizing the political shape, aspirations, and responsibility of the EU. The CEEC's main ambition was that the EC would receive them as late, but legitimate, members of the integrated part of Europe. The CEEC's fundamental motive in joining the EU seems to be the safeguarding of their irreversible escape from the Soviet/Russian sphere of influence. More positively, their concern is to anchor their new democracies in the West and find access to its organizations—EU/WEU (Western European Union), NATO, and, at least, the Council of Europe, which are all perceived as parts of a functioning Western security structure. So the EU's attraction for the CEEC is not only its success in generating prosperity and safeguarding international economic competitiveness through integration. The CEEC argue that the irrevocable acceptance of the CEEC's strategic goal to join the EU by the Union and its member states would be the strongest signal against falling into a gray zone in terms of security or of becoming a new *cordon sanitaire* between the West and Russia.

Basically, both sides share the interest of anchoring the CEEC in the West. For the CEEC, this clearly means membership. The EU and its member states increasingly imagine a variety of solutions as intermediate steps toward membership or maybe even alternative routes to a more voluntary end.

Security Through Membership: A Step Too Far

The EU did not develop a grand design for its new relations with the CEEC and never held a special summit to consider in depth the changes in its neighborhood for the definition of a strong *acquis politique*. It adopted a cumulative and comprehensive approach, which turned out to be more dynamic than expected or even intended. As early as December 1989, the EC/Twelve came up with the proposal for a special type of association coined "Europe Agreements." They are the principal framework[9] for relations and provide for an asymmetrically scheduled opening of markets leading to a free trade area for industrial products, economic and financial cooperation, and political dialogue, all within a multilevel institutional setup for association. Thus, relations with the ten current associated CEEC are built on a complex set of unilateral and reciprocal measures and offers, mostly within a clear legal and institutional framework, conditioned by general political and economic principles, and with a view toward the associate's eventual accession to the Community.[10] At the European Council in Copenhagen in June 1993, the EU made it clear that its principal response to the end of the East-West conflict would be eastward enlargement up to the borders of the former USSR, hence the region of PHARE operations. All three security structures—NATO, WEU, and the EU—proposed, however vaguely, security through eventual membership.

The Europe Agreements are the backbone for all activities of the EU vis-à-vis the CEEC. They work within a more or less "organic scenario" of gradually improving the socioeconomic situation and consolidating democracy in the transforming countries. The underlying idea is "conflict prevention" through cooperation in order building in Europe and assistance in transformation. The assumption that the key toward peace and prosperity in the CEEC is democracy and market economy reflects the ordering principles spelled out in the Europe Agreements and, repeatedly, through the European Council—namely, democracy, rule of law, respect for human rights, and market-type economies. These are eligibility criteria for participation in the PHARE program, as well as the bilateral agreements. For example, in the case of Romania, the EC halted the entering into force of the trade and cooperation agreement for nearly one year, due to the persistent violations of human rights in the country. Political conditionality is even more precisely introduced in the second round of Europe Agreements with Bulgaria, the Czech Republic, Slovakia, and Romania.[11] Whereas the EU in the mid-1990s continues to believe in the validity of the organic scenario, at least some CEEC, such as Poland, tend to assume a more conflict-driven scenario, which considers potential socioeconomic turmoil and danger of a backslide and the "imperial impulse"[12] of Russia more deeply and therefore lets the CEEC argue within a different time frame for their accession. The organic scenario does not schedule measures in a definite way but involves monitoring association and beyond with the chance to agree on medium steps or a route map to accession. The proposals for a white paper to adapt to the EU's internal market and for the approximation of laws are a case in point.[13] The two scenarios also develop different yardsticks for evaluating the Europe Agreements. In the light of the turmoil scenario, the asymmetries of offers by the EU and demand of the CEEC for accountability and stability are striking. The "organic scenario," on the contrary, argues that any weakening, due to political and financial overstretching caused by rapid enlargement, would be counterproductive and would endanger, rather than strengthen, the anchor role of the EU.

An obvious shortcoming of the Europe Agreements is the lack of a security dimension, due, of course, to the limited stage of development of the security component in CFSP. In following its traditional approach of a civilian power, the EU offered its main instruments—market access, financial support, and political dialogue—all crucial elements of a comprehensive security approach. Given the conflicts in the Balkans and the inaccountabilities of a shaky Russian foreign and security policy, with ever stronger tendencies to renounce the freedom of the CEEC to join military alliances—namely, NATO and WEU—the CEEC asked for "hard core security" guarantees. In particular, the Twelve's successive deepening of political dialogue[14] was a reaction to reduce the perceived security vacuum in-between the NATO area and the CIS. The intensity of attraction of the security organizations varied from the CEEC's point of view over the last years. However, a general preference for NATO membership, even after the disappointing holding strategy of NATO's "Partnership for Peace" offer, took shape. With undue optimism, the Commission had argued that intergovernmental settings, such as the WEU forum for consultation and the North Atlantic Cooperation Council (NAAC), "do not fully respond to their desire to belong to a coherent security structure. For this they count increasingly on the Community and the future European Union."[15] Yet clarification of the elements of a European defense policy and their operability have not gained political momentum since the coming into force of the Treaty on European Union. The anchoring of the CEEC in Euro-Atlantic security structures is suffering from the uncertainties and incoherence of the redefinition of the role and scope of NATO, WEU, and EU. Besides the institutional confusion and lack of complementarity between the three organizations, there is no common vision of security for Europe, let alone a strategy to achieve it. Evidently, a balancing of the EU's strategy toward the CEEC and a strategy toward Russia is vital. The attitude toward Russia is the key factor when discussing the different scenarios for the integration or rapprochement of the CEEC in terms of security and defense. At the end of 1994, three scenarios are predominant: (1) parallel accessions of the CEEC to the EU, WEU, and NATO; (2) some open choice or differentiated memberships; and (3) multi-speed and gradual accession with memberships, ultimately, in all three organizations. Whereas the EU had set criteria for membership in June 1993, NATO's criteria are far less transparent.

In spite of the EC/Twelve's intention, the Europe Agreements were not a convincing way out of the Union's dilemma of deepening and widening. Despite their broadness, including substantial provisions for political dialogue,[16] a series of amendments and extensions were acutely demanded.[17] The membership formula had been controversial right from the beginning of negotiating about association. Whereas the various Europe Agreements, in a carefully worded preamble, only recognize that it is the associated country's ultimate objective to accede to the Community and that association, in the views of the parties, will help the associated country to achieve accession, the European Council in Copenhagen went beyond agreeing that "the associated countries in Central and Eastern Europe that so desire shall become members of the European Union" and that "the future cooperation . . . shall be geared to the objective of membership which has now been established."[18] In this, the decisions of Copenhagen were a turning point and attempted to regain the EU's credibility, which had suffered from hollow rhetoric and high expectations, as far as the membership perspective was concerned. Security through short- or medium-term EU membership was a step too fast.

Security Through Effective Association: Structured Relations

Ironically enough, the strategic improvement of Copenhagen, which established that EU membership of the associated CEEC only remains a question of when and how, shifted the political emphasis from membership back to the period of pre-accession. The pre-accession strategy aims at bridging the gulf between association and membership.

Obviously, with the Europe Agreements as the backbone of relations with the CEEC, the EU has several options at hand on how to expand association more effectively and accelerate accession through a bundle of short- and medium-term measures in the pre-accession period. Thus far, the Europe Agreements prove to be a flexible framework for this cumulative, step-by-step approach. The CEEC, however, perceive this flexibility as piecemeal engineering of a reluctant attitude. The criteria for membership—taking over of the *acquis communautaire,* stable institutions, democracy, rule of law, functioning market economy, and coping with competitive pressure and market forces—reaffirm that there will neither be special treatment, as in the case of the German Democratic Republic (GDR), nor a "discount accession," leaving the bulk of adaptation for the period after accession. Besides the more rapid implementation of free trade arrangements and provisions on economic cooperation, the most innovative proposal under the formula "making the most of the Europe Agreements" were the structured relations with the institutions of the Union, which increase institutional complexity considerably.

The European Council of Copenhagen declared that a multilateral structure was to be put alongside the bilateral structures of the association agreements. It proposed to the associated countries to build—as a group of associated countries—structured relations with the institutions of the EU on matters of common interest, to be decided in advance and arising in the Union's areas of competence. Procedures for consultation and dialogue would encompass all three pillars of the EU. They will not be at the expense of institutions and bilateral meetings within the framework of the Europe Agreements. The opinion is held that the European Union is now working with a double institutional net.[19] In view of extending the group of Europe Agreement signatories in the near future from six to ten, perhaps even fifteen, countries,[20] the strategy of membership via ever closer association is no longer a privilege of the most advanced, reformist CEEC. The move toward structured relations also gained momentum from the membership applications by Hungary and Poland in April 1994 and the Commission's efforts to develop a coherent pre-accession strategy that would effectively combine political, economic, and financial instruments. Structured relations are the political side of implementing pre-accession.[21]

Up to the conclusion of association agreements and thereafter, several proposals to stress the credibility of the EU's commitment had been made, but none was really a strategic breakthrough. This is, of course, connected with the fact that the Eastern enlargement "questions the design, policy scope and goals of the Union"[22]—all of them highly controversial among the EU member states. The European Council did not take up the

Commission's proposal for a European Political Area.[23] Commissioner Hans Andriessen's reflections on affiliate membership[24] did not enter an official communication by the Commission, which rather believes that any type of partial membership is a negative tendency, moving away from the single institutional framework of the EU. The Hurd-Andreatta Initiative of December 1993[25] to associate the Europe Agreement signatories with CFSP wanted to redress the perceived economic bias of relations and opted rather for a decoupling of the political and the economic area, nourishing again ideas for partial membership in the intergovernmental second and third pillars of the EU. The Visegrád states promptly reacted by laying down their position about intensifying cooperation in matters of CFSP and Justice and Home Affairs in a joint non-paper.[26]

The structured relations should include joint meetings in Community policies with a trans-European dimension, CFSP and Justice, and Home Affairs. This would introduce a degree of cautious participation of officials from the associated countries in the preparation process that is normally restricted to member states of the EU and its institutions. Practically, the Commission proposes to have joint meetings with the Committee of Permanent Representatives (COREPER), the Political Committee, and relevant working groups. Moreover, the Commission recommends that the European Parliament should also hold joint meetings on particular points of common interest with associated countries. These far-reaching proposals of summer 1994 are partly a reaction to one year of dissatisfaction with the Copenhagen decisions of establishing structured relations. At the ministerial level, there were only two informal meetings of the transport and Ecofin (Council of Economic and Finance Ministers) ministers in November/December 1993 and June 1994, respectively, and one informal meeting of the ministers of the Interior and Justice in September 1994. As far as CFSP was concerned, political dialogue recorded two Troika meetings and a joint meeting of political directors up until the summer of 1994. The first ministerial meeting within the structured relationship took place on 31 October 1994, prior to the meeting of the Council. Actually, CFSP was a pacemaker for structured relations. The Council of Ministers on 7 March 1994 had already developed rules for an upgraded mechanism, with additional meetings at different levels and at a higher frequency, which were entirely adopted in the Commission's communication of July 1994.[27] The European Council in Essen did not consider all of these proposals. It stressed the key function of COREPER, which shall safeguard horizontal coherence of the structured relations. Principally, from 1995 onward, the following meetings should be scheduled by the succeeding presidencies well in advance:[28]

• Annual meeting of the heads of state and government on the margins of the European Council

- Semiannual meetings of the foreign ministers to discuss the full scope of relations—in particular, with a view to the status and progress of the integration process
- Annual meetings of ministers responsible for internal market, economics, finance, and agriculture on the occasion of their Council meetings
- Ministerial meetings on transport, telecommunications, research, and environment annually. Without reference to the level of meetings, the following sectors are indicated: Justice and/or Home Affairs (biannually), culture and education (annually).

Structured relations, confined to consultation and concertation—that is, without joint decisionmaking—could only erode the institutional fortress EU[29] if they became frequent and open to many participants, rather than remaining specialized and somewhat privileged Union-to-region meetings. The character of Union-to-region relations, rather than affiliate or partial membership relations, was emphasized insofar as they should be matched by more intensive relations of the EU with the privileged countries of the Mediterranean. The short- and medium-term measures for pre-accession, which should make association more effective, would probably counteract the strongest internal threats to security, such as economic decline, social unrest, or ethnic conflicts.

Security and Stages of Political Dialogue

A very rich example for institutional complexity and strategic orientation of CFSP is political dialogue with the CEEC. Political dialogue, incorporated into the individual Europe Agreements and currently exercised mainly in a multilateral framework with the group of signatory states, is one ingredient of the European Union's attempts to manage change in its evolving Eastern and Central European neighborhood. Although taken into consideration as early as 1984, the turmoils of 1989 finally provided the opportunity to establish a regular political dialogue with the Eastern European countries.[30] Both sides have been strongly committed to political dialogue ever since, because it constitutes an important channel not only to serve the traditional functions of familiarizing the dialogue partners with the *acquis politique* and demonstrating political solidarity, but also of discussing and preparing the road to membership as far as the noneconomic prerequisites are concerned.

Often described as one of the "unique features"[31] or the "main added value"[32] of the Europe Agreements, the legal anchoring of political dialogue in an agreement based on Article 238 of the EC Treaty figures as the real novelty of these recent association agreements. In addition, the frequency of meetings under the aegis of political dialogue (and its rapid upgrading) emphasizes the strong political and foreign policy dimension in the EU's relations with the CEEC.[33]

Table 11.1 gives a general overview of the agreements of the EC/EU with the CEEC and Russia/CIS since 1989. The following passages are an attempt to portray the various stages of relations between the EU and the CEEC in detail, starting with the informal stage.

The Informal Stage

Political dialogue with the CEEC commenced even before the signing of the various Europe Agreements.[34] From 1989 onward, the Twelve introduced informal political dialogues with leading reform countries—namely, Poland and Hungary, joined by the CSFR in late 1990—and the then USSR, despite its ambiguous reformist profile, was the key country. It had been a long-standing ambition of the Twelve to establish political dialogue with countries of the Warsaw Pact before its dissolution. Even after the general EPC decision of Rhodes in December 1988, controversial discussions continued on the "when and how." So, initially, political dialogue was less a pacemaker for relations with the Warsaw Pact countries but, rather, a companion to the various stages of relations.

In a first stage, from 1989 to 1991, the parties involved developed an informal network, established as a one-sided offer on behalf of the Twelve. The onset of political dialogue resulted from the Twelve's wish to open up channels of regular communication for the management of change and to put a foot in the door as a collective actor in the new European order building. The practice was strictly bilateral in accordance with the then prevailing bilateralism, as part of the so-called parallel approach. In 1989 and 1990 annual gatherings took place at the ministerial level and were also extended to meetings of the political directors at the request of Hungary in 1989. This extension was an early example of the specific interest the three to four Central European countries attached to political dialogue.

The Formal but Latent Stage

Entering a second stage, the Europe Agreements provided, for the first time, a legally binding basis for political dialogue. As the various Europe Agreements follow roughly the same structure, political dialogue considerations and arrangements are as follows. The preamble desires the establishing of a regular political dialogue on bilateral and international issues of mutual interest, to enhance and complete association. Title I concerns political dialogue itself, which shall accompany and consolidate the rapprochement between the parties, support the new political order, and contribute to the establishment of lasting links of solidarity and new forms of cooperation. It is based on shared values and aspirations, recalling the political

Table 11.1   Agreements of the EC/EU with Central and Eastern European Countries and Russia/CIS (February 1995)

Agreements / Countries	Agreements on Trade and Cooperation		PHARE Activities Since	Europe Agreements (plus Multilateral Structured Relationship)	Interim Agreements In force	Application for Membership	Free Trade Agreements In Force	Agreements on Partnership and Cooperation Signed
	1. Generation	2. Generation						
Hungary	1988		1989	Dec. 1991; in force Feb. 1994	1 March 1992 until 1 Feb. 1994	April 1994		
Poland	1989		1989/90	Dec. 1991; in force Feb. 1994	1 March 1992 until 1 Feb. 1994	April 1994		
CSFR[a]	1989/extended in 1990		1990	Signed Dec. 1991	1 March 1992			
CR	—			Signed Oct. 1993; in force Feb. 1995				
SR	—			Signed Oct. 1993; in force Feb. 1995				
Romania	(1980)/1991		1990/91	Signed Feb. 1993; in force Feb. 1995	1 May 1993			
Bulgaria	1990		1990	Signed March 1993; in force Feb. 1995	31 Dec. 1993			
Lithuania		1992	1992	Negotiations since January 1995			1995	
Latvia		1992	1992	Negotiations since January 1995			1995	
Estonia		1992	1992	Negotiations since January 1995			1995	
"Yugoslavia"	1970 Trade Agreement; 1980 Cooperation Agreement; deferred in Nov. 1991		Deferred in Nov. 1991					

Agreements / Countries	Agreements on Trade and Cooperation		PHARE Activities Since	Europe Agreements (plus Multilateral Structured Relationship)	Interim Agreements In force	Application for Membership	Free Trade Agreements In Force	Agreements on Partnership and Cooperation Signed
	1. Generation	2. Generation						
Slovenia[b]	Feb. 1992 preferential treatment	5 April 1993 signed	1992	Negotiations in 1995				
Croatia[b]	Feb. 1992 preferential treatment		Humanitarian and immediate aid 1992					
Bosnia-Herzegovina[c]	Feb. 1992 preferential treatment		Humanitarian and immediate aid 1992					
Macedonia[d]	Feb. 1992 preferential treatment		Humanitarian and immediate aid 1992					
Serbia/Montenegro (Federal Republic of Yugoslavia)	Sanctions/embargo							
Albania		1992	1992					
"USSR"[e]	1989							
Russia			TACIS 1991		Initialled Dec. 1994			June 1994
Ukraine			TACIS 1991		Initialled June 1994			June 1994
Kazakhstan and Other CIS Republics			TACIS 1991					January 1995

Notes: a. Since 1 January 1993: Czech Republic (CR), Slovak Republic (SR)
b. Officially recognized by the EC on 15 January 1992
c. Officially recognized by the EC on 7 April 1992
d. Not officially recognized by the EC
e. Dissolved in December 1991

conditions of association. The objective of "political dialogue and cooperation" is to facilitate the associated country's full integration into the community of democratic nations and progressive rapprochement with the
Community. The interconnectedness of the measures taken to assist transformation is also mentioned in this context, inasmuch as political convergence and economic rapprochement, provided for in the agreement, are
closely related and mutually reinforcing parts of the association. This can be
understood as a codification of the principle of consistency in the
Community's external relations and CFSP.[35]

As usual, the contracting parties hope that political dialogue, through
consideration of the others' position and interest, will bring about better
mutual understanding and increasing convergence of views on international
issues—in particular, on those matters likely to have a substantial effect on
one or the other partner. This specification, as well as a discussion of contributions to a rapprochement of the parties' positions on security issues,
outlines important items on the agenda of political dialogue.

It is noteworthy that the institutionalization of political dialogue will
take place in the Association Council, which was established as the ministerial body that would supervise the implementation of the association agreement. The Association Council is in a key position, as it shall examine any
major issue arising in the framework of association and any other bilateral
or international issue of mutual interest. Moreover, it has the power to make
binding decisions, to delegate to the Association Committee any of its powers, and to set up special committees or bodies for assistance. The
Association Council's probable importance as the political dialogue body
has not been tested so far, since the entry into force of all aspects of the association agreements only occurred, in the case of Poland and Hungary, in
February 1994. The Association Council will meet annually and when circumstances require; given these infrequent meetings, it is unlikely that it
will become the decisive body for political dialogue. Meetings of the foreign
ministers are expected to fuse with those of the Association Council, as was
the case on 7 March 1994 in Brussels. In addition, meetings at the highest
political level are envisaged, including the participation of the president of
the European Council, the president of the Commission, and the head of
state and government of the associated country. The Lisbon European
Council assumed that this kind of meeting would be a systematic preparation for membership.[36]

According to the Council's decision, the hitherto informal practice of
meetings at the level of political directors between officials of the associated country and the presidency of the Council and the Commission was confirmed, and the option to take full advantage of all diplomatic channels was
also stated. This will comprise regular briefings after important CFSP meetings, contacts in the capitals of signatory countries and at international organizations, and conferences such as the United Nations and the Conference
on Security and Cooperation in Europe (CSCE). Political dialogue at the

parliamentary level will take place within the Parliamentary Association Committee. Although by nature without an operative function, its purpose is to build consensus, trust, and familiarity in and with Community policy-making.[37]

This second stage of political dialogue is only on paper and had, at the beginning of 1995, not extended to the Czech Republic, Slovakia, Bulgaria, and Romania.

The Multilateral, Informal Stage

In reality, political dialogue, based on decisions, understandings, and declarations separate from the Europe Agreements, had been practiced in a multilateral framework, starting with the Visegrád group of three/four. In the course of 1992, with two presidencies actively involved in these relations and strongly recommended by the Commission, the "group approach" came to the fore. On this multilateral basis, the Portuguese presidency started implementing provisions of the Europe Agreements. Meetings at the level of foreign ministers and political directors became most prominent, whereas the specific Association Councils remained unestablished until March 1994.[38]

The Structured Stage

In the latent period of the Europe Agreements, the Community made efforts to upgrade the group approach, offering sophisticated procedures and arrangements and lining up the Visegrád states with the group of six signatories. The implementation of the conclusions of the Copenhagen summit opened up a new stage or perhaps even made a qualitative leap. Structured relations in the area of CFSP aim at strengthening the feeling of belonging and familiarizing the aspirant countries with CFSP procedures and involving them through the option of aligning themselves in defined cases.

Although of advisory nature and without decisionmaking abilities, conclusions drawn within the meetings of the structured relations can be implemented through the Association Councils. Meetings at the highest political level, if appropriate, can be held as joint meetings with all the heads of state and government, not only with the president of the European Council and the president of the Commission with their counterparts, as was foreseen in the Europe Agreements and as is the current practice. These summit meetings with full participation would be unique. The invitation to the European Council in Essen in December 1994 was, of course, only for the family photograph album. Substantive meetings at this level are still to be expected.

The multilateral framework and bilateral frameworks should be strongly connected. At the level of foreign ministers and political directors, Troika meetings should take place biannually. More practical and substantive is the establishment of EPC/CFSP Working Groups. In September 1993 the Belgian presidency started implementing the Copenhagen decision, which also became operational in connection with the Council decision of 7 March 1994; but only under the German presidency did structured relations develop more dynamically with a view to the CFSP pillar.

In terms of making the structured relations work, the six Europe Agreement (EA) countries[39] are establishing "contact points" at their embassies in Brussels to communicate the Correspondence Européene (COREU) information to the associated countries. The first meeting of COREPER, with the ambassadors of the six associated countries, was on 14 October 1994 in order to present the strategy of the EU in view of the United Nations. Under the German presidency, twelve Working Groups established contacts with the Europe Agreement countries. They were briefed after the meetings of the respective Working Groups mostly through representatives of the Troika or of all Twelve/Fifteen. These expert-level meetings were quite frequent in the second half of 1994. The Working Groups involved were concerned with disarmament, nuclear nonproliferation, human rights, CSCE, security, CIS, foreign policy planning, arms export, former-Yugoslavia, terrorism, and the UN. This list gives a hint of the items on a CFSP agenda, including those in which a trans-European dimension is evident. Moreover, there are meetings between the European correspondents and the "shadow," or associated, correspondents of the EA countries—in general, before the meetings of the Political Committee with the political directors of the EA countries, in order to prepare the agenda and agree on keynote speakers for various items. Under the German presidency, the first meeting of the correspondents was on 19 July 1994, the second on 18 October 1994. The first meeting of the EU political directors with their counterparts was on 25 October 1994, before the ministerial meeting based on the "Twelve/Sixteen plus Six" formula.

One is tempted only to look on the bright side—that is, functioning arrangements and a satisfactory frequency of meetings—but what about the substance of political dialogue? There was notorious dissatisfaction with the luncheon meetings during the multilateral informal stage, but political dialogue seems to have progressed from that point.

Within CFSP, the EA countries are invited to join CFSP declarations, joint actions, and démarches. The procedures for EA countries associating themselves with the substance of CFSP have not yet been defined. A number of questions arise. Clearly, the EU will decide, for example, on what should become a joint action, and it probably also will decide which actions, in particular, will be open for association. As far as joint actions are concerned, the CEEC are in a peculiar situation. They are objects, as in the case of the stability pact, and simultaneously participants in joint actions.

Through structured relations, the EA countries will have the opportunity to be consulted on the substance of decisions and to indicate their interest early regarding publicly associating themselves. When immediate reactions from the EU are urgently needed—for example, in crisis situations—the consultation machinery within structured relations could be too cumbersome for anything other than ex-post involvement. The structured relations, the "enlarged speaking with one voice" in international conferences, might be attractive to CEEC, as it will serve to broaden and sharpen their profile as international actors. They would, as do other small and medium-sized states in Europe, profit from collective diplomacy. But what about the core CFSP interest of the CEEC—its security dimension? Would the CEEC have a say in formulating the EU's foreign policy toward Russia or in co-determining the enlargement policies of NATO and WEU? Given the EU's weak *acquis politique* on these strategic questions and their political sensitivity, it is likely that the precarious situation of the CEEC as in-betweens will be highlighted, rather than relaxed, within the CFSP activities of structured relations.

Security Through Regional Cooperation

Political dialogue was a forerunner in shifting relations from bilateral to multilateral between the EU and the CEEC. The EU is addressing the CEEC more and more as a grouping based on different formulas: Relations based on the formula EU plus the Visegrád Four (Twelve plus Four) were replaced by the formula EU plus the six EA states (Twelve plus Six) in June 1993; the joint action "stability pact for Europe" is taking place in the formula EU plus Nine, as is the case of the enhanced status of associate partners in the WEU (six EA countries plus the three Baltic countries and Slovenia). With only a little exaggeration, one could say that it is the EU that brings all these groupings into being, and that these groupings are accidental insofar as their making or prolonging originates in Brussels.[40] Reasons for addressing the CEEC as groupings are manifold from the EU's point of view:

- To reduce workload and make the management of contacts, meetings, et cetera, more efficient for the EU
- To balance the EU member states' geopolitical preferences for individual CEEC
- To rationalize measures and make them more effective, given the fact that the CEEC share a host of problems that are connected with basic decisions and consequences of the transformation to market economies and democracies
- To offer, in principle, a fair and equal treatment to all CEEC committed to reforms
- To clarify the pre-accession period

- To strengthen regional cooperation and encourage cooperative conflict settlements between neighboring countries
- To downgrade and sort out conflicts among future EU members before their accession to the EU

Most of the CEEC accept these arguments but downplay the value of the regional approach as a key structure for association, as well as for the pre-accession period.[41] These are the main reasons for thinking of regional cooperation as second-best for solutions that are political as well as economic: The political argument is that any option that could be declared as an alternative to EU membership is counterproductive and not in the interest of the CEEC. The antechamber should not become a permanent residence. On the other side, the EA countries accept that a certain degree of regional cooperation would testify to their EU capability, as far as both political and economic criteria are concerned.[42] Pragmatism and flexibility are indicated, for example, by the openness of Hungary and Slovakia to use the Visegrád summit for talks about the Gabcikovo Dam dispute. The conflict between Hungary and Slovakia is one of the rare examples in which CFSP—with the involvement of the Commission—was instrumental in bringing the conflicting parties together and settling the conflict by bringing it before the International Court of Justice in The Hague.

Strong criticism is voiced against overestimating the impact of regional trade and economic cooperation or misjudging its conditions, because "the development of intra-regional trade among the Visegrád countries will be the consequence of successful integration into the world economy (particularly the economy of Western Europe) and not the precondition for it."[43] From regional economic cooperation, one cannot expect an impact from modernization; as a core for modernization, the economies of the EU are irreplaceable, goes the other argument. "Core for modernization" is the equivalent economic argument of considering the EU to be the political anchor for the CEEC.

Again, there were different stages of establishing the group formula: Whereas the EC was not successful in introducing the promotion of regional cooperation—or even integration—into the association agreements, it did so in key documents for the intensification of relations with the CEEC. In its first communication, "Towards a closer association," the Commission proposed that "the bilateral political dialogues should be supplemented and eventually replaced by a structural multilateral dialogue, involving countries which have decided to cooperate closely among themselves;"[44] obviously, cooperation among the Visegrád countries was meant here. Even after the full entry into force of the EA with Poland and Hungary, Commissioner Van den Broek suggested: "The Union should help create the conditions for membership by breaking out of the separate, bilateral arrangements which link it to each East European country. Instead it should set up with its partners a multilateral political and economic relationship which would be a true precursor of membership."[45] Some academic experts even go beyond that and plead for an association of the associated countries.[46] The idea is to replace the "hub-and-spoke bilateralism" of the EU through the creation of a general free-trade regime with the entire CEEC region and, later, also the Commonwealth of Independent States (CIS). The EU would gradually build a European economic area with the most advanced reform countries, all managed by a newly established "Organization for European Integration." The ideas spread before the Essen European Council, which make the extension of the CEFTA Initiative of the four Visegrád countries to the entire CEEC region a regular criterion for membership—a proposal the summit did not adopt literally—point in a similar direction.

In Lisbon, the EU had thought that a joint action in the area of the CEEC would "contribute to the establishing of [a] political and/or economic framework which [would] support regional cooperation or steps towards regional and subregional integration."[47] Obviously, in the security field the EU must act as a co-optive player.[48] This illustrates the rather ambitious joint action of the EU "stability pact for Europe," which originated in the so-called Balladur Plan.[49] The EU views the participation of the nine CEEC—the six associated countries plus the Baltic states—as part of the association and pre-accession process. The stability pact is an exercise in preventive diplomacy that wants to stimulate neighborhood agreements on borders and on the treatment of ethnic minorities. The setting up of two roundtable discussions on the "Baltic Sea region" and "other CEEC" started a process of talks and negotiations wherein the EU intends to act as an initiator and a moderator. Any bilateral agreements should be placed under the CSCE/OSCE roof. This joint action adds to the political conditions for membership and also forces the EA countries to adopt a more cooperative attitude in perceived key areas of their domestic and foreign policies, which may touch the core of national sovereignty.

The agenda to be treated at the roundtables was widened to include more "soft" subjects, such as economic or environmental cooperation, which should make the controversial issues easier to swallow.

In Essen, the heads of state and government stressed the importance of "intraregional cooperation and good neighbourly relations" as a key to successful implementation of "structured relations." They again earmarked funds for intraregional cooperation within the PHARE program. The summit encouraged, without strict linkages, the extension of free-trade regulations among all CEEC, notably the EA countries. In connection with the stability pact, the Essen European Council proposed a new EU initiative to stimulate regional cooperation—for example, in the Baltic Sea area where countries from the EU/CEEC and CIS shall participate. The setting up of an integrated program for this region clearly indicates the complex approach of the EU, which, during the pre-accession period, attempts to overcome the fixation on the membership question.

Conclusions

There is no alternative to the EU as an anchor for the security and modernization of the transforming CEEC.[50] The categorical statement needs some differentiation, in terms of translating this role into a convincing strategy. Most of all, the initial, but half-hearted, proposals of "security through membership" lacked credibility and caused relations to deteriorate between the EU and the CEEC. The pre-accession strategy is the result of a learning process. It acknowledges that the EU, for its own sake, has to project security beyond its eastern borders, mainly through "effective association." The pre-accession strategy requires the consistent combination of all the traditional civilian instruments of the Community in external relations and also tries to achieve consistency through "structured relations" across all three pillars of the EU. In terms of security, short- and medium-term measures in the economic, commercial, and trade sectors, as well as others, could have an even stronger impact than cooperation in CFSP. However, in this respect the EU is doing more than intensifying a one-way political dialogue. The joint-action "stability pact for Europe" and other incentives for regional cooperation in the PHARE and CIS regions try to enact the good intentions of "conflict prevention." Thus, the real chance for the EU to be an anchor is effective association and transformation in the CEEC. For the time being, as a manager of erupting crises or military conflicts, the EU is considerably overstrained.

As part of the Western security structure and as a virtual cooptive player, the EU must contribute to the broad European strategy a real policy toward Russia, a more solid *acquis* on the defense component of CFSP, and an operational vision for WEU and OSCE.

Notes

1. This contribution will focus on relations with the currently six associated countries, the so-called Visegrád Four—Hungary, the Czech Republic, Slovakia, and Poland—and Bulgaria and Romania. The cases of Russia (see David Allen's Chapter 12 in this volume) and former-Yugoslavia (see Geoffrey Edwards's Chapter 10 in this volume) are treated separately.

2. "Europe and the Challenge of Enlargement," Commission Report, Supplement to the Conclusions of the European Council in Lisbon, *Europe Documents* no. 1790, 3 July 1992, p. 2.

3. See Hugh Miall, *Shaping a New European Order* (London: Pinter Publishers, 1993).

4. See, e.g., in the case of the CEEC: "Joint Memorandum of the Governments of the Czech and Slovak Federal Republic, the Republic of Hungary, and the Republic of Poland on strengthening their integration with the European Communities and on the perspective of accession," September 1992, forwarded to the British presidency on 11 September 1992; see, e.g., in the case of the Community: "Conclusions of the Presidency at the Strasbourg European Council of 8 December 1989," *Bulletin of the EC* 12 (1989), pp. 8–18; and widely in academic literature cited from Barbara Lippert and Heinrich Schneider, eds., *Monitoring Association and Beyond: The European Union and the Visegrád States* (Bonn: Europa Union Verlag, 1995).

5. "Europe and the Challenge of Enlargement," p. 8.

6. There are no bilateral treaties with the successor states of Yugoslavia: Croatia, Macedonia, Serbia/Montenegro, and Bosnia, but only with Slovenia. For Russia and the CIS, the EU developed a special type of agreement, "Partnership and Cooperation Treaties." See David Allen's contribution in Chapter 12 of this volume.

7. Geoffrey Edwards and Elfriede Regelsberger, eds., *Europe's Global Links. The European Community and Interregional Cooperation* (London: Frances Pinter, 1990).

8. "Europe and the Challenge of Enlargement," p. 2.

9. Emphasized, e.g., in "Towards a Closer Association with the Countries of Central and Eastern Europe," Report by the Commission to the European Council, Edinburgh, 11–12 December 1992, *Europe Documents* no. 1814, 9 December 1992, p. 2, and confirmed by the European Council in Essen on 9–10 December 1994, cited from the "Report from the Council to the Essen European Council on a strategy to prepare for the accession of the associated CEEC" (annexed to Conclusions of the Presidency), *Europe Documents* no. 1916, 14 December 1994, p.1.

10. For a more detailed account, see Marc Maresceau, "'Europe Agreements': A New Form of Cooperation Between the European Community and Central and Eastern Europe," in Peter-Christian Müller-Graff, ed., *East Central European States and the European Communities: Legal Adaptation to the Market Economy* (Baden-Baden: Nomos Verlagsgesellschaft, 1993), pp. 209–233.

11. See, e.g., Article 6 in the association agreements with the Czech Republic and the Slovak Republic.

12. See also Zbigniew Brzezinski, "The Premature Partnership," in *Foreign Affairs* 2 (1994), pp. 67–82.

13. See "Report from the Council to the Essen European Council," pp. 3–4.

14. See overview and details below.

15. "Towards a Closer Association," p. 2.

16. See Jörg Monar's contribution on political dialogue in Chapter 14 of this volume.

17. Most articulated in the "Joint Memorandum of the Governments of the Czech and Slovak Federal Republic, the Republic of Hungary, and the Republic of Poland."

18. "Conclusions of the Presidency, European Council of Copenhagen, 21–22 June 1993," *Europe Documents* no. 1844/45, p. 5.

19. Christian Deubner, Heinz Kramer, and Elke Thiel, "Die Erweiterung der Europäischen Union nach Mittel- und Osteuropa," SWP-AP 2818 (Ebenhausen: Stiftung Wissenschaft und Politik, 1993), p. 19.

20. The three Baltic States and Slovenia, as foreseen during the French presidency; see "Conclusions of the Presidency," *Agence Europe* no. 6376 (special ed.— n.s.), 11 December 1994, p. 10.

21. "Report from the Council to the Essen European Council," pp. 2–3.

22. Anna Murphy, *Towards Eastern Enlargement—Scenarios for the European Union* (manuscript, July 1994), p. 9.

23. See "Europe and the Challenge of Enlargement."

24. Hans Andriessen, "Towards a Community of Twenty-four?" Speech held on 19 April 1991, 69th Plenary Session of EUROCHAMBERS Economic and Social Committee, Brussels.

25. *Agence Europe* no. 6134, 22 December 1993, p. 6.

26. Andras Orgoványi, "Die Europäische Integration als Priorität der ungarischen Außenpolitik," in European Cooperation Foundation (Euration), ed., *Euration Konferenz: Der Weg zur Europäischen Union und die mitteleuropäischen assoziierten Staaten* (Budapest, 1994), p. 47.

27. "The Europe Agreements and Beyond: A Strategy to Prepare the Countries of Central and Eastern Europe for Accession," Communication from the Commission to the Council, *Europe Documents* no. 1893, 21 July 1994, second part in *Europe Documents* no. 1897/98, 14 September 1994.

28. "Report from the Council to the Essen European Council," p. 2.

29. Wolfgang Wessels, "Erweiterung, Vertiefung, Verkleinerung. Vitale Fragen für die Europäische Union," *Europa-Archiv* 10 (1993), p. 312.

30. See also Simon Nuttall's Chapter 2 in this volume.

31. Maresceau, "'Europe Agreements,'" in Müller-Graff, ed., *East Central European States,* p. 216.

32. Karel Jezek, "The Multilateralization of Political Dialogue: First Experiences," in Lippert and Schneider, eds., *Monitoring Association and Beyond,* pp. 267–273.

33. Political dialogue on an annual basis was also added, in separate documents, to the trade and cooperation agreements with the three Baltic states, Albania, and Slovenia.

34. See also Elfriede Regelsberger, "Political Dialogue with the Visegrád Group: Only Business as Usual at High Speed?" Lippert and Schneider, eds., *Monitoring Association and Beyond,* pp. 251–266.

35. On consistency, see Horst-Günter Krenzler and Henning Schneider's Chapter 8 in this volume.

36. See the "Conclusions of the Presidency," European Council in Lisbon, 26–27 June 1992, *Agence Europe* no. 5760 (n.s., special ed.), 28 June 1992, p. 6.

37. See, e.g., the recommendations of the first joint Parliamentary Committee, "EU/Hungary," on 26–28 January 1994, PE 207.655/final, 28 January 1994.

38. See overview below.

39. The "Europe Agreement countries" will in the following be abbreviated as EA countries.

40. András Inotai and Magdolna Sass, "Economic Integration of the Visegrád Countries: Facts and Scenarios," *Working Paper* 33 (Budapest: Institute for World Economics, 1994).

41. For the different attitudes and commitments of the Visegrád states to regional cooperation, see George Kolankiewicz, "Consensus and Competition in the Eastern Enlargement of the EU," *International Affairs* 3 (1994), pp. 438–439.

42. See, for a critical view, András Inotai, *The System of Criteria for Hungary's Accession to the European Union* (Budapest: 1994).

43. Inotai and Sass, "Economic Integration of the Visegrád Countries," p. 27.

44. "Towards Closer Association," p. 3.

45. Hans van den Broek, "The Challenge of a Wider Europe," Brussels, ULB, 17 March 1994.

46. See James E. Baldwin, *Towards an Integrated Europe* (London Centre for Economic Policy Research, 1994).

47. See "Conclusions of the Presidency," European Council in Lisbon.

48. Reinhardt Rummel, "Beyond Maastricht: Alternative Futures for a Political Union," in Reinhardt Rummel, ed., *Toward Political Union* (Baden-Baden: Nomos Verlagsgesellschaft, 1992), p. 319.

49. Mathias Jopp, "Strategic Implications of European Integration," *Adelphi Paper* 290 (London: IISS, Brassey's, 1994), pp. 52–54.

50. See Lippert and Schneider, "Introduction and Summary," in Lippert and Schneider, eds., *Monitoring Association and Beyond,* pp. 23–45.

12

EPC/CFSP, the Soviet Union, and the Former Soviet Republics: Do the Twelve Have a Coherent Policy?

David Allen

Before 1989, it was clear that the member states of the European Community (EC) faced changes in their individual and collective roles in the evolving international system. At the beginning of the 1980s, the EC states had achieved a degree of success in managing their own distinct response to the outbreak of the "new Cold War," so that European Political Cooperation (EPC) observers talked of European foreign policy moving toward a "new plateau"[1] and of the EC member states establishing themselves as a "second Western voice"[2] in international relations. However, the effectiveness of that voice in influencing the activities of either superpower was questioned by the circumstances surrounding the U.S.-Soviet summit in Reykjavik in 1986.[3]

Those who saw the Gorbachev détente initiatives, and the positive response to them by the United States, anticipated a time when the EC states would have to play a fuller role in providing for their own security and shaping relations with the Soviet Union; but thinking on both foreign policy and internal EC arrangements remained based on the assumption that European politics would continue to be fundamentally structured by the postwar cleavage. By the end of 1990, however, the Cold War and everything that went with it had all but disappeared. Germany was united within NATO, and NATO and the Warsaw Pact had mutually agreed that they no longer represented a threat to each other. In Paris, in November 1990, all the members of the Conference on Security and Cooperation in Europe (CSCE) had drawn up the Paris Charter, which was seen as the foundation of a "New European Order." The EC was perceived by both superpowers, with apparent enthusiasm, as being the key organization upon which the new Europe would be centered.[4]

These revolutionary changes could be seen as presenting the EC and its member states with a great opportunity to both widen and deepen their integrative experiment in a Europe no longer divided or dominated by the super-power protagonists. The Cold War could, in this view, be seen as having placed definite limits on what was achievable at the collective European level, particularly in the foreign and security policy spheres and especially in relation to the Soviet Union. The end of the Cold War, therefore, might be seen as presenting the EC states with the opportunity to build on their previous success and to rise to the challenge of developing internally and externally, in general, and with regard to the Soviet Union, in particular.

On the other hand, one could see all the European institutions (both Eastern and Western) as being essentially Cold War institutions that might be unlikely to survive its peaceful conclusion. This view would have predicted the collapse of the Warsaw Pact and Comecon but would also have anticipated that NATO and the EC would have problems maintaining internal cohesion once the discipline of the Soviet threat was removed. It is argued here that the initial jubilation about the liberating impact of the events of 1989 on the EC and EPC failed to take account of the dynamic effect of those changes on the position and perspectives of the EC member states. Thus, while the Maastricht Treaty arrangements served mainly to confirm previous practice in the foreign policy area, that practice had made assumptions about the steady convergence of national foreign policies that were to be challenged in the post–Cold War era. Once the national stances of, in particular, Britain, France, and Germany began to diverge, the development of a coherent policy toward the Soviet Union and its successor states was bound to become more problematic.

Policy Toward the Soviet Union

In the late 1980s, the EC had already begun a reconsideration of its relationship with the Soviet Union and its client states.[5] This was partly inspired by their reaction to the 1992 program but was mainly the result of a Soviet desire, evident from 1985 onward, to forge a new relationship with all the potential inhabitants of Mikhail Gorbachev's celebrated "Common European Home." The EC, already dealing with those East European states that had started to show signs of reform potential, was under pressure from Moscow to consider a framework agreement, both with the Soviet Union and Comecon.[6] The EC member states were, however, divided in their reading of Gorbachev's intentions. Britain, in particular, despite Margaret Thatcher's evolving role as an intermediary between Reagan/Bush and Gorbachev, worried that the Soviets were merely pursuing their age-old policy of attempting to divide the Atlantic Alliance and detach the West Europeans—in particular, West Germany—from the United States. West Germany was the EC member state that responded most positively to Soviet advances and, as a result, France demonstrated its traditional concern about a neutralist West Germany "escaping" from the restraints of the EC and NATO in its search for reunification.[7]

These first signs of division between Britain, France, and Germany— the major players in EPC/CFSP (Common Foreign and Security Policy)— were to be reinforced by subsequent developments,[8] so as to raise significant doubts about the ability of the Twelve to develop a coherent and substantial policy toward the Soviet Union in the new environment. At the end of 1988, Gorbachev's UN speech, in which he announced major unilateral military cuts, was received cautiously by Thatcher, who urged that it be "kept in perspective," but with enthusiasm by Hans-Dietrich Genscher, who argued that the anticipated deployment of short-range nuclear weapons by NATO should now be delayed. (Genscher was accused of "renting a room in the common European home before the plans for the building had been drawn up.") The subsequent disagreement, primarily between the United Kingdom and Germany over this planned deployment, was the precursor of much greater differences between the two states (and between them and France, which also viewed Germany's enthusiasm with concern) that were to prevent the emergence of a coherent policy toward Moscow. Moreover, the disagreement was not confined to the Big Three. While British policy reflected U.S. concerns, other EC member states joined the Germans in questioning whether the new circumstances required new thinking in the West as well as the East. The result was that until the NATO summit in 1989, the West Europeans were unable to respond collectively because of their particular national fetishes.

The Western failure to respond effectively was essentially a failure of leadership. The newly elected U.S. president, George Bush, apparently needed time for thought in early 1989, despite his long association with the White House, and it was not until he completed his postinaugural contemplation that the West came up with a response. The disappointment, however, was the failure of the EC member states to fill the vacuum—as they had done in the 1980–1981 transition from Carter to Reagan. Thus, the Western failure was essentially a European failure once the major criteria for dealing with the Soviet Union became political rather than military. Wasn't it surely up to the Europeans to come up with a constructive response to the idea of a "Common European Home"? However, instead it was the United States, supported by its new "partners in leadership" in West Germany, that pulled the West together by offering the Soviets a response—which many, in hindsight, saw as too little too late for Gorbachev.

The EC itself adopted a "carrot and stick" strategy toward the East,[9] applying the principle of conditionality to its offers of assistance and seeking to emphasize separate dealings with individual East European states, rather than collective dealings with Comecon. In April 1989, a political dialogue with the Soviet Union was begun and the EC ambassadors in Moscow started to receive regular briefings from the Soviet foreign ministry. In July

1989 the EC Commission, once again as the result of a policy orchestrated by the United States and West Germany, were given overall responsibility for all PHARE aid, to be provided not just by the EC/Twelve but by the wider Group of Twenty-Four.[10] The PHARE program was initially offered to Poland and Hungary and then extended to all the states of Eastern and Central Europe, Albania, and some of the states of the former Yugoslavia—that is, all the states that had been given reason to believe that they may one day become full members of the EC. Interestingly, the three Baltic states were also eventually made a part of the PHARE program, but aid to the rest of the former Soviet states was organized in a different forum, known as TACIS (Technical Assistance to the Commonwealth of Independent States). The European Commission did not seek and does not have overall responsibility for managing all G24 aid to the former Soviet states (as a result, it is extremely difficult to calculate the exact extent of Western support for Russia, as the figures published by the European Commission, the International Monetary Fund [IMF], and the national donor governments have proved impossible to reconcile).[11] If by distinguishing in name and form between aid to Eastern and Central European states—who can aspire to membership—and aid to former Soviet states—who cannot—the EC/Twelve were attempting to clarify policy, then the inclusion of the Baltic states in the PHARE program served to confuse the issue. One thing was made clear from the start and that was that the Soviet Union and its successors (other than the Baltics!) would not be considered for EC membership. Commissioner Hans Andriessen stated as much at an EC foreign ministers meeting in January 1992,[12] and this view was further endorsed in February by Chancellor Kohl, when he suggested that the former Soviet states should develop their own separate unity and form a bridge between Europe and Asia.[13]

Aid within both the PHARE and TACIS programs is subject to political and economic conditionality that involves a degree of cooperation between the EC and EPC/CFSP processes. The aid process has also, as we shall see, highlighted the conflicting economic and political dilemmas that the EC/Twelve face in trying to develop a coherent policy while trying to balance the political advantages of economic and financial generosity, in the shape of aid, assistance, and improved trading terms, with the economic costs both to the governments of EC member states and to industrial and commercial forces within the Community, who fear that they will lose out to competition with the East. In terms of Community policymaking, this produces a continuous conflict between West European foreign offices and, in particular, Soviet and former Soviet officials, who see the advantages of economic incentives and who work together in the EPC/CFSP process and the trade, industry, and agricultural ministries that feed into the COREPER/EC process, and who fear the short-term economic consequences. This is an old dilemma for EC/EPC coordination, but a definite obstacle to be overcome if a coherent and effective policy toward the former Soviet Union is to emerge. It remains to be seen whether the new "merged" CFSP procedures improve or exacerbate this situation.

German Unification

The fall of the Berlin wall forced West Germans to act quickly and decisively because, for them, the preferred British policy of "waiting and seeing" was not an option. If West Germany's partners in the EC could not act in harmony vis-à-vis the question of German unification and redefining the relationship with the Soviet Union, then West Germany would have to act alone. The sense of urgency was compounded by concern in West Germany about Gorbachev's own position within the Soviet Union. While Britain urged caution and France urged the further development of the EC, the West Germans, ably supported by the United States, perceived that a potentially narrow window of opportunity existed and chose to strive for unity.[14]

The West's approach to German unification further illustrated the divisions within the Community that inhibited the development of new policy toward the Soviet Union. Britain, whose credibility when it came to defining European interests had been sorely questioned by Margaret Thatcher's activities, seemed to prefer the maintenance of the status quo. After the emergency European Council meeting in Paris, called by President Mitterrand to ensure European input into the upcoming U.S.-Soviet summit in Malta, Thatcher repeated her previous assertion that the question of borders (between East and West Germany) was not on the agenda and that the conduct of European affairs within the NATO/Warsaw Pact framework had suited Europe well and should be preserved.[15]

This certainly accorded with what the Soviets were saying and served an agreed upon EC interest in reassuring the Soviets that the West would not take advantage of the changes in Eastern Europe, but it inevitably led to friction with the Germans and with the French, who saw further integration as the way of coexisting with German unification, if it could not be contained by other means (President Mitterrand met with President Gorbachev in Kiev in December 1989 after Chancellor Kohl had announced his "ten-point plan" for unification).[16] In Moscow, to the extent that they were of interest, the signals coming from the EC and its member states must have been confusing at the end of 1989 and the beginning of 1990.

Again, from the perspective of Moscow, the Western approach to German unification in 1990 would have seemed confused at the EC level but effectively dominated by West Germany and the United States. While Britain and France sought to preserve the status quo with a Four plus Two formula designed to reinforce the position of the four occupying powers, the United States was willing to allow the Germans to make their own arrangements (Two plus Four),[17] and it was the United States that orchestrated the NATO summit in London in June 1990, which came up with enough (a joint peace declaration with the Warsaw Pact, an invitation to Gorbachev to address NATO, and the revision of nuclear strategy) to enable Gorbachev— or, more importantly, his military critics—to live with a united Germany inside NATO. The Ottawa and London meetings were crucial to the eventual German settlement, and they both illustrated the continued dominance of, and European dependence on, the United States—despite beliefs and aspirations to the contrary—with regard to policy toward the Soviet Union.

Once the question of German unification was settled, the Paris summit of the CSCE was convened in November 1990, at which all the participants reconfirmed and developed the principles first established in Helsinki in 1975. There was much optimism that Paris was a major turning point in the evolution of Europe and that the Charter of Paris would form the basis of the new European order. To the extent that the EC had a policy toward the Soviet Union, it seemed to be based on the assumption that Gorbachev should be supported with technical and financial assistance (although there was a considerable difference of opinion between Germany and the United Kingdom about the scale of that aid) in his continuing bid to reform and democratize the Soviet Union while keeping it intact. There was broad agreement that the states of Eastern and Central Europe should be encouraged in their progression toward democracy and market economies, without threatening the security of the Soviet Union, and that the Soviet Union should be encouraged to participate constructively in the UN and elsewhere toward the implementation of a wider world order.

To this end, in 1990 the Twelve had agreed at the Dublin summit in June to draw up proposals for short-term credits and long-term support for structural reform in the Soviet Union, and in December in Rome it was decided to grant food aid of up to 750 million ECU (European currency units) and technical assistance of 400 million ECU.[18] The EC had already, in February 1990, concluded a "first generation" trade and cooperation agreement with Moscow,[19] which established most favored nation status for EC-Soviet trade but which left in place a number of quotas restricting Soviet exports of textiles, coal, and steel. It also provided a basis for political consultations between the EC and the Soviet Union.

The first indications that the integrity of the Soviet Union itself might be under challenge came with a deterioration of the situation in Lithuania, and in March 1990 the Twelve issued a statement calling on both Moscow and Vilnius to engage in an "open and fair dialogue" and to show maximum restraint in their handling of the situation.

The objective of engaging the Soviet Union in cooperation on global matters led to the successful negotiation in September 1990 of a joint EC-USSR statement[20] that underlined common positions on both the Gulf conflict (Iraq had invaded Kuwait in August 1990), the Arab-Israeli conflict, and Lebanon. In the case of Kuwait, the EC and the Soviet Union expressed their support for the proposed UN measures, and in the case of the Middle East, the two argued for a comprehensive peace settlement that suggested that their common position might be at some variance from that taken by the United States.

The Baltic States

However, the optimism about future dealings with the Soviet Union that was so apparent in Paris at the end of 1990 was soon to be dashed by events in early 1991. A foretaste of the problems that lay in store for Gorbachev within the Soviet Union came with the resignation of his foreign minister, Eduard Shevardnadze, who had expressed concern that Gorbachev might be backtracking on reforms, under pressure from the Soviet military and Communist Party hard-liners (in particular, Shevardnadze expressed concern about possible Soviet hesitations over the implementation of the Conventional Forces in Europe (CFE) agreements that he had negotiated). This problem of supporting a moderate leader forced to act in an immoderate fashion by hard-line opposition was to arise time and time again in the EC's dealings, first with Gorbachev and the Soviet Union and later with Yeltsin and Russia.

The Twelve, while issuing a statement regretting Shevardnadze's resignation,[21] were nevertheless clear that all their eggs were in the Gorbachev basket. This led them to resist the attempts of Russian president Yeltsin to visit Brussels in his own right. For in backing Gorbachev, the Twelve seemed also, regardless of their sympathy for the stirrings in the Baltics, to be supporting the idea of preserving the integrity of the Soviet Union and resisting the idea that it might itself be split up.

The policy discussed above was immediately challenged in January 1991 when the situation began to deteriorate in the Baltic states. As Soviet forces were sent into action in Lithuania, the Twelve called once again for a peaceful dialogue and referred to the "legitimate aspirations of the Baltic peoples."[22] Referring to the CSCE obligations, so recently renewed in Paris, and disappointed by a Soviet refusal to allow the CSCE to discuss the situation in the Baltics, the Twelve threatened the withdrawal of the only recently agreed upon assistance to the Soviet Union. The problem for the EC was that while some states emphasized the attack on human rights and the right of self-determination, others worried about giving ammunition to the hardliners and therefore further undermining Gorbachev, at a time when the Soviet Union had still to ratify the Two plus Four agreements and initiate the agreed upon process of troop withdrawal from Eastern and Central Europe. This was also a time when the Soviet Union appeared to be contemplating searching for new agreements with the East and Central European states, with the idea of creating a buffer to replace the collapsed Warsaw Pact—a buffer that the West saw as potential "Finlandization."

Nevertheless, the EC did decide to try and bring its economic muscle to bear vis-à-vis the Baltics, with the freezing of some aspects of the Soviet assistance program. Once referenda had been held in the Baltic states and confirmed the will of the majority to leave the Soviet Union, the Twelve repeated their call for a peaceful dialogue and argued that the will of the people could not be disregarded.[23] The Baltic situation raised several problems for the EC/Twelve, in addition to those mentioned above. While the case for supporting Gorbachev seemed sound, it was not clear that there was much that the Community could actually do to impact on events inside the Soviet Union. That being the case, there was an attraction to emphasizing the human rights aspects of the Baltic situation, with some states keen to proclaim their support for "universal self-determination" (this was not popular with the Spanish or the Italians, for obvious reasons). This idea was not compatible with the continued existence of the Soviet Union. However, the real policy debate on this matter seemed to be carried out in the United States rather than in Europe, with some arguing that Gorbachev was a lost cause and others that the memory of the U.S. civil war should lead the United States to support the maintenance of the Soviet Union against demands for secession.

When the Baltic states seized the opportunity occasioned by the August coup to declare their independence, the Twelve were quick to recognize the three new states and soon agreed to their incorporation as beneficiaries of the PHARE program. As stated above, despite their status as former Soviet states, the Baltic states have effectively been treated by the Community as if they were part of Eastern and Central Europe. This may cause the Twelve some problems in the future—the success of the nationalists in the December 1993 Russian parliamentary elections led to nervous Baltic requests for full membership in NATO and closer relations with the EC. Inside the EC, some old members (Britain and Denmark) and some new members (Finland and Sweden) would be sympathetic to a close relationship (possible membership?) between the EC and the Baltic states. However, in their pursuit of an active human rights policy, the Twelve may well find that they are forced to side with the significant Russian minorities in the Baltic states. In July 1993 the EC and the Twelve issued a statement welcoming the amendments that the Estonian parliament had made to the law concerning aliens, which discriminated against Russians, and hoped that other states would follow the Estonian example.[24]

In 1993 and 1994, the central issue concerning the Baltic states revolved around the ultimate withdrawal of Russian troops. Although all Russian forces were formally withdrawn by 31 August 1994,[25] it was only after much prevarication on Russia's part, which caused considerable anxiety in the

Baltic states and provoked numerous statements from the EC/Twelve. In May 1994 the Estonians used the meeting at which the three Baltics states and the six Central and East European states became associate partners of the Western European Union (WEU) to call for support from that organization even though it offered no explicit defense guarantees.[26] However, once again, the credit for the eventual peaceful Russian pullout is generally attributed not to the firm diplomatic line of the Twelve but to the persistence and personal commitment of U.S. president Bill Clinton.[27]

The EU still has some difficult decisions to make with regard to the Baltic states in the future. Despite all attempts to soften the dividing line via the notion of the Partnership for Peace, Europe, however defined, will in the future be divided in some way between those who are either in or moving toward full membership of the EU and those who are not. It will clearly be in the interests of those who are not to reach an accommodation with the EU (free trade area, extension of the single market?), which, in turn, will require the outsiders to cooperate with each other to maximize their effectiveness. At present, it looks as if the states of the former Soviet Union will form that group of outsiders but, as we have noted above, the position of the Baltic states remains ambiguous, with every indication that they are headed for eventual membership of the EU.

The August 1991 Coup

The Twelve's reaction to the events of August 1991, which effectively marked the end of Gorbachev and the beginning of Yeltsin, as well as the beginning of the end of the Soviet Union, was, perhaps understandably, hesitant. Although a meeting of foreign ministers was called within hours of the coup's announcement and although action in the form of a suspension of food aid and technical assistance (this action was revoked two days later when the Twelve "learnt of the collapse of the coup with profound relief and satisfaction") was agreed on, the Twelve were clearly uncertain as to whether they should continue to support Gorbachev or seek some sort of accommodation with the coup's instigators.[28] Once Gorbachev was restored, it was clear that he had lost all authority to Yeltsin and, therefore, that the days of the Soviet Union were numbered. Although the foreign ministers of the Twelve met during the coup in emergency session and declared their concern both for the unconstitutional act and for the fate of the Baltic states,[29] the major Western actors were the United States, Germany, Britain, and France, and they seemed mainly to talk to each other via Washington.

Once the coup was over and Yeltsin predominant, the Twelve had to face the problem of whether to continue to support the maintenance of the "union" or go with the Soviet Republics (it was clear that whatever they chose would make little difference inside the Soviet Union—the problem was to pick winners and the Twelve had already made the mistake of rejecting Yeltsin in favor of Gorbachev).

The Breakup of the Soviet Union

By the time the breakup of the Soviet Union happened at the end of 1991, it was expected, and the Twelve, following a U.S. lead, met twice in December to successfully agree upon a set of "Guidelines on the Recognition of New States in Eastern Europe and in the Soviet Union."[30] The eventual application of these principles to all the former Soviet states was a lot less painful than their application in the case of the former Yugoslavia, where Germany's unilateral decision to recognize Croatia threw the EC's common stance into chaos. The Twelve worried collectively about the control of nuclear weapons and nuclear expertise in the former Soviet states of Russia, the Ukraine, Belarus, and Kazakhstan and sought, wherever possible, to link the prospects for, and content of, any partnership and cooperation agreements with, for instance, the Ukraine, to ratification of the START I Treaty and accession to the Non-Proliferation Treaty. When the Ukraine did eventually sign its partnership and cooperation agreement, concern was also expressed by the EU about the safety of the Chernobyl nuclear plant. A Franco-German initiative sought to use EU leverage and European Bank for Reconstruction and Development (EBRD) funds to coordinate efforts to decommission the remaining reactors at Chernobyl and to develop safer and alternative energy sources in the Ukraine.[31] Despite the EU's efforts, however, it has to be said that the major initiatives designed to resolve the "nuclear problem" in the Ukraine came from the United States and culminated in the Clinton-brokered deal to remove all former-Soviet missiles from Ukrainian territory that President Clinton, President Kravchuk, and President Yeltsin signed in Moscow on 14 January 1994.[32]

The breakup of the Soviet Union also raised the question of EC/Twelve representation, as well as recognition. This is a problem for all the national foreign services who are operating under considerable financial constraints. The British Foreign Office announced that five hundred jobs will be lost over the next three years and that one result might be the sharing of embassies with other EU countries.[33] Britain already shares embassies with Germany in Belarus and Kazakhstan and this may well be a trend in the future—one inspired less by a desire to enhance the principle of CFSP cooperation and more by a pragmatic desire to operate effectively in this new and challenging area. A decision to share embassy facilities occasioned by the multiplication of representational tasks in the former Soviet Union might, in the future, even lay the foundation for consideration of a division of labor between the EU states.

Support for Yeltsin and the
Partnership and Cooperation Agreement

Despite the poor long-term investment that unquestioning support for President Gorbachev had proved to be, the EU soon made support for Yeltsin the main guiding principle for its policy toward Russia. The Twelve produced statements supporting his referendum call in early 1993, as well as his action against Parliament in the autumn, and the EC/EU generally sought to make concessions in the negotiations over the Partnership and Cooperation Agreement in a bid to bolster President Yeltsin. However, when domestic politics were less dramatic in Russia, then the EC/EU tended to backtrack or to pursue more short-term objectives. Thus, in August, just before the action against Parliament, the Community sought to restrict aluminum imports from Russia (they had increased 250 percent between 1989 and 1992), an action that produced a host of complaints from Russia about the Community's general unwillingness to open up markets and treat Russia not as a state trading country but as a market economy.

In March 1993 the Commission was given an enlarged mandate by the Council that introduced the possibility that the Partnership and Cooperation Agreement under negotiation might eventually evolve into a free trade arrangement. This is the economic equivalent of NATO's Partnership for Peace, in that it represents a significant blurring of the distinction that had been established between those states with Europe Agreements that could look forward to full membership and those that could not. The idea of a free trade area (which is also to be found in the agreement with Ukraine) is similar to the past arrangements between the EC and the European Free Trade Association (EFTA), and the Russians may see that as a useful and hopeful precedent.

Despite the new mandate, negotiations with Russia slowed as the Copenhagen European Council approached. The Danish presidency had certainly hoped to round off the European Council with an invitation to Yeltsin to come to Copenhagen for a formal signing ceremony. Sir Leon Brittan appears to have put a stop to this because there were too many outstanding disagreements—including energy prices, the place of human rights, aluminum—that were too serious to paper over. For its part, Russia kept up demands to be treated comparably to the Central and East European states and continued to accuse the Community of erecting "a new iron curtain" to exclude Russia.

However, once Yeltsin took action against Parliament and his position again became delicate, the Union and its member states were quick to back him with immediate support from Britain, France, and Germany—a supportive common position from EPC, with EU willingness to once again speed up the negotiations for the Partnership Agreement. In the end, Yeltsin did get to visit Brussels (the first Russian leader to do so since Peter the Great!) around the time of the December European Council meeting but only to sign a political declaration, not the agreement he wanted. The agreement was held up until 1994 by a disagreement over access to Russia for Western banks and the safety of Russian nuclear fuel, as well as the aluminum dispute. President Yeltsin finally signed the agreement (just a few days after the Ukraine had concluded a similar agreement) at the June European Council meeting in Corfu,[34] shortly after Russia had become the twenty-first member of NATO's Partnership for Peace and shortly before he attended the Naples meeting of the G7—making it briefly the "G8." European Union leaders would argue that this represented a considerable advance for their declared policy of embracing Russia. Certainly, the Partnership Agreement amounts to a major progression in consolidating the growing relationship with Russia.

Even in 1993, Russian exports to the EU accounted for 50 percent of total exports and, with a value of $17.4 billion, considerably outweighed imports from the EU, valued at $13.5 billion. By this agreement, the EU is committed to supporting Russian accession to the General Agreement on Tariffs and Trade (GATT) and the World Trade Organization (WTO), removing all quotas on Russian exports (except steel and textiles) and regulating trade until 1998, when a decision will be made about embarking on the creation of an even more ambitious free trade area. The combination of this greater objective, along with a number of safeguard clauses, should mean that the EU will try to continue its present "stick and carrot" approach in its overall policy toward Russia, with an attempt to link trade concessions and offers of aid and credits to the Twelve's political objectives. The problem that remains is the inability of the EU member states to be that clear about specific, as opposed to general, political objectives.

CFSP Joint Actions:
The Russian Elections and the Balladur Plan

At the European Council meeting held at the end of October 1993 to herald the instigation of the European Union, the EU leaders made their first decisions about the new CFSP category of joint action. They selected five areas, and two of these are directly relevant to the EU's policy toward the former Soviet Union. First, it was agreed that observers would be sent to monitor the Russian parliamentary elections and the referendum on the draft constitution scheduled for December 1993, and second, that a joint action would be directed at the creation of a European Stability Pact along the lines laid out by French prime minister Balladur.

The decision to make the Russian parliamentary elections the subject of the European Union's first joint action was made by the Council on 9

November 1993.[35] The observers were drawn from both the member states and the European Commission and had about five weeks to undertake their task, which culminated in the elections themselves on 12 December 1993. Because other organizations (the Council of Europe, CSCE, and the UN) had also decided to send observers, the Council sought to coordinate "observer activity" via the establishment of a special European Union monitoring unit. This unit was directed by the Belgian presidency in close harmony with the European Commission. The Council decision established that the cost of this operation would be considered as administrative expenditure carried out for the Council[36] and would therefore be borne by the Community budget. The only exception to this was that the expenses incurred by the observers from the member states were paid by the member states themselves.

It was the general consensus of all the foreign observers that the voting process was fair,[37] despite the short notice that the electoral commissions were given to organize things, and that access to the media and media coverage of the elections (but not the referendum) were also fair. The problem for the European Union was not the observation of the elections but the results themselves, which were as alarming for President Yeltsin as they were for a European Union that had placed themselves solidly behind Yeltsin. The elections were a major success for Vladimir Zhirinovsky and meant that President Yeltsin was forced to make some concessions to Russian nationalist thinking in his foreign policy stances toward the European Union and the West in general.

The launch of the French-inspired EU plan for a stability pact at a conference in Paris in May 1994 received a cool response from Russia, which used the occasion to advance its own preference that a "decisive role"[38] be given to the CSCE in the construction of a new Europe with Russian participation. Noting that the stability pact proposals only involved the twelve current and nine aspiring members of the EU, Russian foreign minister Kozyrev argued the need for "a broader effort,"[39] by which he meant not just the CSCE but the North Atlantic Cooperation Council as well.

Russia and the "Near Abroad"

Ever since the breakup of the Soviet Union, the EU/Twelve have produced common positions on the numerous conflicts that have broken out within and between the newly independent states of the former Soviet Union. The EU has shared with the United States the dilemma of reconciling a desire to support President Yeltsin—especially against the demands of the extreme nationalists headed by Vladimir Zhirinovsky—with a reluctance to give Russia carte blanche in an area that it would like to feel came within its special interest. In the United States, Russia's growing diplomatic assertiveness from Bosnia to the Gulf to North Korea, as well as with regard to the "near abroad," has led to a major challenge to Clinton's "Russia first" policy— from the Republican party and from powerful individuals such as Henry Kissinger and Zbigniew Brzezinski.[40] As Cox's article, cited below, records, President Yeltsin's response to the success of the ultra-nationalists in the Russian parliamentary elections has given rise to a considerable debate in Washington about the future of their policy toward Russia. Unfortunately, it is not possible to record or report on such a debate in European Union policy circles, even though developments are obviously being closely monitored in national foreign offices.

Over the past few years, Russia has had cause to intervene in disputes in Ngorno-Karabakh, Georgia, Moldova, Tadijstan, and it has been involved in serious disputes with Ukraine, Belarus, and Kazahkstan. The response of the Twelve to what might be seen as a reassertion of Russian influence over the territory of the former Soviet Union,[41] has been to issue a number of statements, all of which refer to CSCE principles and regret the use of force but are usually supportive of Russian attempts to intervene and keep the peace. The net result is a policy that seems to accept, even welcome, a growing Russian influence over the former Soviet states. Having drawn an implicit distinction between those states that can aspire to EU membership and those that cannot, the EU, and especially Germany, has an interest in the maintenance of both political and economic stability in the former Soviet states. Given the unwillingness of the EU to undertake peacekeeping activities or to contemplate the stronger economic links provided by full membership, it may well be a rational policy to promote the further enhancement of the Commonwealth of Independent States (CIS) and the legitimization of Russian peacekeeping activity.

Some might argue that this is happening already, whether the EU likes it or not. In April 1994 Russia won approval, at a CIS summit chaired by President Yeltsin, for its role as peacekeeper and border guard. The Central Asian states, as well as Georgia and Armenia, agreed formally that Russian troops should police their borders together with their own forces, and Ukraine and Moldova signed a memorandum that went in the same direction. It was also accepted that Russia should send peacekeeping forces to Abkhazia and that it should remain in the chair of the CIS for the rest of the year. By October 1994, the United States had given its approval, albeit with reservations.[42] Furthermore, in recent elections pro-Russian leaders have been elected in both Ukraine and Belarus. Russia's stated desire[43] to create a European security system based on the CSCE but with NATO and the CIS mandated by a ten-state-ruling CSCE Committee to police their respective "spheres of influence" is a clear threat to NATO/EU domination of European security arrangements.

EU governments are already beginning to feel the influence of Russia in the "near abroad," as they are forced to listen to the complaints of business about Russian interference in the deals that they are seeking with the former Soviet states. For example, in Azerbaijan, where BP (British Petroleum) has been leading a consortium of Western oil companies anxious to exploit the large oil reserves in the Caspian Sea, Russia has stepped in and insisted that in return for assistance over the war with Armenia in Ngorno-Karabakh, Lukoil, the Russian state oil company, be cut in on the deal with a 10 percent stake.[44]

While the growth of Russian influence in the "near abroad" is probably inevitable, the way that that influence is exercised is still to be determined and the EU obviously has an interest in a CIS built, as much as possible, on voluntary cooperation. Sergia Karaganov, deputy head of Moscow's European Institute and a Yeltsin foreign policy adviser, has argued that "Russia faces a choice: that between the recreation of a Union and the imposition of an empire."[45] The EU is clearly opposed to the latter, but its interest in the former has yet to be made clear.

Conclusions: The Problem of Leadership

It is the main contention of this chapter that the EU does not have a clear and coherent policy toward Russia and the other former Soviet states. Is this because the member states have drawn the correct conclusion that they can have little impact on political developments, and so, the less said the better? Or, are they handicapped by the CFSP procedures of the EU, which reconfirm the parallel existence of diverging national foreign policies? Was it not unfortunate that in 1993, when President Yeltsin faced his problems, the United States could deliver a new, and still authoritative, president for a Clinton-Yeltsin summit while the best that the Europeans could manage were meetings with the Danish and Belgian presidencies? Is it not inevitable that the EU will always fail to deliver a "grand vision" because there is no central focus for a debate on policy toward Russia, such as is clearly and publicly going on in Washington?

Some would argue that a coherent EU policy is incompatible with the continued pursuit, organization, and implementation of national foreign policies. Despite the new CFSP arrangements and further attempts to ensure "consistency" in external policies, there remains a tendency for EC trade and aid policies to always revert, in practice, to the lowest common denominator and to stances primarily designed to protect short-term interests. The problem with developing an EU policy toward Russia and its neighbors is that it involves long-term thinking and probably the acceptance of short-term economic costs for long-term political gains. At present, policy is being made as much by default as by design. To the extent that the EU has been forced to clarify its intentions vis-à-vis the Central and East European states, it has also been transmitting messages to Moscow and the capitals of those other states that would appear to be excluded from contemplating eventual EU membership.

The danger for the EU is that for some member states, in particular Germany, the development of a coherent policy, supported by the considerable resources of the EU, is a matter of some urgency. If the EU is not able to raise its head above internal squabbles over voting rights in the Council, or the portfolios of commissioners, or the Intergovernmental Conference (IGC) in 1996, then Germany will increasingly be forced to make its own arrangements with Russia and its neighbors. As one seasoned commentator on European affairs has written, "Russia is the really big issue facing Western Europe, and it demands a European strategy. But Europeans are doing what they have done for fifty years: hoping the Americans will take care of it."[46]

One thing is certain—the observation of parliamentary elections in Russia, however fascinating to students of EPC and the CFSP, does not represent much of a response to the challenge suggested above.

Notes

1. See Elfriede Regelsberger, "EPC in the 1980s: Reaching Another Plateau?" in Alfred Pijpers, Elfriede Regelsberger, and Wolfgang Wessels, eds., *European Political Cooperation in the 1980s: A Common Foreign Policy for Western Europe?* (Dordrecht: Martinus Nijhoff, 1988), pp. 3–48.

2. See Christopher Hill, "The Capability-Expectations Gap, or Conceptualizing Europe's International Role," *Journal of Common Market Studies* 3 (September 1993), p. 311.

3. See Elizabeth Pond, *Beyond the Wall: Germany's Road to Unification* (Washington: Brookings, 1993), pp. 48–50.

4. See, for instance, A. Hyde-Price, "Future Security Systems for Europe," in C. McInnes, ed., *Security and Strategy in the New Europe* (London: Routledge, 1992).

5. P. Fraser, "Russia, the CIS, and the European Community: Building a Relationship," in N. Malcolm, ed., *Russia and Europe: An End to Confrontation* (London: RIIA, Frances Pinter, 1994), pp. 200–223.

6. See John Pinder, *The European Community and Eastern Europe* (London: RIIA, Frances Pinter, 1991), pp. 23–36.

7. Ian Davidson, "West Fails to Meet Gorbachev Challenges," *Financial Times,* 18 May 1989.

8. British, French, and German reactions to the end of the Cold War are well documented in Robert Keohane, Joseph Nye, and Stanley Hoffman, eds., *After the Cold War: International Institutions and State Strategies 1989–1991* (Harvard: Harvard University Press, 1993).

9. Pinder, *The European Community and Eastern Europe,* pp. 32–36.

10. S. Haggard and Andrew Moravcsik, "The Political Economy of Financial Assistance to Eastern Europe, 1989–1991," in Keohane, Nye, and Hoffman, eds., *After the Cold War,* p. 259.

11. P. Norman, "Who Gives What in the Aid Stakes," *Financial Times,* 26 March 1993.

12. Ole Norgaard, "The Post-Soviet Newly Independent States and the European Community: Prospects for Trade, Investment, and Aid," in Ole Norgaard,

Thomas Pedersen, and Nikolaj Petersen, eds., *The European Community in World Politics* (London: Frances Pinter, 1993), p. 103.

13. *Financial Times,* 4 February 1992.

14. Pond, *Beyond the Wall.*

15. Ian Davidson, "More of a Sideshow than a Superpower Summit," *Financial Times,* 30 November 1989.

16. Keohane, Nye, and Hoffman, eds., *After the Cold War,* p. 130.

17. Pond, *Beyond the Wall,* pp. 173–191.

18. Norgaard, "The Post-Soviet Newly Independent States," p. 101.

19. Ibid., p. 100.

20. *Bulletin of the EC* (9-1990), 1.4.11.

21. *Bulletin of the EC* (12-1990), 1.5.4, p. 139.

22. *Bulletin of the EC* (1/2-1991), 1.4.12.

23. *Bulletin of the EC* (3-1992), 1.4.2.

24. David Allen and Michael Smith, "External Policy Developments," in Neil Nugent, ed., *The European Union 1993: Annual Review of Activities, Journal of Common Market Studies* 4, vol. 32, Annual Review (August 1994).

25. S. Knights, "Russians Pull Out of the Baltics," *Financial Times,* 31 August 1994.

26. *Financial Times,* 10 May 1994.

27. See W. Safire, "Bill 'n' Boris Fix It in the Baltics," *Guardian,* 10 August 1994, and I. Black, "U.S. Cash Brings Happy Ending to Baltic Saga," *Guardian,* 1 September 1994.

28. *Bulletin of the EC* (7/8-1991).

29. Geoffrey Edwards and Christoper Hill, "A Survey of European Political Cooperation, 1989–91," *The Yearbook of European Law,* 1993.

30. *Bulletin of the EC* (12-1991), 1.4.6, p. 119.

31. *Financial Times,* 15 June 1994.

32. *Financial Times,* 11 January 1994.

33. *Guardian,* 28 April 1994.

34. "Yeltsin Signs Plan to Bring Russia Back into Europe," *Financial Times,* 25 June 1994.

35. See *Official Journal* no. 1: 286, 20 November 1993.

36. See *Treaty on European Union,* Article J.11 (2).

37. Margot Light, "The Russian Elections and After," *The World Today* 3 (March 1994), p. 42.

38. "Russia Rejects French Initiative," *Financial Times,* 27 May 1994.

39. Ibid.

40. See Michael Cox, "The Necessary Partnership? The Clinton Presidency and Post-Soviet Russia," *International Affairs* 4 (October 1994), pp. 635–658.

41. See O. Rumyantsev, "Let's Hear It for the USSR," *Guardian,* 22 August 1994; J. Lloyd, "Russia Begins to Choose Between the Union and Empire," *Financial Times,* 18 April 1994, and "Former Soviet States Bow to Moscow," *Financial Times,* 17 April 1994.

42. "Russia's Peace Role Wins U.S. Backing," *Financial Times,* 7 October 1994.

43. D. Hearst, "Russia Seeks European Security Deal," *Guardian,* 7 May 1994.

44. *Guardian,* 6 October 1994.

45. *Financial Times,* 18 April 1994.

46. Ian Davidson, "Russia Policy Is Vital," *Financial Times,* 30 March 1994.

13

The Twelve/Fifteen's Conference Diplomacy: Has the CSCE/OSCE Remained a Successful Platform?

Heinrich Schneider[1]

It is common knowledge that the CSCE/OSCE process, from its beginning until the present, was one of the most unremittingly emphasized areas of European Political Cooperation (EPC) and that the process has retained its importance, in view of efforts to implement the provisions of the Treaty on European Union (TEU) regarding the Common Foreign and Security Policy (CFSP).

The preparation and implementation of the first Conference on Security and Cooperation (CSCE) in Helsinki is generally considered to be the first successful trial of EPC. At present, perhaps the joint action that was introduced within the framework of CFSP, which aims to work out and realize a European Stability Pact, presents another extremely important test case for the pan-European development of the Community (now transformed into the European Union). This joint action has explicitly been introduced and applied to the CSCE/OSCE.

Structure and Dynamics of a Changing CSCE Process

An Experiment with an Uncertain Outcome

Until today, the CSCE/OSCE had no contractual basis. Its basic documents are, more or less, a solemn declaration of political intent but do not have legal validity recognized by international law. Thus, the Conference does not fulfill the classical criteria of organizations of international law,[2] which may suggest an inappropriate comparison with EPC.

EPC was established between the member states of an integrationist community that was striving for an ever closer union of the European people through economic integration; and to this aim, it has established an independent legal order and supranational institutions. From the beginning, EPC could rely on a fundamental premise that promoted cohesion. The CSCE lacked such a foundation.

Consequently, two antagonistic blocs of states existed within the framework of the CSCE and waged a cold war on each other. Of course, there were also the neutral and nonaligned states ("N plus N"), which, from the beginning, attempted to utilize the CSCE as a means to promote détente.[3] Despite this, one might raise the question as to why the CSCE was able to become a success story at all, under such conditions.

Especially in its first phase of development, the CSCE was judged skeptically by not just a few observers. It was argued that since the agreements lacked the validity of international law, they were more a case of political rhetoric that, in the best case, was meant well, but, nonetheless, carried only limited political weight. Advocates of a fundamental détente often labeled the CSCE an "alibi operation," which distracted the public from the absence of concrete disarmament and détente agreements. Commentators worrying about Eastern imperialism considered the CSCE to be an undertaking that implemented Moscow's coexistence strategies and therefore was detrimental to the Western position. Others hoped that the CSCE would furnish the West with new possibilities to influence the Communist sphere of control and anticipated that it might be possible to relax the atmosphere in the Eastern bloc and provide the forces of reform with more freedom of action through the influence of human rights principles and efforts regarding "Basket III." A few optimists—mostly those of a leftist-liberal or socialist background—considered the CSCE to be the basis or focal center for a new, structurally safeguardable, and thus reliable, détente—which, in the long run, could lead to a humanization of the social and political systems in Eastern Europe.

However, the undertaking was by no means an experiment devoid of risks. After the decision in favor of its adoption had been made, the participants assured each other that they would attempt to introduce cooperation in certain areas for the benefit of everyone involved and that they must strive to overcome mutual distrust. In reality, however, each side emphasized both its own trustworthiness and the right to be distrustful of its opponent.

The protagonists of the respective factions viewed the CSCE as a field of strategic interaction. A network of relations was to be established, but preferably with the result that one's opposing faction would be integrated more effectively than oneself. The Conference was considered to be an instrument of the nonviolent competition of systems. The East, incidentally, had for some time been toying with the idea of a European "people's movement" for peaceful coexistence and international cooperation as a counterpart to the "European movement"—which in the early phase of Western integration policy was by no means considered unimportant in public opinion—and as a "would-be predecessor" of the new peace movement, which arose in connection with the decision to deploy new arms and which was by no means supported solely by Communists. The Communist parties, the unions, organizations active in the surroundings of the CSCE, and sympathizing "fellow travelers" would form the core of this envisaged "mass basis." In response to this, the West supported the idea of a diplomatic conference of closed ranks. Not a few of those involved were very much surprised that matters took a completely different course when nongovernmental organizations (NGOs), in the form of human rights organizations and sympathizers of dissident groups—though hardly proponents of Eastern concepts—made their appearance (for example, the "Helsinki Watch Committees," et alia). This led to the West's support of public sessions, the accreditation of NGOs, and a public popularization of conference projects, while, at the same time, the East wanted to restrict even the admission of the press to certain official occasions.

The Change of the "Sociogram"

The CSCE policy was valued quite differently by various participating states. This resulted in a concept that overlapped and broadly modified the original "sociogram," which was made out of the delegations of the two "blocs" and the "N plus N" group.

There were a number of participating states that were particularly attached to the continued existence and success of the process, whether because of interest in détente or other reasons. Among those countries:

- The two German states, which had respective interests due to domestic, foreign, and security policy reasons
- Most members of the "N plus N" caucus, because of motives already addressed earlier (with Switzerland playing a special role)[4]
- Certain Central European states included in the Eastern caucus, such as Hungary (because of recently developed economic relations with the West and their own reasonably liberal cultural policy) and Poland (for which the consolidation of its economic and financial relations with the West had to be just as important as its satisfactory relations with the former USSR)
- States that, for whatever reasons, despised bloc unity and recognized that the pan-European framework promoted tendencies to loosen bloc conformity (e.g., Romania and, to a certain degree, France)

This provided at first an occasional and later a constant incentive to create ad hoc coalitions (and "instant" cartels) between those states that supported a strengthening of the CSCE process beyond their respective caucus limits.[5]

At times, one had the impression that the respective group was even in opposition to the "hawks" and "hard-liners" in its own camp, a circumstance that put caucus unity into question. The "hawks," for their part, had to show consideration for the position of the advocates of détente in order to retain caucus unity. The latter were in a strong position to argue that they would trigger an alliance crisis if the "hawks" decided to set off a CSCE crisis. Overall, this proved to be crisis dampening and, thus, regime stabilizing.

It is noteworthy that the unity of the "N plus N" caucus was also subjected to centrifugal forces, especially by the continuing inclusion of topics relating to military security. In this respect, the common interests of states such as Finland, Sweden, Yugoslavia, Malta, Cyprus, Austria, and Switzerland became less viable. What proved to be even more difficult was explaining to both alliances what genuine European security interests were or proposing the way in which an individual country's national vision could be expanded enough to be valid regarding the "pan-European" security interest.

Hence, a configuration developed that no longer fit the original dramaturgical scheme of the CSCE—namely, a policy that, against background competition between East and West, attempted to create dependency in one's opponent, increase one's own influence, and even provoke a moral-political exchange of blows. This became obvious as new procedures concerning the submission of texts were developed in the course of the Vienna meeting. Previously, it was customary to have "Western proposals," on the one hand, and "Eastern proposals," on the other, from which the coordinators worked out the first compromise texts, which mainly served to test the reaction of the two primary camps. Then trial proposals were made by "mixed" authors or sponsor groups, first by several Eastern and "N plus N" delegations, or by several Western and "N plus N" delegations. Finally, proposals were submitted for single elements of the final document by ad hoc sponsor groups that consisted of members from all three caucuses—naturally, on less politically significant issues, such as cultural exchange.

At any rate, the "sociogram" was in motion long before the "great change" of 1989–1990. At the time the radical change actually took place, the exponents of the new policy in Central and Eastern Europe, along with the representatives of the West, used the CSCE to lay down the new social and constitutional principles and to make solemn mutual promises of solidarity against all efforts at revision.[6]

This tendency toward consolidation also played a role in the early admission of those Eastern states, even the Central Asian ones, which had gained their sovereignty after the breakup of the Soviet Union. The attempt was made to stabilize these countries by including them in the pluralist-democratic, social-market economic, social, and state orders under the rule of law within the framework of the CSCE. It was feared that they would otherwise be subject to the sphere of influence of powers in the Muslim world.

However, the proclamation of a new age of democracy, peace, cooperation, and European unity (Charter of Paris, November 1990), under the care of the CSCE, had something of an eerie nature if one considers the fact that armed conflicts had already broken out months before between hostile people in southeastern Europe (i.e., in Knin, which was ethnically Serbian but belonged to the Croatian state) and that Zbigniew Brzezinski had already warned of a "Balkanization" of Eastern Europe and of a "Lebanization" of the Soviet Union in the fall of 1989.[7]

It was clear that the structures and resources of the CSCE would scarcely be capable of stopping these tendencies. Nevertheless, the CSCE was again proclaimed to be a major element of the European security architecture—at the minimum, in order to give the Soviet Union (and later the Russian Federation) the impression that it was fully integrated into the development of this security architecture. From a Western point of view, this was necessary because following the establishment of German unity and the agreement to grant the united Germany membership in NATO, on the one hand, and because of the dissolution of the Warsaw Pact, on the other, it became clear that the security architecture had become rather asymmetrical and that the initiative to act would now rest with the West (especially with NATO). At the same time, however, this meant that the factual "architectural" function of the CSCE, in view of the unambiguous Western center of gravity, remained open.[8]

Meanwhile, the CSCE/OSCE region, and Europe particularly, was on the way toward becoming a new order, and the OSCE would continue to play an important role. The complete arrangement, however, has not yet been laid down.[9] The OSCE will receive those tasks that the participating states assign to it, and the degree to which the OSCE fulfills expectations will depend on how the political will of those states and associations of states represented in the OSCE enable and permit the organization to do so. In this respect, at least, the European Union will play a key role.

European Political Cooperation and the CSCE

The Helsinki Conference: A Stroke of Luck for EPC

It has often been stressed that the CSCE was the first testing ground for EPC and that it passed the test successfully.[10] Perhaps because of this success, expectations regarding other activities of EPC were set too high. Its positive performance was associated with the fact that the conditions of success for EPC were far more favorable in the case of the CSCE than in other areas of action (for example, in the Middle East). This is based on structural and situational circumstances.

From a structural point of view, it was beneficial to EPC that the conference was an interaction characterized by a specific correspondence of tasks. In its beginning, EPC was primarily concerned with "exchanging information and consulting regularly," with the aim of promoting "greater mutual understanding with respect to the major issues of international politics," and, above and beyond that, EPC wanted to "increase their solidarity by working for a harmonization of views, concertation of attitudes, and joint action when it appears feasible and desirable."[11] It would be too ambitious to require common actions to be a permanent EPC task, rather than an option in only isolated cases; and it remains open which joint actions were eligible and whether they should not, at first, be exceptions to the rule. At any rate, even in these cases, joint operations were not guaranteed via EPC but were merely "encouraged."

Another factor cropped up: As was discussed previously, the "sociogram" in the early days of the CSCE was determined by the triad of caucuses. The Eastern and Western camps opposed each other, and the "N plus N" group attempted to converge common positions and joint interests, among which the success and the strengthening of the CSCE and détente played an important role. A main function of the "N plus N" delegations was to render presentation and coordination services. The East presented itself as a closed group under the leadership of the Soviet Union. The dominant power of the Western Alliance, the Unites States, showed no inclination to act strongly. As a result, the then nine member states of the EC had the chance to transform their own cooperation into a focal point for the formulation of Western positions—yet only with regard to those topics that foresaw a joint formation of opinion or will. This was especially the case for topics of "Basket II" (concerning economic relations), which fell under the responsibility of the Community, but also for other "baskets"—excluding however, the subject of military security, the latter not playing a central role in the first Helsinki Conference anyway. Overall, the Nine became the Western "party to address" in matters included within the scope of the EC and EPC.[12]

The preparation and implementation of the CSCE constituted a challenge for EPC; a better test could not have been planned. The challenge corresponded to the areas that the EPC had made its business, and excessive demands were not to be feared, for the time being. There was no competition from either NATO or any Western leader. On the other hand, the Nine, after presenting themselves as a coherent group, were exposed to a certain degree of pressure as a result of expectations from outside.

The course of the CSCE conveyed the impression to those immediately involved that the EC states had made their mark on the conference right from the beginning.[13] Although this may be an overstatement, the role that the Nine played during the conference was nevertheless more pronounced than people (even in the capitals of the EC member states) had generally expected.

This impression was also reinforced at a later stage by the fact that, for example, the French delegation—up until the "great change" of 1989–1990—emphasized that the CSCE was an endeavor by participating sovereign states and that it was out of the question that the alliances appear as collective actors throughout the conference. Hence, what was right for the EC/EPC was, in the view of the French, in no way proper for NATO.[14]

Besides joint appearances, cooperation in the context of the CSCE policy contained certain other aspects:

- Role allocation: France took over the role as spokesman for the Nine in the cultural and politico-educational part of "Basket III"; the Danish delegation endeavored to convey the opinions of the EC states to its partners in the "Nordic Council"; Italy and France undertook similar efforts with regard to other states participating in CSCE in the Mediterranean region.
- It soon became obvious that the development of pan-European economic cooperation, according to CSCE intentions, would require a linkage of CSCE efforts with the European Economic Commission (EEC) of the UN in Geneva, led by a joint effort of representatives from the EC states at the EEC, the result being that the EC began to function as a focal point for the coordination of Western, neutral, and bloc-free EEC delegations.[15]

The Community and the member states' involvement in the CSCE was also effective for the development of EPC itself:

- The persons responsible were motivated to expand and intensify cooperation in the field of foreign policy.
- EPC acquired a reputation for being effective that lasted beyond the 1970s and that camouflaged other, less successful, experiments of EPC.
- On the other hand, this involvement and the experiences therein had an effect on the "internal dynamics" of the organization, creating an awareness of problems regarding the structural relations between Community integration and EPC and also, at least reflectively, in view of the question of the inclusion of "gray area policies" into the integration process.

The EC and EPC in the Continuation of the CSCE Process

Soon after the results of the Helsinki Conference were evident, a several-hundred-page document was drafted in order to evaluate the conference and its results, with the aim of creating a suitable basis for the continuation of the CSCE policy of the EC/EPC. In the run-up to the subsequent Belgrade

Conference, a Community CSCE Working Group was formed in Brussels, taking over the agenda of the ad hoc group that was set up in 1971 and that was strongly tied to EPC. The CSCE Working Group on EPC continued to exist. After the "mixed group" had moved more closely into the "force field" of Brussels, it became more difficult for the two working bodies to reach an agreement.[16]

At the subsequent Belgrade meeting, a changed constellation came to light: U.S. president Jimmy Carter's decision to follow a more aggressive human rights policy prompted stronger U.S. engagement in Belgrade. The EC states again acted in common, on the basis of a permanent cooperation of delegations—the delegation of the presidency acting as spokesman, actively supported by the Commission, which was also in the plenum.

Yet the United States now took over the leadership in the Western caucus, which meant increased importance for the NATO group in terms of coordinating unified Western positions. Nevertheless, because of the marked polarization between East and West, very few problems were encountered.

The final document, however, was rather sketchy. On the occasion of its official adoption, the representative of the state holding the presidency issued a declaration on behalf of the Community and stressed the view that in present and future areas of competence, the EC was to be regarded as a single participating state. Earlier, the representative had reminded the audience that the member states had founded a community sustained by certain sovereign rights that, prior to the inception of the EC, had only existed on a national level. Moreover, the representative argued that the Community's jurisdictions and activities included a wide range of subjects.[17]

In Madrid, matters remained unchanged in principle. Various perspectives on the CSCE process were discussed, and papers, as well as draft proposals, were presented in the framework of EPC and under the inclusion of the Commission. Their focus was particularly on human rights and the topics of "Basket II" and "Basket III." As they had been in Belgrade, Western positions were strongly coordinated within the circle of NATO: The United States, which had become quite receptive to CSCE policies, retained its leadership role. During this time, the East-West confrontation escalated again because of the Afghanistan conflict and after martial law was declared in Poland. Incidentally, this Polish declaration of martial law was issued just as the "N plus N" group had worked out a promising draft for the final document. The events in Poland brought the conference to the brink of a crisis and led to an adjournment of over six months. Even after the resumption of negotiations, discussion proved difficult and only massive intervention from the head of the Spanish government succeeded in easing the blockade.

One reason that might explain why efforts that aimed to harmonize Western viewpoints were put under the spell of NATO was that this enabled the host state, Spain, to be included: Spain was not yet a member of the EC.[18] Furthermore, the fact that decisions were scheduled to be made regarding an extension of agendas and projects of the CSCE in the area of military confidence and security building certainly played a major role in this shift to NATO. It would have been difficult to imagine holding consultations on this topic only within the framework of the EC and not in conjunction with the partners of the Atlantic Alliance.

A few months after the conclusion of the Belgrade meeting, France submitted a proposal to all states participating in the CSCE, calling for a "disarmament conference in Europe" to which all European countries, as well as the United States and Canada, were to be invited. First, agreements were to emphasize confidence-building measures and, as a second step, the limitation and reduction of conventional offensive air and land war machinery and military personnel in a zone stretching from the Atlantic to the Urals.[19] In May 1979 the Warsaw Pact states had made a similar proposal (this proposal was put into concrete form during a conference in East Berlin in December 1979), in which the Eastern states wanted to include only the western part of the Soviet Union (to a distance of 250 km [155 miles]) and, moreover, wanted to emphasize a binding agreement to renounce the first use of nuclear and conventional weapons. The Eastern states were also reluctant to admit any new members into the alliance systems.

In November 1979 the EPC foreign ministers declared their readiness to evaluate all initiatives that discussed these matters. They particularly accentuated the French proposal and pronounced themselves in favor of working out and deciding on the mandatory negotiations at the Madrid meeting of the CSCE. NATO, as well, had judged the CSCE a suitable foundation for the project and declared its solidarity with the French proposal in December 1979—after it turned out that this new conference would be embedded in the CSCE process (the original proposal had not provided for this, due to the unfavorable atmosphere in Belgrade). The agreement reached among the NATO states was accepted by all the member states of the EC. However, three aspects were especially remarkable.

First, the EC states played a more moderate role within the Western caucus than the United States and other participating states, who toyed with the idea of pursuing a tough stance in view of the newly escalated East-West confrontation. It was decided to submit only a brief, final declaration that documented the dissent and to relinquish all preliminary agreements on individual topics, including the disarmament conference. In particular, German foreign minister Hans-Dietrich Genscher labored fiercely in order to ensure further negotiations that aimed to achieve more substantial results. He finally succeeded in winning the partners over to his viewpoint, although certain EC countries wished to support the U.S. position, at least with respect to its strong language. The now ten member states finally decided to vote for a continuation of the CSCE process. Their spokesman, Belgian foreign minister Leo Tindemans, gave expression to this in Madrid in February 1982, and the European Council confirmed the decision in favor of a continuation once again at the end of March.[20] At this point, the regime-stabilizing effects of individual delegations that were behaving more favorably to the CSCE made themselves felt.

Second, the original differences proved to be surmountable, because they were less a result of an operative decision than of declaratory policy. Most EC member states were not in favor of concrete, drastic sanctions against the East anyway.[21]

Third, in view of the strengthened importance of security-related negotiation topics, it again became clear that the exclusion of security questions from the agenda of EPC reduced the influence and effectiveness of the Community and its member states.[22]

The declarations of the presidency, issued on behalf of the EC member states—at the beginning (1984) and especially at the end (1986) of the disarmament conference (the Conference on Confidence- and Security-Building Measures and Disarmament in Europe [CDE]), which had taken place in Madrid—dealt extensively with problems of confidence and security building. And this, despite the fact that only the political and economic dimensions of European security had, at that time, been formally included in EPC responsibilities. Neutral Ireland—which had demanded an exclusion of the military aspects of security during negotiations on the Single European Act (SEA)—was satisfied. Apparently, the military aspect of confidence and security-building measures could be downplayed. However, when the CDE had concluded, the SEA was signed and sealed—though not yet in force.

By and large, the leadership of the Western group of states during the disarmament conference (CDE) was, to a large extent, in the hands of NATO, especially as Ireland—a member state practicing restraint in military matters because of its neutrality—held the presidency of the EC/EPC in the last six months of 1984. France also demonstrated occasional self-willed behavior in Stockholm, which did not help the now twelve member states to define common positions. At the minimum, there was a certain distrust toward German "Genscherism"—that is, an accommodating German attitude toward the Soviet Union—which helped the United States use its hegemonic position within the NATO framework in order to make everyone toe the line.[23] Despite this, the Twelve (through the voice of the president of the Council, the Dutch foreign minister) positively assessed not only the results of the conference, but also their own role, arguing that the Twelve had contributed considerably to its success.[24]

Soon after the end of the CDE, the third follow-up conference began in Vienna in November 1986 and was to be concluded in January 1989. During this conference, the Twelve again became more visible, especially because of the broad scope of the topics, which were backed by a range of proposals. Again, representatives of the Commission participated actively in the context of the respective delegations of the presidency, presenting numerous proposals for "Basket II"—among them, a CSCE economic conference that would be held in Bonn. A tug-of-war between Bonn and Prague, regarding the site of the conference, was decided in favor of Bonn; this was a decision that signaled the major role that the Community would play at the economic conference. It is noteworthy that the United States attempted, in the course of working out the conference mandate, to reduce the ambitious program of the Commission, which had also been strongly supported by Genscher. Once again, there existed clear implications between the positions of the United States and the Community with regard to "Basket II": The United States insisted that the COCOM criteria should be extensively taken into account and thus proposed a very modest Western position regarding technological cooperation. Genscher tried to circumvent the issue by introducing the idea of cooperation into the technical educational system, thereby transferring one aspect of the subject into "Basket III."

The joint appearance of the EC states was not only limited to "Basket II"; their contributions, for which they always sought to enlist other states as co-sponsors, had a determining influence on all phases of the negotiations. With regard to more important questions (generally economic matters), the common standpoint was, for the most part, presented by the delegation of the state holding the presidency. It nearly became a ritual for spokesmen of other member states' delegations to emphasize at the beginning of their statement that the presidency had also spoken in their name and that they would only like to make some additional remarks.

Differences existed, however, in the realm of security policy. This was demonstrated even by the seating arrangements. While the delegations in formal plenum and Working Group sessions were arranged in alphabetical order at the conference table, they sat with their state groups during informal sessions. For example, the Irish delegate initially took her or his seat with the delegates of the EC states, at the table occupied by the members of the Western caucus, and, when the topic of "security" came up on the agenda, later sat with the delegation of the "N plus N" states.

Shortly after the conference had begun, Poland proposed to proceed to the second phase of the CDE, in which negotiations were not only to be held on confidence-building measures but also on actual disarmament plans; at that point, the negotiation process became more difficult. It became clear that the acceptance of this proposal—which was already agreed upon in the Madrid mandate for the CDE of Stockholm—would imply the end for Mutual Balanced Force Reduction (MBFR).

There were now contrary positions within the Western caucus. The United States wanted continuing negotiations between the alliances. France rejected this idea and was able to win over a number of allies to support its position—understandably so, from the group of "N plus N" delegations, but less expectedly from the Eastern caucus (i.e., states that believed they would have an improved chance of emancipation from Soviet domination by means of "more open" negotiations). There was, however, another French motive:

For quite some time in Paris, the idea had been discussed that it would be beneficial to gradually elevate the commitment of the CSCE regime to the level of binding international law (this could be seen as a step toward a pan-European federation). Agreement was soon reached on the plan to legally enact the anticipated arms control agreements. If this could occur definitively within the framework of the CSCE, then a segment of the CSCE commitments would acquire the status of international law.

In NATO, however, there was resistance to giving up the current principle of "bloc-to-bloc" negotiations, and negotiations between all thirty-five CSCE states were viewed as problematic. This created a problem of dual loyalties for a number of EC states, as they were members of both NATO and the EC.

It soon became clear that the United States was not willing to give in. This resulted in setting up parallel negotiations, on the theory that the Conventional Armed Forces in Europe (CFE) negotiations were to take place "autonomously," but within in the framework of the CSCE process (not, however, within the framework of the CSCE), while further extensive confidence- and security-building measures were negotiated between the member states of the CSCE. This compromise was acceptable to all participants. Finally, the results of the negotiations were presented, in connection with the Paris CSCE summit of 1990. The problem was finally solved when the second Helsinki CSCE summit decided, in July 1992, to "harmonize" the commitments of the states subject to the CFE Treaty with those of the partners of the Confidence- and Security-Building Measures agreements. This was declared a priority task for the "Forum for Security Cooperation," which was founded at that time; but even after two years, the negotiations had not yielded any results.

A comprehensive conference and negotiation program was implemented, outside the area of military security-related problems, after the end of the Vienna follow-up meeting in 1989, in which the Community, as such, participated regularly.

The Twelve, the CSCE, and the "Change"

The fundamental change of the pan-European scenery and the consequent restructuring of the CSCE was understood by the Twelve to be a new challenge; this had remarkable effects on its position and action in the CSCE process. The end of East-West polarization and the breakdown of Communist dictatorships led to a dismantling of "system antagonism," on the one hand, and brought about the chance to develop social, economic, and political orders throughout Europe that were comparable to the ones existing (inter alia) in the member states of the EC. The new political elites in Central and Eastern Europe declared their support for a similar policy. On the other hand, old and new tensions and conflicts arose, which led, for example, to the summit declaration of Helsinki (July 1992) addressing these developments in a tone that contrasted strongly with the proclamation of the Paris "Charter for a New Europe" (1990):

> This is a time of promise but also of instability and insecurity. Economic decline, social tension, aggressive nationalism, intolerance, xenophobia, and ethnic conflicts threaten stability in the CSCE area. . . . There is much work to be done in building democratic and pluralistic societies. . . . For the first time in decades we are facing warfare in the CSCE region. New armed conflicts and massive use of force to achieve hegemony and territorial expansion continue to occur.[25]

Having heard pretentious declarations from EC officials, the Central and Eastern European states expected the Community to take over the role as center of gravity, anchor of stability, and trustee for joint European interests (i.e., maintaining or restoring peace and the development of prosperity). As a result, the Community had to develop a new *Ostpolitik* that took the new realities into account and that more and more exceeded its engagement in the CSCE process. This engagement, however, continued to be important.

This was made clear in an exemplary fashion at the economic conference of the CSCE (1990) in Bonn. In a certain sense, it caused a breakthrough with regard to the EC realizing its leadership functions. As has already been mentioned, not only had the conference mandate been worked out on the basis of a draft by the Commission, but the draft of the final document (which served as a basis for discussion and which grasped the opportunities of the situation in order to suggest to all participating states the political principles and norms of the EC) was also worked out by the Twelve and was based, for the most part, on the work of the Commission. The economic conference ended with an only slightly modified adoption of this draft.[26]

As a result of this gain in prestige for the EC and, particularly, for the Commission, the Paris summit document was not only signed by the "actual" heads of state and government but also by the president of the Commission, Jacques Delors.[27] On the occasion of its meeting in Dublin in mid-1990, the European Council had already stressed that the Community would continue to play a "leading role" in the CSCE process. The Community also sought to meet this requirement in the following period: During the second Helsinki follow-up conference, numerous member states, fully supported by the EC or in the name of the Community, submitted proposals on nearly all areas of cooperation, such as CSCE peacekeeping (Germany), the strengthening of conflict-settling mechanisms (France), the taking over of the regional arrangement function according to Chapter VIII of the UN Charter (Belgium), the appointment of a high commissioner for national minorities (Netherlands), and, last but not least, numerous proposals regarding "Basket II." In these cases, the Commission, on the basis of its extension of areas of responsibility in connection with the provisions of the Single European Act, took initiatives that went far beyond classic trade policy. These included areas such as scientific and technological cooperation, the development of telecommunications, transport-infrastructure projects, energy, and ecological policies. Perhaps it sounds too much like political self-aggrandizement, prompted by motives of "status enhancement," when an official of the Commission argues that the EC was, and will remain, the driving force behind new ideas for the strengthening of the CSCE.[28] Nevertheless, such statements do have a *fundamentum in re.*

The importance of the EC and European Political Cooperation for the recent development of the CSCE process is not only limited to initiatives regarding the classic "Baskets" and to their determined implementation. It deserves to be noted that the Community of Twelve, including its EPC, has served as a role model for the CSCE in several respects.

First, clearly the CSCE has learned from the EPC process as to what effects the establishment of a more dense and substantial communications network might have on the views and, consequently, on the positions of participating states and their political, diplomatic, and administrative elites— and especially the impact of such a network on the process of political interaction based on unanimity rule. Even before the formal institutionalization of the CSCE, the first measures of which had been implemented in Paris in 1990, the web of communications networks became denser and more complex. The number of conferences and meetings continually increased. Between the follow-up conferences in Belgrade and Madrid, from 1978 until 1980, three expert conferences were held. In the period of time between the conferences in Madrid and Vienna, the number of meetings increased to six (among them, the particularly long and intensive CDE in Stockholm). Between Vienna (1989) and Stockholm II (1992), however, an even larger number of intermediate meetings took place. Aside from the Vienna negotiations on military security and the follow-up meetings for the exchange of information and opinions, there were three meetings on the "human dimension," six additional conferences, expert meetings, forums, and seminars. This meant two nearly permanent negotiation rounds, as well as three or four official CSCE events that usually lasted several weeks. Subtracting the usual holiday periods, this amounted to one weekly session per month, not including the permanent negotiation committees. Thus, the decision had been made to intensify the process of communication to a degree that was at least comparable to the heavy schedule in the first developmental phase of EPC. Apparently, as the traditional bipolar (or tripolar) constellation became weaker, intensified efforts to promote understanding and agreement became more useful.

Second, the Paris summit, held in response to the changes in the East, brought about innovations in the form of a continuing institutionalization. The setting-up of the "Council" (on the level of foreign ministers), the

"Committee of High Officials" (made up of political directors), as well as a secretariat, appears to be a copy of the EPC model (ministerial meetings, "political committee," and secretariat). In accordance with a Helsinki summit resolution of 1992, the CSCE adopted, at a later stage, several instruments of the EC/EPC, such as empowering the respective chairman with the authority to manage the administration, as well as the quasi-institute of the "Troika" (present, incumbent, and future chair delegation).

Third, the establishment of functionally orientated institutions and agencies (the Conflict Prevention Center in 1990, the Office for Democratic Institutions and Human Rights in 1990/1992, and the High Commissioner for National Minorities in 1992) under the overall responsibility of the CSCE steering committees corresponds more to the role model of functional cooperation or integration as it existed in the early times of Western European policy.[29]

Fourth, before the Paris summit began, the participating states had agreed on a "CSCE Communications Network." The multilateral communications system of EPC (COREU) was the model for this, as may be deduced from the fact that the Netherlands, having had previous experience with COREU, made this proposal and set up the technical headquarters.

Finally, the idea also seems to suggest itself that a number of interaction patterns, thinking styles, and strategies that were observed in the EC integration process were introduced and used in the CSCE process—for example, in the concept of "package deals," in the method of one state compromising with another by "splitting the difference," or in efforts at the "upgrading of common interests." Therefore, deductions could be made regarding the appropriation of specific patterns of integration policy before the developments following the epochal events in the fall of 1989.[30]

However, this at no time led to the Community of Twelve, at the expense of its identity, "integrating" itself into the system of the CSCE, with the latter adopting features of integration. On the other hand, one can raise the question of whether and to what extent the CSCE/OSCE has become a structure of interaction in which the EC itself—or, nowadays, the European Union—can develop its power of attraction and can express its own political intentions. Accordingly, perhaps the EC/EU should, to some extent, "integrate" the OSCE into itself.

The CSCE/OSCE as a Challenge and a Chance for CFSP

The Connection Between the Union's Integration and Foreign Policy

The above headline points to the current constellation of tasks and problems in the relationship between the European Union and the OSCE.

It is a sign of peculiar dialectics: The OSCE is an interaction process in which the broadening policy of the EU is embedded; however, this broadening policy is itself delicately connected to intentions of deepening integration and is not really a part of the "foreign policy" of the Union. On the one hand, the Central and Eastern European associated partners are third-party states; on the other, they are already, to a certain degree, included in the integration process of the Union.

The unified representation of viewpoints within the OSCE, and, even more, the unified execution of rights of co-decision regarding the selection, design, and implementation of operative OSCE tasks, is part of the Union's foreign policy. In this connection, however, there are peculiar links and transitions.

This is exemplified in the case of applications for membership, not only regarding "theoretical" considerations—for instance, the question of where the "limits of the political system of the EU" lie—but in concrete terms. One sign, for example, is that since the conclusion of the accession negotiations with Austria, Finland, Norway, and Sweden—in other words, since the meeting of the European Council in Corfu in the summer of 1994—the EU presidency, as a rule, not only issued its declarations on behalf of its twelve member states, but also on behalf of the four candidates (and this, despite the fact that the membership treaties were not ratified and, consequently, not yet in force at the time).

A similar course of events can most likely be expected concerning the Central and Eastern European associated partners. Should the efforts regarding the intensification of the "political dialogue," as laid down in the Europe Agreements, yield positive results, then it seems conceivable that the EU would speak within the framework of the OSCE on behalf of a more comprehensive group of states in the near future—thus including significantly more countries than the ones already in its own group of member states. Efforts in such a direction are obvious since the drafting of the so-called Hurd-Andreatta Initiative. If things should progress in such a manner, the importance of the EU in the OSCE context would increase steadily and, in fact, make it a decisive center of gravity. This is especially important because, since the development of the OSCE's "operative" dimensions, the formal structure of a system supported by fifty states on the basis of "sovereign equality" is overlapped more and more by new power configurations, as the old configuration of bloc antagonism, with a weaker "N plus N" group, was bid farewell.

Thus, in the foreground of the Budapest follow-up conference, the idea of an "executive committee," consisting of permanent and nonpermanent members, had already been considered. This took the "iron law of oligarchy," within the framework of the CSCE/OSCE, into account—a "law" already apparent in the development of factual, structural, and procedural patterns, as the chair delegation creates ad hoc groups for the treatment of specific problems. Aside from the Troika, representatives of the more influential states and groups (as previously mentioned)—namely, the United States, the EU, and the Russian Federation (on behalf of the Commonwealth of Independent States), as well as those states particularly involved in these matters—participate regularly in such ad hoc groups. This observation also corresponds to an insight had by regime researchers in political science—namely, that "cores of strength" stabilize international regimes.

The creation of such groups implies that, at times, "nothing goes" without the goodwill of such supporters of regime oligarchy, and that the group's success depends primarily on those who are able to impose their will on the others—even if, in the end, the consensus of all participating states needs to be established for an agreement to be reached within such a closed circle.[31] If a member of the leadership oligarchy is not itself a strong state but an organized group of states or an "association of states" (*Staatenverbund*) in the process of integration, then, obviously, the inner solidness of such a construction is of considerable importance for its ability to carry weight within the OSCE context. Therefore, "deepening," "broadening," and the ability to observe pan-European stabilizer and trustee functions are clearly interconnected.

There is an initiative of the European Union that attempts to take this interconnectedness into account. The initiative was introduced as one of the first joint actions, according to the provisions of the Treaty of Maastricht, and it is possibly the first important test of the CFSP within the framework of the CSCE/OSCE.

The Project of the Stability Pact as an Example

The initiative for this first joint action was taken by the French government on 9 June 1993, with a memorandum directed first to the German, then to the British, and finally, to the U.S. government. The so-called Balladur Plan[32] assigned to the European Union the task of ensuring that existing minority problems in Central and Eastern Europe be solved in a satisfactory manner for all parties concerned, and that subsequently, the inviolability of frontiers should not only be reaffirmed but also effectively guaranteed. In this way, the development of tensions and conflicts shall be avoided and stability, security, and cooperation in Central and Eastern Europe—with the active participation of the European Union—shall be strengthened.

Those countries that are possible future members of the European Union should first be asked to participate. It is worth remembering that the European Council has assured all Central and Eastern European associated states (i.e., presently, the four Visegrád states [Poland, the Czech Republic, the Slovak Republic, and Hungary] plus Bulgaria, and Romania) full membership, under the condition that they meet the structural (economic and constitutional) requirements. In the meantime, similar treaties were signed with the three Baltic states and Slovenia. The expansion of the Union to other European countries and regions seems possible at a later phase, provided they are not noticeably embroiled in violent inner- or interstate conflicts.

It should be the task of the European Union to play the role of an initiator and a catalyzer and to support negotiations through its economic and political weight.[33] Agreement on minority and frontier questions should take place on a bilateral or subregional level (i.e., between small groups of neighboring states). The Union makes itself available for the summoning and presentation of such negotiations, so to speak, out of consideration for its neutrality and its catalytic weight. At the conclusion of these efforts, the agreements reached should function as parts of a greater whole—which is more than merely the sum of its parts. They shall play a role in a multilateral "pact," in which the European Union wants to participate as a trustee-guaranteeing power. The key elements of the treaties should be supported by agreement on a process of securing amity and on a "codex of proper behavior." A linkage with the CSCE/OSCE was foreseen, although the sphere of realization would not cover the entire CSCE/OSCE area.

The project skillfully combined different elements and intentions: First, it was an attempt to implement the frequently proclaimed theory that the European Union should serve as an anchor of stability for Central and Eastern Europe. The project attempts, in a specifically political dimension, to do justice to the European Union's responsibility for the pan-European peace and security order, above and beyond broadening association and economic aid.

Second, in this manner the influence of the European Union shall be strengthened in the pan-European context and the CSCE/OSCE process—not in an "imperialist," but rather in a "benevolent," fashion—by rendering services in the interest of the development and stabilization of the region.

Third, specific French interests apparently played a role, too. Paris wanted to insure, with its initiative, that the *Ostpolitik* of the Union will not merely be developed and pursued from a German perspective.[34]

Fourth, the initiative presented itself as an opportunity to use the possibilities that the CFSP provisions of the Maastricht Treaty offer for the initiation of a joint action—at an early stage and in a consensual and convincing manner, thus profiting the Union project.

Fifth, while the project is not able to effectively end the violent conflicts in Europe—for example, the conflict in Bosnia-Herzegovina—it can sometimes counteract the repetition of similar conflict escalations. This could help to appease the public's disappointment over the inability of the European Union (and other international organizations) to solve the conflicts in the Balkans (and elsewhere), by producing other positive results, particularly as the problems of national minorities have sensitized and worried the European public for years.

Sixth, the initiative grappled with an internal problem of the CSCE/OSCE: For many years, the CSCE Forum of Security Cooperation in Vienna had worked on a "Code of Conduct" that would consolidate and broaden the binding political principles, norms, rules, and procedures that are likely to stabilize European security. There is agreement that this "Code of Conduct" shall, among other things, affect a number of politico-military areas of behavior—for example, regulations governing the use of armed forces within a state, the commitment of armies to enforce humanitarian international law, and other legal norms. No consensus was reached on whether or not this "Code of Conduct" shall include all relevant security problem areas (or minority problems), according to the comprehensive security plan of the CSCE/OSCE. The Balladur Initiative made it possible to address such problems in a different type of negotiation process, in the event that no consensus could be reached regarding their inclusion into the "Code of Conduct," and also possibly to elevate the solutions to the level of treaty obligations bound by international law.

Seventh, the French plan to transform certain CSCE/OSCE agreements into legal norms was advanced and introduced with this initiative. One may be reminded of a concept propounded by François Mitterrand at the pan-European confederation, although the basic idea was clearly modified by Balladur.[35]

Finally, the initiative had a specific use, in view of the eventual enlargement of the European Union to the East. It was primarily concerned with reducing potential conflict among those states that were considered to be candidates for an accession to the Union. From this point of view, at least the first phase of the project appeared to be not only the Union assuming responsibility beyond its own area for the whole of Europe, but also a policy of conflict settlement that would help secure the political maturity of future members. It is certainly in the Union's interest that its neighborhood form a zone of stability. First and foremost, the Union must do its best to prevent or dispel instabilities or conflict potential within its own frontiers. In other words, the EU can have no interest in acquiring new member states if this leads to an incorporation of those states' dangerous conflicts. As much as the European Union must address the prerequisites for an Eastern enlargement in view of the issue of the economic consolidation of its future members, the EU must also think of political stability requirements. These issues must particularly be addressed because the Union, as a community of integration striving for an "ever closer Union among the peoples of Europe," needs nothing less than incitement created by nationalism or irredentist tendencies.[36] This connection between the policy of broadening and the promotion of stability can also be seen in a different light. It is precisely because the Central and Eastern European states—which the Union wants to win as partners for the Stability Pact—have shown a marked interest in membership in the EU that the Union has a chance to induce possible candidates to adopt a constructive stance concerning minority questions, by making the adoption of such a position a requirement for future membership.

The Balladur Initiative was picked up by the Union and, with a few modifications, was made the subject of a joint action according to CFSP provisions.[37] What seems remarkable, with regard to the modifications, was the stronger link with the CSCE/OSCE, as management and implementation control will be put under the aegis of the CSCE/OSCE. German foreign minister Klaus Kinkel declared succinctly, before the Permanent Committee and at the Forum for Security Cooperation of the CSCE in Vienna on 17 May 1994, that "the pact itself will merge with the CSCE."[38] This turned the joint action into an important first trial for CFSP in the direction of the CSCE/OSCE and, at the same time, within the second pillar itself. Its actualization began with the inauguration conference[39] held in Paris at the end of May 1994.[40] Among other things, it led to the setting up of two regional "roundtables" that have meanwhile begun to operate. The linking of the roundtables' functions with the CSCE/OSCE was consolidated in "evaluation meetings," at which the presidency of the EU invited, besides the members of the roundtable, all the representatives of interested CSCE/OSCE member states. The final conference, held at the end of March 1995, was to complete the Comprehensive Stability Pact.

The manner in which the CSCE/OSCE will keep to the agreements and translate them into action has not yet been agreed upon—nor has it been decided in which manner the CSCE/OSCE will look after the further development of the stabilization process on the basis of the pact. Altogether, however, the project is a remarkable and intelligent pan-European–CFSP action and will not be the last action we see that relates to the CSCE/OSCE.

Prospects:
The Enlarged EU as Power Center of the CSCE/OSCE

As was argued previously, the Community of Nine had found a field of action in the CSCE in which it was suitable to challenge the formation and development of European Political Cooperation in a productive manner. The Community of Twelve has not missed an opportunity to make its mark and to influence the pan-European political field of interaction.

Even before the broadening of the Union of Twelve, the CSCE/OSCE delegation of the EU presidency issued declarations, not only on its own behalf and on behalf of the Twelve, but also on behalf of the four candidates—Austria, Finland, Norway, and Sweden. The prerequisite for this was an intensive, on-the-spot effort to develop a mutual viewpoint and united political will among the Sixteen.

There are exceptions to this rule of presenting an appearance of acting in concert, but they are rare.[41] However, other "group formations" within the CSCE/OSCE can also be observed.[42] Nevertheless, the appearance of "acting in concert" by the EU is surely the most striking aspect of states participating in the CSCE/OSCE—one that is now almost taken for granted.

Providing that unexpected changes in the European constellation do not occur, one can assume that this development will continue and will be strengthened. This may contribute to a consolidation of CFSP, but may also give the CSCE/OSCE process a characteristic feature, as has happened in the past but perhaps may happen to an even greater extent in the future.

For this purpose, it may be worthwhile to look at the material circumstances of CSCE/OSCE activities. Compared with its wide range of topics and tasks, the CSCE/OSCE is a very modestly equipped "organization."[43] Whereas the organization of the United Nations has an annual budget of several billion U.S. dollars (not including the funds for auxiliary institutions and peacekeeping operations) and the 1993 EC budget amounts to 65.5 billion ECU (roughly $48.5 billion),[44] the budget of the CSCE for 1994 only amounted to $25 million.[45]

Twenty-nine thousand employees work for the United Nations, roughly 50,000 in all, if one includes the specialized agencies. The number of employees working for the European Union amounts to 26,000, of which 16,700 work for the Commission. The staff of the CSCE/OSCE, on the other hand, numbers less than 150 employees.[46]

The modest number of staff and equipment does not mean that financial problems are unimportant. On the contrary, negotiations have increased in intensity and energy since the CSCE/OSCE has become "operative," and the results will be decisive for its activities and public standing, since the budgetary and financial problems are of increasing importance for the entire institution. It may be that the financial contributions are a factor of rather limited consequence, but they are hardly irrelevant.

In view of all this, it is remarkable that the Fifteen, which appear jointly in the context of the CSCE/OSCE since the European Council of Corfu (mid-1994), contribute 60 percent of the budget (the contributions of the Twelve alone amount to over 50 percent).[47]

In other words, the European Union will continue to be in a position to play the role of a decisive power center within the OSCE. For a host of reasons that were explained or, at least, mentioned previously, it is in the interest of the European Union to strengthen the OSCE and to use this important field of interaction in order to promote the goals of its CFSP.[48] Conversely, it is in the interest of the OSCE region and in the interest of the whole of Europe if the EU uses its power to strive for peace, security, the strengthening of human rights, democracy, and prosperity, all within the framework of the OSCE process.

Notes

1. The author's contributions rest primarily on many years as a participating observer, and, from these experiences, he has written articles for numerous publications, such as: "Über Wien nach Gesamteuropa? Der KSZE-Prozeß nach dem dritten Folgetreffen," *Integration* 2 (1989), pp. 47–60; "Vom KSZE-Prozeß zum Gesamteuropäischen Kooperationssystem: Die europäische Sicherheit und ihr Architekturdilemma," *Integration* 4 (1990), pp. 150–164; "Wolken über Gesamteuropa: Der KSZE-Prozeß nach dem Gipfeltreffen in Helsinki," *Integration* 4 (1992), pp. 189–205. Furthermore, many contributions were made on the CSCE and pan-European cooperation in the following yearbooks: Werner Weidenfeld and Wolfgang Wessels, eds., *Jahrbuch der Europäischen Integration* (Bonn: Europa Union Verlag); yearbooks: 1990–91, pp. 41–52; 1991–92, pp. 29–43; 1992–93, pp. 27–40; 1993–94, pp. 27–40. Moreover, he made a series of contributions, such as: "Das Wiener Nachfolgetreffen 1986 der KSZE-Teilnehmerstaaten," in Alfred Stirnemann and Andreas Khol, eds., *Österreichisches Jahrbuch für Politik 1986* (München und Wien, 1987), pp. 583–561; "Die KSZE und die gesamteuropäische Zukunftsordnung," *Actio Catholica* (1991–92), pp. 27–40; "Die Bedeutung der KSZE für die Religionsfreiheit," *Kirchliche Zeitgeschichte* (1993), pp. 35–47.

2. It is by no means a matter of course that the United Nations has recognized the CSCE as a regional organization in accordance with Chapter VIII of the UN Charter. The reason for recognition seems to be the strong interest of the UN in managing its own overload via the support of other international institutions and groupings.

3. Not all participating states could be classified into one of the three groups. One position, sui generis, was occupied by the Holy Seat, although the Vatican had decided to participate fully and not merely to send a delegation of observers. This proved to be a correct decision, as the delegation from the Vatican became particularly effective in matters of Principle VII, especially because the West had decided to attribute, in the struggle for agreement on human rights issues, an exemplary function to the matter of religious freedom. See, in addition to the previously mentioned contributions of the present author, also: Victor-Yves Ghebali and Marlis Steinert, "Religionsfreiheit als Thema des KSZE-Prozesses," *Kirchliche Zeitgeschichte* (1993), pp. 47–61.

4. Yugoslavia had a few additional motives. Because of its inner structure and in view of stabilizing its chances to increase tourism, Yugoslavia had to be particularly interested in regional stability.

5. This became evident, e.g., in the different types of implementation critique, in the course of which one was more cautious regarding certain states than with others.

6. See the above reference to the "Charter of Paris," as well as the documents of Bonn (1990), Copenhagen (1990), and Moscow (1991).

7. Zbigniew K. Brzezinski, "Post-Communist Nationalism," *Foreign Affairs* 5 (1989), pp. 1–25.

8. The East obviously understood the Western comment on the fundamental role of the CSCE in the general context of the European security policy differently than the West did; otherwise, the Russian Federation would not have attempted, even as late as 1994, to propose the idea of subordinating NATO to a strengthened CSCE as a serious alternative to a NATO-dominated "Partnership for Peace." It is noteworthy that this Russian idea was not taken seriously.

9. See Heinrich Schneider and Simon Palmisano, "Europäische Sicherheitsarchitektur," *Nationale Sicherheit—Trends und Alternativen* 5 (1994) (Schriftenreihe der Landesverteidigungsakademie), pp. 1–96.

10. See Götz von Groll, "Das Debüt auf der internationalen Bühne: Die Neun auf der KSZE," in Reinhardt Rummel and Wolfgang Wessels, eds., *Die Europäische Politische Zusammenarbeit* (Bonn: Europa Union Verlag, 1978), pp. 121–138; Wolfgang Wessels, "Die Europäische Politische Zusammenarbeit," in Werner Weidenfeld and Wolfgang Wessels, eds., *Jahrbuch der Europäischen Integration 1980* (Bonn: Europa Union Verlag, 1981), pp. 115–127. See also Fraser Cameron, "Das Krisenmanagement in der KSZE und den Vereinten Nationen—Die EG und ihre Mitgliedstaaten als bedeutende Kraft und bescheidener Beobachter," in Elfriede Regelsberger, ed., *Die Gemeinsame Außen- und Sicherheitspolitk der Europäischen Union* (Bonn: Europa Union Verlag, 1993), pp. 95–105.

This section partly relies on the above contributions, as well as on analyses of EPC by Wolfgang Wessels (1980–1984) and Elfriede Regelsberger (since 1985) included in the *Jahrbuch der Europäischen Integration.*

11. "The Luxembourg Report" (Part Two), *Bulletin of the EC* (11-1970), pp. 9–14.

12. See von Groll, "Das Debüt auf der internationalen Bühne," p. 133.

13. Ibid., p. 123.

14. As a result, there was always a reference to "sixteen delegations" (in the case of the member states of NATO) or to "seven delegations" (in the case of the member states of the Warsaw Pact) in the official conference papers; the naming of the alliances, on the other hand, was frowned on. What was even more important than the official semantics was the fact that France denied the wish of other Western states to formally link the CSCE with the MBFR, arguing that the latter had been arranged by individual alliance. Similar problems came up at a later stage, at which time the discussions focused on some sort of linkage between the CFE negotiations and the CSCE.

15. See von Groll, "Das Debüt auf der internationalen Bühne," p. 132.

16. Ibid. Whether or not the fact that the pressure to reach an agreement was not as intense between the two major meetings and played some role is an open question.

17. Original text in Hermann Volle and Wolfgang Wagner, eds., *Das Belgrader KSZE-Folgetreffen* (Bonn: Verlag für Internationale Politik, 1984), p. 186.

18. See Wessels, "Die Europäische Politische Zusammenarbeit," in Werner Weidenfeld and Wolfgang Wessels, eds., *Jahrbuch der Europäischen Integration 1981* (Bonn: Europa Union Verlag, 1982), p. 297.

19. Original text in Hermann Volle and Wolfgang Wagner, eds., *Das Madrider KSZE-Folgetreffen* (Bonn: Verlag für Internationale Politik, 1994), pp. 112–115. The proposal was already made by President Valéry Giscard d'Estaing on the occasion of the special disarmament session of the UN General Assembly. On the one hand, it was generally argued that the French government wanted, by means of this proposal, to take part in the multilateral European security policy because France was not actively integrated into NATO and was thus isolated in this regard. On the other hand, it was believed that Paris aimed to include an addition, or even a possible alternative, to the bloc-to-bloc constellation, which had always been unpopular in France. See David S. Yost, "Rüstungskontrolle im KSZE-Prozeß," in Volle and Wagner, eds., *Das Madrider KSZE-Folgetreffen,* pp. 37–44.

20. See Jörg Kastl, "Das KSZE-Folgetreffen von Madrid," in Volle and Wagner, eds., *Das Madrider KSZE-Folgetreffen,* pp. 37–54 (especially pp. 48–54); and also Wessels, "Die Europäische Politische Zusammenarbeit," *Jahrbuch der Europäischen Integration 1981,* p. 297; and Wolfgang Wessels, "Die Europäische Politische Zusammenarbeit," in Werner Weidenfeld and Wolfgang Wessels, eds., *Jahrbuch der Europäischen Integration 1982,* pp. 231–240.

21. Europeans were not fond of the U.S. strategy to use the regulation of eco-

nomic relations with the East as a political weapon. This became evident in the case of the gas pipeline deal with the Soviet Union, which led to a crisis in the relationship between the United States and Western Europe. See ibid. (Weidenfield and Wessels), p. 232.

22. Whether these experiences essentially promoted the incorporation of security issues into EPC by means of the Stuttgart "Solemn Declaration," and to what extent the issues experienced within the framework of the Stockholm CDE possibly co-motivated the decision to include the corresponding perspectives in the Single European Act cannot be answered in this present analysis.

23. See Wolfgang Wessels, "Die Europäische Politische Zusammenarbeit," in Werner Weidenfeld and Wolfgang Wessels, eds., *Jahrbuch der Europäischen Integration 1984* (Bonn: Europa Union Verlag, 1985), pp. 235–244; and Elfriede Regelsberger, "Die Europäische Politische Zusammenarbeit," in Werner Weidenfeld and Wolfgang Wessels, eds., *Jahrbuch der Europäischen Integration 1985,* pp. 239–248.

24. Speeches held at the end of the CDE in Stockholm and on the occasion of the expiry of the presidency at the European Parliament. See Elfriede Regelsberger, "Die Europäische Politische Zusammenarbeit," in Werner Weidenfeld and Wolfgang Wessels, eds., *Jahrbuch der Europäischen Integration 1986/87* (Bonn: Europa Union Verlag, 1987), pp. 243–252.

25. "Helsinki Summit Declaration" (10 July 1992), sec. 12 and 13.

26. See Cameron, "Das Krisenmanagement in der KSZE und den Vereinten Nationen," p. 97.

27. Hence, this was the first time that the idea, which had originally been expressed at the first conference in Helsinki, to regard the EC in areas of its competence as a member state, was taken into account.

28. See Cameron, "Das Krisenmanagement in der KSZE und den Vereinten Nationen," p. 100.

29. The "special authorities" serving functionally defined tasks, some of which were established and others merely planned, were—according to the prevailing ideas of the early 1950s—to be set up and were to operate under the aegis and control of the Strasbourg Council of Europe. This concept only became obsolete at the time the Community of Six emancipated itself from this Strasbourg desire for "subordination."

30. Schneider, "Über Wien nach Gesamteuropa. Der KSZE-Prozeß nach dem dritten Folgetreffen," pp. 54–60.

31. The rule of consensus formally gives every participating state a right of veto, but its use can be very costly for smaller states.

32. The text is reprinted in Ingo Kolboom and Ernst Weisenfeld, eds., *Frankreich in Europa* (Bonn: Europa Union Verlag, 1983), pp. 180–186. See also Ernst Weisenfeld, "Frankreich und Mitteleuropa—Der Plan für einen Europäischen Stabilitätspakt," ibid., pp. 167–179.

33. View expressed by Prime Minister Edouard Balladur and Chancellor Kohl in their joint article in *Le Monde* and in *Frankfurter Allgemeinen Zeitung.*

34. Weisenfeld, "Frankreich und Mitteleuropa—Der Plan für einen Europäischen Stabilitätspakt," p. 175.

35. See also ibid., p. 169 and p. 174.

36. On the occasion of the inaugural conference, Edouard Balladur and Helmut Kohl published a joint article in *Le Monde* and in *Frankfurter Allgemeinen Zeitung* in which both addressed the following question: "What would the Europe Agreements be worth, even their [the relevant countries] future accession to the European Union, if grave political crises—set off by frontier and minority problems—would question this progress?" (Author's translation.)

37. The modified concept, adopted by the European Council, was published as Annex 1 to the Conclusions of the European Council in Brussels, 10/11 December 1993, reprinted in *Europa-Archiv* 1 (1994), pp. D24–D26.

38. Author's translation. *Europa-Archiv* 15 (1994), p. D439. The project thus served a ninth function—namely, to transfer a new productive task to the CSCE, which, due to its own ambivalence and shortcomings, had been put into a state of uncertainty.

39. Apart from the member states of the European Union, the following states were "full participants": nine states interested in an accession to the EU (the six associated states and the three Baltic states—the Czech Republic, the Slovak Republic, Poland, Hungary, Bulgaria, Romania, Estonia, Latvia, and Lithuania)—and a number of other states participating in the CSCE that had expressed their particular interest: Albania, Austria, Canada, Finland, the Holy See, Iceland, Malta, Moldavia, Norway, the Russian Federation, Sweden, Switzerland, Slovenia, Turkey, the Ukraine, the United States, and White Russia. The remaining states participating in the CSCE were invited to send observers.

40. The final document was reprinted in *Europa-Archiv* 14 (1994), pp. D403–D407.

41. For example, if the spokesman of the presidency is incapable to speak on behalf of the member states and the Union on matters concerning the former-Yugoslav Republic of Macedonia, at a time that Greece was blocking its recognition.

42. Proposals are, for example, submitted from the member states of NATO, occasionally from the "Central European Initiative," and recently, also from the "triad": France, Germany, and Poland.

43. The word "organization" is put in quotes because the CSCE constitutes a system of interaction that does not portray only "classical" features of an international organization: The CSCE is not based upon a founding treaty; the basic principles, norms, and rules are merely laid down in political declarations; in its structural dynamics, it more resembles an "arena" for the interaction of participating states than a crystallized "collective actor," because of the validity of the principle of unanimity and the fact that the bodies' competence of action, which makes consensual decisions without the participation of every member state, is rather weak.

44. Figures taken from Volker Rittberger, *Internationale Organisationen— Politik und Geschichte* (Opladen: Westdeutscher Verlag, 1994), p. 15.

45. According to the annual report of the general-secretary of the CSCE.

46. See ibid.; 110 people work in the secretariat, including interpreters and translators for conference meetings; without the language service, this number totals 75. In addition, there are 19 employees at the Office for Democratic Institutions and Human Rights in Warsaw, as well as 7 employees of the High Commissioner for Minorities in The Hague.

47. The contribution of the United States is 9 percent, Canada's is 5.25 percent, the Russian Federation's is 9 percent, and the Commonwealth of Independent States' (including Russia) is 13.75 percent.

48. According to Article J.1 (2) of the Treaty on European Union.

14

Political Dialogue with Third Countries and Regional Political Groupings: The Fifteen as an Attractive Interlocutor

Jörg Monar

"Political Dialogue": The Meaning of the Term

It is commonly accepted that the Fifteen's "political dialogues" with third countries are one of the main features—instruments as well as achievements—of their cooperation on the international stage. Yet, the term is mentioned neither in the long series of constitutive texts of European Political Cooperation (EPC) nor in the Union Treaty, and its meaning needs clarification.

In the London Report of 1981, the foreign ministers took the view that the member states should be able to respond adequately to demands of third countries for "more or less regular contacts."[1] In a carefully drafted official information brochure on EPC established by the EPC secretariat in 1988, mention is made of the "close links" the member states have, "whether informal or institutionalized," with many third countries and groups of third countries.[2] This suggests a basic distinction between "more or less regular" and "institutionalized" contacts and other contacts that are more of an ad hoc and informal nature.

In the past, the term "dialogue" was not always used consistently. It did happen that in public declarations, a second or third occasional meeting with representatives of a third country was referred to as having taken place as part of a "dialogue," although there had been no previous agreement on regular, institutionalized contacts. Nowadays, however, the term is only used (at least, by the Union) if three conditions are fulfilled:

1. There has to be a formal decision of the Political Committee and/or the ministers to engage in a "dialogue."
2. There has to be a formal agreement with the third state(s) concerned, which can take the form of an informal arrangement between the

presidency and the third state(s), of a common understanding through an exchange of letters (e.g., Australia), of a joint declaration (e.g., Japan), or of a formal treaty obligation (e.g., "Europe Agreements" with the countries of Central and Eastern Europe, the Visegrád group).

3. The agreement must provide for regular political contacts at one or several levels, in addition to the normal diplomatic relations.

These conditions show that the "dialogues" have become a quite specific form of contact with third countries, which—although committing neither side to any sort of political alliance—goes clearly beyond occasional meetings and normal diplomatic business.

Forms of Dialogue

Not only have the dialogues become a specific form of contact, they have also grown to a quite comprehensive set of institutionalized contacts, consisting at present of well over thirty dialogues, with individual countries as well as regional political groupings. The forms they take vary considerably from one dialogue to the other. They mainly differ in three respects:

1. Level(s) of the meetings
2. Size of the Union delegations attending the meetings
3. Frequency of the meetings

These may also be seen as criteria for the intensity of the dialogue. Unlike some of the EU's dialogue partners, however, one should not simply equate the formal "intensity," in terms of level, delegation size, and frequency, with the political importance of the dialogue. It is obvious, for example, that the political dialogue with China, which has been resumed by a decision of the Political Committee in June 1993, is politically much more important than the one with applicant country Malta, although the latter dialogue provides for contacts at one level more.

There are three main levels at which the dialogue meetings can take place. In each case the representative(s) of the Fifteen, accompanied by representatives of the Commission of similar rank, meet their counterpart(s) of the dialogue partner(s):[3]

At the *level of the presidency of the European Council,* it is the head of state or government of the country holding the presidency, together with the president of the Commission. This is the "highest" possible formula and it was limited until now to the dialogues with Canada, Japan, Russia, the

United States, and the group of the Central and Eastern European countries (CEEC). The frequency of the meetings—at least, as it is foreseen—varies from occasional ad hoc meetings (e.g., CEEC) to biannual meetings (e.g., the United States).

At the *ministerial level,* it is either the foreign minister of the presidency, or the ministerial Troika, or all the foreign ministers together with one or (sometimes in the latter case) several members of the Commission. The "one minister formula" is applied, inter alia, in the dialogues with Cyprus and India; the "Troika formula," inter alia, in the dialogues with Australia and China; and the "Fifteen formula" mainly in the dialogues with regional political groupings. The latter formula being the "heaviest" from the point of view of organization, meetings under this formula are, in most cases, held on the occasion of association council meetings (e.g., dialogues with the ACP groups [Africa, the Caribbean, and the Pacific area] and the Baltic countries), of the openings of the United Nations General Assembly (e.g., dialogues with the Rio Group and Russia), or in combination with ministerial meetings provided for by cooperation agreements (e.g., dialogues with the ASEAN countries and the San José Group). An exception is the dialogue with the United States, which provides for biannual ministerial meetings on the basis of the "Fifteen formula," biannual ministerial meetings of presidency and Commission, and additional ad hoc ministerial meetings that can take various forms (including Troika). Contacts at the ministerial level still add some luster to dialogues, not only because ministers are involved but also because some of the dialogues (e.g., Pakistan and the Ukraine) do not provide for contacts at this level.

At the *level of the political directors,* it is either the political director of the presidency (e.g., dialogues with New Zealand and Switzerland) or the Troika (e.g., dialogues with Russia and Turkey). With the exception of some major group-to-group dialogues (Andean Pact group, ACP countries, Rio Group, Gulf Cooperation Council, and Central America), most of the dialogues provide for contacts at the political director level, so that this level of contacts can be regarded as a kind of backbone of the Union's dialogue activity. Some of the dialogues provided for at least one meeting during each presidency (Canada, Japan, and the United States), a circumstance that has put increasing strain on the directors' heavily charged agenda, and meetings at the deputy political director level only are, until now, limited to the dialogue with Pakistan.

Apart from these three main levels, some dialogues also provide for regular contacts at *senior official or expert level* (normally, the heads of the divisions being in charge of relations with the country concerned in their national foreign ministries and the Commission) or at *parliamentary level* (members of the CFSP [Common Foreign and Security Policy] committee and/or of the corresponding delegation of the European Parliament).

Reasons for Engaging in Dialogues:
The Perspective of the Fifteen

Seen from a historical perspective, the main reason for setting up dialogues has been a strong demand from third countries to enter into somewhat more structured relations with the emerging political actor, EPC. The Six (and then the Nine) had to meet this demand, which at the same time allowed them to strengthen their collective diplomacy via a set of regular high-level contacts with third countries.

This "reactive" component of the dialogues' origins does not mean, however, that there were and are no other good reasons for engaging in dialogues on the European side.

First, the dialogues are a very flexible instrument. They can be established by a mutual agreement that does not even need to be formalized. They can precede or complement intensified economic relations. They commit both sides only to more or less regular contacts at one or several levels—not to any common political position—and even the commitments entered in respect to contacts can be handled flexibly according to interests and time constraints. Also, each dialogue can easily be intensified through additional ad hoc meetings, an increase in the number of regular meetings, or meetings at a higher level. Last but not least, a dialogue can also be "frozen" with relative ease; for example, meetings can simply be suspended in the event of perceived misbehavior of the dialogue partner, as has happened, for instance, to the dialogue with China after the violent repression at Tiananmen Square in June 1989.[4] In sum, the dialogues are a form of structured political relations that can easily be adjusted to the Fifteen's political ends without creating any substantial political obligation for them.

Second, the dialogues are a convenient way to convey political positions the Union has agreed on to third countries and a way to try and convince them to support these positions, or even an international initiative of the EU, for example, in the framework of the UN or the Conference on Security and Cooperation in Europe (CSCE). The regular contacts and the regular flow of information they entail create a favorable climate for better comprehension of the Fifteen's positions and more willingness to support or, at least, not to oppose these positions. Although no third country will publicly admit that it has adopted this or that position partly under the influence of its political dialogue with the EU, diplomats of the Fifteen frequently point to this "conveyer role" of dialogues as one of their essential "raisons d'être."

Third, dialogues can be a valuable instrument in pursuing certain mid- or long-term political strategies. Such aims can be the preparation of applicant countries for membership (as was done—not with overwhelming success, with respect to the CFSP chapter—in the dialogues with Austria, Finland, Norway, and Sweden), the adding of a political dimension to formerly almost exclusively economic relations (dialogue with the ACP countries), or the encouragement of regional cooperation or peaceful conflict resolution (Rio Group, San José Group).[5] Using the dialogues for the protection of human rights in third countries is also among the Union's long-term strategies. Yet the fact that most of the member states reacted negatively to the strong emphasis the last Portuguese presidency laid on human rights in the dialogue with the ASEAN countries (i.e., the East Timor problem) may be taken as an indication that they are not really prepared to make the existence of a dialogue dependent on human rights issues.

Fourth (and closely linked with the two previous points), dialogues allow the EU to affirm their collective identity vis-à-vis the dialogue partners. It is true that normally all, or at least most, of the Fifteen have more or less developed bilateral relations with the dialogue partners and that these partners can become familiar with all major positions adopted by the Union through their official statements on international issues; but in bilateral relations between the EU and a third country or a group of third countries, the Fifteen usually only appear as an "acting" collective identity through the high-level contacts of the dialogues in which they explain common positions and listen and react to the positions taken by the dialogue partners.

Fifth and finally, there are the advantages of an increased level of information, such as the possibility of complementing the information collected through bilateral contacts, of getting a clearer idea about the positions (and internal divisions) of other regional political groupings, and of creating new contacts at various levels, which may afterwards ease the flow of information.

If these reasons for engaging in dialogues are valid for the Fifteen as a group, one should also not forget that some of the member states may appreciate dialogues for more national reasons. Some of them may see a dialogue as a means of supporting certain national positions on the international stage (such as France, in the dialogue with ACP countries), others simply as an occasion—when holding the presidency—to add some political prestige to their diplomacy. Some of the smaller member states would certainly have many fewer high-level contacts with third countries if the EU's set of dialogues did not exist. This adds to the willingness to bear the organizational burden of the dialogues, which is particularly heavy for the smaller foreign ministries.

Reasons for Engaging in Dialogues:
The Perspective of the Third Countries

Most of the Union's dialogues have been established on the demand of third countries. Recent examples for such demands are those of the CEEC, of several countries of the former Soviet Union, and of Switzerland. What are the reasons for this strong and apparently still increasing demand?

Some of the EU's reasons for engaging in dialogues are certainly also valid for their dialogue partners. The flexibility of the instruments has its advantages for them as well, and so has the conveyor role of dialogues and the increased level of information they can provide. Yet, the mid- or long-term strategies they pursue by engaging in dialogues can be quite different from those of their European partners.

For a quite considerable number of third countries, dialogues with the Union appear very attractive because of the huge economic power of the European Community. It is true that in formal terms the Fifteen only pursue intergovernmental cooperation in the field of foreign and (only recently) security policy. But many third countries have never really accepted the legally rigid, but politically subtle, distinction made by their European partners between "pure" foreign policy issues to be dealt with by the Union and "pure" economic and financial issues to be dealt with by the Community. Quite understandably, it has been difficult to convince them that ministers who meet as the General Affairs Council in Brussels to decide on major Community issues have no power over the Community's external economic relations and development policy when talking to their counterparts in the framework of "political" dialogues. The presence of Commission representatives in these meetings has only added to the impression that the distinction between foreign policy and economic and financial issues is more declaratory than real.

Contacts with the Fifteen in the framework of dialogues, therefore, mean for many dialogue partners a convenient way to have regular contacts with high-level representatives of the economic giant—namely, the Community. This is particularly true for the developing countries of the Andean Pact Group, the San José Group, the Central American Group, and the ACP Group, but also for groups with more specific economic interests, like that of the Gulf Cooperation Council.

No less important for many dialogue partners is the symbolic political value of being engaged in a structured political relationship with the EU. For some of them, it helps to assert their independent standing in international relations. Examples here are the position of Australia vis-à-vis the United States and (with a more dramatic note) of the Ukraine vis-à-vis Russia. For others, having a dialogue means to underline their claim to political nearness to the Europe of the Fifteen and to future membership in the Union. Examples here are the Baltic states and the CEEC, which are both bringing their strong security policy into the dialogues, and Turkey, which has always regarded its dialogue as one method of paving the way for membership. Finally, a dialogue with the Union may simply be a precious instrument for increasing international diplomatic prestige or paving the way for a general political rehabilitation. An example of the latter has been the recent resumption of the dialogue with China, which gave a strong signal on the international stage.

There are, of course, also the countries that—mainly due to their economic and/or military strength—do not have to seek a dialogue for economic reasons or for asserting their political positions in international relations. These countries are nevertheless interested in a structured political relationship with the Fifteen, which is appropriate for the importance of their international status and for the importance of the EU's collective weight. The interest of the Fifteen in such a relationship being normally at least as strong as the third country's, dialogues then take a particularly intense form, which also, for the outside world, underlines the importance given to this kind of structured relationship. Examples here are the dialogues with the United States (whose broad range and frequency of contacts is particularly impressive),[6] Canada,[7] Japan,[8] and Russia.[9] In these cases, the demand to establish a dialogue cannot be located on one side only but takes the form of a more or less common initiative. Needless to say, these "big" dialogue partners sometimes try to convey their political positions to the Union in a much more than informative manner, for which the U.S. gatherings with the Twelve during the Gulf crisis are a good example.

Last but not least, there is also the aspect that dialogues largely function as a consensus operation, which means that dialogue partners have ample opportunities to avoid those topics that are particularly unpleasant for them. Also, one dialogue partner normally avoids blaming the other partner publicly for positions taken within a dialogue or for the disappointing results of a meeting.

Major Trends of Development

The number of dialogues has significantly increased during the last ten years and—taking into account the continuing external demand—is likely to increase further. A number of major development trends that have emerged during the last years are likely to persist as well.

First of all, the European Union is consistently expressing its interest in dialogues with regional political groupings and its group-to-group dialogues cover, at present, over one hundred third countries. For the Fifteen, dialogues with regional groupings have advantages with respect both to practicability and to political content.

Taking into account the heavy organizational burden for the presidency and the increase in timetable problems each new dialogue brings with it, agreeing on regular contacts with a group of countries rather than with each of them individually is a very powerful practical argument in favor of dialogues with regional groupings. This argument has played an important role in the establishment of all the group-to-group dialogues existing until now.

But there are reasons of political content as well. The central elements of the *acquis politique* of the EU encourages regional cooperation and peaceful regional conflict resolution. Group-to-group dialogues are obviously the most appropriate means to encourage such developments and to influence regional groupings in this direction, if necessary with the help of various economic and financial incentives of the Community. The dialogues with the San José Group and the Central American states are successful examples in this respect.

The political interest of the Fifteen in dialogues with regional groupings is even greater in the case of groupings that are geographically on the doorsteps of the Union, such as the CEEC, the Baltic countries, and the Arab League. Here, the Fifteen try, through the dialogues (the one with the Arab League has been downgraded to the technical level for some time, due to the Libyan problem), to stabilize their immediate environment, which gives a particular quality to these contacts.

It should be noted, however, that the group-to-group formula also creates problems. Many of the countries, being part of regional groupings, would have preferred individual dialogues with the Union and have reacted with some disappointment to the establishment of a group-to-group dialogue instead. This is true, for instance, for many of the ACP countries. In the case of the CEEC, the Union even had to press quite strongly for the establishment of a group-to-group dialogue; the CEEC have always expressed a clear preference for having individual political dialogues with the EU, as this is, in fact, provided for by the Europe Agreements.[10] Poland even went so far as to press for the establishment of a joint EU/Polish political committee. Consequently, the Union's objective to establish a dialogue with the entire group met with little enthusiasm—in some cases, even clear resistance. In the end, the CEEC accepted a group-to-group dialogue, but only after the EU had renounced the idea of replacing the individual dialogues with the group dialogue and after they had established an explicit link between the group dialogue and preparation of the CEEC for membership.[11] Although the group-to-group dialogues are normally not too much affected by such initial disappointments or reticences, there is a risk that countries that are particularly keen to cooperate with the Fifteen lose some of their enthusiasm if they are forced to bring it to bear only from within a large grouping of their own region.

Another problem is that regional groupings (and the Fifteen themselves are a good example of this) tend to agree only on the least common denominator when it comes to common positions on foreign affairs issues, which makes it difficult for the Fifteen (if they can agree on such an intention) to go very far. A case in point here is the dialogue with the huge group of the ACP countries, which has not produced very substantial results until now.

A fairly new, but nevertheless important, trend is to include obligations to enter into a political dialogue in association treaties concluded with third countries, as has been done in the case of the Europe Agreements with the CEEC. The advantages of such a formalization are that the dialogue is thereby put on a treaty basis and that it is directly and firmly linked with the close relationship established at the Community level. A possible disadvantage is that dialogues entered into on such a solid basis may be less easy to adjust to changing political circumstances. "Freezing" a dialogue that was provided for by a Europe Agreement will certainly be a much bigger step than suspending the informal dialogue arrangements that existed with China before 1989. Nevertheless, the first Europe Agreements have established an important precedent that may become a model for other association agreements as well.

Another trend is that of a growing decentralization of meetings. In order to avoid the timetable and other organizational problems of organizing special meetings in capitals of the dialogue partners, more and more meetings (particularly at the ministerial and political director level) are organized in the margin of other international gatherings, such as association council meetings (e.g., dialogue with Turkey), CSCE summits (e.g., dialogue with the Baltic states), or the opening of the United Nations General Assembly (e.g., dialogue with China). This helps to keep up to the frequency of meetings as provided for by the existing agreements, but, at the same time, it is somewhat to the detriment of the solemnity and the political prestige of the high-level meetings, which appear to be a marginalized event compared to the main international gathering.

Finally, there is yet another trend, mainly due to problems of time and organization, and this is the growing decrease in participation at meetings. For the past couple of years, it has become a growing practice that ministers of foreign affairs send junior ministers as their deputies to dialogue meetings at the ministerial level. This has not always been appreciated by dialogue partners but may be inevitable, at least in many cases. The agenda difficulties of the political directors (which play a key role in most of the dialogues) have increased quite considerably as well. In order to discharge them, there is a growing tendency in dialogues to provide for regular meetings at the deputy political director level only (e.g., dialogue with Pakistan) or senior official level (e.g., dialogue with the Baltic countries). Such official arrangements with dialogue partners for meetings at a slightly lower level are certainly preferable to a situation in which partners would have to see an increasing number of meetings scheduled at political director level, the Fifteen silently replacing their directors by more junior officials.

Problems of Performance

Some performance problems of the dialogues have already been mentioned: the heavy burden the ever increasing set of dialogues places on the Union and, in particular, on the member state holding the presidency; the substance problem of some of the group-to-group dialogues; the dissatisfaction of some individual third countries with the group-to-group formula; the "marginalization" of dialogue meetings on the occasion of other international gatherings; and the decrease in the level of participation in meetings.

To these, one may add the old problem of discontinuity—that is, the fact that due to the rotation of the presidency, dialogue partners have to deal with a different set of representatives every sixth month, except for those of the Commission, which represents the only element of continuity. It has been said that this increases the influence of Commission representatives in dialogue meetings, and this may be true to some extent. It should be noted, however, that there are still some regular contacts provided for at the level of the presidency only (one example is the dialogue with Australia at the ministerial and political director level). Since the Commission participates in all other types of dialogue meetings, we have here another element of discontinuity that—in addition—is not in line with the "full association" of the Commission provided for by Article J.5(3) of the Union Treaty.

Yet the biggest problem of performance the Fifteen have to face with respect to their many dialogues is that of how to keep all of them manageable, particularly in the light of the prospect of even more dialogue commitments coming up in the future. It hardly seems an exaggeration to say that many third countries are competing for "upgradings" of their dialogues with the Union, asking for higher levels of meetings and/or more frequent meetings. There is a serious risk that the dialogue system will become the victim of its own success.

The Fifteen have already started to react to this challenge. On the one hand, they are trying to play down the political importance of the dialogues in their relations with third countries. On the other hand, they are pursuing a more restrictive approach to dialogue commitments than in the past. In November 1992, the member states already agreed on a number of nonbinding guidelines, such as adapting political dialogue commitments to the changing importance of dialogues, limiting meetings at the ministerial level to one per presidency (in whatever formation), spreading contacts over successive presidencies, and allowing presidencies to deploy deputy political directors or regional directors or to ask any one member state of the Troika to conduct a dialogue on behalf of all partners. Provided that such pragmatic adjustments are made in full agreement with the dialogue partners, they can certainly be useful. In addition, the Fifteen could consider the possibility of presidencies entrusting certain dialogue contacts to other members of the Troika or to the enlarged Troika and of reducing the commitment to regular annual or biannual contacts to the level of the political directors or the deputies, providing for meetings at the ministerial or head of state or government level only on an ad hoc basis or a biannual basis. Some of the briefing of third countries could also be carried out by the CFSP Unit (former EPC secretariat) in the Council secretariat. Such solutions may not please some of the member states, but a certain streamlining and a partial shrinking of many dialogues may prove necessary to keep the entire dialogue system operative.

Conclusions

The persisting strong interest of third countries in political dialogues and the impressive set of dialogues that has been set up until now clearly show that the dialogues have become a major policy instrument of the EU. The increasing regional and global responsibilities the Union has to face will only add to the value of this instrument.

Yet, like any instrument, the dialogue system needs to be handled with some circumspection. This means, for example, that however attractive group-to-group dialogues may seem, they should not lead the Fifteen to overlook the importance that political contacts with individual group members or subgroups of countries might have. This also means that the flexibility of the instrument—perhaps one of the main reasons for its success— should be protected against greater and more increasingly stiff commitments. In consequence, a too rigid codification of commitments, as well as an overload by too many and too frequent multilevel dialogues, needs to be avoided. In this respect, more dialogues with less frequent meetings at fewer levels seem to be preferable to fewer dialogues with very intense commitments.

Also, like any instrument, the dialogue system needs a certain amount of regular restructuring. In view of the increasing load in terms of organization and time, this means, above all, that new procedures to reduce the burden of the presidency, new formulas for contacts with third countries, and new divisions of tasks between the various levels of contact have to be found.

Notes

1. *Bulletin of the EC,* Supplement 3 (1981), p. 14.
2. European Political Cooperation, Luxembourg: 1988 (Office for Official Publications of the European Communities), p. 15.
3. The following details on a number of dialogues are mainly drawn from an unpublished report established by the Political Committee in November 1993. They have been updated by more recent information from the CFSP Unit of the general-secretariat of the Council.
4. See *EPC Bulletin,* 1989, Doc. 89/171.
5. See the "overall objectives" defined in the joint declaration concerning relations between the European Community and the Rio Group of 20 December 1990, *EPC Bulletin,* 1990, Doc. 90/474, pp. 524–525.

6. The basis for the dialogue with the United States is the "Declaration on EC-U.S. relations of 23 November 1990," *EPC Bulletin,* 1990, Doc. 90/432, pp. 463–466.

7. See "Declaration on EC-Canada relations of 22 November 1990," *EPC Bulletin,* 1990, Doc. 90/431, pp. 461–462.

8. See "Declaration on EC-Japan relations of 18 July 1991," *Bulletin of the EC* (7/8-1991), pp. 109–110.

9. See "Conclusions of the Copenhagen European Council of 21/22 June 1993," *Bulletin of the EC* (6-1993), p. 14.

10. Title I of the agreements provides for regular bilateral meetings at various levels, including the parliamentary. See S. Benyon, "Les accords européens avec la Hongrie, la Pologne et la Tchécoslovaquie," in *Revue du marché unique européen* 2 (1992), pp. 37–38, and Franklin Dehousse and P. Vincent, *L'accord européen de 1991 entre la Communauté et la Hongrie* (Liège: Centre Européen Fernand Dehousse, 1993), pp. 68–69.

11. See the "Conclusions of the Copenhagen European Council of 21/22 June 1993," *Bulletin of the EC* (6-1993), p. 18.

15

The Twelve,
the United Nations, and Somalia:
The Mirage of Global
Intervention

Patrick Keatinge

Many of the changes in the international system since 1989 have quite naturally focused our attention on the redefinition of the European region, and of the European Union's (EU) role in that regard. Nevertheless, one of the most fundamental of these changes lies in the very structure of the system, transformed from a marked bipolarity to an uncertain diffusion of power, with consequences for global security. The way in which the international order is managed is no longer viewed as a byproduct of East-West relations; rather, the point of reference has become the "international community," and the redefinition of that somewhat amorphous concept has, in turn, revived interest in the United Nations (UN).

Thus, any consideration of how the Union has adapted its collective efforts to the post–Cold War era requires a reassessment of its relationship with the UN. There is a particular relevance to the most acute problem of international security inside the European region, the war in former-Yugoslavia, which is examined in a separate chapter.[1] However, the concentration on the crisis in the Balkans has perhaps obscured the less widely noticed, but sometimes equally important, changes in the ways in which the policies of the Union mesh with those of the world outside Europe. Indeed, it is argued here that this has become an increasingly significant aspect of the evolving Union's "presence" as a collective entity in the international system; however, experience to date also suggests that the EU is still far from being a full-fledged "international actor" in the domain of international security.

Chris Hill has identified six "conceivable future functions" for the EU in the changing international system, or ways in which it might enhance its presence, and these provide an initial benchmark to assess the current situation.[2] Three of these are of particular relevance to security issues outside Europe. As a "global intervenor," the EU might find itself either competing

275

with or substituting for the United States in interventions on a global basis. As a "mediator of conflicts," it might use its diplomatic assets or even act as a "coercive arbiter," while as a "bridge between rich and poor," it might take effective action to reduce the degeneration of North-South relations. The explicit inclusion of "security" and "defense," in the language of the Maastricht Treaty, together with the revival of the UN's role in global security, at least suggests the possibility of the European Union extending its activity in these ways. The aim of this chapter, therefore, is to assess the extent to which the Union seems to have moved in this direction in the early 1990s.

It is first necessary to summarize the recent changes in the UN, in themselves affecting a familiar pattern of behavior in European Political Cooperation (EPC), and to review the EC (European Community)/EU's involvement in the UN's response to security crises in the post–Cold War era. The UN intervention in Somalia, from 1992 on, is then examined in more detail. This particular episode became an important test case for the definition of UN practice, as well as demonstrating the major dilemmas confronting the member states in their attempts to mesh a strong regional identity with global systemic security. Finally, the analysis concludes that although the EU's presence has been enhanced in some respects, the proposition that the Union is on the verge of achieving its "conceivable future functions" remains in doubt. The Union's commitment to global security has come up against constraints that can only be removed by significant adjustments to both the Common Foreign and Security Policy (CFSP) and the security policy of the UN.

From the "Old UN" to the "New UN"

For the greater part of the history of European Political Cooperation, the United Nations remained in the background of the EC states' attempts to establish a collective presence in the international system. Although the UN Charter was the central legitimating element in the formal structure of the international system, political behavior was determined mainly by East-West antagonism, and a major effect of that antagonism was to paralyze the UN as an instrument of global security.

Thus, it was only after a significant improvement in East-West relations resulted in the Federal Republic of Germany gaining membership of the UN in 1973 that the politics of the General Assembly made some mark on the evolution of EPC.[3] The Nine were faced with the challenge of formulating a collective response to a broad "global" agenda beyond their control and sometimes to initiatives that they would rather have avoided. The annual sessions of the General Assembly thus became something of a test-bed on which the performance of EPC was demonstrated. The analysis of voting behavior, notwithstanding its limitations in evaluating the quality of solidarity, showed both the durability and the limits of collective commitment.[4] The presidency's opening statement came to be regarded as an embryonic "state of the union message."

All of this contributed to the distinctive diplomatic profile that the Nine, and later the Twelve, acquired in New York. However, the significance of this achievement must be qualified in two respects. First, New York was rarely at the center of world politics during the bipolar era, and, second, even when it was the Security Council remained out of bounds for EPC. As permanent members, France and the United Kingdom insisted on their freedom of action, and discussion of ways to moderate the divisive effect this might have on the Union's position was itself taboo. Thus, so far as collective action on security policy was concerned, the UN's influence on the EU was limited and indirect. UN resolutions provided policy legitimation that was stitched into the Union's common positions (especially on the Middle East), but when it came to the broader question of how a global security regime might best be organized, the Assembly remained on the sidelines. As recently as 1988, the Twelve joined in resisting an insistent Soviet attempt to bring a more comprehensive and politicized concept of security into the Assembly's First Committee.

Participation in the low-profile peacekeeping operations of the UN was also a matter on which the member states of the EC would go their separate ways. Military cooperation remained outside the domain of EPC, mainly because of fears of decoupling the Atlantic Alliance, but also in response to Ireland's reluctance to become involved in any military alliance. The restriction, in the Single European Act (SEA), to the "economic and political aspects of security" confirmed what had, in any case, become the prevailing practice. That did not preclude member states from contributing to either UN or ad hoc peacekeeping operations, but their decisions to do so remained essentially national.

From the late 1980s, however, the image of a generally weak UN and, in particular, a paralyzed Security Council no longer corresponded to reality. The "end of the Cold War" may be most readily associated with the dramatic events in European politics in 1989–1990, but one of its first manifestations was the unfreezing of the Security Council following the superpowers' arms control breakthrough in the Washington Treaty of 1987. The major powers now saw it as a forum for creative multilateral diplomacy rather than the sterile ritual of confrontation. There was renewed interest in the UN Charter as the central source of global norms, and a change in emphasis from the General Assembly, with its inherent Third World bias, to the original concept of a United Nations with a strong political leadership exercised in the Council.

The nature and extent of this transition is still far from clear, but there can be no doubt that it has already posed fundamental challenges to all the

UN's member states and is bound to affect the ways in which the Union, as a uniquely cohesive group of states, see themselves within the UN context. There is no little irony in the over-representation of the EU (with two out of five vetoes) in that UN organ, where they find it most difficult to act as one; nor is it certain that they can agree on the reforms of the UN's structures and procedures required by the increased demands being made on it. Yet it is in meeting these demands, often in a rather haphazard and pragmatic way, that the new "rules of the game" are being written, both for the UN and for the emerging Common Foreign and Security Policy of the European Union.

Global Security: The Post–Cold War Experience

The Security Council (SC) was the institutional focus of the international community's response to the first major crisis of the post–Cold War system, Iraq's invasion and annexation of Kuwait in August 1990. During the next four months, there were no less than twelve SC resolutions, condemning Iraqi behavior and authorizing stringent economic sanctions.[5] The twelfth, Resolution 678, went further by authorizing member states to "use all necessary means"—the late-twentieth-century euphemism for "force." This formed the basis for the subsequent war, in which an ad hoc coalition led by the United States expelled Iraq from Kuwait.

The Twelve shared general interests in such a serious crisis for global security; it was, at the same time, a blatant challenge to the international rule of law, a further destabilization of regional politics in the Middle East, and a threat to oil supplies. They also had their individual concerns. The larger member states had significant commercial interests, not least in the arms trade to both sides up to the invasion of Kuwait. Even smaller countries had significant direct interests at stake; Ireland, for example, suffered serious losses in beef exports, and more than four hundred Irish citizens were hostages in Iraq.

There were, therefore, strong incentives for the Twelve to coordinate their own position and, thereby, to influence the UN's collective policy. The impending Intergovernmental Conference (IGC) on Political Union, already scheduled for December 1990, increased the awareness of all concerned that their solidarity was being exposed to a critical test. However, a divergence of national positions, particularly in participation in the eventual war, became evident.[6]

In the initial stage of the crisis, EPC action meshed reasonably well with the mobilization of a consensus in New York. The Twelve deployed the instruments of "civilian power"—a coherent declaratory policy and agreement on economic sanctions. In the subsequent war of nerves, however, the collective response was less impressive. Even implementation of the agreement to compensate front-line states for losses unfairly incurred as a result of sanctions was bogged down (in the *communautaire* rather than EPC side of the policy process). The agreed on position not to engage in bilateral deals with the Iraqis on the hostage issue looked decidedly patchy well before all the hostages were released.

The military implications were problematic from the beginning. The UN's repertoire of deliberate escalation from "soft" to "hard" measures was clear in theory, but not in practice. The Charter's development had been stunted by the Cold War, and the full rigors of collective security (particularly in Article 43) would not necessarily be exercised. Some of the Twelve (e.g., Italy and Spain) were anxious to seek additional legitimation by coordinating positions in the Western European Union (WEU) and, together with France especially, by the same token sought legitimation for WEU. Others either did not want to be associated with such a body (Ireland) or simply seemed to need very little external legitimation at all (the United Kingdom).

The fact that the Security Council, and not the General Assembly, was the formal setting in which these ambiguities were explored no doubt put the Twelve's political coordination at something of a disadvantage. Nevertheless, this procedural weakness was probably less important than the substantive differences that were clear in the attitudes of the two permanent EC members on the Council. The British were quick to revive the special relationship with Washington, while the French were inclined, right up to the onset of hostilities, to indulge in bouts of solo diplomacy.

Even more importantly, the overwhelming dominance of the United States at that particular juncture meant that consultations in the Council were less significant than bilateral and unilateral actions involving the Bush administration. In particular, the vital threshold between a strategy that relied primarily on economic coercion and one that used force was, in effect, crossed by the U.S. decision to increase its deployment in the Gulf four weeks before Resolution 678 was agreed upon. The conduct of the war itself was almost wholly removed from effective influence by the Security Council as such; moreover, at that stage the Twelve had no collective role other than as an occasional cheerleader.

On the other hand, the collective influence of the Twelve in the aftermath of the war should not be dismissed. For example, the linkage with the Palestinian issue, for some time a less controversial issue for the Twelve than for the United States, was implicitly acknowledged in the subsequent U.S. approach to the Arab-Israeli peace process. More immediately, the postscript of the Gulf War seemed to suggest that a new concept of "humanitarian intervention" was in the making. The establishment of "safe havens" in northern Iraq in the spring of 1991, following the failed Kurdish revolt, also offered a chance for some rehabilitation of the Twelve's credibility. British, French, and Dutch participation in "Operation Provide Comfort" was presented in the context of WEU coordination, and the whole exercise received a measure of legitimation at the Special European Council at

Luxembourg, which was also dealing with the Intergovernmental Conferences on Economic and Monetary Union (EMU) and Political Union. In these circumstances, it was perhaps easy to overlook the rather tenuous nature of UN legitimation for the intervention.[7]

Yet, at the same time that the Security Council seemed ready to delegate much of its newly found authority in the cases referred to above, it was also becoming more directly involved in a quite unprecedented expansion of UN peacekeeping as a whole. By the middle of 1993, the number of forces deployed was five times greater than in mid-1991, and seven times greater than in 1987.[8] In October 1993, seventeen operations were under way, only five of which owed their existence to the Cold War era.[9] The costs of UN peacekeeping are now more than three times the order of the organization's regular budget, though still very small in relation to national defense budgets.[10] Perhaps more important than this change in overall volume have been changes in the range of tasks undertaken (including ambitious attempts at political reconstruction), the involvement of a wider range of contributing countries, including the major powers to a much greater extent than previously, and the sheer size and complexity of some of the missions.

The participation of the individual member states of the Twelve in all of this was very considerable by the autumn of 1993. Table 15.1 shows that, taken together, they provided more than twenty-four thousand military and police personnel—that is, just about one-third of the world total. Six member states (Belgium, Denmark, France, Ireland, Italy, and the Netherlands) were each contributors to between six and nine of the current total of seventeen operations. Of the others, the United Kingdom had sizable deployments in former-Yugoslavia and Cyprus, while Germany, Greece, Portugal, and Spain were becoming involved in an activity hitherto outside their experience. Even Luxembourg sent military personnel to the UN operation in former-Yugoslavia. If the four European Free Trade Association (EFTA) candidate countries (Austria, Finland, Norway, and Sweden) are taken into account, the potential capacity of the European Union is yet more striking, with close to 40 percent of the total personnel deployed.

However, as far as the capacity of the EU, as such, is concerned, these figures represent an ambiguous mixture of potential and actual influence. They are, after all, aggregates of national contributions, and the extent to which they have collective significance will depend on the circumstances pertaining to particular operations. The Twelve's peacekeeping presence in former-Yugoslavia is an obvious case in point. The considerable political demands to participate, from domestic public opinions and some governmental interests (both national and *communautaire*), are matched by serious hesitations on the part of the major actors; the outcome has fallen far short of original expectations.[11]

If it is difficult to reach a positive assessment of the Union's capacity to act as a regional peacekeeping organization within the European region,

Table 15.1   The Twelve's Contributions to UN Peacekeeping Operations (as of 31 October 1993)

	Civilian Police	Troops	Military Observers	Total Personnel	Number of Operations
The Twelve					
Belgium	5	1,989	17	2,011	9
Denmark	44	1,314	59	1,417	6
France	63	8,457	74	8,594	8
Germany	4	1,859	—	1,863	3
Greece	—	101	7	108	3
Ireland	36	783	46	865	9
Italy	12	3,697	25	3,734	8
Luxembourg	—	35	—	35	1
Netherlands	2	1,077	67	1,146	6
Portugal	35	293	12	340	2
Spain	106	1,189	46	1,341	4
United Kingdom	—	2,754	30	2,784	4
The Twelve's Total	307	23,548	383	24,237	63
Candidate Countries					
Austria	9	808	37	854	8
Finland	—	1,104	37	1,141	7
Norway	30	1,587	73	1,690	7
Sweden	38	1,882	72	1,992	10
The Candidates' Total	77	5,381	219	5,677	32
World Total	1,020	72,152	1,933	75,105	

The Twelve's Share of the World Total   32.23%
The Sixteen's Share of the World Total   39.78%

Source: United Nations, "Summary of Contributions to Peacekeeping Operations by Countries as of 31 October 1993."

where the incentives for common policy are relatively high, what are the prospects for enhancing the EU's presence in global security issues outside Europe? A closer look at the case of Somalia, which was the occasion for a significant degree of experimentation on the part of the UN as well as the involvement of six of the EU's member states, provides an indication of the opportunities and limitations that may be expected.

The UN and Somalia

The overthrow of the Somali dictator, Siad Barre, at the end of 1990 was followed by serious divisions among his former opponents, which led to civil war, widespread famine, and a state of anarchy throughout much of the country by the following winter. In April 1992 the UN Security Council established a United Nations Operation in Somalia (UNOSOM), which con-

sisted of fifty military observers to monitor a ceasefire and a small force of
five hundred troops to protect aid workers.

None of this was effective. The ceasefire was a fiction, arms were
already in plentiful supply as a result of years of Cold War military assistance, and it was impossible to distribute the most basic famine relief.
At U.S. instigation, as an interim measure the Security Council then
authorized a large-scale intervention in December 1992, the Unified
Task Force (UNITAF), which, at its peak, included twenty-eight thousand U.S. troops out of a total of thirty-five thousand. Although authorized
under the enforcement provisions in Chapter VII of the Charter, this was not
a UN operation proper since it remained under Washington's command. The
massive show of force did succeed in creating a secure environment for
humanitarian assistance, but UNITAF did not make much progress in disarming the Somali factions or in the complex business of political reconstruction.

These ambitious tasks were included in the mandate of UNOSOM II,
authorized by Security Council Resolution 814 on 26 March 1993, and operational from 4 May. The scope of its activity was broad and varied, ranging
from the immediate objective of reestablishing basic order to the virtual
rebuilding of the state. By the autumn of 1993, it was the largest of the new
breed of large-scale UN operations, with nearly twenty-nine thousand personnel. More important, UNOSOM II was a pioneering experiment in terms
of its legal basis. It was not dependent on the consent of the local lawful
authorities—since there were none—and it went beyond the traditional limits of peacekeeping, which have been indirectly legitimated under Chapter
VI of the UN Charter. For the first time, under Chapter VII an enforcement
action was authorized under direct UN command. UNOSOM II thus represented an important test for the UN's credibility in the field of global security, and, by the same token, it could be seen as a significant challenge to the
Twelve's capacity to project a security presence outside the European
region.

The Politics of Involvement

On what grounds did the member states of the Twelve decide whether or not
to contribute to UNOSOM II? To what extent did these decisions reinforce
the image of a collective presence? The legal basis of the decisions themselves was, of course, wholly national; even had the provisions of the
Maastricht Treaty been in force, it is not clear whether Article J.4 (Treaty on
European Union, or TEU) would have changed that position significantly.
The criteria on which such choices are made vary from the altruistic—the
immediate demands of the humanitarian disaster in Somalia—to broader
political considerations for the intervening countries. The latter will include
the desire to preserve or develop bilateral links in the region, the effects on

the contributing state's diplomatic reputation, and the costs it will face, especially in the context of the military capabilities required. The wish to support a collective policy, to promote the Union's presence as such, may also be a factor, particularly in the foreign ministries, but may not be so persuasive in the context of the domestic policy process. In that respect the national political contexts, the relative weight of foreign and defense ministries, and the organization of special interests and public opinion as a whole can lead to quite different national responses.

In the case of UNOSOM II, the response of six member states was *not* to participate. For Luxembourg, there is the obvious constraint of both diplomatic and military capability. That does not apply to Portugal and Spain; however, neither has a long tradition of multilateral peacekeeping. Spain's main efforts have been directed to the former-Yugoslavia (UN Protective Force, or UNPROFOR), and Portugal's to its former colony, Mozambique (UN Observer Mission in Mozambique, or ONUMOZ). Neither has distinctive links with the countries in the Horn of Africa. Denmark and the Netherlands, on the other hand, are very much in the mold of "UN activists," with a small-state foreign policy profile that puts a high premium on multilateral peacekeeping and development policy. Although both are still major development aid donors, this may reflect a more long-term change of emphasis to European, rather than extra-European, security concerns; certainly both were already heavily committed in former-Yugoslavia. Finally, numbered among the absentees is the United Kingdom, a former colonial power in Somalia and a permanent member of the Security Council. It may be that in this case there is a "tacit recognition" that even a major actor cannot do everything. British military capabilities were very stretched, not least in UNPROFOR and the continuing commitment in Northern Ireland.

Notwithstanding these abstentions, half of the member states and two of the four candidate countries did decide to contribute to UNOSOM II (see Table 15.2). Pride of place, in terms of military capability but with some historical irony, goes to the other former colonial power in the region, Italy. The direct colonial links, though by now rather remote, may account for Italian policymakers' confidence that they possess an understanding of the local political culture. During the 1980s, Italy had (somewhat controversially) supported the Barre regime.[12] In the subsequent chaos, Rome took more trouble than most to maintain a direct diplomatic presence in Mogadishu. The Italian decision may also be attributed to a more general activism and assertiveness, which has characterized Italian foreign policy since the end of the Cold War. This includes increasing the country's presence in multilateral diplomacy outside Europe, in Mozambique as well as Somalia. Thus, it was not surprising that Italy responded to the U.S. initiative on UNITAF and transferred this commitment to UNOSOM II. A notable feature of the policy process in the Italian case was the incoherence of domestic political debate at this time; the virtual collapse of the party system meant that little

Table 15.2   The Twelve's Contribution to UNOSOM II (as of 31 October 1993)

	Number of Troops	Type of Unit	Number of Fatalities (as of 11 October 1993)
The Twelve			
Belgium	989	Infantry battalion	3[a]
France	1,113	Brigade HQ infantry battalion	1
		Aviation unit	
		Logistical battalion	
Germany	1,731	Logistical units	—
Greece	101	Medical units	1
Ireland	79	Transport company	—
Italy	2,590	Brigade HQ	6
		Three infantry battalions	
		Aviation unit	
		Logistical/engineering unit	
		Medical unit	
The Twelve's Total	5,604		
Candidate Countries			
Norway	136	HQ company	—
Sweden	133	Field hospital	—
The Candidates' Total	269		
Total UNOSOM II	28,980		
The Twelve's Share of Total UNOSOM II	19.34 percent		
The United States' Share of Total UNOSOM II	11.97 percent		

Note: a. Incurred under UNITAF (March 1993).

Sources: United Nations, "Summary of Contributions to Peacekeeping by Countries as of 31 October 1993." United Nations, "Report of the Secretary-General, 12 November 1993," S/26738. "Report to the Congress on U.S. Policy in Somalia," October 13, 1993.

attention was paid to foreign engagements. In the short term at least, the foreign ministry seemed to have a considerable freedom of maneuver, constrained mainly by considerations of military costs.

France, too, has encouraged an enhanced role for the UN, with the evident corollary that as a permanent member of the Security Council it is very much a major player in this regard. Indeed, there is quite a contrast with British commitments here; as Table 15.1 shows, France deploys three times as many "blue helmets," in twice as many operations, as its partner on the Security Council. Is it stretching the point to suggest that this is a deliberate policy to confirm French credentials to speak for "Europe" in this context?

As far as the specific involvement in Somalia was concerned, a further motivation was to be found in the insistence of the then minister for health and humanitarian action, Bernard Kouchner, that force would have to be used to end the famine in Somalia in the summer of 1992. The first government minister from any of the Twelve to visit the country, Kouchner's flair for publicity and direct access to President Mitterrand served to overcome the hesitation of the minister of defense. Not that military capabilities were lacking—with a base in neighboring Djibouti and a distinctive "African vocation," the French army was well placed to contribute to both UNITAF and then UNOSOM II.

Of the contributions by the three smaller member states, that of Belgium was, in military terms, the most substantial. Belgium, like Italy, France, and Greece, participated first in UNITAF, an involvement that was carried over from the initial decision to join UNOSOM I. The Belgian contingent was actively and successfully engaged in the sensitive task of disarming local factions, in the course of which three fatalities were incurred in March 1993. This did not alter the government's policy to continue its commitment, in the context of UNOSOM II, through to the end of 1993 as originally decided. Belgium's former colonial links elsewhere in Africa may suggest that an empathy with the predicament of Somalia was a general background factor in the formation of policy, but, by the same token, it seems that the prospect of having to respond to a similar crisis in Zaire may have influenced the decision to restrict the duration of the contribution. A novel aspect of Belgium's participation from the outset, which is examined in more detail below, was partial funding from the Community budget.

The background to the Greek decision to send a medical unit is less clear. Greece does not have a tradition in UN peacekeeping, but the new government's initial response to the post–Cold War era had been to attempt a more constructive approach to political cooperation in general, including an emphasis on security. However, the Twelve's policy on the breakup of Yugoslavia caused an abrupt and fundamental reappraisal of the new orientation. Throughout 1992 Greece was in a difficult relationship with its partners, especially over the status of Macedonia. Clearly, the government would not have anything to do with UNPROFOR, and, in any case, UN orthodoxy precludes direct participation by states bordering on an area in dispute. Participation in UNOSOM II may be seen as a signal that at least it retained a commitment in principle to multilateralism.

Ireland's decision to participate was initiated by very strong domestic pressures concerning the humanitarian aspects of the Somali crisis. These, in turn, may be explained by the generally high profile of nongovernmental development groups in Irish public life and the direct involvement of some of these in Somalia. The Irish foreign minister, David Andrews, was not far behind Kouchner and was followed to Somalia in October 1992 by no less than the head of state, President Mary Robinson. A decision to contribute to the original UNOSOM was thus no surprise, but implementation was overtaken by events. However, participation in UNITAF was precluded by the legislative constraint restricting overseas peacekeeping operations to those established—that is, both authorized and directed—by the UN. While UNO-SOM II fulfilled that requirement, its mandate to "enforce" implied a formal amendment to Irish legislation. Domestic debate thus acquired a much broader scope, involving an important redefinition of the state's commitment to multilateral security. The fact that by the time this debate took place, the operation was already in serious trouble did nothing to ease the government's task. Opposition parties' sensitivities about the use of force, the exposure of Irish troops, and even the policy of neutrality were assuaged by repeated reassurances, including the claim that Irish troops were not going to Somalia in a combat role.

Many of these themes were amplified in the German decision to contribute to UNOSOM II, a decision that was part of a major adjustment to German foreign policy with potentially far-reaching consequences—not just for Germany, but for the UN and the overall development of the European Union's diplomatic persona.[13] The issue of national legitimation for multilateral commitments arose not just on the legislative level, as in the case of Ireland, but as a question of constitutional politics. Varying interpretations of the Basic Law's restriction on the deployment of combat troops "out of area" were hotly contested—not merely between the government and the SPD opposition, but between the government partners themselves. For some, the debate concerned a traditional polarization between pacifism and militarism, but its significance for foreign policy also lay in defining the international status of a Germany "whole and free."

The government's initial intention to amend the Basic Law was overtaken by Chancellor Kohl's insistence on some degree of de facto participation in enforcing the UN-authorized "no fly zone" in Bosnia early in 1993. The tension between the coalition partners was only resolved by a favorable preliminary and interim decision of the Constitutional Court on 8 April 1993, confirmed with respect to Somalia on 23 June, and this paved the way for the decision to make a sizable contribution to UNOSOM II. In a similar tacit reservation to Ireland's, and showing a similar degree of sensitivity to domestic opinion, these troops were assigned a logistical mission, with the inference that they were not in a combat role. Nevertheless, the significance of the German decision should not be underestimated; by participating in a Chapter VII operation, Germany was reinforcing its claim to a permanent seat on the UN Security Council.

Taken together, the Twelve's collective presence in UNOSOM II is significant. At the end of October 1993, it amounted to nearly one-fifth of the total personnel (and a little more when the contributions of two of the candidate countries, Norway and Sweden, are taken into account). This exceeded U.S. participation (by this stage being reduced), but was almost matched by the biggest single national contingent, that of Pakistan. However, this aggregated image must be qualified by the way in which the commitments were made or, indeed, declined, in a series of essentially national decisions.

Motivations varied from one case to the other, as did the sensitivity of government policy to public pressures. Similar variations were also evident in the Twelve's subsequent experience in Somalia.

Operational Realities

Barely a month after the official commencement of UNOSOM II, it became clear that expectations of a largely voluntary disarmament process (with the UN's coercive capability only as a last resort) would not be met. On 5 June 1993, twenty-four Pakistani troops were killed in a deliberate attack by one of the main factions, the Somali National Alliance (SNA), led by General Mohamed Aidid. Between then and 9 October 1993, the SNA waged a persistent guerrilla campaign against UN forces, especially in south Mogadishu. The loss of life by UN contingents naturally reduced the confidence of the affected countries, but the greater numbers of Somali fatalities led to accusations of partiality by the UN, thereby reducing the overall credibility of the operation. Attempts to capture General Aidid were fruitless, and one, in particular, marked a turning point; on 3 October 1993, eighteen members of an elite U.S. unit were killed, seventy-five wounded, and one captured. The effect on U.S. opinion was decisively negative, with President Clinton announcing U.S. withdrawal from UNOSOM II by 31 March 1994, a year earlier than originally envisaged.

As far as the EC contributing states were concerned, the brunt of the violence and consequent political controversy was born by Italy. On 1 July 1993, three Italian soldiers were killed, an event that attracted much attention at home, particularly as these were the first combat fatalities in the Italian army since World War II. Tensions between the Italian military commander, General Bruno Loi, and the local UN command now became increasingly exposed and were soon translated to the highest political level, between Rome and UN headquarters in New York (*Agence Europe*, July 1993). The latter publicly demanded the recall of General Loi, complaining of his failure to coordinate operations with the local UN military commander, General Bir of Turkey, and accusing him of virtual insubordination. The Italian government claimed General Loi took his orders from Rome and threatened to redeploy the Italian contingent out of Mogadishu. Underlying these mutual recriminations were fundamental differences concerning the appropriate enforcement measures to be taken against the armed Somali factions. The Italian preference for small-scale, localized negotiation in the traditional peacekeeping mode was opposed to the UN (and U.S.) predilection for a more visible and proactive intervention relying on its U.S. helicopter gunship capability.

This can be seen, in effect, as a microcosm of a more general divergence between U.S. and European diplomatic and military cultures. Nevertheless, the role of the United States was central; Somalia was as much a test case for U.S. commitment to the development of multilateralism as it was for the UN itself.[14] Washington's leadership and military capabilities were seen as essential elements in the eventual success of a new world order, and at the time the experience of UNOSOM II promised to offset the difficulties simultaneously encountered in Bosnia. Thus, it was necessary to contain the dispute between the Italians and a UN leadership that was strongly influenced by and dependent on U.S. policy toward Somalia. By the end of July, this appeared to have been achieved; General Loi was still Italian commander, the Italians remained in Mogadishu, and improved consultation procedures were adopted in New York, while UN strategy was focused as before, on the pursuit of General Aidid. There were further Italian fatalities in September 1993 and further tensions over specific incidents, but, on the whole, an uneasy modus vivendi lasted until the Clinton administration radically changed its approach, following its humiliation at the beginning of October 1993. By that time, the overall credibility of UNOSOM II was in jeopardy. Though immediate humanitarian objectives had been realized, the prospects for durable political reconstruction were poor, and the collective agent of that reconstruction—the UN—appeared to be considerably less than the sum of its parts.

Indeed, it was sometimes easy to forget that UNOSOM II was a collective endeavor, when considering the Italian experience. Yet if the limitations of the UN were self-evident by the autumn of 1993, it is also pertinent to ask to what extent the Twelve acted as a collectivity in the Somalian crisis. The answer begins, not in the sphere of political cooperation, but in that of the Community's development policy.[15] In 1991–1992 the EC was the principal donor of humanitarian and food aid to Somalia, accounting for two-thirds of the Red Cross distribution alone; in 1992, in addition to 101 million ECU (European currency units) provided by the EC, bilateral contributions by member states amounted to 57 million ECU. The prospect of such a significant expenditure achieving little, primarily because the aid could not be distributed, was a strong incentive for the direct intervention that followed, and this, in turn, brought Somalia into the ambit of EPC.

A visit of the Troika foreign ministers on 4 September 1992 was followed by the decision to commit Community funding (20 million ECU) to the protection of humanitarian convoys, which, as we have seen, was applied in the case of the eventual Belgian contribution to UNITAF and later UNOSOM II. This decision might appear, in effect, as an experiment foreshadowing the provision in the Treaty on European Union that allows for operational expenditure being charged to the Community budget (Article J.11.2); however, no such justification was offered. The immediate political context did not favor signaling advances in integration, however small. The decision was agreed upon on 10 September 1992, little more than a week before the controversial French referendum on Maastricht and with the currency crisis looming. The British presidency's discomfort could be seen in an insistence that it should not be taken as a precedent, and the foreign ministers contented themselves with a much more general declaration on 13 September 1992, of a largely exhortatory nature. However, it is difficult to disagree with the observation that "it was a remarkable precedent nevertheless."[16]

With the evident failure of the original UNOSOM and in the context of the UNITAF initiative, on 7 December 1992 the Council agreed to a declaration supporting the relevant Security Council resolution (794), describing it as "an important development in international law," and welcoming "the contributions of a number of member states to the force as a European initiative." The conclusions of the European Council in Edinburgh shortly afterwards confirmed this legitimizing statement at the highest level, though in a more concise form that omitted, inter alia, the description of the member state contributions as "a European initiative."[17] Behind the scenes, it may be presumed that the Twelve's "cooperation reflex" assisted both the U.S. mobilization of the interim force and the UN Secretariat's "recruitment" of its successor, at a time when military commitments were being unexpectedly stretched elsewhere.

A further example of the Twelve providing declaratory support occurred after UNOSOM II itself was established, in response to the initial killing of UN troops at the beginning of June 1993. A declaration on 8 June 1993 strongly condemned what was described as a premeditated act and reiterated full support for the UN. The conclusions of the European Council on 21–22 June 1993 continue in a similar vein, but the first signs of the operational dilemmas facing the UN are reflected in an expression of regret for civilian casualties.[18] These were causing concern in the European Parliament at this time, although in the event, the Parliament continued to support UNOSOM II in principle.[19]

Indeed, the subsequent exposure of UNOSOM II's internal tensions made it difficult simply to repeat these themes. After all, the issues at stake now had to do with the performance of the UN itself and with differences between the contributing countries on how to run the operation. Thus, the heated and very public dispute in early July 1993, involving the Italians with both the UN and the United States, resulted not in high-profile declaratory statements, but in "quiet diplomacy" on the part of the Belgian presidency. A meeting of the Council on 19 July 1993 appears to have authorized the presidency to express the Twelve's concern to the UN Secretary-General, though it is not clear what degree of emphasis was agreed upon. The Spanish and Italian foreign ministers were reported to have understood that a clarification of the UN mandate was called for; the presidency, however, claimed its task was to "remind" the UN leadership of the political aims of UNOSOM II.[20] In any case, the Belgians, as a contributing country, were well placed to mend the broken fences in New York. By the time the next meetings of the European Council took place, in Brussels on 29 October 1993 and 10–11 December 1993, the situation in Somalia had changed to a tense stalemate, in which several contributing countries were more intent on withdrawal than commitment. Somalia did not appear in the conclusions of these summit meetings, which were now (in the context of CFSP) in any case adopting a more selective approach to the publication of declarations.

Below the level of ministerial involvement, the Somalian crisis was characterized by a complex web of bureaucratic coordination. Consistency between the Community and EPC spheres of activity was involved from the outset, given the Commission's responsibilities for development aid. In March 1992, DG VIII set up a special unit, the European Community Humanitarian Office (ECHO), to deal with disaster relief. As far as Somalia was concerned, two difficulties were encountered. The first was the absence of a Somali government with which to relate concerning the normal financial procedures of development policy. The solution adopted was to work through procedures established under the Lomé framework, thus involving the Commission's ACP Working Group (which covered countries in Africa, the Caribbean, and the Pacific area). The second difficulty lay in establishing a presence in the field, close to the nongovernmental organizations that were the main implementors of aid in these circumstances. Coordination with member state governments, through EC Working Groups on Development and ACP Relations, was channeled through the development divisions in the foreign ministries, which are generally separate from the political divisions. Thus, consistency was as much a question of the internal organization of the foreign ministries as it was of procedures between the Commission and the member states. There appears to have been no attempt to anticipate or experiment with CFSP "joint action" procedures.

Within the EPC sphere of activity, it was the Africa Working Group, rather than the United Nations group, that was most closely involved on a day-to-day basis with UNOSOM II. The latter, with its orientation toward the agenda of the General Assembly, reflects something of the modus operandi of the pre-1990 EPC/UN relationship. It deals with peacekeeping issues in a general, thematic way, coordinating the Twelve's positions in the context of their New York representations' post-Assembly session assessment in mid-December and a pre-session report in June. The UN Working Group thus acts as a sort of feedback mechanism that may contribute to the formulation of common views in the medium term.

However, the fact that the operational questions to do with peacekeeping fall within the aegis of the Security Council means that the much larger and more heterogeneous group of UNOSOM II contributing countries was the primary focus of consultation in New York. The issues raised there, as far as the Twelve were concerned, were examined in the Africa Working Group, in which the volume of business has grown significantly since the end of the Cold War.

On the whole, then, the policy process dealing with the Twelve's involvement with Somalia has been, if anything, more than usually complex, incorporating several Working Groups on both Community and EPC sides and a corresponding multiplicity of operational units within national foreign ministries. The level of collective decision, however, remains the Political Committee–Council nexus. The main bureaucratic input from outside the foreign ministries consisted of national defense ministries and their armed forces. However, with respect to the latter, there was little evidence that policies were directly influenced by the "division of labor" debates (being conducted at the same time as the Somali crisis) on possible peacekeeping functions for either NATO or WEU.[21]

The Politics of Exit

The abrupt U.S. decision, in October 1993, to drop its policy of coercive disarmament of the Aidid faction and to leave Somalia a year earlier than originally envisaged, was an important turning point. There appears to have been no real consultation between Washington and its European allies, and it left the UN and the other contributing governments in a quandary. Although the short-term humanitarian aims of UNOSOM II had largely been achieved, many nongovernmental aid groups were critical of its assertive approach.[22] The prospects for political reconstruction were uncertain, the more so following the failure of reconciliation negotiations in mid-December 1993. In his report to the Security Council on 12 November 1993, the UN Secretary-General defined three options for the future of the intervention: maintaining the enforcement mandate (though "enforcing" only as a last resort), in which case yet more troops would be required; reverting to a classical peacekeeping approach, at about half of the existing level of deployment; or reducing the scope of the operation to securing essential supply routes with a much smaller force.[23] The stage was set for "the politics of exit"—the decision whether, and under what conditions, to withdraw from a collective commitment.

Such a decision may be difficult, involving as it does the credibility of both the contributing state and the collectivity that has legitimated the intervention.[24] In the case of UNOSOM II, the reputation of the UN obviously stood to be affected by hasty or unanticipated withdrawals; but to the extent that the Twelve had approached Somalia as "a European initiative" (as the Council had phrased it on 7 December 1992), their collective reputation was also at stake. The most straightforward solution to this dilemma, at least from a national point of view, is to make the commitment for a fixed term in the first place. This approach had been adopted by both Belgium and France; thus, their withdrawal from UNOSOM II at the end of 1993 could be presented as a routine event, quite independent of second thoughts by the Clinton administration or the actual situation in Somalia.

Germany's decision on withdrawal, like its decision to participate in the first place, was more problematic. The foreign ministry, keeping Germany's overall credentials as a future member of the Security Council in mind, was anxious to avoid a precipitate departure, but the defense ministry did not seem to share these apprehensions. This debate was at least partly colored by personal and coalition rivalries at the political level, but the more fundamental, long-term question of the commitment of German forces outside of the area was, in any case, in the hands of the Constitutional Court. The latter eventually delivered a favorable verdict at the end of June 1994, well after Germany's departure from Somalia.

Italy, on the other hand, having been (quite literally) in the front line of UNOSOM II, appeared at first to rest its reputation as much on an outcome that was successful in terms of the eventual rehabilitation of Somalia as on the timing of a possible withdrawal. However, this issue of substantive policy, like most others, was submerged in the run-up to an extraordinary general election at the end of March 1994, in which the party system, rather than policies, was at stake. By the time the election took place, Italy joined most of its partners in quitting UNOSOM II. Greece, too, withdrew its unit, with as little fuss as had accompanied its original involvement—and a great deal less fuss than was associated with its concurrent policies in the Balkans.

Ireland's commitment, being quite closely related to the situation of Irish nongovernmental aid organizations and, in any case, being on a small scale, remained the only one of the six EU contributing states in Somalia and then only until mid-September 1994. There was evidence that the government was disillusioned with the enforcement aspect of the original mandate, and the more restricted mandate subsequently adopted made little impression on the overall situation in Somalia, which steadily regressed into a state of violent anarchy.

Conclusions:
The Limits of the EU Presence in Global Security

It would be invidious to generalize on the basis of the case of UNOSOM II alone, but there can be no doubt that, together with the difficulties the UN has recently experienced elsewhere, it suggests the limitations of, rather than the potential for, a more assertive type of multilateral security regime. The paralysis of the international community in the face of the genocidal civil war that broke out in Rwanda in April 1994 underlined the point, in what was almost a ghastly parody of the "lessons of Somalia." Belgium again seemed destined for an active role, until ten of its soldiers were murdered in a single incident at the outset of hostilities; France made a unilateral intervention three months later, when the civil war became a refugee crisis. The fact that there was now a European Union made little difference to the outcome.

With that in mind, it may seem superfluous to ask whether the involvement of the Twelve in Somalia demonstrated an enhancement of their collective presence, but it can hardly be said that any other element of the international community—whether state, group of states, or multilateral organization—performed any better. The criteria of effective international action should not be pitched too high. Reverting to Hill's "conceivable future functions," the effort to be a "bridge between rich and poor" was substantial, in terms of humanitarian assistance, but marred to some degree by association with the UN and U.S. insistence on an ineffective coercive approach to disarmament. As a "mediator of conflict," the Twelve as such played a secondary role to the UN, mainly in the form of declaratory policy; at the local level, though, the participating member states may have made positive, if short-lived, contributions.

The "role of global intervenor" was even less evident. It proved costly enough for the one power with the apparent capabilities to bring its influence to bear through the UN framework, but UN cover proved to be no defense against the U.S. administration's vulnerability to abrupt swings in domestic opinion—the "CNN factor." However, there was little to indicate that the Twelve were either willing or able to replace an uncertain U.S. leadership in mobilizing the international community on security issues outside the European region. The extent of commitment remained the prerogative of the individual member states, and while it was endorsed by all Twelve, in practice it was uneven. Nor is it clear that the application of the European Union's CFSP procedures would have made a significant difference in this respect. Those member states that did contribute directly to the enforcement experiment were not all necessarily in a stronger political position to sustain significant losses of ground troops than the United States had been. Domestic opinion in Germany and Ireland was clearly sensitive on that point; even Italian and Belgian resolve, which was tested in practice, did not appear to be limitless.

An initial assessment of the Twelve's experience in Somalia, together with the immediate postscript of Rwanda, therefore suggests that global security is not a promising field for the development of their international presence. Yet such a conclusion may discount the effects it may have on future policies, now within the CFSP context. After all, the history of EPC over nearly twenty-five years demonstrates a capacity to learn. If there was a common lesson to emerge from Somalia for the Twelve, it was the primacy of political ends over military means. This was a persistent theme at the UN General Assembly session in 1993, in the contributing countries' national statements, as well as in the Belgian presidency statement. The use of force might be legitimate, but as the Italian foreign minister said, the real issue was "its advisability and timing."[25] Moreover, doubts about peace enforcement do not preclude the possibility that UN peacekeeping, in the more traditional sense of the word, will continue to expand. There is little evidence of a decline in demand for such services; the issue rather, for those states that can supply them, is whether to do so through the UN, regional organizations, ad hoc coalitions, or a mixture of these.

For the evolving European Union, the desire to stress an almost exclusive role for regional security organizations concerning issues arising in the European region has already been tempered by the experience in former-Yugoslavia. As far as issues outside Europe are concerned, the UN framework still seems to be an indispensable source of legitimacy, but that begs the basic question that now confronts the Union: Is the UN to be developed as a serious multilateral security agency, or is it to be merely an acquiescent and occasional legitimator of ad hoc coalitions? The answers to this question will be formulated in the context of the debate on the reform of the UN, and they may prove to be quite difficult, if not divisive, in the development of CFSP. The composition of the Security Council is a case in point. That Germany (along with Japan and one or more major Third World powers) should be a permanent member is a proposition that is hard to deny.[26] Yet, apart from arguably over-representing the EU on the Security Council, it crystallizes the privileged position of a de facto *directoire* that the other nine (or more) EU member states may find difficult to live with. The answer to that quandary might lie in a more generous interpretation of Article J.5.4 (TEU) than seems to prevail at present.

At least as important as the question of institutional prerogatives will be that of operational capacity. The demands of financing an extended UN, and its quid pro quo, a very thorough reform of the global body's internal organs and procedures, are matters for the CFSP agenda. With particular regard to the UN's broad peacekeeping capacity, the question of providing standing forces or other procedures for the more rapid deployment of troops with more specific peacekeeping training is an important aspect of UN reform, and one in which an advanced regional organization (as the EU aspires to be) should have a role to play.[27] Indeed, it may be that it is with regard to preparations for peacekeeping as an instrument of crisis management that all of the multilateral security institutions—UN, CSCE (Conference on Security and Cooperation in Europe), NATO, and WEU—"interlock" with the European Union in a practical way.

At least, it cannot be said that the agenda is insubstantial. The challenge is for the European Union, at a time of considerable internal change, to take it seriously. It may be, after the experience of Somalia, that the member states will approach these issues with less unrealistic expectations than they had in the early 1990s. Although it is true that the European Union's "civilian power" capacity looks more promising than its security attributes, and this is reflected in the extent to which the first CFSP joint actions mostly concern issues that are in a relatively benign phase, it is difficult to envisage a European Union with no presence at all in the difficult field of global security.

Notes

1. For a detailed analysis of the EU's performance during the Yugoslav crisis, see Geoffrey Edwards's Chapter 10 in this volume.
2. Christopher Hill, "The Capability—Expectations Gap, or Conceptualizing Europe's International Role," *Journal of Common Market Studies* 3 (September 1993), pp. 312–315.
3. Simon Nuttall, *European Political Cooperation* (Oxford: Clarendon Press, 1992), pp. 136–139.
4. Elfriede Regelsberger, "EPC in the 1980s: Reaching Another Plateau?" in Alfred Pijpers, Elfriede Regelsberger, and Wolfgang Wessels, eds., *European Political Cooperation in the 1980s: A Common Foreign Policy for Western Europe?* (Dordrecht: Martinus Nijhoff Publishers, 1988), p. 48.
5. *Strategic Survey 1990–1991* (London: IISS, Brassey's, 1991), p. 55.
6. Trevor C. Salmon, "Testing Time for European Political Cooperation: The Gulf and Yugoslavia, 1990–1992," *International Affairs* 2 (April 1992), pp. 236–248.
7. Adam Roberts, "Humanitarian War: Military Intervention and Human Rights," *International Affairs* 3 (July 1993), pp. 436–439.
8. John Roper, "A Wider Range of Tasks," in John Roper et al., eds., *Keeping the Peace in the Post–Cold War Era: Strengthening Multilateral Peacekeeping* (New York: The Trilateral Commission, The Triangle Papers 43, 1993), p. 3; and Enid C. B. Schoettle, "Financing UN Peacekeeping," in Roper et al., *Keeping the Peace,* pp. 17–18.
9. United Nations, "Summary of contributions to peacekeeping operations by countries as of 31 October 1993."
10. Schoettle, "Financing UN Peacekeeping," pp. 17–26.
11. See also G. Edwards in Chapter 10 of this volume.
12. European Parliament, "Report by the Committee on Development and Cooperation on the Situation in Somalia," (*Rapporteur:* Mr. Luciano Vecchi), 8 November 1993 (PE 205.695/fin.), p. 7.
13. Masashi Nishihara, "Trilateral Country Roles: Challenges and Opportunities," in Roper et al., *Keeping the Peace,* pp. 54–56.
14. See Mats Berdal, "Fateful Encounter: The United States and UN Peacekeeping," *Survival* 1 (Spring 1994), pp. 30–50.
15. *Humanitarian Aid of the European Community: Annual Report 1992,* pp. 21–23.
16. *Strategic Survey 1993–1994* (London: IISS, Brassey's, 1994), p. 114.
17. Presidency conclusions, 12 December 1992, Part D, par. 20.
18. Presidency conclusions, 22 June 1993, Annex IV.
19. *Agence Europe,* 25 June 1993.
20. *Agence Europe,* 20 and 21 July 1993.
21. On WEU and peacekeeping, see Mathias Jopp's contribution in Chapter 9 of this volume.
22. See European Parliament, "Report by the Committee on Development."
23. United Nations, "Report of the Secretary-General," 12 November 1993, S/26739.

24. L. Freedman, "The Politics of Military Intervention in Europe," in Nicole Gnesotto, ed., *War and Peace: European Conflict Prevention* (Paris: WEU Institute for Security Studies; Chaillot Papers 11, 1993).

25. Andreatta speech at the UN General Assembly, 30 September 1993.

26. Olara A. Otunnu, "Maintaining Broad Legitimacy for United Nations Action," in Roper et al., eds., *Keeping the Peace,* pp. 72–73.

27. See Roper, "A Wider Range of Tasks."

16

Transatlantic Dimensions of CFSP: The Culture of Foreign Policy Cooperation

Roy Ginsberg

This chapter analyzes the political aspects of EU (European Union)–U.S. relations, which have grown more sophisticated in the 1990s. It also introduces the notion of an EU-U.S. "foreign policy cooperative culture" to describe and explain the bilateral consultative process and to identify examples of coordinated and complementary foreign policy responses related to that process. There is a broad consensus, based on a new pragmatism, that the two need each other to address international problems too big for any one state to solve alone.

EU-U.S. foreign policy cooperation now covers the world's major regions and key issues (e.g., Asia, weapons proliferation); takes different forms (sanctions against repressive regimes, diplomatic recognition); operates at different levels (bilateral, multilateral); varies in composition of its key players (EU–United States–Canada); is organized into scheduled and ad hoc consultations (from Working Groups to heads of government); draws on a dense web of bilateral links and communications (EU–United States, EU member states–United States); entails meetings around the world (Washington, New York, Brussels, other EU-member capitals, third country capitals, and international conferences and organizations); and draws on considerable resources of the participant governments (to prepare, schedule, attend, participate, and implement the results of bilateral consultative meetings).

Policy differences remain, but their number and velocity pale in comparison to the tensions of 1970–1980, when the two sides were at odds over how to respond to regional conflicts across the planet. The end of the Cold War has unleashed the potential of bilateral relations to develop over time into a foreign policy partnership for which leaders on both sides have expressed public support.[1] First, the EU will need to sustain the political will to make Common Foreign and Security Policy (CFSP) and Western

European Union (WEU) work to its advantage. This means backing its powerful economic diplomacy with a politico-military capability. The development of the Eurocorps, the integration of WEU into the EU, and NATO's green light for WEU to draw on NATO assets in the service of CFSP in order to enable the EU to act more effectively are steps in the direction of such a capability.

CFSP in the mid-1990s is more an objective than a reality.[2] It is torn between integrationists and intergovernmentalists and between minimalists and maximalists, so common foreign and security policies will not materialize overnight, as contending forces battle over the future of CFSP. Yet the quest for CFSP is as old as the EU itself; it draws on the *acquis communautaire* of the European Community (EC) and the *acquis politique* of European Political Cooperation (EPC). Until CFSP materializes, the EU remains an important civilian foreign policy power and a potential partner of the United States. The student of these relations must temper the logic of cooperation with the hearty perennial of interstate competition and is cautioned to avoid extremes of optimism and skepticism over how far international cooperation can go. Foreign policy differences in the new framework of EU-U.S. political relations do not occur at the expense of consultations and cooperation in seeking the means to achieve common objectives.

Efforts to end the war in Bosnia illustrated both the reach of and limits to CFSP and how EU-U.S. cooperation and consultation went hand-in-hand with policy differences in 1993. Despite its limited impact on actually ending the war in former-Yugoslavia, the EU provided significant and continuous leadership in the international mediation effort since the outbreak of the conflict in 1991. Sharp EU-U.S. (and intra-EU) divisions over the use of outside military force in, and the lifting of the UN arms embargo against, Bosnia did not deflect the two from sustaining the most intense period of consultations and coordination in the history of their bilateral political relationship (finally leading to a joint strategy carried out through NATO in early 1994).

Ethnic cleansing and other atrocities committed in Bosnia go against everything for which European integration stands. Yet, unlike events in 1914 and 1939, the conflict has been contained and has spared Europe a wider conflagration as a result of EU, the United States, NATO, UN, and Russian policies. The EU states stuck to a common line despite the many stresses that tested their unity. EU members through NATO and WEU have joined NATO members in monitoring the UN embargo and have been engaged in the largest and longest humanitarian aid effort (to air drop food and medicine to isolated Bosnians) since the Berlin Airlift. Seven thousand troops from several EU member states remain on the ground in former-Yugoslavia at the service of the UN Protective Force (UNPROFOR). Others have served in the European Community Monitoring Mission (ECMM), and dozens of these monitors have lost their lives or sustained injuries in the service of the European Union.

Thus, a balanced assessment reveals what specialists know: Competition and cooperation are uneasy concomitants. Despite advances made in the development of political relations in the 1990s, those relations are little understood outside a narrow band of practitioners and scholars. Why the mystery? The EU is still anachronistically viewed by some as the "common market," perpetuating the myth that European integration has no foreign policy dimension. Realists neglect the EU as an international actor (because it is not a state) and assume the EU-U.S. relationship is politically unimportant (because it is not one between equals). What the EU is (and is not), what it does (and does not) do in the world, and how its multivaried relationship with the United States operates require some basic knowledge not generally possessed by many students of international relations, much less the wider public. When the U.S. press covers the EU's role in the world, it more often focuses on the EU's shortcomings than on its common policies, whose impact is felt by many states and regions. When the press covers the EU-U.S. relationship, it tends to focus on trade and foreign policy disputes. Coverage of foreign policy cooperation and joint positions rarely, if ever, occurs.

EU-U.S. foreign policy consultations and negotiations tend to factor into the decisionmaking in other bilateral (e.g., Washington-Bonn) and multilateral forums (NATO, UN), thus contributing to the illusion that EU-U.S. deliberations do not matter, as their effects are not readily transparent. For different reasons, both sides tend to be cautious in publicly revealing the extent of their bilateral diplomacy, so there is an element of mystery in what they do together in international politics. Although all the EU member governments accept in principle and practice the need to cooperate with the United States, some prefer not to bring public attention to it, instead stressing the independence of EU foreign policy. In response, the U.S. government has chosen not to publicly stress the particulars of the workings of EU-U.S. foreign policy cooperation, thus contributing to the mystery as well. Yet over time, the EU-U.S. political relationship is likely to gain more exposure; after all, the Transatlantic Declaration, which provided a framework for EU-U.S. cooperation, has only been in operation since November 1990.

This chapter seeks to demystify political relations and foreign policy cooperation against the backdrop of what was EPC and what is not CFSP. It asks five questions: What are the new concepts and rhetoric of EU-U.S. political relations? How have those relations changed over time? What is the process of consultations and what effects may be attributed to it? And how will CFSP change relations?

The New Concepts of EU-U.S. Political Relations

EU-U.S. political relations refer to the formal and informal, scheduled and ad hoc, diplomatic exchanges between the EU and the United States over bilateral, multilateral, and international political and security issues and developments. Whereas relations have been traditionally characterized as largely commercial, those relations always had a political component, one that has grown in importance in the 1990s as the EU itself has been catapulted into a position of European leadership as a result of the collapse of communism.

Within the context of political relations, there is a "foreign policy cooperative culture"—that is, a relationship between actors of roughly comparable economic and demographic size (e.g., GDP) who are at similar levels of societal and political development (advanced industrialized democracies) and who are: bound by similar political values and principles, which affect foreign policy behavior (human rights, respect for international law); bound to a framework of bilateral policy consultations, which entails mutual commitments and responsibilities (Transatlantic Declaration); committed to minimizing policies that work at cross purposes and seeking common or complementary approaches to international problems (arms proliferation); prepared to agree to disagree over certain policy issues without endangering overall cooperation (response to Bosnian War); prepared to harness considerable diplomatic and financial resources to obtain similar objectives more effectively than if each acted alone (aid coordination to Eastern Europe).

The EU-U.S. culture of foreign policy cooperation, with its various processes and manifestations, neither replaces nor competes with bilateral relations between the individual EC states and the United States. Instead, EU-U.S. foreign policy cooperation draws from, is an outgrowth of, and thus complements strong and historically deep bilateral interstate ties. The EU and the United States have, or are developing, special cooperative relationships (or partnerships) with other states. However, few partnerships between major powers share the historical resonance that distinguishes the EU-U.S. relationship.

The culture of foreign policy cooperation is, in part, a product of complex interdependence and posthegemonic cooperation among industrialized democracies.[3] These concepts, designed to develop understanding of the wider relationships among advanced industrialized democracies, offer rich explanatory insights into the EU-U.S. political relationship.[4] Realism, a standard explanation of interstate behavior since the 1950s, has limited application to EU-U.S. politics, although neomercantilism, one of its offshoots, offers insights into the economic nationalism that underpins some of the more fiercely contested bilateral trade disputes.[5]

Complex interdependence exists when military force is not used within an interdependent area, although it may be used vis-à-vis outside countries (the idea of an EU-U.S. war is unthinkable); there are multiple channels of various types that connect societies (commerce, diplomacy, energy, education, etc.); the agenda of international relations consists of multiple issues that are not arranged in a clear or consistent hierarchy (there are interacting governmental and nongovernmental political, economic, and social dimensions at work in EU-U.S. relations); and there are reciprocal effects of policy decisions that limit the autonomy of national decisionmaking (European opposition scuttled the Clinton administration's support for lifting the arms embargo against Bosnia, just as U.S. opposition to sending ground troops to Bosnia puts pressure on the EU states).[6] Interdependence affects the interactions between actors, and there is scope for both harmony (establishment of the September 1990 Gulf Crisis Financial Coordination Group) and disharmony between them (Western loans to Iran in 1993).[7]

The operation of interdependence can be gauged in terms of processes (contacts and meetings concerned with matters of mutual sensitivity—e.g., nuclear proliferation, drug trade, and terrorism), patterns of behavior (apparent commitment to abide by and expand the coverage of functional cooperation under the rubric of the Transatlantic Declaration), and results (common and complementary foreign policy activities—e.g., aid coordination to Central and Eastern Europe and démarches against repressive regimes).[8] Taking part in the game (the process) is as important as the results.[9] The results of foreign policy consultations are difficult to measure because they are linked to NATO, G7, CSCE (Conference on Security and Cooperation in Europe), UN, and to bilateral relations between the individual EU members and the United States. However, principals on both sides testify to the narrowing of differences and the mutual need to avoid working at cross purposes that underline EU-U.S. dialogue and point to a growing number of specific examples of common or complementary foreign policy activities (actions, declarations) that are linked to EU-U.S. cooperation. The section on the implementation and effects of the Transatlantic Declaration identifies and analyzes some of the thirty examples of common or complementary foreign policy activities that spring, in large part, from EU-U.S. dialogue. They are the outcomes of the process, although many other outcomes linked to the process take form in other multilateral and bilateral forums.

Hegemons provide partners with leadership and create a pattern of order in return for deference but cannot make and enforce either without accepting a degree of consent from other states.[10] The profile of U.S.-EC relations generally fits this definition of hegemony during the first two decades after the end of World War II. During 1970–1980, the United States began to downsize its international leadership role and was less willing to defend its interests in terms complementary to those of Europe. As the Europeans were less inclined to defer to U.S. interests, the EC began to develop the external dimension of the customs union by executing policies toward many of the world's regions and international issues. During this period of EC and U.S. adjustment to hegemonic decline, the EC and the United States were deeply divided over how to respond as a Western bloc to many regional and international economic and political problems. In the present period of bilateral relations, the United States has largely ceased to behave as a hegemon vis-à-vis the EU in response to an acceptance of its own limitations, the rise in EU abilities and influence, and the changes in Europe and the international system at the end of the 1980s. Now neither side has the means or the will to play a hegemonic role in the world. Keohane argued that there will be no more hegemons in the twentieth century, yet states need to cooperate without hegemony.[11] The pragmatic necessity of solving problems too big for any one state to handle—not any form of neo-Atlanticism—drives the level of EU-U.S. cooperation in the absence of hegemony. A "politics of scale" is at work, whereby the benefits of international cooperation outweigh the costs of states acting alone. The logic of cooperation, which gave rise to European Political Cooperation, has begun to spill over to the EU-U.S. arena, despite the expected limitations of how far the Europeans want to see EPC develop trans-Atlantically.

The New Rhetoric of EU-U.S. Political Relations

The rhetoric of EU-U.S. political relations is changing. Whereas in 1989–1990 key leaders pointed to the need for upgraded relations and intensified cooperation at the end of the Cold War, leaders in the mid-1990s have pointed to the need to go beyond cooperation to policy coordination and acting in concert and even a foreign policy partnership. Indeed, during the course of the 1990s, the EC and the United States have gone beyond the practice of consultation to several acts of posthegemonic cooperation.

Despite its interest in deepening trade ties with the Pacific (Asia Pacific Economic Cooperation forum) and Canada and Mexico (North America Free Trade Area), the United States has challenged the EU to forge a new partnership. President Clinton has stated: "A strong and united EC as a key partner in the pressing problems around the world is very much in [U.S.] interests";[12] "Our partnership [needs] to be effective in finding solutions to the problems we face together and to those few problems which continue to divide us";[13] "My administration supports European Union and Europe's development of strong institutions of common purpose and action";[14] "We will benefit more from a strong and equal partner than from a weak one";[15] and, "We believe that a strong and unified Europe makes for a more effective economic and political partner."[16]

Secretary of State Christopher stated that "the U.S. is absolutely committed to European security and to a full range of economic and political interests that we will pursue together,"[17] reaffirmed "U.S. support for a strengthened EC," and concluded that "European integration can also lead to a strengthened U.S.-EC partnership."[18] In the heat of battle over how to conclude the Multilateral Trade Negotiations (MTNs) and end the Bosnian War, Christopher was quoted as saying the United States is "too European-centered" and that "Europe is no longer the dominant area of the world,"[19] yet these remarks ought to be taken in context and balanced against the many strong affirmations of U.S. support for close relations. For example, Undersecretary of State Tarnoff spoke of the "unity of purpose between the U.S. and the EU" in looking for ways actively to work together to bring an end to the conflict in ex-Yugoslavia.[20]

Despite its intense preoccupation with Central and Eastern Europe, the EU, too, has endorsed strengthened ties with the United States. German chancellor Kohl called on the partnership to be further developed, as the United States and EU need each other now more than ever before.[21] Commission president Delors called for the EU and the United States to "combine their efforts and act together . . . to create living structures for concertation and coordination"; "We see the EU as an honest and cooperative protagonist, a genuine partner for the U.S. . . . the Transatlantic Declaration . . . provides a good foundation for a substantial dialogue."[22] External Political Relations commissioner Van den Broek stated that EU-U.S. meetings have helped achieve the "adoption of compatible, and often identical, positions on foreign policy over the past two years."[23] European Parliament president Klepsch stated that "The U.S. and the EC must work and act together in contributing to stability and constructive change in [the world]."[24]

The rhetoric of relations points to a quality of political ties not previously known in the EU-U.S. context. In time, observers will be able to judge whether form will follow rhetoric and whether the notion of a foreign policy consultative culture will result in the kind of policy concertation about which President Delors has spoken. As CFSP is heir to EPC, a brief historical review of EPC-U.S. relations will provide a useful and necessary backdrop to understanding prospects for the next step in the evolution of political relations.

EPC and the United States, 1970–1990

Prior to 1970, the EC states had no mechanism to formulate common foreign policy positions. There were too many constraints on the EC's international margin of maneuver in an era of U.S. hegemony and Cold War bipolarity. The EC was also preoccupied with setting up the internal policies of the customs union. Yet by the 1970s, internal integration had made headway, the outside world was making demands on the EC to act externally, and the EC states were ready to enter into political cooperation. The margin of EC maneuver in international politics began to widen as a result of the decline of U.S. (and Soviet) hegemony and the stabilizing impact of East-West détente on the EC's eastern borders. The birth of EPC in 1970 marked the beginning of a new phase of EU-U.S. relations—an explicitly political one.[25]

The United States was caught off guard when EPC made its international debut in 1973 by taking a common negotiating position at the CSCE talks (to which the United States had to adapt). After years of U.S. neglect of, or even hostility toward, the EC (e.g., the United States did not have the support of EC members for its involvement in the Vietnam War and tensions over the end of the Bretton Woods monetary order left deep wounds), the Nixon administration attempted to move closer to EPC in the ill-fated Year of Europe Initiative. Not interested in allowing the United States a seat at the EPC table, EPC rebuffed the United States but consented to begin briefing like-minded nonmember states, beginning in 1974, whose interests are affected by EPC deliberations (this move became known as the "Gymnich Formula"). In 1974 the EC Commission and the U.S. Cabinet initiated biannual ministerial meetings, and EC and U.S. foreign ministers initiated ad hoc consultations. These patchwork consultative meetings were not related to any overall strategy of bilateral political ties and tended to concentrate on the sharing of views rather than on the unification of policies.

The United States was stunned by EPC opposition to its efforts to resupply Israel during the 1973 Yom Kippur War and to forge a unified Western opposition to the oil cartel's embargo and price hikes. The breakdown of EC unity over how to respond as a unit to the oil embargo of the Dutch and EC support for the "legitimate rights" of the Palestinians sent shock waves through the U.S. foreign policy establishment, scuttled U.S. expectations of EU unity, and ushered in an era of strained relations. Differences over how far the Allies should move to develop East-West détente after the Soviet invasion of Afghanistan in 1979 and in the course of North-South relations presaged more foreign policy disputes in the next decade.

In the 1980s, the United States continued to battle with a more assertive EPC. The United States faulted EPC for a weak response to the Iranian hostage crisis and for slow responses to support U.S. sanctions against both Poland (for the imposition of martial law) and the Soviet Union (for its support of Polish martial law). The United States was shocked by EPC's Venice Declaration, which called for a Palestinian homeland and Palestinian participation in the peace process, a move that contradicted U.S. diplomatic efforts. The United States opposed participation of EC members in the scheme to build a Soviet natural gas pipeline by imposing an embargo on construction equipment exports, and the EC opposed the extraterritorial reach of U.S. law when the Reagan administration sought to apply its embargo to U.S. subsidiaries in Europe. EPC opposed U.S. support for the repressive regime in El Salvador (in its war against leftist rebels) and U.S. support for the right-wing rebels battling to overthrow the democratically elected government in Nicaragua. The United States opposed the EPC-backed Contadora peace process. EPC condemned human rights violations by the U.S.-backed Pinochet government in Chile. EPC opposed U.S. support for the Israeli invasion of Lebanon. Friction occurred over the U.S. bombing of an airstrip under construction by the Communist regime in Grenada (with EC funds), which it claimed would have given the Soviet bloc another strategic foothold in the area.

EC governments opposed the U.S. bombing raid on Libya, a raid the United States maintained was in retaliation for Libyan complicity in acts of international terrorism. The United States was disappointed in EPC's lackluster response to its concerns over Libya just prior to its decision to take punitive military action. Discord continued over U.S. problems with EPC's operation itself—its variable leadership, slow responses to crises, difficulty in keeping to unified stances, and lack of institutionalization.

The United States inadvertently played a catalytic role in EPC's early development simply by being the hegemon against which the Europeans could rebel, from which they could seek independence, and over which they could rally internal support for foreign policy cooperation. EPC members were driven, in part, by the need to develop common foreign policy positions that reflected indigenous or self-styled European interests.[26] For all intents and purposes, EPC was a declaration of EC independence from the United States. The United States responded adversely to any EPC position that conflicted with its policies. EPC would not succumb to U.S. pressures and the United States was eventually forced first to accept EPC as a fait accompli and then to work with EPC. EPC, too, would eventually develop along lines more acceptable to the United States, but that would not happen until the 1990s.

All was not fractious during the period of hegemonic decline. Despite the rise in foreign policy (and trade) disputes, the two sides completed two rounds of General Agreement on Tariffs and Trade (GATT) negotiations to liberalize international trade, helped finalize the 1975 Helsinki Accords, and helped end Israeli occupation of the Sinai peninsula in 1979 (troops from some of the EC members participated in the multinational force that oversaw Israeli disengagement). What is significant about the hegemonic decline period is that the two had to adjust to their new relative roles in the world. Part of the problem of adjustment was that U.S. policy flip-flopped between ignoring or discounting the Europeans and overpowering them with calls for cooperation. The EC sought recognition of its international interests but failed to develop a coherent "U.S. policy." There was no formalized EPC-U.S. consultative framework during the 1970s and much of the 1980s: Political relations developed in a slipshod fashion and those consultations that did occur were not linked to explicit policy objectives.

As many of the foreign policy conflicts during 1970–1980 centered on divergent views over how to deal with the return of the Cold War in 1979 and its impact on East-West détente, the ending of the Cold War ten years later removed many of the tensions associated with earlier political relations and paved the way for more cooperative relations, based on pragmatism, to develop. The entry into force of the 1987 Single European Act (SEA) gave EPC a small but permanent secretariat to better anchor its operations and provide institutional memory, strengthened the hand of the Council presidency in political cooperation, and included the economic and political aspects of security in EPC deliberations. These developments led to a renewed U.S. effort to develop closer ties with EPC, though this time not from a position of hegemony.

Thus in 1984 the EPC Troika political directors and the assistant secretary of state for European and Canadian affairs began meeting biannually to discuss foreign policy issues. In 1987 the EC foreign ministers, EC commissioner for external relations, and the U.S. secretary of state began meeting on an annual basis in New York in the fall (since 1991, they also meet in the spring in Brussels). Subcabinet meetings between the EC Commission director-general for external relations, the U.S. undersecretary of state for economic and agricultural affairs, and other officials began on an ad hoc basis in the 1980s.

Just a few months prior to the adoption of the Transatlantic Declaration in November 1990, the EC and the United States set up new ad hoc consultations between the EPC Troika Working Groups and deputy or assistant secretaries of state for regional/functional areas (these meetings have doubled between 1990 and 1994 so that now there are ten to twelve per presidency; all areas of the world and most international issue areas are covered in these deliberations). In February 1990, U.S. president Bush and EC Council president Haughey agreed to set up biannual EC-U.S. presidential summits. Thus, before German unification and the collapse of the Soviet Union, the EC and the United States were already putting their bilateral political relationship on a more pragmatic and posthegemonic footing. The United States instigated the adjustments because it knew that the EC was going to become a more powerful political unit, and the EC recognized how valuable the U.S. anchor in Europe was.[27]

Prelude to the Transatlantic Declaration

The Transatlantic Declaration came out of a major overhaul of U.S. foreign policy toward the EC in 1989 and an exchange of mutually enforcing comments from leaders on both sides about the need to upgrade relations in 1989–1990.[28] The change in U.S. administrations from Reagan to Bush was a healthy corrective to what had become a decade of trade wars. A more proactive—less NATO-centered—U.S. policy toward the EC emerged from the interagency review of U.S. foreign policy that occurred in spring 1989. The U.S. government had begun to recognize the central role of the EC in the future of post–Cold War Europe and sought to reach out to it in new and constructive ways. The first breakthrough came with strong U.S. support for the EC Commission to coordinate the G24 aid effort in Central and Eastern

Europe. This gave the EC a major boost to its prestige as a responsible international actor, symbolized U.S. recognition of the important role of the EC in Europe, and helped usher in a new era of U.S.-EC policy coordination. The breach of the Berlin Wall on 9 November 1989 confirmed the need to give a more concrete structure to relations. The democratic revolutions that followed in Eastern Europe and the collapse of Soviet power increasingly reminded the Bush administration of the need to improve relations with the EC. The new U.S. policy was pragmatic: If the United States were to have influence with the EC, it could not be seen opposing further EC unification. Thus, it would be best for the United States to work with the EC to develop a relationship in which the responsibilities and burdens of management of Western interests would be more evenly shared.

The emergence of a Bush administration "EC policy" was aided by positive signals from Brussels. President Delors had broached the idea of closer EC-U.S. political links as early as February 1989. Secretary of State Baker's December 1989 Berlin speech stressed the need to "achieve, whether in treaty or some other form, a significantly strengthened set of institutional and consultative links."[29] Baker said "as [Europe's] institutions for political and security cooperation evolve, the link between the U.S. and the EC will become even more important. We want our transatlantic cooperation to keep pace with EC integration and institutional reform."[30]

At the December 1989 EC-U.S. ministerial meeting, the two sides concluded that "as Europe changes, the instruments for western cooperation must adapt; world stability is enhanced by a strong [bilateral] relationship."[31] At the February 1990 meeting between President Bush and Irish prime minister Haughey (also EC Council president), the two agreed to institute biannual summits between the U.S. president and the EC Council president (with the EC Commission president) and biannual consultations between the presidency foreign minister and the U.S. secretary of state.

The idea of a declaration came from the Germans. In April 1990 Foreign Minister Genscher called on the two to "issue a joint declaration heralding a new Atlantic partnership, a declaration encompassing all . . . aspects of our relationship and capable of meeting the challenges confronting mankind."[32] The Germans subsequently set out to work on a draft declaration, which arrived in U.S. hands through the Italian presidency in late summer 1990, and by November the two sides agreed to a final text at the end of the Paris CSCE summit. After months of negotiations on the final text, the drafters faced an inglorious conclusion to their efforts. Pressing issues pertaining to German unification and last-minute French opposition to some of the wording of the text meant that the signing ceremony got pushed off the agenda of the CSCE summit. On 23 November 1990, the two sides simply announced their agreement to no fanfare and to little or no press coverage. Yet the Transatlantic Declaration has become a benchmark in bilateral relations during the transition years of the current decade. It remains a valuable blueprint each side continues to take seriously even if the public awareness of this document remains low.

The Foreign Policy Consultative Culture

The Transatlantic Declaration captured the shift in mentality from hegemonic decline during the Cold War to posthegemony at the end of the Cold War and ushered in a new culture of foreign policy cooperation. The declaration reiterated principles of bilateral relations that go back to the 1940s: human rights, democracy, market economics, social progress, and multilateral cooperation. It also reiterated areas of bilateral cooperation already in practice (consultations on important matters of common interest "with a view to bringing their positions as close as possible without prejudice to their respective independence"). New areas of bilateral cooperation were identified, for example, exchanges and joint projects in science and technology, education, and culture. New areas of cooperation in which the EC and United States committed themselves to act on a multilateral basis were also identified: antiterrorism; combatting the production, trafficking, and consumption of narcotics and related criminal activities; protecting the environment; and stopping nuclear, chemical, biological, and missile technology proliferation. In terms of foreign policy, the Declaration listed the various new and continuing EC-U.S. consultations.

Implementation and Results
of the Transatlantic Declaration

Keohane and Nye argued that the processes of a complex interdependent relationship are as important as its results. This section evaluates the process as an end in itself and as a means to achieve desired results. The process of consultations is important. It enables the two sides, according to principals, to share information, narrow differences, reduce risks of misunderstanding, and seek common approaches. With an occasional exception due to schedule conflicts, the consultative meetings are scheduled and held, testifying to the parties' commitments to follow the outline of meetings provided for in the Declaration.

Indeed, a new set of consultations was added in 1991. EU and U.S. ambassadors now meet regularly in fourteen third country capitals to consult on issues pertaining to the host country (Algiers, Brasilia, Cairo, Damascus, Kinshasa, Luanda, Port au Prince, Pretoria, San José, Beijing, Bangkok, Seoul, Tel Aviv, and Tokyo). These post-Declaration meetings testify to the dynamic of EU-U.S. cooperation, which continues to take new forms. For example, in 1992 the EC, the United States, and Canada set up a Working Group on Iran to seek coordination of policy questions pertaining to Iran's accumulation of weapons of mass destruction and its support of terrorism. The two sides have undertaken separate and joint reviews of their consultations and have concluded that they are valuable and ought to be retained. Recommendations have been made to improve the quality of preparations and to allow more flexibility in calling for meetings on quick notice. The sizable resources each side expends to prepare for, attend, and follow up the consultative meetings are themselves testimony to the value each side places on them.

Evaluating the results or outcomes is a methodological challenge: (1) Consultations are designed more to coordinate policy than to deliver joint action—the former is more difficult to measure than the latter; (2) there is no chronicle of bilateral foreign policy activities and agreements (e.g., common/complementary actions and declarations), so the analyst must work extensively with primary sources to develop such data; (3) some diplomats, keen to preserve the confidentiality of diplomatic exchanges, are reticent to speak about EU-U.S. meetings; and (4) EU-U.S. discussions roll over into wider consultations among like-minded states in other forums, thus making it difficult to attribute specific outcomes to the EU-U.S. negotiations. Yet in some cases, specific acts of cooperation can be linked directly to EU-U.S. consultations.

The Center for European Policy Studies (CEPS) developed a methodology that identified thirty-one examples of foreign policy cooperation that occurred between July 1990 and February 1994.[33] Principals involved in each of these areas of cooperation were interviewed to determine if bilateral consultations were a key factor in arriving at coordinated or complementary actions and declarations.

Of the thirty-one examples, two variants were identified: coordinated actions and declarations, in which the two undertook actions or took declarations together in pursuit of common objectives following bilateral consultations; and complementary actions and declarations, in which the two undertook actions and declarations separately in pursuit of common objectives following bilateral consultations. There were thirteen coordinated and eighteen complementary actions and declarations.[34] Coordinated actions and declarations included instances when the EC (or EU) and the United States:

- Agreed in the context of the 1989 G7 to charge the EC Commission with coordinating Western aid to Central and Eastern Europe with a U.S. aid coordinator posted inside the Commission since 1990.
- Established the Gulf Crisis Financial Coordination Group in 1991 to coordinate assistance to countries suffering adversely from the effects of the Iraq-Kuwait War and the allied liberation of Kuwait.

- Created safe havens for Kurds in northern Iraq and aid to refugees in 1991.
- Aligned sanctions policy on Serbia in 1991.
- Tied the granting of further development aid to the cessation of political violence and government repression in Malawi in 1991.
- Condemned the rejection of civilian control by the military in Yugoslavia in 1991, pledged support for international observers to monitor a ceasefire, and underscored EC-U.S. cooperation on the matter in the CSCE.
- Rejected any outcome to the conflict in Yugoslavia that violated CSCE principles with regard to borders, minority rights, and political pluralism in 1991.
- Reaffirmed willingness to assist Central and Eastern Europe with democratic and market reforms in 1991.
- Resolved in 1991 to work together to set up an arms transfer registry under UN auspices to obtain more transparency in arms transfers and to urge global cooperation.
- Urged the Burmese authorities in 1991 to permit family visits and medical treatment for Nobel Laureate Daw Aung San Suu Kyi, held under house arrest.
- Coordinated diplomatic recognition of Slovenia, Croatia, and Bosnia in 1992 and accepted their pre-crisis borders as legitimate.
- Agreed in 1992 to work to resolve the outstanding issues between Greece and the former-Yugoslav Republic of Macedonia.
- Agreed to a two-pronged strategy in 1994 to lift the siege of Sarajevo through NATO auspices and to work toward a negotiated settlement based on the revised EU action plan.

Complementary actions and declarations included instances when the:

- EC barred a visit to Europe by the Iraqi foreign minister in December 1990 in advance of his trip to the United States.
- EC and the United States reviewed their respective assistance programs for the USSR following the use of force by the Soviet government in the Baltic republics in January 1991.
- EC, following consultations with the United States, granted $213 million in emergency assistance to Israel in 1991, given the losses it sustained by Iraqi missile attacks.
- EC joined the United States in imposing an arms embargo on Burma in 1991 to protest government repression in that country.
- EC and the United States suspended economic assistance to Haiti in 1991 to protest the military coup and political violence occurring there.
- EC, following negotiations with the United States and USSR,

assumed the chair of the Economic Regional Development Group of the Madrid-based Middle East multilateral peace conference in 1991.

- EC and the United States condemned the removal of President Gorbachev from power in 1991, called on the reform process to continue and on the USSR to abide by its international treaties, and threatened withdrawal of support for economic aid if constitutional order was not reestablished.
- EC endorsed in 1991 the warrants for the arrest of two Libyan nationals by France, the United Kingdom, and the United States in connection with the bombings of Pan Am 103 and UTA 772 and condemned terrorism.
- EC and the United States called on the Burmese military authorities in 1992 to stop human rights violations, release political prisoners, and transfer power to a civilian government.
- EC and the United States condemned Sudanese authorities for the execution in 1992 of EC and U.S. employees.
- EC and the United States applauded new diplomatic initiatives in the UN and Organization of American States (OAS) in 1993 to find a solution to the crisis in Haiti and urged all parties to show flexibility.
- EC and the United States (with Canada) set up a Working Group on Iran in 1992 to seek a coordinated response to Iran's accumulation of weapons of mass destruction and support of terrorism.
- EC and the United States levied sanctions against Nigeria in 1992 after the government suspended the results of the presidential elections.
- EC and the United States condemned the setback to the democratic process in Togo in 1993 and tied aid to the cessation of political violence.
- EC in 1993 endorsed U.S. efforts to open North Korea to international inspection of its nuclear facilities.
- EC and the United States condemned the bombing of civilian populations by the Sudanese air force and urged all parties involved to work toward a negotiated settlement of the conflict.

Interpretation of the Foreign Policy Consultative Culture

The inventory of coordinated and complementary actions/declarations underscores the existence of an EU-U.S. culture of foreign policy cooperation in the 1990s. Operational cooperation (i.e., cooperation that gets implemented into policy) covers many of the world's regions (Central and Eastern Europe, the former Soviet Union, Asia, Africa, the Middle East, Persian Gulf, and the Caribbean); many key international problems (weapons proliferation, terrorism, political repression, human rights violations, and inter-state warfare); some of the (nonmilitary) means to punish violators of inter-national norms of behavior (economic sanctions, threat of sanctions, and condemnations); and some of the "carrots" used to stabilize states and regions (foreign aid coordination, diplomatic recognition, and diplomatic mediation). The actual range of international concerns raised in the context of the EU-U.S. foreign policy dialogue is much wider than the examples of coordinated and complementary actions and declarations. The range of dis-cussions is as important as the outcomes of discussions.

Each area of cooperation is linked to the consultative framework ini-tially provided by the Transatlantic Declaration and since expanded and refined. When compared to the absence of cooperative activity during 1970–1980, the record of the 1990s points to a significant change. The con-sultative framework enables each side to strengthen the effectiveness of its own foreign policy through negotiating coordinated or complementary actions with the other. Of the hundreds of foreign policy actions the EU gov-ernments and the United States take each year, the examples of EU-U.S. cooperative acts inventoried above seem relatively small. Yet their number represents more a sample than the universe of total activity, given the absence of a chronicle of all actions and declarations (not all are captured by the Center for European Policy Studies) and the newness of EU-U.S. foreign policy cooperation itself. The EU and the United States have coordinated démarches to third country governments since the 1980s, but these docu-ments are treated confidentially and rarely become public. They are exam-ples of cooperation that cannot be currently quantified.

Most examples of cooperation were found in areas where the EU posi-tion was clear, as were the cases regarding Kurdish safe havens; G24 aid to Central/Eastern Europe; sanctions against Serbia, Haiti, Burma, and Nigeria; a nuclear-free Korea; and a UN Conventional Arms Transfer Register. The more developed and unified the EU position, the more the United States found itself adjusting to the EU's position, a pattern likely to continue as the EU develops new foreign and security policies.

Complementary activities were more frequent in number than coordi-nated ones. This should not come as a surprise. There are few fundamental differences in the general global outlook of the EU states and the United States. Differences tend to be more over means and policy styles than end results. Many EU and U.S. actions/declarations were already being formu-lated when they got discussed in the context of EU-U.S. consultations. Coordinated activities require a much higher level of interaction and thus are harder to achieve.

In sum, the previous analysis sought to identify and explain the out-comes of EU-U.S. foreign policy cooperation. The premium on cooperative acts is pragmatically driven, yet is still striking when compared to the roughness of political relations and the paucity of foreign policy cooperation in 1970–1980.

EU-U.S. Political Relations in the Mid-1990s[35]

What is the state of the EU-U.S. political relationship in the mid-1990s? Four developments in 1993–1994 unleashed the potential for a new chapter in the development of the EU-U.S. political relationship because they pierced previous constraints on foreign policy cooperation: the entry into force of the Treaty on European Union (TEU) on 1 November 1993; completion of the Uruguay Round of Multilateral Trade Negotiations on 15 December 1993; the NATO summit on 10–11 January 1994; and the North Atlantic Council on Bosnia on 9 February 1994.

Indeed, a new chapter in EU-U.S. political relations has opened as the result of the coming into force of the TEU, with its provisions for a Common Foreign and Security Policy and a European Security and Defense Identity (ESDI). As the EU develops a more effective means of conducting foreign and security policies and can back its powerful economic diplomacy with a politico-military capability, the prospects for EU-U.S. foreign policy cooperation expanding into new areas of security are increased in ways previously not thought possible. It will take years for the EU to put CFSP into operation, but the potential alone for CFSP will enliven EU-U.S. political relations in the years ahead. EPC was flawed and its limitations restrained EU-U.S. foreign policy cooperation. CFSP will be welcomed by those who want to see the culture of foreign policy cooperation turn into a full EU-U.S. foreign policy partnership.

Conclusion of the Uruguay Round after seven years of negotiations enables the EU and the United States to put aside many long-simmering commercial disputes of the past decade and turn to improving other areas of the bilateral relationship, including foreign policy. Had closure of the Round failed, fratricidal trade wars would likely have erupted over the many unresolved bilateral disputes of the past decade, endangering cooperation in foreign policy and other areas of bilateral cooperation. The EU would have been thrown into disarray, drawing its attention inward, at the expense of addressing the many international responsibilities at its own doorstep, and the United States might have taken a decisive step away from its traditional multilateralism in favor of regional and bilateral trade policies.

The NATO summit was a historical turning point in EU-U.S. political relations. For the first time, NATO: (1) gave its full support to CFSP and ESDI, which it maintained would strengthen the European pillar of the Alliance; (2) concluded that the EU and NATO share common strategic interests; (3) endorsed the notion of Combined Joint Task Forces (CJTF) to allow WEU to draw on NATO assets in support of CFSP outside the NATO area; and (4) supported and commended the EU action plan of 22 November 1993 to secure a negotiated settlement in Bosnia.

The reaching out of NATO to WEU reflects a sea change in the thinking of the U.S. government. The shift in U.S.-WEU policy is a breakthrough, as some officials in the U.S. government have been (and probably still remain) loath to give support to an organization (whose membership is not open to the United States) that they think competes with NATO (which the United States has long dominated). The NATO decision is a boost to prospects for an ESDI related to, yet separate from, NATO, and it also pays tribute to the thankless task of mediation in former-Yugoslavia that was assigned to the EU. It was extraordinary that a NATO summit communiqué should refer to the EU seven times, to the ESDI seven times, to WEU nine times, and to the CFSP two times. A major strain in trans-Atlantic security relations has been alleviated as a result of NATO (U.S.) recognition of the role of WEU as a means to strengthen the European pillar of NATO and to serve the future security of the EC.

The February 1994 North Atlantic Council ultimatum on the belligerents around Sarajevo (following the bloody mortar attack on a crowded Sarajevan marketplace) to withdraw, or place under UN command, all heavy weapons or else face air strikes reflected intense consultations between the United States, the EU, and EU governments; drew heavily on EU experience of mediation in the conflict in general and on its action plan for a negotiated settlement in particular; brought divergent Allied positions over how to end the war much closer together; eased severe bilateral tensions over the extent of U.S. involvement; and served as the basis of new Allied and international coordination.

After a year of bitter recriminations over how to advance peace to Bosnia in 1993, Europe and the United States finally agreed in February 1994 on a two-pronged strategy to lift the siege of Sarajevo through NATO auspices and to work for a negotiated settlement based on the EU's revised action plan (first broached in November 1993). The United States agreed to press the Bosnian Muslims to be more flexible on the territorial issue, the Europeans agreed to press the Bosnian Serbs to accept the EU action plan and to agree to an improvement in the quality of the territory offered to the Muslims, and both accepted the need for a NATO ultimatum on the belligerents in and around Sarajevo to lay down their heavy weapons. Subsequent coordination took place on 22 February 1994 in Bonn between the EU, UN, United States, and Russia as the four sought to build on the momentum from the ceasefire in Sarajevo to ensure free access to humanitarian aid and the negotiation of ceasefires elsewhere in the country. In April 1994 the four established a contact group on former-Yugoslavia and called for a four-month ceasefire, during which time a proposed new map for Bosnia could be negotiated. In short, although Bosnia was a key source of

EU-U.S. conflict, it was also a key source of intense Allied cooperation and coordination over diplomatic efforts, sanctions monitoring via NATO and the WEU, and humanitarian airlifts.[36]

Taken together, these key developments at mid-decade potentially widen the scope of EU-U.S. foreign policy cooperation. Political relations now appear to blend pragmatic cooperation based on national (and European) interests with the common values and principles, complex interdependence, and security cooperation of a mature bilateral relationship. EU-U.S. relations draw on and complement rich bilateral relations that exist between the individual EU states and the United States. The next stage in the development of EU-U.S. political relations will depend on how the EU develops CFSP and WEU as a result of the 1996 Intergovernmental Conference on Political Union.

Conclusions

Operationalization of the culture of foreign policy cooperation comes at a unique confluence of historical developments. First, the foreign policy behavior of democratic states is guided by common values and principles, so there is a philosophical basis for cooperation. Second, foreign policy cooperation is built on time-tested pillars: an economic partnership based on complex interdependence and the world's most successful political-military alliance. Third, pragmatic necessity drives foreign policy cooperation in the 1990s. The world's problems are too big for any one state to handle in the absence of hegemony. The logic of cooperation, which gave rise to EPC, has begun to spill over into the trans-Atlantic arena. There will be limits to how far European political cooperation can develop trans-Atlantically, but the evidence provided in this chapter suggests some spillover has already occurred.

This chapter has sought to demystify EU-U.S. foreign policy consultations and to introduce the notion of a foreign policy cooperative culture. As this culture deepens, it will not be unreasonable for the EU and the United States to develop a foreign policy partnership—a professed goal of many of those leaders quoted in this chapter. Although the EU and the United States are developing partnerships with other states (e.g., Russia), few partnerships between major powers share the historical resonance found in the EU-U.S. relationship. However, prospects for a EU-U.S. partnership hinge on how well the EU develops CFSP and ESDI.

The United States has a deep stake in how the EU develops CFSP. It needs the EU to succeed in CFSP because it wants an interlocutor of scale as a partner in solving international problems. CFSP is bogged down in internal EU philosophical debates over decisionmaking, institutional divisions of labor, budgets, and semantics; and it is also captive to the crises associated with other aspects of European integration during the period between the ratification of the TEU in 1993 and the next Intergovernmental Conference on Political Union in 1996. In the end, there is no certainty that the member governments will find the political will necessary to allow political cooperation to graduate from EPC to CFSP. Surely, CFSP faces many hurdles ahead, yet there have always been uncertainties associated with the various stages of European integration. As the quest for CFSP is as old as the EU itself, it will not be easily snuffed out by the crisis of the day. The United States—indeed, the outside world—needs the EU to succeed in developing common foreign and security policies that will enable it to act responsibly in the void of power created by the collapse of the Soviet Union and the absence of U.S. hegemony.

Notes

1. For a more in-depth analysis of the notion of foreign policy partnership, see Thomas Frellesen and Roy H. Ginsberg, *EU-U.S. Foreign Policy Cooperation in the 1990s: Elements of Partnership* (Brussels: Center for European Policy Studies, 1994); and Roy H. Ginsberg, "The United States, the European Union, and Acts of Post-Hegemonic Cooperation in the 1990s: The Elements of Partnership," in David Allen and Christopher Hill, eds., *The Changing Context of European Foreign Policy* (London: Routledge, 1994). The author wishes to thank Thomas Frellesen for permitting him to draw on the results of the study by the Center for European Policy Studies for the purpose of this chapter and to thank Peter Ludlow, Director of CEPS, for his collegial support during his stay at CEPS as the 1993–1994 Fulbright Fellow in residence.

2. For further analysis of gaps between expectations and capabilities, see Christopher Hill, "The Capability-Expectations Gap, or Conceptualizing Europe's International Role," *Journal of Common Market Studies* 3 (September 1993), pp. 305–328; and Ginsberg, "The United States."

3. Robert Keohane and Joseph Nye, Jr., *Power and Interdependence* (Boston: Little Brown, 1977, revised 1987), introduced the notion of complex interdependence as an ideal model of international relations, and Robert Keohane, *After Hegemony: Cooperation and Discord in the World Political Economy* (Princeton: Princeton University Press, 1984), introduced the notion of posthegemonic cooperation.

4. Keohane and Nye did not apply their ideal model of complex interdependence to the EC-U.S. relationship that existed during the time of their writings. For an analysis of how complex interdependence can be applied to EU-U.S. relations, see Chapter 2 in Kevin Featherstone and Roy H. Ginsberg, *The United States and the European Community in the 1990s: Partners in Transition* (Boulder: Lynne Rienner, 1993).

5. For an analysis of the application of neomercantilism to EU-U.S. economic relations, see Chapters 2 and 4 in Featherstone and Ginsberg, *The United States and the European Community.*

6. Keohane and Nye, *Power and Independence,* 1977, pp. 9–37.

7. Ibid.

8. Ibid.

9. Ibid.

10. Keohane, *After Hegemony*, p. 46.

11. Ibid., p. 183.

12. *USIS Wireless File,* 12 January 1994, pp. 9–10.

13. *USA Text,* USAT PL 17, 7 May 1993.

14. "Remarks by the President," Hotel de Ville, Brussels, January 9, 1994, *USA Text,* USAT PL2, 9 January 1994, U.S. Mission to the EU.

15. *USIS Wireless File,* 12 January 1994, pp. 9–10.

16. Ibid.

17. Statement by Secretary Christopher, *USA Text,* USAT PL 20, 8 June 1993.

18. Ibid.

19. Cited in Mark Nelson, "Transatlantic Travails," in *Foreign Policy* 92 (Fall 1993), p. 79; and in *The Economist,* 30 October 1993, p. 15.

20. "Tarnoff Briefs on Discussions with Allies on Bosnia on February 11, 1994," *USIS,* Embassy of the United States, 15 February 1994.

21. Helmut Kohl, "Address to National Governors Association," Washington, 31 January 1994.

22. Address by Jacques Delors to the 1993 World Leadership Conference, International Management and Development Institute, Washington, 18 March 1993.

23. Hans van den Broek, "The Future of Transatlantic Relations," address at Chatham House, London, 3 June 1993.

24. Egon Klepsch, "Speech to the American Chamber of Commerce," 9 October 1993, as cited in *Agence Europe,* 21 October 1993, p. 4.

25. President Kennedy in 1962 attempted in his Grand Design to forge a foreign policy partnership with the EC states, but it was an idea whose time had come much too early in the EC's development. For in-depth analysis of EPC-U.S. political relations during the early years, see Chapter 6 in Roy H. Ginsberg, *Foreign Policy Actions of the European Community: The Politics of Scale* (Boulder: Lynne Rienner, 1989).

26. Ibid.

27. An example of how the U.S. government was affected by EC assertiveness, despite the advent of new consultative mechanisms, came in January 1990 at a meeting of the EC foreign ministers in Dublin when the European Council accepted Mikhail Gorbachev's proposal for a CSCE summit before consulting with the U.S. government. This action appeared to be at odds with the spirit of the Gymnich Formula of 1974 (the EC's response to the Year of Europe, in which the EC committed itself to consultation with the United States before action was taken).

28. For in-depth analysis of the run-up to the Transatlantic Declaration, see Roy H. Ginsberg, "The United States and the Transatlantic Declaration," in Wolfgang Wessels, ed., *The Transatlantic Declaration—the First Lessons* (Bonn: Europa Union Verlag, forthcoming).

29. James Baker, "A New Europe, A New Atlanticism," prepared address delivered in Berlin on 12 December 1989 (Washington: Bureau of Public Affairs, U.S. Department of State, December 1989), no. 1233, pp. 2–3.

30. Ibid.

31. "European Community and the U.S. Must Forge Closer Ties," *European Community News,* no. 45.89, 18 December 1989.

32. Hans-Dietrich Genscher, "The Future of a European Germany," speech delivered to the American Society of Newspaper Editors, Washington, 6 April 1990 (New York: German Information Center, April 10, 1990), vol. 8, no. 9.

33. See Frellesen and Ginsberg, *EU-U.S. Foreign Policy Cooperation in the 1990s.*

34. Ibid.

35. This section draws heavily from Roy H. Ginsberg, "Transatlantische Beziehungen," in Wolfgang Wessels and Werner Weidenfeld, eds., *Jahrbuch der Europäischen Integration 1993/94* (Bonn: Europa Union Verlag, 1994).

36. For a more detailed analysis of the EU's performance in former-Yugoslavia, see Geoffrey Edwards's contribution in Chapter 10 of this volume.

Part 4

The Future: Challenges and Limitations

17

The Potential and Limits of CFSP: What Comes Next?

Günter Burghardt

Three years after the agreement at Maastricht to establish a Common Foreign and Security Policy (CFSP), it has become abundantly clear that the Treaty is insufficient as a basis for the European Union (EU) to meet a mounting array of external challenges. The pillar structure, which the Dutch Council presidency had tried to avoid when presenting its draft Treaty in September 1991, has proved cumbersome and inefficient, as forecasted by the Commission during the negotiations. There has been little progress on the security front. The development of operational capabilities needed in order to support a European Union defense identity is proceeding slowly. The implementation of the newly defined relationship between the European Union and the Western European Union (WEU) leaves much to be desired because of some member states still not having overcome their initial political and institutional reservations. Indeed, the WEU has been tempted to assert its own role as an independent organization, to acquire a foreign and security policy role—notably through political dialogue with Central and Eastern Europe, including Russia, with obvious risks of overlapping with EU activities. Work on subjects already identified for eventual joint action by the European Council as far back as 1992—in particular, concerning economic aspects of security—has been delayed because of some member states refusing even to have recourse to the intergovernmental procedures of Article J, as the artificial compromise over the setting-up of an informal expert group on a European armaments policy outside the Treaty framework has illustrated. On another front, there have been constant wrangles over the legal base and financing of CFSP. Perhaps these problems could have been overcome more swiftly if there had been the political will to move forward in a coherent and consistent manner, but a review of the first year of CFSP in operation sadly reveals the opposite. There has been an almost total lack of strategic planning, a repeated disregard for EU procedures, coupled with

321

regrettable ups and downs in the performance of the Council presidency system, and a failure to commit the necessary resources to deal with major problems of direct concern to the EU, with the effect that the very notion of a CFSP sounds increasingly hollow. The change of labels from European Political Cooperation (EPC) to CFSP has raised expectations but, regrettably, these have not been matched by appropriate actions.

As a result of the lengthy struggle to secure the ratification of the EU Treaty, CFSP did not come into operation until 1 November 1993. This is, however, no convincing justification for the poor results so far, since CFSP could look back to more than twenty years of EPC *acquis*. The Belgian presidency made laudable efforts to use most of the short time remaining under their six-month stewardship to mark the difference with "classic" EPC, by launching the first five joint actions at the 29 October 1993 European Council meeting; but much of the momentum was subsequently lost in the controversies characterizing the first half of 1994. As a result, we have again witnessed a tendency for member states increasingly to portray themselves through uni-, bi-, and trilateral initiatives—for example, the Contact Group on Bosnia, the revival of the "Group of Four" (notably in preparing the Budapest CSCE summit meeting), the embargo by Greece against the former-Yugoslav Republic of Macedonia, uncoordinated French initiatives concerning Rwanda in other forums, "bilateral" visits of the Council presidency foreign minister to sensitive countries like Iran, just to mention a few examples on a list growing ever longer. Bilateral initiatives, such as the Hurd/Andreatta Proposals on reinforcing political dialogue with Central and Eastern European countries or the Kinkel/Kooimans Initiative concerning strengthening of the Conference on Security and Cooperation in Europe (CSCE), in response to Russian proposals can, of course, underpin or trigger collective European Union action, albeit at the risk of creating confusion with respect to EU procedures. But the policy of three member states (Germany, France, and the United Kingdom), starting under the Greek and further developed during the German presidency, of virtually taking over EU policy toward Bosnia left other partners no choice but to accept grudgingly an evolution brought about by the incapacity of the international community to deal effectively with the most important challenge for CFSP in Europe, while being in no way able to prevent the Bosnian Serbs from flouting the most basic international standards. Other examples, although less visible, are the tendency for "Group of Four" coordination at the expense of agreed upon structures for EU-U.S. consultation and cooperation, or trilateral (again Germany, France, and the United Kingdom) concertation concerning relations with Ankara. Dealings with the tragedy in the former Yugoslavia have illustrated more than any other issue the declining impact of the European Community/European Union on events. While, at the beginning of the drama, the European Council dispatched Presidents Santer (Luxembourg European Council presidency) and Delors in April/May 1991 to Belgrade, in

December 1994 the foreign ministers of the two member states holding a permanent seat on the United Nations Security Council decided to go to Belgrade to explain the latest version of the Contact Group's peace plan.

The 1996 Intergovernmental Conference (IGC) will offer an opportunity to assess and hopefully improve CFSP procedures; but it will also produce the risk that some member states may try to renationalize CFSP (and possibly other parts of the integration process) by pushing it onto an even more intergovernmental track. It is too early to speculate about the IGC proper. The time between now and the IGC must rather be used to improve the performance of CFSP by fully implementing the Treaty on European Union (TEU) and preparing the ground in practical terms for institutional changes to be agreed on later.

For its part, the Commission has made a start in reorganizing itself to cope with the new challenges with the decision of the third Delors Commission to create an external political relations portfolio under Hans van den Broek, the experienced former Dutch foreign minister from 1982 to 1992, and the establishment, in the spring of 1993, of a separate Directorate-General for External Political Relations (DG 1A). Because of the limited two-year mandate of the last Delors Commission, these changes were not accorded sufficient time to prove themselves. Indeed, there had been various problems in the functional separation of political and economic external portfolios at the political level, which led President Santer to reorganize external relations into four mainly geographical portfolios while maintaining functional responsibilities, particularly with regard to CFU's and trade policies. Santer has retained CFSP in his own portfolio, in agreement with Van den Broek, whose services remain in charge of coordinating CFSP matters while receiving added responsibilities for all aspects of relations with Europe—the main priority issue both for external relations of the Community and within CFSP. The Commission thus underlined its determination, politically and in terms of organizational decisions, to fully contribute to the success of the new Treaty in the sovereignty-sensitive field of foreign and security policy.

The Potential of CFSP

It is important to remind ourselves about some of the main factors contributing to the inherent potential of CFSP. CFSP is the constituent element, the spinal cord of the Political Union concept, which, together with Economic and Monetary Union, form the two sides of the medal called "European Union." The Maastricht Treaty has become the first comprehensive constitution accommodating economic and political affairs in one single framework defined as "European Union" and which maintains the impetus toward the *finalité politique*. It is equally true that the areas of the Treaty characterized by intergovernmental cooperation derive their strength from the dynamics of economic and monetary integration. The dynamics of the integration process provide *the* powerful engine of the Union, which, according to Article A, is *based* on the Community. Intergovernmental cooperation alone, through CFSP and "pillar III" issues, would almost certainly result in the Union ending up in a "Jurassic Park" of powerless European organizations. As the twin brother of the Community's external economic relations, CFSP should enable the Union to put its full economic *and* political weight to bear on international affairs. The single institutional framework is the tool provided by the Treaty to create this synergy and to allow the effects of integration to encourage more determined foreign policy cooperation. The notion of the Union's global action under Article C of the Treaty, combining the potential of economic, development, political, and security instruments of external action, is the clearest constitutional expression of this concept. It puts the Council presidency *and* the Commission into the driving seat of more coherent and comprehensive European Union external action.

While the Community was still digesting the lessons of the Gulf War, the 1989 revolution and the need to organize post-Communist Europe quickly became the overriding challenge in the run-up to the Maastricht Treaty. The actualization of German unification within the framework of the European Community institutions provided the most formidable additional reason for adding Political to Economic and Monetary Union. The rhetoric of Germany's division being part of the division of Europe as a whole suddenly became political reality when the newly emerging democracies behind the former Iron Curtain voiced expectations not only for assistance in economic and political reform but also—and more importantly—to be anchored in the process of European unification from which they had been excluded through no fault of their own. While German unification already changed the Community's center of gravity, the emerging European Union found itself quite unprepared to face up to the challenges of Central and Eastern European geopolitics, the disintegration of the former Soviet Union, and the polarizing factor of Russia's new assertiveness. The drama of the brutal disintegration of the former Yugoslavia, coupled with an unacceptable ideology of ethnic cleansing, put the spotlight on the inadequacies of the combined effects of traditional external economic policy instruments and the limited diplomatic clout of EPC. The absence of the willingness and the capacity of member states to add a credible military threat to the otherwise full spectrum of external action condemned the Community and its member states to no more than a collective appeasement policy. The use of military force, not the European Union's diplomatic efforts, drew the map on the ground. However, CFSP in post-Communist Europe is confronted with a formidable challenge and an opportunity to derive strength and motivation from the historical task of providing the greater Europe with an anchor of stability. To take on this challenge successfully, it must learn the lessons from its inadequacies in the former Yugoslavia. The EU initiative for a Stability Pact in Europe is an important example of preventive diplomacy. If the EU's pre-accession strategy to prepare Central European states for eventual membership, agreed upon at Essen in December 1994, is to succeed, it will oblige the Union to strengthen its capacity for integration—otherwise, there is a danger of disintegration and a return to the failed approach of shifting alliances.

Since its inception in the early 1970s, EPC has been dogged by persistent worries from the more "Atlanticist" member states about the impact that a too tight coherence between European powers might have on the Europe–United States alliance. The United States did not send clear messages during the Cold War; its attitude sometimes resembled what psychology calls a "double bind": On the one hand, it approved in principle of the idea of harmonizing the foreign policy of EC members (along with support for wider European integration), and actively pushed for "burden sharing"; however, it also sometimes seemed to indicate that it liked European cooperation only if it reinforced, rather than challenged, U.S. influence. Thus, for example, it showed distaste at EPC moves on the Arab-Israeli dispute in the mid-1970s and early 1980s—and U.S. efforts, exemplified by the Dobbins-Bartholomew Memorandum of February 1991, to influence directly the difficult IGC negotiations on the defense component of a future common foreign policy—by providing arguments to the "Atlanticists." The TEU's provisions for a CFSP coincide with a fundamental U.S. review of the nature of its commitment toward a post–Cold War Europe, East and West. The new uncertainties make the question of the U.S. reaction to any European Security and Defense Identity (ESDI) more pressing than ever. Would the United States respond to, say, a coherent CFSP and a respectable defense force by withdrawing its troops faster and washing its hands of future crises among the EU's neighbors? Or is U.S. involvement unaffected by the development of European unity? Or would, indeed, a united European stand, effective foreign policy mechanism, and proper burden sharing and even resource pooling in defense and security measures actually facilitate cooperation with the United States in a more balanced Euro-Atlantic Alliance?

After a year of reassessment, the Clinton administration has come up with a clear answer to these questions by genuinely and unambiguously supporting a European Security and Defense Identity. This, in turn, has helped to clarify the internal European debate about the relationship between ESDI and the Transatlantic Alliance. The NATO summit on 10–11 January 1994 led to agreement on resource pooling: The United States would allow the WEU/Eurocorps to use NATO personnel, equipment, and infrastructure for operations in which the United States decided not to take part: the formula of "separable but not separate" structures. President Clinton used his first

European tour to NATO and EU headquarters in January 1994 to state that the future security of Europe lies in its integration—militarily, politically and economically. He recognized that a strong, confident Europe will make a better partner than a weak, divided one, whether in promoting free trade or in spreading stability eastward. It is a recognition that shared European-U.S. interests in foreign policy far outweigh the differences. CFSP can thus derive strength from a return of Europe's most important partner to its traditional support of European integration. CFSP and the transformation of the Euro-Atlantic Alliance will either both succeed, or both fail.

The Weaknesses of CFSP

Despite considerable preparatory work before the entry into force of the TEU, concentrated particularly on the definition of common interests and the putting into place of the necessary institutional arrangements, the very first experiences at this initial stage of CFSP do not allow for the conclusion that the credibility gap between the ambition of the vocabulary and the reality of practical policy has been reduced by any sizable degree. Although CFSP can build on the major achievements of the European Communities' external relations and those—admittedly less significant because largely declaratory—of EPC, foreign policy has not become more unified and security policy has not even entered its embryonic stage, as outlined in Article J.4. This is particularly disquieting on the eve of enlargement of the EU, since the introduction of CFSP was part of the indispensable prior deepening.

Proposals on what to do next require a thorough diagnosis of shortcomings. They also need to consider the subsequent stages of the political agenda ahead of us. The change of vocabulary from the more modest EPC to the more ambitious CFSP has not modified basic underlying weaknesses, which can be subdivided into three categories: systemic, substantive, and institutional.

Are some member states "more equal than others"? This appears still to be the perception in the case of the United Kingdom and France, both of which assume responsibilities as permanent members of the UN Security Council and as nuclear weapons states. It might also become the case for Germany, now that it is in the process of overcoming its domestic impediments with regard to the defense-related dimension of the TEU. But this perception leads to a vicious circle: The larger states are not prepared to trust the EU to represent and implement their foreign policies, hence they create ad hoc coalitions—which, in turn, makes it more difficult to achieve EU visibility, responsibility, and coherence.

Although Article J recognizes the specificities of member states' foreign and security policy status, it is hardly reconcilable with systematically putting individual nations' political interests "first," instead of acting in solidarity and facilitating the task of the Union to speak with one voice. Enlargement without deepening would inevitably reinforce such centrifugal attitudes and lead to—in particular—big member states looking for smaller and more intimate circles within an ever larger club.

Do member states recognize the existence of "common important interests"? Are they ready to exercise these interests in common? Are they willing and able to put at the disposal of the Union the necessary means to do so? These questions, raised by President Delors during the 1991 IGC on Political Union, still remain largely unanswered. The first modest set of common actions launched at the end of the Belgian presidency and the absence of any sizable new initiative since then are witness to the insufficient political will generated by the new system. Moreover, looking into the substantive ingredients of what has been qualified to be "joint action" under Article J.3, these consist largely of Community instruments mobilized in support of joint actions rather than committing member states' own—national—means for the benefit of common European Union foreign policy.

Apart from the built-in limits of any intergovernmental framework based on consensus, CFSP so far has neither improved visibility nor continuity of the Union's global external action. Discontinuity of widely overburdened six-month rotating "presidencies" is, on the contrary, the main feature of the system. Elements of continuity that would compensate for this, like a more active role of the Commission or more systematic use of the Community budget for CFSP expenditure, are still met with utmost mistrust by defenders of intergovernmentalism. The resulting lack of visibility is especially regrettable when compared to the importance of the EU's contributions in the field of trade, cooperation, and finance. While the U.S. superpower teaches us how to achieve maximum publicity with often little cash, the EU is the champion of maximum, notably financial, contributions and minimum political gains.

The Political Agenda Ahead

What the EU requires between now and the year 2000 is an inspiring concept comparable to "1992," which was set in motion by the first Delors Commission in 1985. While the Single European Act (SEA) translated the 1992 program into treaty obligations, the revised Maastricht Treaty and its evolving geopolitical environment will need to lead the way into the next century. Such a political agenda should comprise the following three stages: (1) full and dynamic implementation of present Treaty provisions while integrating successfully into the Union the new European Free Trade Association (EFTA) members by 1996; (2) an IGC on how to prepare for the final phase of Economic and Monetary Union (EMU) and the further strengthening of CFSP (including common defense policy and common defense, as sketched out in Article J.4), as well as the necessary institutional reforms with ratification in 1996/1997; and (3) eventual subsequent enlargement negotiations with a new wave of applicants mainly from Central Europe, in light of the results of the IGC and of progress made by these countries on their rapprochement to the Union. The single currency and full-fledged CFSP are the indispensable two "tigers in the tank." If the Union does not wish to turn out to be a toothless tiger because of a lack of consensus on these strategic objectives, it might become inevitable for a nucleus of member states to take on the motor function.

This notion is currently at the heart of an intensive debate on a "multi-speed" Europe, launched by the CDU/CSU (Schäuble/Lamers) Paper on the future of the Union. While various other models[1] are being considered, in capitals and academic circles, to reconcile the pursuit of integration with the prospects of enlargement, "variable speed" seems to be the only option that allows for maintaining unity of purpose in the integration project, while taking into account the (uneven) capacity of individual member states to commit themselves to "inner core" policies at a given time. Under this scheme, all member states would be bound to participate eventually in all common policies (and, in fact, are called to contribute to the latter's development, albeit indirectly), but some could delay—or phase in—their commitment to selected policies (EMU, Defense, etc.) over time. A degree of variable speed is already foreseen by the mechanism envisaged in Maastricht for the construction of EMU; and in many ways, the current status of Ireland and Denmark with regard to WEU and prospects for a common defense policy can be considered as part of an evolutionary process of the same kind. More of this flexibility (timewise) will no doubt be needed to integrate fully the acceding (EFTA) countries, as well as the associate countries of Central Europe, whose full integration in several policies will likely need a longer time-span than that required for accession proper. On the other hand, the coherence of the Union's institutional framework may be put under severe strain should several "circles" of countries be established under this scheme, each proceeding with its own pace and timetable. More reflections are clearly needed, in the period leading up to the next IGC, on institutional issues and on the impact of "variable speed" options thereupon.

The fact that since July 1994 until the end of 1997, not less than five out of the six Communities' founding members will successively hold the Council presidencies, together with Euro-committed Spain and Ireland, provides a unique opportunity for more continuous political leadership. The newly elected European Parliament and five-year Commission, which took up office in January 1995, will provide much needed additional continuity.

While it would seem too early to speculate about the possible outcome of the 1996 IGC, much remains to be done during the period leading up to the 1996 phase immediately ahead of us to ensure full implementation of present CFSP provisions and thus to prepare practically the ground for the next Treaty revision. The shortcomings of CFSP, summarized above, need to be scrutinized and significantly improved during each of the four main phases of CFSP: analysis of EU interests, policy proposals, decisionmaking, and implementation. There is an obvious need for more efficient CFSP instruments and mechanisms corresponding to each of these four steps.

A European Capacity for Foreign Policy Analysis

The lack of any systematic assessment capability at Union level directed toward the concept of defining important common interests and properly geared to the decisionmaking process:

- Has confined CFSP to excessively limited joint action with a disappointingly meager record, and makes the selection of subjects for joint action look haphazard
- Precludes well-prepared substantive discussion about long-term implications of foreign policy options
- Prevents the emergence of a pro-active, rather than re-active, foreign policy (preventive diplomacy rather than crisis management)

While in the Community framework, the Council is working on the sole basis of Commission proposals designed to reflect Community interests. Member states arrive in CFSP—as in former EPC—each with their individual analysis based on respective national interests. Hence the proposal that the Commission, in close cooperation with the Council secretariat, should take the initiative, with the help of the national planning units in the member states' foreign offices, to move toward the creation of a permanent structure akin to the United States National Security Council. The Commission's specific contribution consists of injecting forward planning capacity based on a synthesis of Community interests in the external economic and development policy fields into broader analysis of the Union's long-term interests and objectives in foreign and security policies. The Commission's approximately 120 permanent representations in third countries are ready to step up cooperation with member states' embassies in order to collect information and provide joint assessments. The Union structure should moreover link up with WEU's military planning capacities to include, at an early stage, security and defense-related elements into a global analysis of objectives and the means necessary to achieve them. WEU has offered such cooperation at the ministerial meeting at Noordwijk in November 1994.

Joint Actions and Priorities

The lack of any focal point for devising and proposing foreign policy action as part of global action (Article C, TEU) mobilizing the economic, financial, diplomatic, and security-related resources of the Union, results in member states making disproportionate use of their liberty to take individual action or engaging "à la carte" bilateral initiatives without sufficient regard to the constraint of the Union's interests or guarantee that the positions of member states as a whole are being taken into consideration. Early experience with the first set of joint actions decided by the October 1993 European Council illustrates the need for systematic cooperation between the Council presidency, supported by the secretariat, and the Commission.

Joint action without sufficient genuine foreign policy content either tends to be extremely limited (observe the elections to the Russian Duma in December 1992) or simply to provide a CFSP label to what would largely be possible to achieve with Community instruments (securing increased humanitarian aid in the former Yugoslavia; financial support for the Palestinian police force in the occupied territories) with limited added value. On the other hand, joint action to achieve maximum impact needs to be part of a global action of the Union in all fields of external policies. Accompanying the Middle East peace process, support of democratic transition in South Africa, promotion of stability among Central and Eastern European countries affected by problems of national minorities, and the search for a negotiated political solution to the conflicts in the former Yugoslavia are cases in point, where diplomatic action committing member states to common objectives has to be combined with "sticks" and "carrots" resulting from Community external economic instruments (sanctions; development of relations with the Community; financial assistance). In fact, in many cases where joint action will be required, all three pillars of the TEU might be concerned, including the field of security policy (from arms exports control to nonproliferation).

A decisive upgrading of the efficiency of CFSP action, however, will depend primarily on the ability of the member states to spell out clearly their common interests, starting with the need to define strategically the Union's role in its area of geographic proximity, that is, the rest of Europe and the Mediterranean region. There is no doubt that the wider continental dimension should constitute the most immediate geopolitical priority for CFSP. This includes the process of association and eventual integration of Central European countries; striving for peace and the protection of what remains from a multi-ethnical society in former-Yugoslavia; promoting stability in Europe in the widest sense; helping the transition in Russia and the Ukraine; forging new cooperative links with the whole space of the Commonwealth of Independent States (CIS); and working for stability and prosperity in the Mediterranean. In the longer run, the Union will have to establish its role beyond this area of geographic proximity, as a leading world player—be it with regard to trans-Atlantic relations, to development and peace in Africa, or to establishing closer relations with the increasingly important Asia/Pacific region.

Strengthening the Decisionmaking Capacity

The holy cow of the consensus rule in an ever wider Union, if strictly applied, will most certainly result in bringing the embryonic CFSP to a grinding halt. Replacing unanimity by some qualified majority rule would be a task for the 1996 IGC. Meanwhile, two existing provisions would have to be effectively implemented:

- Qualified majority decisionmaking on modalities for joint action on the basis of Article J.3 (2)
- Urging dissenting member states to avoid preventing decisions for which unanimity is required, and where a qualified majority exists in favor of that decision, according to the Declaration (No. 27) attached to the TEU on CFSP voting procedures

The Need for a Single Voice

The lack of visibility and continuity is particularly apparent when it comes to implementing foreign policy and representing the Union on the international scene. It is perhaps not too early to consider evolving the current Troika system (which, in reality, is a quadriga of three member states and the Commission) to a system that includes the current and following presidencies plus the Commission. The basic principle that the Union must speak with a single voice, however, goes beyond the matter of presentation; it addresses the problem of substance. When dealing with the outside world, European Union representatives need to be able to explain and to defend the overall external action of the Union. A *bicephalous* voice of combined presidency/Commission spokesmen would therefore seem to ensure both coherence and flexibility. This should therefore become the standard rule of European Union representation as such, without precluding other, Troika or full, representation whenever necessary.

Conclusion

The Maastricht Treaty on European Union was the result of an inevitable, and thus far unconvincing, compromise between economic and monetary integration and intergovernmental cooperation in foreign policy and home affairs. Yet the Common Foreign and Security Policy, including its still to be defined common defense component, is one of the essential innovations of the new Treaty meant to justify the ambitious label of "European Union." What was intended to provide the postwar European unification process with additional strength and political *animo* to face the challenge of post-Communist European geopolitics risks turning into one of the principal reasons for disenchantment and Euroskepticism. It is indeed fair to say that at this stage, the Union has not succeeded sufficiently in translating its enormous economic potential into political weight.

Not only in the former Yugoslavia has the Union not lived up to the expectations of its own citizens and of the people in the new democracies in Central Europe. In the Middle East, in Rwanda, in setting out a strategic approach to future relations with Russia, and in redefining the trans-Atlantic security link, the EU's record of political achievements remains very meager, and totally inadequate in comparison with the very substantial economic efforts that the EC deploys worldwide.

A few lessons should thus be drawn from the preceding sobering analysis:

- The EU needs to develop the political will to identify and pursue common objectives decisively. In this respect, CFSP starts in capital cities, not in Brussels.
- Full use should be made of all the instruments available to the Union—namely, by developing a more coordinated and global approach to external actions. Even though the pillars structure of the TEU represents a weakness in terms of efficiency, there is much scope for improvement in this respect, even under the present framework.
- Structural flaws in the decisionmaking, exposed by the first year of operation of CFSP, should be tackled as appropriate, either in advance or in the framework of the next IGC. This concerns the need to create mechanisms to define common interests and plan possible responses in advance of crises erupting (planning and analysis capacity), as well as the need to overcome the continuing adherence to the unanimity principle and to ensure more consistency in the executive and representation functions.

Strengthening and revising CFSP goes hand-in-hand with another objective (still unfulfilled) of the TEU: in other words, that the Union, in symbiosis with WEU (which is "an integral part of development of the EU"—Article J.4) should become a serious player in the field of security and defense. "Collective defense" engagements and guarantees will have to be prudently reassessed over time, as the EU, WEU, and possibly NATO prepare for future enlargements.[2] Yet even more compelling priorities (time-wise) have arisen with regard to new subregional or diffuse threats to European security and stability. Wars, tensions, and massive socioeconomic disarray rage close to the Union's borders, calling for common responses (threat assessment, conflict prevention, crisis management, and intervention where needed) that are not forthcoming, due to the insufficient development of a European Security and Defense Identity. Much political determination is needed to deal with these and other closely related issues, such as the need to avoid or reduce costly duplication of resources in the defense field, through the establishment of rational and complementary defense collaboration. All those issues are already referred by the TEU to the future IGC, but only modest collaborative steps are being taken in preparation thereof, including establishing closer relations within the "security triangle" (EU, WEU, and NATO).

The success or the failure of the Common Foreign and Security Policy will—together with the full implementation of the Economic and Monetary Union and the strengthening of the Union's institutional framework—decide the future course of European unification—the capacity of the Union to further enlarge into Central and Southern Europe; the role of the Union as an anchor of stability for greater Europe and as a meaningful partner within a renewed trans-Atlantic alliance to the West and with Russia to the East; and the potential of the Union to defend the common interests of its member states on the international scene and to contribute to international solidarity. Further enlargement without the necessary internal strengthening would produce yet another "Eurosaure" in a Jurassic Park full of acronyms, which would be in the interest neither of present nor of future members.

Notes

The content of this chapter is the author's own view and is not that of any organization or institution.

1. Such as "variable geometry," which implies varying inner circles of member states committed to different policies (EMU, Defense, etc.); or "Europe à la carte," basically relying on the extension of "opt-out" practices.

2. For a more detailed analysis of the relationship between WEU and EU, see Mathias Jopp's contribution in Chapter 9 of this volume.

18

Enlargement as a Challenge and Incentive for Reform[1]

Paul Luif

The enlargement of the European Union (EU) in the 1990s basically concerns three groups of countries:

1. The European Free Trade Association (EFTA) countries: Austria, Finland, and Sweden, which joined the EU in 1995. In Norway, membership was rejected by a majority of the population in November 1994. The Swiss government suspended its membership application after plans for joining the European Economic Area (EEA) were rejected in a referendum in December 1992. Iceland and Liechtenstein have not (yet) applied for EU membership.
2. Three Mediterranean countries that have already applied for EU membership: Turkey, Malta, and Cyprus.
3. Several Central and Eastern European countries (CEEC), all of which have already applied for EU membership.

These (potential) enlargements have simply raised the question of numbers: how to maintain and perhaps even improve the efficiency of decision-making with fifteen, eighteen, or even more member states.

The problems concerning the membership of the Mediterranean countries and the CEEC will not be touched here.[2] This chapter concentrates on the accession of the EFTA countries. The fact that most of the applicant EFTA countries have had a long tradition of neutral foreign policies poses the question of the quality of Common Foreign and Security Policy (CFSP). Will the new members influence the contents of the CFSP statements and decisions, and if yes, in what way? Will there be the possibility of joint actions?

The origin of European Political Cooperation (EPC) had much to do with the first EFTA enlargement. In particular, the (political) weight of the

United Kingdom made it necessary to find a platform for foreign policy coordination among European Community (EC) member states. It was significant that this foreign policy cooperation was started *before* the United Kingdom (as well as Denmark and Ireland) became a member of the EC.[3] The neutral status of Ireland played no role in the membership negotiations. The southern enlargement brought the "Greek problem" and the reduction of consensus among EC members on EPC questions.

Security (especially "hard" security, in a military sense) has never been part of European integration—except in the unsuccessful attempt of the European Defense Community (EDC) of the 1950s.[4] It often lingered in the background—in particular, during enlargement negotiations (United Kingdom 1961–1963, Spain in the 1980s),[5] but it never became part of EC decisionmaking.

Why Did the EFTA Countries Apply for EC Membership?

Looking at Figure 18.1, the preliminary question to answer is why the EFTA countries did *not* apply at an earlier date for EC membership. They all have had a large and growing amount of trade with the EC. The answer used to be quite simple. Four of the EFTA members have been neutral countries that

Figure 18.1   Exports of EC and EFTA Countries to Both Integration Groups, 1990, Percentages of Total Exports

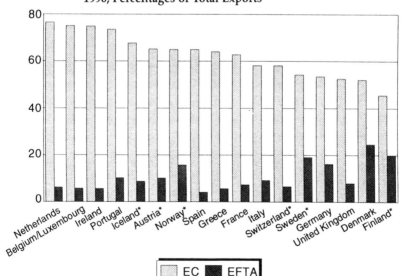

Sources: External trade, *Statistical Yearbook 1991*, Brussels/Luxembourg 1991; *EFTA Trade 1990*, Geneva 1991.
Note: Asterisks show EFTA member states.

were militarily not aligned to the West. Neutrality used to be seen as an obstacle for EC membership. Norway, a NATO member, tried to join the EC in 1972, but the Norwegians rejected membership in a referendum. Iceland, a NATO member as well, never thought of joining the EC because it did not want to open its fishing waters to Community fishing industries. Liechtenstein, which was a member of EFTA since 1 September 1991, has generally followed Swiss behavior in external affairs.[6]

Why has this attitude toward the EC/EU changed? A study by John Redmond suggests the following reasons:

- The creation of the European Economic Area would not be sufficient to offset the handicap of being outside the EC's internal market
- The rapid collapse of the Soviet bloc
- A growing sense that nonmembership in the EC implied, in some sense, exclusion from "Europe"
- There has been a "bandwagon" or "domino" effect, which has been accelerated by the sheer pace of change of the political map of Europe[7]

There can be no doubt that all four factors played a role in the decision of the EFTA countries to apply for membership. It is clear that the offer of the EC, and, in particular, Commission president Jacques Delors, to start negotiations on the EEA gave some of the EFTA countries a possibility of avoiding the issue of EC membership. When it turned out that the EEA would not be an alternative to EC/EU membership, the countries most eager to reach an agreement with the EC (Sweden and Switzerland) did change their integration policy. However, Redmond misses several important points.

The answer on the foreign policy change of the EFTA countries given here consists of three elements: transformation of domestic structures, new interpretation of neutrality in connection with change in international politics, and public opinion.

The economies of the EFTA countries had a relatively bad performance in the second half of the 1980s and the early 1990s. Figure 18.2 summarizes one aspect—economic growth. Between 1973 and 1978, the economic growth rate in the EFTA countries did not exceed the EC average. In Switzerland, economic development was actually quite bad. The best performance was by the Austrian economy. For the late 1970s and early 1980s, figures indicate a stronger economic performance of the EFTA countries compared to the Community average.

In the mid-1980s, the EC but also the EFTA countries attained higher economic growth—except Austria. Just at a time when the "new dynamics" of the Community bestowed it with renewed prestige, the Austrian success story came to an end.[8] The "Austrian way," the so-called

Figure 18.2   Average Annual Growth Rates of Real Gross Domestic/National Product (Percentages)

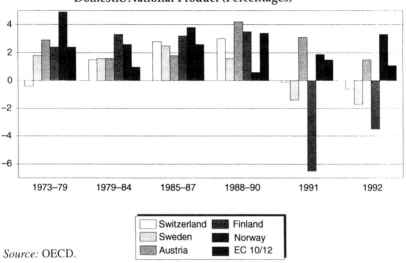

Source: OECD.

Austrokeynesianism, where the government tried to maintain, through "deficit spending," higher economic growth rates than its competitors, as well as full employment even under adverse (international) conditions, was no longer possible. The relative low growth rate of Austrian GDP in connection with various scandals (wine, Waldheim, etc.) led to a decline of Austrian self-confidence.

In 1987/1988, business circles, but also the Austrian People's Party (ÖVP—Christian Democrat, conservative), the junior partner in the government coalition, saw the EC as a way to improve the performance of the Austrian economy. The push for EC membership also had some ideological overtones. Important factions of the business sector and then the ÖVP wanted a "modernization" and "liberalization" of the Austrian economy and society.[9] The trade unions were split—the workers and employees of the modern, competitive sectors opted for EC membership whereas the trade unions of the protected sectors were against membership application. The final compromise was a cautious support for EC membership by the Trade Union Council.

The farmers were very cautious. Since the early 1980s, the prices for farming products were rising much faster in Austria than in the EC. At the end of the 1980s, they were, on the average, some 30 percent higher in Austria. But since their party, the ÖVP, was pushing toward membership application and EC membership was very popular (in 1987, there was a 30 to 50 percentage point majority in favor; see Figure 18.3), the representatives of the farmers accepted membership application as long as their

Figure 18.3 Attitudes of the Populations on EC/EU Membership (Differences of percentages "For" minus "Against" membership)

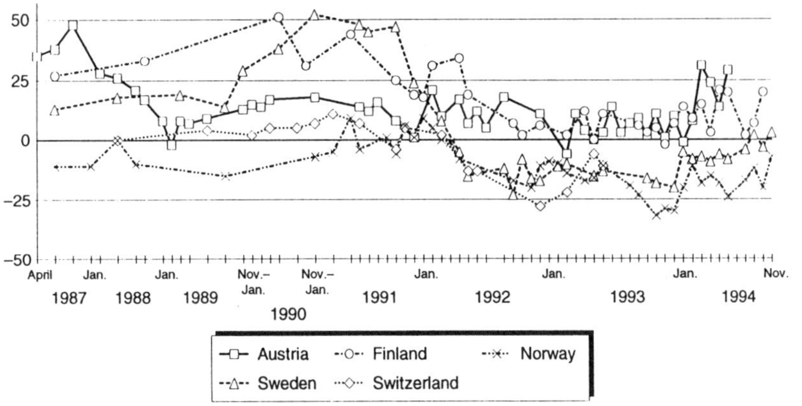

Sources: Paul Luif, "Die österreichische integrationspolitik," in Hanspeter Neuhold and Paul Luif, eds., *Das Außenpolitische Bewußtsein der Österreicher: Aktuelle Internationale Probleme im Spiegel der Meinungsforschung,* Vienna: Braumüller, 1992, p. 71; and additional polls.

possible losses would be compensated. Among the Social Democratic Party (SPÖ), a group of "modernizers" also pushed for membership, but it took some two years to make an official decision. As the leading government party, its decision was crucial. It was under pressure because the EC question seemed to be—at least, until mid-1988—quite popular. Most economists predicted advantages for the Austrian economy through EC membership. Not to take this chance would have given the ÖVP a big issue in the campaign for the next general elections.

In April 1989, the SPÖ finally decided for membership application. But the ÖVP had to accept two conditions: a neutrality clause in the formal application letter and no reduction of social standards by EC membership.

Looking again at Figure 18.2, one can also see the big problems in the Swedish economy in the late 1980s and early 1990s. Its growth rate was far below the EC average and below the growth rates of the other neutrals. In the Swedish case, there was another indicator that pointed to a difficulty in the economy of the late 1980s—the large direct investments of the Swedish companies abroad. This used to be a sign of strength for Swedish business (compared, e.g., with Austria) but the tremendous increase of outward foreign direct investments in the late 1980s (especially in the EC countries)[10] turned out to be a significant liability for the Swedish economy. The problem was slowly recognized by the trade unions and then by the Social Democrats. Finally, the Social Democratic government decided—quite surprisingly for some observers—to opt for EC membership in October 1990.

Significantly, this turnaround was announced in a government report on "Measures to Stabilize the Economy and to Limit the Growth of Public Expenditure." The Swedish government stated: "Swedish membership in the EC, while maintaining Swedish neutrality policy, is in our national interest."[11]

Figure 18.2 also shows the problems Finland had in 1991 with its economy, after an outstanding economic performance in the 1980s. The loss of the markets in the former Soviet Union,[12] due to its breakup, and the transformation of the successor states to market economies made Western Europe the only viable alternative. In January 1992, Finland agreed on a new treaty with the Russian Federation, which replaced the old Treaty of Friendship, Cooperation, and Mutual Assistance (FCMA Treaty) with the now defunct Soviet Union. The new treaty did away with any restrictions Finland would have to take into account in its relations with the EC. At the end of February 1992, the Finnish government "decided that it will apply for membership of the European Community." According to the Finnish government, it "is essential for the Finnish economy to be able to operate on equal terms with its competitors on its principal markets."[13]

In Switzerland, EC membership has been—except for a short period in early 1991—never really popular (see Figure 18.3). According to Figure 18.2, Switzerland also began to be a "candidate" for EC accession. Its economic performance in 1991 was quite bad. The economic difficulties brought uneasiness about Switzerland's special position and identity ("*Sonderfall*") in the center of Europe. For a long time the Swiss government denied the necessity of EC membership, but the slow economic growth and the applications of the other neutrals put a heavy pressure on the Swiss government. In March 1992, the Commission started discussions on enlargement of the EC. Switzerland was in danger of "missing the train." In early May 1992, Commission president Jacques Delors remarked that the EC would now be quickly enlarged by Austria, Sweden, and Finland. Thus, one day after the Swiss public agreed in a referendum to membership of Switzerland in the Bretton Woods institutions (18 May 1992), the government decided to apply for EC membership. The rejection of the EEA Agreement by the Swiss population in the referendum of 6 December 1992 led the government to suspend the membership application.

A similar negative public opinion has developed in Norway. After EC membership was rejected in the referendum in 1972, membership never became popular (see Figure 18.3). The performance of the Norwegian economy was quite bad in the late 1980s, but in 1991 it had improved, as Figure 18.2 clearly shows. One important factor in the Norwegian economy has been the large oil and gas revenues from the wells in the North Sea, which help in financing the state budget.

Conflicting opinions on the EC question ended the rule by a nonsocialist coalition after only one year, in October 1990. The small Center party, which represents the interests of the farmers, rejected any closer cooperation with the EC, even in the context of the planned EEA. In contrast, the biggest party of the coalition, the conservative Right, had pushed for membership application. The new Labor party minority government, although supported by the Center party, started to move toward EC membership application. Nevertheless, it was very late in 1992, when the "membership train" had almost left the station, before the government submitted its application for accession to the EC in Brussels.

Iceland, being a small country and economically relying on its fisheries exports, has not applied for membership in the Union because it would have meant opening up the Icelandic fishing grounds to all EU fishermen. But in early June 1994, the Social Democrats ended their opposition to EU membership. Iceland's foreign minister announced that the country could apply for membership if the Independence party ceased resisting accession to the EU as well.[14] The population of small Liechtenstein did—in contrast to Switzerland—accept the EEA in a referendum on 13 December 1992. But in order to accede to the EEA, the government had to first solve the problems caused by combining EEA with the Liechtenstein-Swiss customs union. The government has no intention applying for EU membership.

To conclude this section, it is clear that one important cause of the "new dynamics" of the EC as well as the "problems of corporatism" were the changes in international economic relations. The increased competition from Japan and the United States had to be faced by the Europeans. The completion of the internal market, caused by opening up the economies of the member states and increasing economic growth by more competition, challenged the tight corporatist structures of most of the EFTA states. Their application for EC membership was a sign of the weakening of these structures and indicated a (West) Europeanization of their societies. They were ceasing to be "special cases" where politics and economics differed notably from the West European "standard."[15]

Figure 18.3 is also an indicator of a differentiation between Austria and Finland, on the one hand, and Sweden and Norway, on the other. In the latter countries, EC/EU membership had become or had remained unpopular well before the referendums. In the former countries, the positive attitudes toward accession to the EC also decreased in late 1991 and 1992, but in most opinion polls, the share of people wishing EC/EU membership was practically always larger than the percentage of the population opposing membership. One could interpret this difference according to the precarious geographical position of these countries—vis-à-vis the conflicts in former-Yugoslavia (for Austria) and the turmoil in Russia (for Finland). As will be shown below, political reasons—in particular, increasing one's security by joining a larger group—have supplemented the economic arguments for EU membership in the applicant countries. This reasoning seems to have fallen on fertile ground, especially among the political elites in Austria and Finland.

The Attitudes of the
Applicant Countries Concerning CFSP

Austria

In Austria, discussions about EC membership had already started in the mid-1980s. As we have seen, only after a long debate of the pros and cons of accession did the two big parties in government, the social democratic SPÖ and the conservative ÖVP, agree on an application. The report of the Austrian federal government to Parliament from April 1989 commented on the foreign policy aspects of the Community:

> The cooperation which includes military aspects actually does not take place in the framework of EPC. . . . Therefore, the participation of a permanently neutral state in the EPC seems to be without risk from the point of view of neutrality law. However, Austria could under no circumstances partake in an eventual future progress of the EC towards a defense community; the same would be true for a binding foreign policy of the EC with majority decisions, as far as they would include areas of relevance for neutrality.[16]

The EC membership application was submitted by the Austrian foreign minister some three months later (17 July 1989) in Brussels. Austria made this application on the understanding that

> its internationally recognized status of permanent neutrality, based on the Federal and Constitutional Law of 26 October 1955, will be maintained and that, as a member of the European Communities by virtue of the Treaty of Accession, it will be able to fulfill its legal obligations arising out of its status as a permanently neutral State and to continue its policy of neutrality as a specific contribution towards the maintenance of peace and security in Europe.[17]

The Austrian government quickly realized the importance of participating in the foreign policy cooperation of the EC. In an *Aide mémoire* (February 1990), the government acknowledged the basic aims of the EC treaties and the Single European Act (SEA). Austria would participate fully in their realization with a spirit of solidarity.[18] The cooperation of Austria in the Kuwait crisis—allowing, inter alia, planes of the Gulf allies to overfly Austrian territory—also helped to increase its credibility in this area.

The EC Commission published its opinion on Austria's application more than two years after Austria had sent its letter to Brussels. The relatively long duration of this procedure points to the fact that the Austrian application had met some opposition inside the Commission. It seems that during the final stages of the decision on the *avis,* the Commission was split. Jacques Delors and Frans Andriessen wanted to postpone negotiations on Austria's application until after the reform of the EC's institutions and the planned treaty revisions on defense policy in 1996. Others, like Henning Christophersen from Denmark—who wanted to keep the EC open for the Scandinavians—pleaded for the prompt start of negotiations with the Austrians.[19]

In the ensuing compromise the *avis* confirmed that on the basis of economic considerations, the Community should accept Austria's application for membership. From the political standpoint, the application had to be situated in the general context of the future development of the Community and of Europe in general.

> In this connection, Austria's permanent neutrality creates problems for both the Community and Austria. The first issue which arises is that of the compatibility of permanent neutrality with the provisions of the existing Treaties. In addition, developments in the intergovernmental conference on political union would also require the Community to seek specific assurances from the Austrian authorities with regard to their legal capacity to undertake obligations entailed by the future common foreign and security policy.
>
> Subject to possible further developments in the discussions under way in the intergovernmental conference, these problems should not, however, prove to be insurmountable in the context of the accession negotiations.[20]

The results of the European Council at Maastricht, December 1991, were widely regarded as "positive" by the Austrian representatives. Just before the European Council in Lisbon (26–27 June 1992), Austria sent another *Aide mémoire* to the Twelve. It stated that "Austria identifies itself fully with the objectives of the Common Foreign and Security Policy of the European Union and Austria will participate in this policy and in its dynamic development actively and in a spirit of solidarity."[21]

The situation in neighboring former-Yugoslavia—in particular, the Serb aggression, the plight of Bosnia-Herzegovina, and the danger of an escalation and spreading of the violence—initiated a change in the attitudes of the Austrians. They began to feel more insecure and to think that the Austrian armed forces would not be able to defend Austria against armed intervention.[22] Even by mid-1992, the conservative ÖVP started to maintain that the prime reasons for joining the EC would be security issues. It was admitted that stressing the economic aspects of EC membership had been a mistake and that the ultimate goal of Austria's accession would be the political union. Austria should join the Western European Union (WEU) and more or

less "forget" neutrality.[23] The Social Democrats started to talk about security aspects of EC membership as well, but still favored neutrality until an
alternative security system developed in Europe.

As a compromise, the *Aide mémoire* of June 1992 was welcomed by the
socialist and conservative majority of the Lower House of the Austrian
Parliament (*Nationalrat*). It supported the aims of the Common Foreign and
Security Policy. The Parliament called upon the government

> to ensure that Austria can participate in the development of a system of col-
> lective security in Europe; in this connection it will be assumed that the
> European peace and security organisation developed by the European
> Union and possibly other institutions will be a regional arrangement
> according to Chapter VIII of the Charter of the United Nations.[24]

A complete abandonment of neutrality has not been proposed by the
government. Many officials stated that the neutral status should be maintained until a working European security order can replace it.[25] An important reason for this quite cautious approach was the still existing popularity
of neutrality among Austrians. A large (but diminishing) majority of
Austrians would rather renounce EU membership than abandon neutrality, if
gaining EU membership would only be possible by their abandoning neutrality. No party—except for the right-wing, liberal-national Freedom party
(FPÖ)—has demanded a formal abrogation of the neutrality law.

Sweden

After the Swedish Social Democratic government had announced its favorable attitude toward EC membership, the Swedish Parliament prepared a
report on the integration question. On 12 December 1990, this report was
approved by a large majority of Parliament, with only the Greens and the
Left party (former Communists) voting against. It stated that "Sweden
should strive to become a member of the European Community while maintaining its neutrality policy."[26] To prepare the application for membership,
the Swedish foreign ministry conducted a comprehensive study on the
development of the foreign and security policies in Europe during the spring
of 1991. The study concluded that the security concept of the EC countries
was not as closely connected with defense and military matters as the
Swedish discussions would suppose. In the EC, "security" included questions of disarmament, the Conference on Security and Cooperation in
Europe (CSCE), minority conflicts, and security aspects of North-South
relations.[27]

Prime Minister Ingvar Carlsson explained the Swedish application in
Parliament on 14 June 1991. Questions concerning EPC got a prominent
place in his speech. According to Carlsson, most EC members were still very
cautious about adding a defense dimension to the Community. There was no

reason to assume that the EC was in the process of turning into a military alliance. Any decision on defense matters would be based on unanimity, and there would be a continued readiness to find solutions for states that do not wish to or cannot participate in such a cooperation. The government concluded that the EC decisionmaking structures would assure the possibility of safeguarding fundamental Swedish security interests. Membership in the EC would be compatible with the requirements of the policy of neutrality.[28] In the official request for EC membership, Swedish neutrality policy was—in contrast to the Austrian application—not mentioned.

After the general elections in September 1991, the new Conservative-led government started to formulate a more restricted interpretation of neutrality. For Prime Minister Carl Bildt, it was obvious that the notion of "neutrality policy" did not represent an adequate description of Sweden's foreign and security policy. Sweden would, for now, not join any military alliance and would maintain a strong defense. But Sweden wanted to pursue a policy with a clear *European identity.* It had a great interest in the establishment of a new security structure in Europe.[29]

In reaction to the outcome of the European Council in Maastricht, Prime Minister Bildt advocated Swedish participation in a European defense and security cooperation, but he excluded participation in a military alliance.[30] The foreign policy spokesperson of the Social Democratic opposition, Pierre Schori, expressed an idea that has been widely held among politicians in the neutral countries. The Swedish policy of freedom of alliances should be valid as long as it were not replaced by a common security, a real and enduring all-European peace order.[31]

As the discussion about Swedish EC and security policy continued, some parties—especially the Social Democrats—started to criticize Prime Minister Bildt for going too far in stressing the European identity. In May 1992, a compromise was found between the main parties (except for the Left party). The Swedish Parliament accepted two reports of its foreign policy committee. In one report, it was agreed upon that Sweden's *alliansfrihet* (freedom of alliances, nonalignment) should remain. It was now interpreted to mean that Sweden will try to be able to stay neutral in the event of a war in the *vicinity* of Sweden.[32] This was a slight change over the previous Swedish position, where the intention was to retain the credibility to stay neutral in all circumstances (and not only to maintain the possibility of staying neutral) in case of war.

In the second report, the Swedish Parliament agreed with the government that the request for EC membership was based on the understanding that Sweden participated in all parts of EC cooperation. Sweden had a strong interest in being able to participate in the development of the European Union. The Maastricht Treaty was compatible with Sweden's aim of becoming a member of the EC.[33]

The EC Commission published its opinion on the Swedish request for membership in July 1992. Similar to the opinion on the Austrian case, it affirmed that the EC "will, on the whole, benefit from the accession of Sweden." But there was also a caution on foreign policy cooperation:

> In the area of Foreign and Security Policy, the Commission notes that Swedish policy has evolved significantly, especially since the beginning of the nineties. There seems to exist a consensus in Sweden in relation to a full participation in the Common Foreign and Security Policy of the European Union. Sweden will be required to accept and be able to implement this policy as it evolves over the coming years. There seems, however, to remain reservations in the Swedish position relative to the eventual framing of a common defence policy and, in an even more marked way, regarding the possible establishment in time of a common defence. The Commission recommends that in the context of the accession negotiations, specific and binding assurances from Sweden would be sought with regard to her political commitment and legal capacity to fulfill the obligations in this area.[34]

In Sweden, this generally positive, but slightly critical, attitude of the Commission regarding defense started a new round of discussions about Sweden's security policy. One prominent scholar of Sweden's neutrality, who in the past strongly supported the traditional foreign policy line, now even suggested that the government should use the occasion to proclaim that it would participate fully in the security cooperation of the EC. That would enhance Sweden's security. Sweden should abandon the neutrality policy, which has lost its value.[35]

Foreign Minister Margaretha af Ugglas suggested that Swedes should start thinking about the advantages and disadvantages of WEU membership.[36] In a speech to the Fondation Paul-Henri Spaak in Brussels, Prime Minister Bildt argued that enlargement would strengthen key policies of the Union, not least CFSP. Along with Norway and Finland, Sweden would, as a member of the European Union, be able to make a decisive contribution to the security of the northern part of the Union. Recalling that Moscow regarded the three Baltic states as its "near abroad," Bildt stated that "it is our task to make it clear that they are just as much the 'near abroad' of the European Union and all its member states."[37] He also drew attention to the fact that Sweden, though not a member of any military alliance, makes a far bigger contribution to military peacekeeping operations than the leading members of NATO in Europe. This, in Bildt's view, demonstrated the limited relevance of dividing countries into those that are part of a military alliance and those that are not. Commenting on the Western European Union, the Swedish prime minister said that Sweden's relationship with WEU could only be defined when Sweden had become a member of the Union.[38] This was also the position of the new Social Democratic government that came into power after the general elections of September 1994.

Finland

In Finland, the government and all relevant parties and interest groups debated for a long time, clearly against EC membership. Finland (like Switzerland) tried to play the "EFTA card." It wanted to gain access to the internal market of the EC via the EEA. In early 1991 it was clear to the Finnish officials that as a condition for participating in the internal market, the EFTA countries would have to accept the *acquis communautaire* and would not be granted co-decision rights for new legislation. In addition to these difficulties with the EEA, the fact that Sweden, the most important economic partner of Finland, had applied for EC membership on 1 July 1991, put additional pressure on the decisionmakers.

During 1991, the economic situation deteriorated dramatically (see Figure 18.2). By summer 1991, the consensus among the political groups in Finland concerning EC policy finally dissolved. The party congresses of the Conservative party and the Swedish party, both parties being members of the government, redefined their official integration policies more favorably toward eventual EC membership. The party leadership of the main opposition party, the Social Democrats, began to support an accession to the EC during the summer of 1991 as well.[39]

The question was now the attitudes of the president and the agrarian-influenced Center party, the biggest party in the Finnish Parliament. The breakup of the Soviet Union and the new treaty with Russia seems to have helped to diminish the relevance of the neutrality question and to have more or less removed the last obstacles to a membership application. In the decision of the government on EC membership at the end of February 1992, the security issue was dealt with in a similar way to Sweden's resolution of the problem:

> In a changed Europe, where the Cold War division has vanished, the core of Finnish neutrality can be characterised as military non-alignment and an independent defence. The central goal of this policy is to maintain and strengthen stability and security in Northern Europe. . . .
>
> In the European Community, Finland's point of departure is the maintenance of an independent defence. . . . Membership in the Western European Union is not a precondition for membership in the European Community. Finland's future decisions in this respect will depend on how the role of the Western European Union in carrying out the foreign and security policy of the European Community is elaborated.[40]

On 18 March 1992, Finland—like Sweden—applied for EC membership without any neutrality clause. The rising turmoil in the former Soviet Union led the Finnish government to look for support for its security. It participated as observer—the first "neutral" country to do so—at the North Atlantic Cooperation Council (NACC) in Oslo, 5 June 1992. According to President Koivisto, Finland got useful information on the development of the military situation in areas adjacent to it by participating as an observer in meetings of the NACC. When applying for membership of the European Community, Finland stated that it would accept the objectives of the Maastricht Treaty, also with regard to the defense dimension, but Koivisto did not see any immediate action to be necessary. Finland "will, in due time, consider and develop its relations with the WEU."[41]

In the *avis* on the Finnish application for membership, the Commission admitted that Finland's neutrality is not rooted in international law. However, problems could arise if Finland would "oppose itself systematically to certain actions which, in its view, could be prejudicial to its policy of neutrality, or what is left of it."[42]

The developments in Russia—in particular, the strengthening of the nationalist and Communist elements—intensified the discussion on the security aspects of EU membership. Some thought that WEU membership would not be sufficient and argued for joining NATO. In October 1993, the government saw no urgency in considering NATO membership, but did not exclude accession to NATO in the future.[43] Social Democrats dismissed NATO membership and demanded that adjustment to the coming EU security cooperation should proceed according to Finland's economic and political possibilities.[44]

Norway

In Norway, the emphasis in the debate on EU membership was on economic aspects and the question of national sovereignty. As a member of NATO, Norway has been granted associate membership status in WEU. Influential Norwegian elites still reflected the traditional Norwegian preference for an "Atlantic" security framework by voicing concern that further integration with the EU would have negative consequences for West European–United States security cooperation. A pragmatic, status quo approach characterized official Norwegian arguments regarding EU and security policy. The idea of a European security and cooperation order found general support, but only as long as it did not seriously call into question the existing security structures.[45]

In a report by the foreign ministry of the Social Democratic government from June 1994, CFSP was seen as giving new possibilities to advance Norway's priorities in international relations. The general goals of CFSP, as laid down in the Maastricht Treaty, were in agreement with Norwegian foreign policy and would enable its continuation. The areas of the planned joint actions were also central for Norwegian foreign policy. Norway would be able to play an active role in international politics, something it would not be capable of doing on its own. Finally, the foreign ministry stressed the consensus rule and the intergovernmental cooperation of CFSP.

The two options available to Norway if it would have joined the EU would have been either observer status or full membership in WEU. An observer status would definitely have been a step backward from associate membership, since observers have no voice in WEU. It seems this was the reason why the foreign ministry in its report made a clear statement that Norway would join WEU should the country become a member of the European Union.[46]

The Membership Negotiations

The European Council in Maastricht (9–11 December 1991) agreed that negotiations on accession to the Union on the basis of the Treaty agreed upon in Maastricht could start as soon as the Community had terminated its negotiations on its own resources and related issues in 1992. In a similar vein, the participants of the European Council in Lisbon (26–27 June 1992) stated that "the official negotiation will be opened immediately after the Treaty on European Union is ratified and the agreement has been achieved on the DELORS-II package."

During the fall of 1992, one could detect a significant movement in the French attitude to enlargement. France used to be very insistent on the EC getting its house in order before admitting new members. In early December 1992, President Mitterrand started to blur the preconditions of the Lisbon summit and called for accelerated talks with Austria, Sweden, Finland, and Norway. For him, compatibility of neutrality with EC membership would be the main negotiating issue for the first three of these countries—but that was "a problem for them, not for us."[47] The Edinburgh European Council (11–12 December 1992) thus agreed to accelerate the enlargement process, allowing accession negotiations to commence even before all formal preconditions had been fulfilled. Doubtless, the main motive behind this French change of policy was a wish to accommodate Germany, but the move was also meant to help the Danish government in its campaign for a "yes" to the Union in a second referendum.[48]

On 1 February 1993, at the formal beginning of the negotiations with Austria, Finland, and Sweden, the president-in-office of the Council, Danish foreign minister Niels Helveg Petersen, outlined the conditions for the accession of the applicant countries. He made special reference to the (still not ratified) Treaty on European Union and its provisions on CFSP:

- Enlargement should strengthen the internal coherence of the Union and its capacity to act effectively in foreign and security policy.
- Applicants must, from the time of their accession, be ready and able to participate fully and actively in the Common Foreign and Security Policy, as defined in the Treaty on European Union.

- Applicants must, on accession, take on in their entirety and without reservation all the objectives of the Treaty, the provisions of its Title V, and the relevant declarations attached to it.
- Applicants should be ready and able to support the specific policies of the Union in force at the time of their accession.[49]

On the one hand, these conditions excluded the option that the applicant countries could obtain the special status concerning the EU's defense policy that Denmark had obtained at the Edinburgh summit. On the other hand, it was not yet clear if they would have to sign up to the so-called potentiality of the Maastricht Treaty.

At the same meeting, the delegates of the applicant countries referred to CFSP in their introductory statements. Austrian foreign minister Alois Mock explained:

> Austria is prepared to accept the principles and the *acquis* of the European Union. Austria is fully committed to the content of the Treaty on European Union and will prove its solidarity by participating in its implementation.
>
> Austria is conscious of the fact that its security is indissociably linked to that of Europe and that it is in Austria's own vital security interest that effective mechanisms are developed to repel and punish aggressions and violations of law. Austria is therefore committed to the perspective of further development of security structures as provided for by the Treaty on European Union in order to achieve the objectives of the Common Foreign and Security Policy.[50]

In the statement, no mention was made of Austria's neutrality status. The Finnish foreign trade minister, Pertti Salolainen, did not see any major difficulties, but mentioned Finland's international status:

> We do not expect great problems in the field of foreign and security policy. We share with you the same values and general international goals. On the basis of our own views, we will actively participate in the development of the common foreign and security policy.
>
> In the post–Cold War Europe, the core of the Finnish policy of neutrality consists of military non-alliance and an independent defense, which in our view is a positive element in the overall situation in Northern Europe.
>
> As to the future, we have an open mind and are ready to contribute constructively to the development of the defense dimension of the European Union. For us, it is essential that future decisions will enhance stability and security in Northern Europe.[51]

Ulf Dinkelspiel, minister for European affairs and foreign trade, also stressed the importance of CFSP for Sweden. He mentioned Swedish non-alignment:

We wish to participate in the construction of a new European security order on the basis of the UN Charter, the principles and decisions of the CSCE, and other relevant principles of international law. To this end, we wish to participate fully in the Common Foreign and Security Policy (CFSP) within the framework of the Union.

Our political commitment to become a full and active partner in the CFSP is based on broad parliamentary support. Sweden is not bound by any legal restraints with regard to such participation. We are prepared to assume the same treaty rights and obligations as the present members of the Community.

As recently stated by the Swedish parliament, Sweden's policy of nonparticipation in military alliances remains unchanged. At the same time, we recognize that the eventual framing of a common defense policy, which in time might lead to a common defense, is one of the CFSP goals which is to be further discussed in the context of the 1996 review conference. We will not hamper the development of the European Union as it moves towards this goal.[52]

Obviously, these remarks were an attempt by the three applicant countries to dispel concerns that their traditions of neutrality would compel the Community to slow down ambitions to develop a collective foreign and defense identity.[53] However, their representatives did not renounce the nonparticipation of their countries in military alliances. Domestic sensitivities would not have allowed such a bold move.

At the start of the negotiations with Norway, 5 April 1993, the head of the Norwegian delegation, Minister for Trade Bjørn Tore Godal, explained the position of his country. This statement had a slightly different character from the previous ones. Whereas membership in NATO was stressed, Norway's representative did not mention WEU in any way:

Norway looks forward to participate fully in the Common Foreign and Security Policy. Membership in the Atlantic Alliance and cooperation between Europe and North America will continue to be vital to Norway's security. The foreign policy challenges of our European partners are also ours. . . .

As a member of the Community, Norway would bring in a strong tradition of broad cooperation in the field of foreign and security policy, a tradition which has been built up over the years in the process of consultations in the Atlantic Alliance with eleven of the present member states.[54]

Negotiations on CFSP could only start after the Treaty on European Union came into force on 1 November 1993. Surprisingly enough, the talks on CFSP were concluded in quite a short period of time. The EU member states could not find any common position toward the applicant countries. Some member states wanted far-reaching commitments to the future development of CFSP from the applicants, while other EU countries rejected these demands. Therefore, the permanent representative of the EU presidency, Belgian ambassador Philippe de Schoutheete de Tervarent, was put in charge of the negotiations on CFSP with the applicant countries. After talks with the EU member states and the applicants, a compromise was found. The Union noted that CFSP was considered "nonproblematic" by all the applicant countries. At the Ministerial Meeting of the Conference on Accession of 21 December 1993, it was agreed that a joint declaration would be added to the Final Act of the accession negotiations.[55]

In this Joint Declaration on CFSP, the applicants confirm their full acceptance of the rights and obligations attached to the Union and its institutional framework (the *acquis communautaire*), as it applies to the present member states. The acceding states declare that they will be ready and able to participate fully and actively in CFSP. They will adopt, in their entirety and without reservation, all the objectives of the Maastricht Treaty. Concerning CFSP, the new member states will make their legal framework compatible with the *acquis*.[56]

The agreement on this declaration was particularly welcomed in the applicant countries. The gist of the understanding was that the new members would not have to promise more than the present members are obliged to do in CFSP.[57] In the report by the European Parliament on enlargement and neutrality, the applicant countries' constructive attitude toward CFSP was commended. The explicit assurance that they would not follow Denmark's example and insist on derogations allowing them to opt out of the consideration of security and defense policy questions was welcomed. The applicant countries thus satisfied the "main criteria on which membership of the European Union should be based where the provisions of Title V of the Union Treaty are concerned."[58]

The membership negotiations for Austria, Finland, and Sweden ended on 1 March and for Norway on 16 March 1994. The formal completion of the negotiations was reached only on 30 March 1994, after the internal quarrel on the threshold necessary for a qualified majority (for the enlarged Council of Ministers) was solved by a declaration of the present twelve member states. The declaration was a face-saving device for the United Kingdom, which opposed any increase of this threshold, attempting to make decisions by qualified majority more difficult to attain. It states that the Council will do all in its power, within a reasonable time and without prejudicing the obligatory time limits, to reach a solution that could be adopted by a larger majority than necessary (sixty-five votes instead of the obligatory sixty-two votes).[59]

The Accession Treaty between the twelve member states of the EU and the four acceding countries was signed on the Greek island of Corfu on 24 June 1994. Some days before, on 12 June 1994, the Austrians voted overwhelmingly in favor of EU membership.[60] The vote was the first in a series of referendums that decided on the accession of all four applicant countries. Economic advantages seem to have been the main reason for voting yes in the Austrian referendum. The second most important argument was the fear that Austria would be isolated outside the EU. Next came a positive view of European integration in general and the preservation of jobs through membership. In fifth place, internal and external security arguments influenced the decision of the Austrian voters.[61]

In Finland, the referendum on EU membership brought a clear, but somehow smaller than expected, majority for accession.[62] During the referendum campaign, security issues played a relatively minor role in public discussions. In fall 1994, before the referendum, Finns were asked about forty issues that could be influenced by EU membership. Ranked by positive effects, "Finland's military security" was in eleventh place, after mostly economic topics. Thirty-one percent of Finns thought that joining the EU would positively affect Finland's security, whereas 30 percent expected a negative influence. A year before, only 25 percent assumed a positive effect and 34 percent negative consequences for Finland's security.[63]

The margin of the "yes" side in the Swedish EU referendum was much smaller than in Austria and Finland. The country was almost split in the middle.[64] Security issues played a minor role in the debate. In October 1994, only 6 percent saw "peace" as an advantage of EU membership. The "disappearance of neutrality" was regarded as a disadvantage by 2 percent of the voters.[65] However, it seems that in the last phase of the campaign the importance of the peace issue did increase.

In Norway, the share of people opposing EU membership practically always surpassed, by a large margin, the percentage opting for membership (see Figure 18.3). So the negative outcome of the referendum came as no surprise.[66] For 18 percent of the "yes" voters, defense and security policy was an important reason to prefer EU membership; only the economy and jobs (24 percent) and Nordic cooperation (21 percent) were more significant. Among the "no" voters, a mere 2 percent saw defense and security as an important reason for their decision—no surprise, in view of Norway's NATO membership.[67]

With the signing of the Accession Treaty, all four acceding countries became "active observers" in most EU institutions.[68] The acceding states could take part in all elements of CFSP; they could raise their voice but were formally not (yet) part of the decisionmaking procedures.

Since then, the foreign ministries of the four states have experienced a much higher work load. The officials in the ministries have to prepare and attend the various CFSP Working Groups and the meetings of the Political Committee. They have to handle the COREU telexes; there are now some one hundred telexes per day to read, to forward, and to answer; but the foreign ministries also get much more information, particularly through the COREU network. The participation in the CFSP Working Groups and in the meetings of EU embassies in third countries provides new information as well. In general, the officials in the ministries must act faster than before because, in many instances, they have to react to EU information, have to answer COREU telexes on short notice, and so on.

In the last few years, a *réflexe communautaire* has already developed in the foreign policies of the acceding states, but there is no doubt that officials must now respect the EU positions even more, notably in international organizations. On the other hand, as (future) EU member states, the acceding countries have become more important interlocutors and have more prestige in their contacts with other states, in particular with Third World countries.

Until full membership, the acceding countries had the possibility for "opting in" and could associate themselves with CFSP declarations of their own choice. The first time this happened was when Austria and Sweden associated themselves with a presidency statement on behalf of the EU on Tadjikistan (28 July 1994). Austria and Sweden also took part in the EU joint action in Mostar, Bosnia-Herzegovina. There are indications that East Central Europe will be among the priorities of Austria; for the Nordic countries, the Baltic area will be of great importance.

The Enlarged Union: Scenarios for Its Development

At the European Council, Brussels, 10 and 11 December 1993, the EU member states agreed on the place of the applicant states in the institutions and bodies of the enlarged Union. Each of the new countries had one member in the Commission, bringing the total to 20. The European Parliament increased the number of its members from 536 (including the 18 members from former East Germany) to 624. There was a slight increase in seats for the bigger countries, to make for a more proportional representation (but without changing the number of seats—99—for Germany). Here, the EU decided to go beyond the status quo and moved toward a "pragmatic evolutionary concept" in its institutional adaptations for enlargement.[69]

When weighing the votes in the Council, the new members got four votes (Austria and Sweden, respectively), and three votes (Finland). The rotation of the presidency maintained its six-months' duration; the first new member country to hold the presidency will be Austria in the second half of 1998. This most probably means that for the Council, the EU will retain the (adapted) status quo. The European Free Trade Association enlargement has not brought any "streamlining" of EU institutions.

All applicants—in particular, the neutral (or "postneutral") countries— progressively adjusted their foreign policy behavior to EPC/CFSP. What will these developments mean for the future of CFSP? It is clear that the new member countries will, in most areas, only have a marginal influence. However, enlargement will add to the EU's international economic and political clout. The Union will gain voting power in multilateral organizations, such as the CSCE.[70] The (post)neutral EFTA countries could enrich the security policies of the Union because they traditionally have diplomatic and personal ties with East European countries and Moscow. Moreover, all have a long-standing experience of peacekeeping activities.[71]

Irrespective of these positive aspects of enlargement, more or less uncertain implications remain for the security and defense dimension of the EU. Since 1991, the EC/EU, WEU, and NATO have had to deal with the question of enlargement. All three organizations have given different responses to this question.[72]

The EU has been the first of these organizations to really increase its membership. The early experiences of the acceding states in CFSP have shown that neutrality, or the policy of military nonalliance, have not played any role in the day-to-day process of EU's foreign policy. The first CFSP joint actions have posed no problems for the acceding states regarding participation. They have not been obliged to join WEU when they enter the EU. Representatives of the (neutral) acceding states have all declared that they will only participate as observers in WEU. Thus, the number of EU countries that are not full members of WEU will increase, making a merger of WEU and the Union in the next coming years less likely and possibly also affecting their close relationship.[73]

During the referendum campaigns, the questions of security and, in particular, neutrality played a relatively minor role in the debates. Nevertheless, after the referendums the future shape of security policy and neutrality will again be on the political agenda in the new member states. In May 1994, Finland and Sweden started to cooperate in NATO's Partnership for Peace. In Austria, the Social Democrats (in contrast to the conservative ÖVP) opposed this move for some time and accepted participation in Partnership for Peace only in September 1994.[74] In the meantime, cabinet members from the ÖVP renewed their pledge for Austria to accede to WEU. There was even talk that a narrowly interpreted neutrality could be made compatible with WEU membership.[75] These ideas were rejected by the Social Democrats and the other political parties.

This raises the question of what the long-range effect of the participation of the new member states will be in the decisionmaking processes of CFSP and, eventually, WEU, "which is an integral part of the development of the Union" (Article J.4, TEU). One cannot really predict the future behavior of the new members, but merely can present some scenarios of the evolution of CFSP and make an educated guess on how the new members will fit in.[76]

Starting from the most pessimistic scenario, one can imagine a situation in which many EU members will try to "veto" any CFSP decision that is against their interests and in which cooperation is at a minimum. An example could be the behavior of Greece in the conflict about the former-Yugoslav Republic of Macedonia. It is hard to imagine that any new member would act in such a way and systematically block numerous decisions.

They finally did adjust their foreign policies in recent years—if not always to conform exactly to the views of the core of the EU countries, then at least close enough.

Another possibility of CFSP development could be more an *active neutrality* stance in international affairs, something the EU is, in effect, practicing in the conflicts of former-Yugoslavia. The (post)neutral countries would fit in quite well. They have ample experience in peacekeeping missions and the Nordic countries have cooperated closely with the EU in former-Yugoslavia. The problem could be that one of the new countries would like the EU to go further and take sides—but it avoids committing itself to tasks like peacemaking or peace enforcing because of its tradition of neutrality.

A similar problem could arise when CFSP develops at *different speeds* or evolves even into *different tiers.* The fact that none of the new members would join WEU at the beginning of their membership could strengthen the position of Ireland and Denmark and make the gap between (economic) external relations and foreign and security policy larger than before or larger than intended by the Maastricht Treaty. It is difficult to predict if and when the new member states will join WEU. A lot will depend on public opinion in the new member states, on the distribution of political forces in these countries (the center-right parties are more likely to opt for WEU membership than the Social Democrats), but also on the security situation in Europe (notably Russia) and the relations between NATO and EU/WEU (or U.S.-EU).

It could also be that inside the EU, member states will push for a *European defense identity* and move beyond its "civilian power" profile. It is hard to imagine that the new members—in particular, the (post)neutral countries—will follow this path in the near future. The 1996 Intergovernmental Conference (IGC) could show how far the new (and old) members are ready to go here.

There can be no doubt that the IGC will have to take into account that early expectation for a "qualitative" leap forward by introducing the provisions on a Common Foreign and Security Policy in Title V of the Maastricht Treaty have not been realized. With fifteen or even more member states, the Union cannot avoid a thorough revision of its decisionmaking processes in foreign policy matters if the EU wants to gain the capacity to act in the years ahead. The EFTA enlargement could be an incentive to start this most difficult task if the Union and its members wish to contribute to maintaining and restoring peace and security on the European continent and beyond.

Notes

1. The final version of this contribution was written in December 1994.
2. For an analysis of the relationship between the EU and the Eastern and

Central European countries, see Barbara Lippert's contribution in Chapter 11 of this volume.

3. In a similar way, the original EC members agreed on the first common fisheries policy in 1970, just before countries that had fishing interests far greater than those of the Six joined (or intended to join—Norway's membership was discarded after a negative vote in a referendum); see John Redmond, "The Wider Europe: Extending the Membership of the EC," in Alan W. Cafruny and Glenda G. Rosenthal, eds., *The State of the European Community, Volume 2: The Maastricht Debate* (Boulder: Lynne Rienner Publishers—Longman, 1993), p. 211.

4. See Klaus Dieter Harwig, *Verteidigungspolitik als Moment der westeuropäischen Integration* (Frankfurt/Main: Haag and Herchen, 1977).

5. One big bone of contention during the first phase of accession negotiations between the United Kingdom and the EC was the close security relationship of the United Kingdom with the United States. Spain, having joined NATO in 1982, drew a clear link between its participation in the Alliance and membership in the EC.

6. Liechtenstein is connected with Switzerland through a customs union.

7. See Redmond, "The Wider Europe," pp. 213–214.

8. For a quite explicit praise of Austrian economic and social policies, see Peter J. Katzenstein, *Corporatism and Change: Austria, Switzerland, and the Politics of Industry* (Ithaca and London: Cornell University Press, 1984).

9. See Heinrich Schneider, *Alleingang nach Brüssel. Österreichs EG-Politik* (Bonn: Europa Union Verlag, 1990), pp. 208–209.

10. For the first time in 1989, Swedish firms invested more capital abroad than at home. According to the Swedish central bank, some 70 percent of the country's record foreign direct investment, or about SKr 35 billion ($5.5 billion) went to the EC; see "Swedish Firms Set Sail for Europe" in the *Economist*, 1 September 1990, p. 59.

11. "Regeringens skrivelse 1990/91:50 om åtgärder för att stabilisera ekonomin och begränsa tillväxten av de offentliga utgifterna, 26 Oktober 1990" (Stockholm: Norstedts Tryckeri, 1990) (= Riksdagen 1990/91. 1 saml. Nr. 50), p. 5 (translation Paul Luif).

12. In the mid-1970s, more than one quarter of Finnish exports went to the Soviet Union; in 1991, only 5 percent of all Finnish goods were exported to the (former) Soviet Union.

13. "Government's Decision Regarding the Communication to Parliament on Finland's Membership in the European Community" (Helsinki, February 1992, manuscript).

14. According to *Wiener Zeitung*, 14 June 1994, p. 4.

15. See, e.g., for Austria, Anton Pelinka, "Österreich: Was bleibt von den Besonderheiten?" in *Aus Politik und Zeitgeschichte* B 47-48 (13 November 1992), pp. 12–19, for Sweden Leif Lewin, *Samhället och de organiserade intressena* (Stockholm: Norstedts, 1992) (= Riksdagen och de organiserade intressena, 1).

16. "Bericht der Bundesregierung an den Nationalrat und den Bundesrat über die zukünftige Gestaltung der Beziehungen Österreichs zu den Europäischen Gemeinschaften. Manuskript, Wien, 17. April 1989," III–113 der *Beilagen zum Stenographischen Protokoll des Nationalrates*, p. 38 (translation Paul Luif).

17. This translation of the neutrality clause in the Austrian "letter" is taken from Austria's application for membership. Commission Opinion, Brussels: 1 August 1991 (= SEC[91] 1590 final), p. 6.

18. "Aide mémoire der österreichischen Bundesregierung vom 16. Februar 1990," in *Österreichische außenpolitische Dokumentation. Texte und Dokumente* (April 1990), p. 17.

19. Otmar Lahodynsky, "Ein neuer Nettozahler für die Gemeinschaft," *EG-Magazin* 9 (September 1991), p. 30.

20. Austria's application 1991 (see note 17), p. 29.

21. "Aide Mémoire an die Mitgliedstaaten der Europäischen Gemeinschaften, Wien, im Juni 1992," in *Österreichische außenpolitische Dokumentation. Texte und Dokumente,* no. 4 (October 1992), pp. 50–52.

22. Poll reported in *Der Standard,* 8 January 1993, p. 1, where 84 percent of Austrians thought that the danger of war has increased during the last years and 63 percent maintained that the Austrian army would not be capable of protecting Austria against an armed intervention (telephone poll, December 1992, n=504).

23. Helmut Spudich, "Die EG, eine Sache des Gefühls. Busek: Politische Union eigentliches Beitrittsziel—Fehler in bisheriger Kampagne," in *Der Standard,* 12 June 1992, p. 6.

24. "Bericht des Außenpolitischen Ausschusses über den Antrag 364/A (E) der Abgeordneten Dr. Gugerbauer und Genossen betreffend österreichische Neutralität und kooperatives Sicherheitssystem in Europa," in *724 der Beilagen zu den Stenographischen Protokollen des Nationalrates XVIII.* GP, Vienna, 20 October 1992, p. 3 (translation Paul Luif). On 12 November 1992, this resolution was adopted with the votes of the two government parties, SPÖ and ÖVP.

25. Andreas Khol, "Neutralität—ein überholtes Instrument österreichischer Sicherheitspolitik?" in *Österreichisches Jahrbuch für Politik 1990,* pp. 677–709.

26. "Sverige och den västeuropeiska integrationen," Riksdagen, Stockholm, 22 November 1990 (= Utrikesutskottets betänkande 1990/91:UU8).

27. See *Sverige, EG och den säkerhetspolitiska utvecklingen i Europa* (Stockholm: Utrikesdepartementet, 1991) (= UD informerar, 1991:4); the Swedish researchers are pointing here to what Keatinge calls "soft security" in the EPC context. See Patrick Keatinge, "The Foreign Relations of the Union," in Patrick Keatinge, ed., *Political Union* (Dublin: Institute of European Affairs, 1991), p. 139.

28. Ingvar Carlsson, "Statement to the Riksdag by the Prime Minister on 14 June 1991, on Sweden's application for membership of the EC," manuscript, p 7.

29. Carl Bildt, "Schweden—vom zögernden zum begeisterten Europäer." Ausführungen von Ministerpräsident Carl Bildt im Büro der Kommission der Europäischen Gemeinschaften in Bonn, on 13 November 1991, manuscript, p. 13.

30. *Le Monde,* 28 December 1991, p. 5.

31. *Dagens Nyheter,* 14 January 1992, p. 4.

32. "Säkerhet och nedrustning," Riksdagen, Stockholm, 28 April 1992 (= Utrikesutskottets betänkande 1991/92:UU19), p. 17.

33. "Sverige och EG," Riksdagen, Stockholm, 28 April 1992 (= Utrikesutskottets betänkande 1991/1992:UU24), pp. 9–10.

34. "Sweden's application for membership. Opinion of the Commission," Brussels, 31 July 1992 (= SEC[92] 1592 final), p. 29.

35. Sverker Åström, "EG:s försvarssamarbetet gagnar Sverige," in *Svenska Dagbladet,* 9 August 1992, p. 3.

36. Margaretha af Ugglas, "Överväg WEU-medlemskap!" in *Dagens Nyheter,* 1 October 1993, p. 4.

37. Carl Bildt, address to "La Fondation Paul-Henri Spaak," Palais des Académies, Brussels, 16 September 1993. Manuscript, pp. 12–13.

38. See also Thomas Pedersen, *European Union and the EFTA Countries. Enlargement and Integration* (London and New York: Pinter Publishers, 1994), p. 91.

39. Esko Antola, "The End of Pragmatism: Political Foundations of the Finnish Integration Policy Under Stress," in *Yearbook of Finnish Foreign Policy 1991,* p. 21.

40. "Government's Decision Regarding the Communication to Parliament on

Finland's Membership in the European Community," Helsinki, February 1992, manuscript, pp. 2–3.

41. "Meeting Between Dr. Mauno Koivisto, President of Finland, and Mr. Manfred Wörner, Secretary-General of NATO, in Brussels on 28 October 1992." Manuscript, Embassy of Finland, Vienna, p. 1.

42. "Finland's Application for Membership. Opinion of the Commission," Brussels, 4 November 1992 (= SEC[92] 2048 final), p. 30.

43. Bjarne Nitovuori, "Säkerhetspolitiken allt viktigare i EG—men inte på grund av Ryssland," in *Hufvudstadsbladet,* 8 October 1993, p. 5.

44. Paavo Lipponen, "EG, inte NATO," in *Hufvudstadsbladet,* 7 October 1993, p. 2.

45. Martin Sæter, "Norwegian Integration Policy in a Changing World: The Primacy of Security," in Brent F. Nelsen, ed., *Norway and the European Community. The Political Economy of Integration* (Westport, CT, and London: Praeger, 1993), p. 39.

46. See Utenriksdepartementet, Om medlemskap i Den europeiske union, St.meld. nr. 40 (1993–94), p. 84.

47. David Buchan and Andrew Gowers, "Gambler Eyes His Crowning Glory. François Mitterrand Is Determined that Maastricht Will Be Ratified," in *Financial Times,* 9 December 1992, p. 12.

48. See Pedersen, *European Union,* p. 140.

49. "Draft Statement by Mr. Niels Helveg Petersen, president-in-office of the Council, at the Ministerial Meeting Opening the Conferences on the Accession of Austria, Sweden, and Finland to the European Union," Brussels, 1 February 1993, manuscript, p. 9.

50. "Erklärung des Bundesministers für auswärtige Angelegenheiten auf der Ministertagung zur Eröffnung der Verhandlungen über den Beitritt Österreichs zur Europäischen Union, Brüssel, am 1. Februar 1993," in *Österreichische außenpolitische Dokumentation. Texte und Dokumente* 2 (March 1993), p. 48; English version according to *Agence Europe,* 5 February 1992.

51. "Statement by Pertti Salolainen, Minister for Foreign Trade of Finland," Brussels, 1 February 1993. Manuscript, p. 3.

52. "Statement by Ulf Dinkelspiel, Minister for European Affairs and Foreign Trade, at the opening of Sweden's accession negotiations," 1 February 1993. Manuscript, pp. 5–6.

53. See David Gardner, "New Applicants to Give Up the Neutrality Habit," in *Financial Times,* 2 February 1993, p. 2.

54. Inlegg av Handelsminister Bjørn Tore Godal i forbindelse med åpningen av Norges medlemskapsforhandlinger med EF i Luxembourg, 5 April 1993. Manuscript, p. 2.

55. "Austria–Sweden–Finland–Norway, Conference on Accession to the European Union." Meeting Document No. 1 (Rev 1). Brussels, 21 December 1993, p. 1; see the "Accession Treaty," *Official Journal of the European Communities,* C 241 (29 August 1994), p. 381.

56. This last provision directly aims toward Austria, the only applicant country that has a legal obligation (a federal constitutional law) to maintain its neutrality status. France seems to have unsuccessfully tried to get a separate declaration from the Austrians, which would have practically meant—looking at the public opinion polls in Austria—preventing Austria's membership in the EU; see Otmar Lahodynsky, "Mangelnde Sensibilität in Brüssel," in *Die Presse,* 22 December 1993, p. 8.

57. In particular, the Swedish Social Democrats were happy with the outcome

of this round of talks. They thought that now the negative opinion of the Swedes would change; see Ewa Thibaut, "Nu vänder opinion," in *Dagens Nyheter,* 22 December 1993.

58. "European Parliament, Report of the Committee on Foreign Affairs and Security on Enlargement and Neutrality," *Rapporteur:* Martin Holzfuss. PE 206.084/fin., pp. 13–14.

59. The decision (*Beschluss*) of the Council was agreed upon with the acceding states. However, it neither forms part of the Accession Treaty nor of the Final Act, but is noted in the minutes of the Accession Conferences and was published in the Official Journal ("C" series).

60. With 82.3 percent of the electorate participating, 66.6 percent of the Austrians voted yes and 33.4 percent no to EU membership.

61. According to a telephone exit poll, see Fritz Plasser and Peter A. Ulram, "Meinungstrends, Mobilisierung und Motivlagen bei der Volksabstimmung über den EU-Beitritt," in Anton Pelinka, ed., *EU-Referendum. Zur Praxis direkter Demokratie in Österreich* (Wien: Signum Verlag, 1994), p. 111.

62. On 16 October 1994, 56.9 percent of the Finns voted for EU membership and 43.1 percent against, the turnout being 74 percent. On public opinion polls, which predicted a larger "yes" majority, see also Figure 18.3.

63. *Finnish EC Opinion. Autumn 1993* (Helsinki: Centre for Finnish Business and Policy Studies [EVA], 1993), p. 24, and *Finnish EU Opinion. Autumn 1994* (Helsinki: Centre for Finnish Business and Policy Studies [EVA], 1994), p. 25.

64. In the referendum of 13 November 1994 52.3 percent voted yes to EU membership, 46.8 percent voted no and 0.9 percent cast a blank vote; 83.3 percent of the eligible population participated in the vote.

65. See Toivo Sjörén, "Svårt ange fördelar med EU-medlemskap," in *Opinioner & trender* 6 (October 1994), pp. 5–12.

66. On 27–28 November 1994, 47.8 percent voted yes and 52.2 voted no, the turnout being a high 88.6 percent. Compared to the referendum in 1972, the "yes" side gained 1.3 percentage points.

67. Data from an MMI analysis; see *Dagbladet,* 29 November 1994, p. 26.

68. After the negative outcome of the EU referendum, Norway lost this status.

69. See "Enlarged Community: Institutional Adaptations. Final Report," *Study on Behalf of the European Parliament by the Trans European Policy Studies Association* (TEPSA), Luxembourg: European Parliament, Directorate General for Research, June 1992 (= Political Series, 17); the European Council has followed here the Bocklet/De Gucht proposals, pp. 43–44.

70. Thomas Pedersen, "The Common Foreign and Security Policy and the Challenge of Enlargement," in Ole Nørgaard, Thomas Pedersen, and Nikolaj Petersen, eds., *The European Communities in World Politics* (London and New York: Pinter Publishers, 1993), p. 44.

71. Mathias Jopp, "The Strategic Implications of European Integration," *Adelphi Paper* 290 (London: IISS, Brassey's, 1994), p. 25.

72. See Eric Remacle, "La dimension 'sécurité-défense' de l'élargissement de l'Union européenne," in Mario Telò, ed., *L'Union européenne et les défis de l'élargissement* (Bruxelles: Editions de l'Université de Bruxelles, 1994), pp. 79–106.

73. Jopp, "The Strategic Implications," p. 26.

74. "Dem Ansuchen steht nichts mehr im Wege," Bundeskanzler Vranitzky über Neutralität und NATO-Partnerschaft, in *Der Standard,* 16 September 1994, p. 5.

75. Defense Minster Werner Fasslabend (ÖVP) argued with Article XI of the Modified Brussels Treaty ("The High Contracting Parties may, by agreement, invite

any other State to accede to the present Treaty on conditions to be agreed between them and the State so invited . . ."); see Andreas Unterberger, "Fasslabend: Neutral auch in WEU. Ja zu kollektiver Verteidigung," in *Die Presse,* 26 September 1994, p. 5.

76. I have taken inspiration for these scenarios from "Enlargement and the CFSP: Political Consequences." Preliminary Report for the European Parliament by the Trans European Policy Studies Association (TEPSA), coordinated by John Pinder, Brussels: TEPSA, 15 October 1993, pp. 36–40.

19

The Intergovernmental Conference 1996: How to Reform CFSP?

Reinhardt Rummel

The Common Foreign and Security Policy of the European Union is to some degree a misnomer. For the CFSP is less a policy, in the sense of a specific course of action, than a process. It is a means to bring to bear the combined resources of the Union to achieve certain political objectives . . .

Hans van den Broek[1]

In fact, not only the "policy" in the notion "common foreign and security policy" needs explanation, but the other three words as well. Is this policy/process really a "common" one? Do all the member states of the European Union (EU) fully participate in it—Denmark and Ireland, too? How "common" is the Western European Union (WEU) in this regard? Does each member state share the degree of commonality, either the present or the one to be achieved in the future? Can "common" be translated into a certain amount of solidarity among member states? What does "foreign policy" mean in CFSP? Is it not rather "pure diplomacy," deliberately excluding subjects like economics, trade, foreign aid, and cultural affairs? Is it a modern, future-oriented policy that includes the new challenges in global relations: environmental diplomacy and international migration policy? What does the term "security" represent? Is it identical with the traditional defense policy, or does it try to convey a somewhat larger concept reaching into non-military areas? Is human rights policy part of it? Are humanitarian operations, such as food transport by military vehicles in crisis areas, included?

Any revision of CFSP will want to either confirm, redefine, or specify each of the four letters of the acronym. At least, it may want to clarify them. At the same time, a reconsideration of the provisions and the goals for CFSP will decide on the EU's role as a partner in international politics—especially, if this reconsideration is not limited to a small group of civil servants.[2] In other words, an acronym does not—and this may have been the illusion in

363

the past—lead to a self-fulfilling process. Successful revision presupposes a union-wide discourse and acceptance. In this sense, the following reflections will not only discuss the crucial subjects of CFSP revision, but will make a strong case for the need of a revision strategy that connects the experts' concepts to the expectations of the publics of the EU member states.

Context for Revision: External Pull or Internal Push?

Europe and its international environment have changed significantly since the negotiation of the Maastricht Treaty in 1991. Economic deterioration has questioned some of the assumptions for establishing Economic and Monetary Union (EMU) as envisaged. Challenges from regional crises, such as those in former-Yugoslavia, Central Africa, the former Soviet Union, and the Caribbean have shed new light on the rationale and the scope of the EU's CFSP. At the same time, the sociopolitical distress in countries south of the Mediterranean and the consequences of the transformation process in Eastern Europe have caused hundreds of thousands to migrate to Western Europe—a tough test for the cooperation among member states of the EU in areas of domestic affairs and law enforcement. All of the three pillars of the EU have been strained and need repair or strengthening. CFSP (and its connection with the Western European Union) is just one element of it.[3]

CFSP Within Europe's New Political Order: The Pull from Outside

The revision of Title V of the Maastricht Treaty needs to be placed in the context of ongoing reform in the institutional setup of Europe as a whole, of which it is a corresponding part. As NATO is adjusting to new tasks of collective security and to the dynamics of the EU and the European Security and Defense Identity (ESDI), the Alliance is rebalancing and reorganizing itself. The January 1994 NATO summit in Brussels decided upon some major changes in the Alliance's military structure, with a view to regaining more flexibility and to allowing NATO to make its means available to the WEU through Combined Joint Task Forces (CJTF), and also to tackle the threat of proliferation of weapons of mass destruction through a common political and military approach.

The Alliance has opened up to new members and has invited partners of the North Atlantic Cooperation Council (NACC), as well as all other members of the Organization of Security and Cooperation in Europe (OSCE) to take part in the Partnership for Peace (PFP) program. For some East European countries, this program will lead to full membership, for others, to closer ties with NATO. These initiatives add to those of WEU, which has invited prospective members to participate in a dialogue and to join some of its Working Groups. These and other cooperative security measures have been stimulated and complemented by the EU's Europe Agreements with associated countries of Central and Eastern Europe, by its structured foreign policy dialogue with these countries, by the Stability Pact aimed at preventing violent conflict in Europe, and by the Partnership and Cooperation Agreements with countries of the Commonwealth of Independent States (CIS).[4]

The interface of EU and NATO is in the making. The interconnection of the two organizations with the UN and with OSCE needs to be improved. OSCE is about to fine-tune its instruments and improve its capabilities of early warning, normative intervention, and mitigation of disputes. The roles of the Council of Europe and the European Bank for Reconstruction and Development (EBRD) are growing more strategic. The position of all the organizations in the cooperative order of Europe will co-determine the future size, fabric, and function of CFSP and WEU within this structure, and this pull process is complemented by driving forces from within the EU.

CFSP as an Answer to Renationalization: The Push from Inside

A comprehensive assessment of the reforming Europe and the range of new regional challenges ahead shows that the continent is in need of the EU as a strong actor in security and stability matters and that neither the United States nor Russia are opposed to the emergence of such an actor, while Central and East European countries encourage Brussels to take a more forceful international stand.[5] With regard to CFSP and its potential revision, Western Europe has moved away from the pre-Maastricht constellation into a new regional and international context that is characterized by a revival of nationalism, a disappointing performance of the EU's foreign and security policy since its inception in 1993, and the pressure for an early enlargement of the present membership. In a more fundamental sense, post–Cold War Europe is challenged by a growing fragmentation of states and regional authorities, a trend that demands some countervailing movement.[6]

All these factors add to those motives that originally led to a CFSP-related revision clause in the Treaty of Maastricht: The Twelve were unsure and divided, at the time, on how far and how fast to proceed with integration in the sensitive areas of foreign, security, and defense policy.[7] Today's motivating factors would most likely trigger a reconsideration of the Maastricht Treaty on their own grounds. Depending on the historical context chosen (a 1991 point of view or a 1996 approach), the CFSP revision process will most likely produce substantially different results: either narrowly focused on security and defense matters or entailing CFSP as a whole and placing it in the wider context of the entire Maastricht Treaty. To meet the wider demand for revision, some observers in the European public and some portions of the

European Parliament have reintroduced the long-standing idea of a constitution for the Union. For them, CFSP revision leads right to the heart of the
European integration process.

Subjects of Revision: Obligatory and Facultative Agendas

The Maastricht Treaty specifies that in 1996 an Intergovernmental
Conference (IGC 96) will revise the provisions of Article J.4 on security and
defense cooperation. Such reconsideration needs to be completed before the
Brussels Treaty on Western European Union, after fifty years of duration,
comes to a provisional end in 1998. Should the Brussels Treaty be continued
and revised? Should WEU remain autonomous? Should it become more
interconnected with EU or be merged into the EU, either as an identifiable
body or be dissolved altogether? Should EU develop a military component
of its own, in addition to WEU, or should military policy be banned from the
integration process and be organized either in NATO, on a strictly intergovernmental basis, or just unilaterally? This is the startup set of questions for
IGC 96. In the spring of 1995, all of these questions were raised in the
public debate and one can find advocates for all of these very diverse models.

Obligatory Revision: Moving from the Core to the Periphery

At present, WEU is part of the development of EU, not part of EU as such.
If WEU were to give up most of its autonomy to EU, either by merging or
by extensive interaction with EU, the West European defense organization
would become an integral part of EU. In this case, WEU would go beyond
its present duties in EU. It would deal not only with defense-related aspects
of the Union's policy, but also with common defense policy or even common defense as projected in Article J. 4 (1). Given the reluctance of many of
the EU member states to give up sovereignty in the core of their defense and
given the complicating factor of the principles of neutrality of the three new
member states, a common defense policy of the EU does not seem to be a
realistic goal for IGC 96. Rather, it seems likely that the WEU Treaty will
be extended beyond 1998 while WEU's functions within the framework of
EU will grow.

   The potential growth area for the WEU-EU relationship could be all the
military-backed missions that are neither part of Article J.3-type joint
actions nor do they belong to defense-related functions of WEU, as laid
down in Article J. 4 (2).[8] Such missions would cover all kinds of "collective
security" tasks (as opposed to "collective defense" and "nonmilitary foreign
policy"), such as peacekeeping and peace enforcement as well as humanitarian interventions and disaster relief operations. A catalogue of such mis-

sions is part of the WEU Petersberg Declaration. Similar to those in NATO, these operations should not necessarily engage all WEU member states, while WEU planning and infrastructure could be used to support ad hoc coalitions formed of individual states. This raises profound questions of intra-EU and intra-WEU burden sharing. A collective budget for collective security? The question of commitment comes up as well: Should there be a notion of solidarity introduced in these collective, yet ad hoc, responsibilities? Will all EU/WEU member states have to comply with Article 5 of the WEU Brussels Treaty? A third question is: How is collective security, how is peacekeeping, connected with collective defense?[9]

WEU, like NATO, did not have any reference to this kind of challenge in the treaty. Article 4 of the WEU Treaty allows for military actions globally. It does not limit WEU's competencies to a geographically confined area such as NATO does with respect to collective defense commitments. The question now is whether the WEU members want to limit collective defense within WEU geographically and functionally. The view of the European Parliament (EP) is that CFSP's J.1, which formulates five goals, should be extended by one more goal: to defend the EU at and within its political boundaries. This would include, for example, the French DOM but not the TOM—that is to say, all geographical areas that have been Community areas in the past are protected collectively.[10]

It may be very hard to obtain agreement for an extensive territorial defense, but it is part of the logic of the Union. Germany and, more specifically, the German defense establishment need to get acquainted with that view.[11] It is quite natural for Paris to extend defense guarantees to its overseas departments. Former colonial powers may have other military obligations that they have extended to countries outside of Europe. France has given such guarantees to some of its partners in Africa and the Middle East. Continental powers will not want to take over these burdens,[12] but how about defense guarantees for the three new members of the EU and for those countries that are on a medium-term accession track, such as the Visegrád countries?

If Finland were to be attacked, it is almost unthinkable that the EU member states would regard this to be solely a Finnish problem. EU member states will find a way to defend Finland, given that the internal market has included Finland in the large economic space of the Union, which includes free movement of EU citizens and economic activity and assets of other member states in the Finnish region. De facto, the EU member states extended the territory to be protected by NATO and WEU at the moment when they agreed to extend the economic space of the EU all the way to the Russian border. At the same time, NATO and the United States have been committed as well, nilly-willy. These were not called security guarantees by the backdoor, but they should have been. These were *implicit* guarantees. A second, now direct and *explicit,* guarantee will be given, once the WEU observer countries become members of WEU. Certainly, WEU will want to cooperate with Russia and the CIS countries in order to help avoid any aggressive action.[13]

To put the emphasis on defense in the reform process of CFSP is therefore very important but also less important than collective security. Collective defense has been handled and will be handled one hundred percent by military policy and by military instruments. Collective security is only partly a military duty. It is a diplomatic and political duty that includes economic external relations, development policy, and financial cooperation, among other things. The military may be involved here but, most of the time, not in a central way and, in any case, only with a certain percentage of its assets. The EU is relatively well equipped for this mixture of policies and instruments, especially since the inception of the Maastricht Treaty, which, at least theoretically, allows combining the necessary military and nonmilitary means. WEU and NATO, focusing on political-military missions, are much too narrow to deliver all the required instruments. The EU should build its security policy on the comprehensive mixture of instruments rather than on military capacity alone, which the Union as such can ask from WEU but, for the time being, does not possess or command. In many cases, WEU needs the support and the consent of NATO and, more specifically, of the United States to be able to operate.[14]

Another issue to be considered in the IGC 96 revision process is the acquisition of common infrastructure (airlift capacities, communication, and surveillance capabilities) for EU-decided and WEU-backed missions. Such assets could either be contracted from NATO or the United States, or they could be developed as a common basis of EU and WEU. These assets would be used for both collective security missions and UN Charter defense actions, such as those of Chapter VIII, Article 53. These assets are needed badly when it comes to military actions of EU/WEU without direct involvement of either NATO or the United States. To the extent that the EU takes on a wider range of security tasks in Europe and in other critical regions of the world, such support will be indispensable. At present, NATO Allies are in the midst of sketching solutions to WEU's dependence on NATO and the United States in this regard, while gradually trying to build up some forces of its own (such as the Eurocorps)[15] and some infrastructure of its own (such as the surveillance satellite).[16]

As of now, WEU does not have any troops at its direct and exclusive disposal—a fact that also makes it difficult, if not impossible, to comply with the eventual decisions of the European Council concerning defense aspects, as they are enshrined in the current version of the Maastricht Treaty. As it stands, Article IV of the Brussels Treaty categorically excludes any military organization proper to WEU, referring instead to NATO-assigned military forces. This avoids duplication of military forces, but also somehow contradicts the obligation for mutual defense listed in the Brussels Treaty. If

WEU is supposed to play a more assertive role and represent a new ESDI, it will not only need infrastructure but also military forces. The way in which these are brought about and made effective needs to be further specified. How exactly can the European Council draw on WEU for military support of CFSP's diplomatic action? This is a question that increases its relevance the more EU and WEU memberships diverge.

Major subjects for revision are political guidance and military command. In this respect, recent experience with the enforcement of the UN embargo on the states of former-Yugoslavia in the Adriatic has demonstrated confusion as well as conflict among the Allies. On the insistence of Washington, NATO has declared itself to remain the prime framework for security consultations—yet it will be the European Council that gives political guidelines to WEU for Article J.4 actions. The relationship between the European Council and the NATO Council needs clarification beyond the provisions of Article J.4 (5) of the Maastricht Treaty and those of the Declarations from WEU and NATO connected with it. The revision of these Declarations must be an item on the IGC 96 agenda, which, in turn, will trigger the need for parallel adaptation of the trans-Atlantic relationship beyond the provisions of the Washington Treaty.

Likewise, the command structure needs to be clarified to avoid West European troops receiving orders from both NATO Headquarters and WEU operational staff. So far, the Maastricht Treaty does not contain any reference to the problems of military command. It might, however, be wise to introduce a respective clause or add a declaration, in order to specify the division of labor between NATO and WEU. The concept of CJTF allows for the possibility of overcoming some of the problems of incompatibility and duplication of efforts between WEU and NATO. It is a pragmatic solution that also meets the position of WEU member states like France and Spain. Following a political principle, these two countries prefer to remain outside the permanent military integration of NATO forces. The central idea of CJTF consists of a mobile headquarters that, in a sense, is ranked above Western defense organizations and will be assigned forces for specific missions on an ad hoc basis. Such clarification on the practical level needs to be translated into appropriate language connected to the IGC 96 revision. Article J.4 (5) will certainly require some specification.

Depending on the experience with CFSP joint actions, it could be examined whether the instrument of joint actions should also be introduced for collective security purposes. As of now, this proposition seems to be a long shot. Hardly any member state will be prepared to have its soldiers committed to fight by the procedure of Article J.3 (2) [qualified majority decision]. However, with respect to sharing support structures, a start could be made, especially to the extent that WEU possesses such assets of its own. Moreover, the joint actions approach for collective security tasks could be mentioned explicitly in Article J.4 (1) (along with common defense policy), as one of the long-term goals for the development of the EU. Finally, the EU needs provisions for the integrated use of military and nonmilitary instruments in order to deal effectively with the new types of security challenges, including preventive and post-conflict measures. The combination of military and nonmilitary security policy will need particular attention in case WEU is regarded to be the fourth pillar.

As a consequence of changes to Article J.4, the provisions of other articles of Title V may be affected. In this case, IGC 96 will have to examine further changes according to Article J.10. Such alterations will—generally speaking—liberate security matters from their ghetto in Article J.4 and introduce them into other articles of Title V. One example would be the mentioning of collective security in Article J.1 (3), expressing that the Union could use military means to support the principles of the UN Charter and the OSCE Charter. Another example would be to change Article J.8, in order to extend to WEU bodies some of the rights to launch initiatives within the EU/CFSP framework.

While the prescriptions for revision in Article J.4 and Article J.10 remain within the field of CFSP as defined by Title V, Article B (hyphen 5) calls for a revision of the policies and procedures of CFSP in the event that the Community cannot operate effectively. Therefore, it should be part of the deliberations of IGC 96 to discuss and clarify the interconnection of policies in all three (four) pillars. Here are some exemplifying questions: To what extent should Community trade and economic cooperation policy be connected with CFSP? Is CFSP nonproliferation policy to be harmonized with foreign aid policy? Should cooperation in Justice and Internal Affairs and CFSP be connected to deal effectively with immigration problems and, thus, to allow the full implementation of the Community's internal market? Answers to these questions are likely to lead to a wider change of the Maastricht Treaty than just Title V. The issue is whether to abolish or transcend the present pillar system, in order for a new and much wider "external policy of the Union" to emerge.

Facultative Revision: Moving from the Periphery to the Core

While IGC 96 was originally scheduled and motivated by the expiring Brussels Treaty, the revision process will substantially be influenced, promoted, and hampered by more recent events. Among them is the factor of a growing nationalism that causes ambivalent dynamics with respect to European integration. On the one hand, rising nationalistic political forces within member countries of the EU are trying to slow down further integration and to reduce multilateralism. This attitude is not limited to foreign and security policy. It extends into almost all areas of the EU and is part of the opposition that emerged during the ratification period of the Maastricht Treaty. Part of this trend away from further union building has its roots in the end of the Cold War and the disappearance of the formerly uniting factor, the Soviet threat. Another part of the rejection of integration is stimulated by the poor record of the EU's recent performance in international crisis management. In this view, linking one's foreign and security policy to a group of indecisive countries leads to inefficiency and paralysis, which justify and even necessitate the option for unilateral action. Some observers, moreover, argue that a deepening of CFSP would undermine NATO; others see a French or a German or a Franco-German hegemony in the making and therefore oppose the evolution of CFSP.

Conversely, other political leaders draw exactly the opposite conclusion from the same analysis. They regard most of the new challenges in the field of foreign and security policy as requiring intensified multilateral cooperation and intend to control any newly rising nationalism or hegemonism by enhancing CFSP and connecting it to a multitude of security-related organizations in Europe. Some of these proponents will ask for an inclusion of CFSP in the communitarian framework of decisionmaking or, at least, the formulation and implementation of a common defense policy, if not a common defense. To them, the modest record of CFSP's crisis management in the recent past is due to the incomplete competence and construction of the Union.[17]

Thus, if IGC 96 were not required by Article N (2) of the Maastricht Treaty, Article N (1) would have been used by one of the member states of the EU or by the European Commission to call for a revision, in order to try to repair some of the weaknesses of the current system as mentioned above: lack of competence in new areas of security, missing military infrastructure and forces of the EU, underdeveloped orchestration of the various foreign policy and security instruments of the Union, as well as unstructured WEU-NATO relations. Moreover, beyond the military aspect, CFSP has been suffering from its clumsy decisionmaking process, its conceptual and planning weaknesses, as well as its budget rules.[18]

Decisionmaking Process

This contrasts with the fact that CFSP was meant to make progress as compared to European Political Cooperation. It is true that eighteen months of CFSP do not yet allow for a thorough judgment.[19] On the other hand, the period was long enough and enriched with a variety of challenges that provided ample evidence of most of the deficiencies. It is unlikely that some of the structural problems will go away by themselves. Let us look into a recent example. In early February 1995, President Mitterrand proposed that the EU should deal with the brewing conflict in Algeria. It was obvious at that time that French policy had reached a stage in which it was lacking credit and influence with both contending political camps in that North African country. Will the EU be able to develop a greater impact? An EU approach could be shaped as a preventive measure under the regime of joint action.[20] What would be the means of influence that the EU could bring to bear, in addition to what already has been in place and what Paris has mounted so far? The fact is that CFSP lacks the ability to put these types of external challenges on its agenda in a way that produces an assessment, designs a policy, has member states agree on the means, and implements the decisions taken. Given the negative experience of the past, there is little confidence in the abilities of the EU to run complex foreign policy operations.

There is significantly more trust in the EU when it comes to international trade diplomacy, such as the negotiations of General Agreement on Tariffs and Trade (GATT) rounds. They are difficult and complex as well, but Brussels finally delivers. To make CFSP stronger, it needs to organize a process of initiative that is analogous to the one in the Community. Part of this role can be played by the European Commission. The Commission has not yet used the room for an active role in CFSP. The Maastricht Treaty gives the Commission a role of initiative alongside the member states. It seems, however, that the Commission does not yet know how to exploit that possibility. One reason may be that it is used to holding the monopoly on initiative in communitarian matters and finds it hard to come to grips with sharing this role with the Council or the member states. Another reason might be that the directorate-general (DG IA) was psychologically overburdened with the new role in CFSP. In a kind of appeasement approach, the Commission did not want to overdo its new position, fearing that some of the member states would crack down on it. Certainly, the lack of initiative was also due to lack of expertise, which made it hard to take on an assertive role. Finally, the buildup of personnel from roughly thirty to three hundred within a year added to inactivity and paralysis. The Commission will have to develop more imagination and innovation despite and because of the new team of commissioners and the new assignment of dossiers and departments.[21]

The ability of the Commission to take initiatives needs to be strengthened. For the time being, there is a lack of knowledge and expertise. Part of the recent recruitment process of DG IA has been to assign "political" officers. At least some have been named, in central places like the UN in New York, but they are career officers from the Commission, not trained for the political job, and, in any case, there are not enough of them. Their reporting has been much too sporadic to make an impact and to let the DG IA compete with the diplomatic services of the member states. Van den Broek sits in on the Contact Group meetings but cannot talk, because he has not enough information and has too little to offer.[22] Will this deficiency go away soon or stay for ever? Should the Commission install a diplomatic school of its own to train its personnel, and should trained young diplomats from member states be recruited?

The Commission's place and function in the context of CFSP needs clarification and development in the 1996 reform exercise, but first of all, the commissioners and their staff need imagination and "statecraft" to take initiatives in the EU's external relations. The dispatch of external competencies of the Santer Commission certainly deserves all the criticism that has been raised, but it needs to be transcended and applied constructively from now on. Doesn't this allow the overcoming of the pillar structure, at least within the Commission's activities? This opportunity should not be missed. A reassessed external relations agenda should be established, and the Commission and its departments should cooperate to demonstrate where and how they have something to offer in coping with the items on the list. Just to mention two ways in which the Commission should make such an offer to the other actors of the Union:

Generic approach. The Commission can compile a list of the instruments at its disposal and specify which capabilities have not been used in the way they could have been and what they could be used for. It is a comprehensive demonstration of the realistic potential of the Commission, which could come to bear if the context for using this potential could be made favorable or if the other institutions of the EU would be willing to do business. The Commission should make better use of its position as a provider of instruments, of continuity, and of cohesive solutions.

Case study approach. The Commission could select a few examples from the external issue agenda, design a comprehensive strategy to cope with these issues, and locate its own role (as well as those of other institutions) within such strategy. It is very important to stress the comprehensiveness of the strategy because this allows both to demonstrate knowledge and seriousness and to define the proper (relative) role for the Commission within a multi-institutional policy process. Thus, the Commission may come in with some of its instruments in a mixed-policy strategy; it may either come in from the start or be indispensable at the end of a longer process. The art is to make it clear how useful it would be to have the Commission on board all the time.[23] Again, the first step for the Commission is to get its act together internally, and the second step is to invite the other institutions to do business according to their competencies and duties.

Assessment Unit

Today's external challenges are, most of the time, very complex and include many components: military and nonmilitary, economic and diplomatic, official government and nongovernmental organizations. The Commission should demonstrate within the framework of its competencies and abilities that high-quality concepts of policy can be developed that live up to the demands of an issue.

One of the most widely shared proposals for an improvement of CFSP is to establish an assessment unit. It seems to be a plausible suggestion to have such an objective voice, but what should it look like? Here are some features of such a unit:

- All EU institutions should be allowed to draw on it. It should be funded via a foundation that is created by the profiting institutions.
- The unit should give assessments and develop options but refrain from narrow policy recommendations.
- It should not play with the public and try to beef up its status and influence. Its reports would be reserved exclusively for the EU institutions. Publication may be allowed after six months.
- It should be independent of any single institution but be prepared to accept demands for studies and fact-finding missions. Part of its duty would be to look into areas chosen by its own consideration.
- The supervisory board should represent the mainstream thinking in the EU and seek to avoid that the unit tilts into extremist directions. All major political fractions should be represented there.
- Those who do the assessment should be experts in international relations and security, with a research background and an operational interest. They should produce policy options but leave it to the EU institutions to choose from these options.
- The unit would consist of a small research and research management section. It would mainly commission work at member states' research institutes. It would bring in, on a temporary project and case-related basis, specialists for particular questions (ethnologists, for example). It would draw on communication networks (Internet).
- The main feature of the unit would be that it takes an EU perspective on international challenges, not a *national* and not an *international* one, and that it does not narrow down its view to just one institution's perspective within the EU.

The concept should make a significant difference to similar units and research bodies, such as the WEU Institute, the Planning Cell, the CFSP group of heads of planning staffs, the Cellule de Prospective, the Political Committee, and the cabinets of the commissioners.[24]

Budgetary Scheme

Instead of developing the CFSP-WEU liaison, it would be more beneficial and more appropriate, with respect to the dimension of security challenges, to look into the strengthening of links between Community policies and CFSP. Deficiencies in this regard are aggravated by the fact that the two modes of decisionmaking continue to be at odds with one another. They are one of the major reasons why dossiers such as the one on the Ukraine and Rwanda have been internally blocked for a long time. The reason is not a lack of consensus concerning the subject matter but rather the dispute over the course of integration, partly expressed by the quarrel over financial resources: EU budget or contributions by individual member states.[25] Article J.11 of the Maastricht Treaty will have to be amended in order to reduce the high degree of uncertainty and the high risk of blockage.

The Ukraine was analyzed by the EU and is regarded to be a strategically important country that needs all available help for stabilization. The EU worked out a program of support for the Ukraine in the summer of 1994 (Corfu), but it has been stuck for many months because of those interinstitutional frictions concerning the financing of the actions and the competencies of the involved institutions. This does not seem to be a very successful method of conflict prevention. On the other hand, one can turn the issue around and claim that the interinstitutional disagreements were not overcome because the case lacked urgency and eminence. If this is a valuable argument, then there are not that many cases in which the EU will act early, before a crisis breaks out. In fact, there are probably only two geographical areas that are, in this sense, vital to all EU Europeans: the stabilization of East Central Europe, including the countries bordering that region, and the Mediterranean region. Perhaps there may be one or two functional areas, in addition—such as proliferation of weapons of mass destruction—which are of the same vital quality.

The report on the performance of CFSP, as required for the Article N (2) revision process, will probably reveal a number of further deficits concerning the functioning of the EU's institutions, the instruments at its disposition, the decisionmaking mechanism, and the range of issues treated on the EU level. The subject of institutional reform is primarily triggered by the enlargement of 1995 and the commitment to further enlargement—starting with Malta and Cyprus, then turning to the countries of Central and Eastern Europe, as well as Slovenia.[26]

Many institutional issues have already emerged since Maastricht and many more are to come: the size of the European Commission, the majority quota in the Council, the relationship of Commission to Council. Does the Treaty clause of "the single nature of the institutional framework" enhance the role of both the European Commission and the European Council? Following up on Article C provisions: What is the record concerning the responsibility of the Commission and the Council to ensure "coherence and continuity of the Union's external actions as a whole"?[27] Which institution should be determinant in those areas where cooperation and Community subjects, as such, meet or are superimposed (for instance, in the field of external relations)? Should such influence be left to a pragmatic process? What is the experience of the interlocking of the Committee of Permanent

Representatives (COREPER), Council secretariat, and the Political Committee? The sizing of the liaisons (member states/EU/WEU; within EU; EU/WEU/NATO) will be crucial for the performance of the future CFSP.[28]

Revision Strategy: Doing Better than Maastricht

How to officially start the reform of CFSP? Article J.4 (6) points out that a report on the experience and progress of security cooperation (Report 96) should be the basis for such an exercise. The Council, which will present its report to the European Council, began drafting it in June 1995 when the Revision 1996 Group, consisting of special advisers to the fifteen foreign ministers and of two representatives from the EP, was established in Nice. Several institutions, particularly the European Commission and the European Parliament as well as WEU, have completed specific reports of their own.[29] They all reveal one trend: They do not confine themselves to the narrow notion of Article J.4 (6), they go beyond an assessment of the current state of security cooperation and open up the debate about CFSP, as such, in the context of an institutional setup of the EU, which needs a reformative push.

Assuring Political Acceptance

Given the negative experience with public acceptance of the Maastricht Treaty, its revision, which will have to be ratified in the end, should avoid the same mistake. A large part of the criticism toward the Maastricht Treaty referred to its technocratic nature and its lack of appeal to the European citizen. The European public at large learned too little too late of the far-reaching intentions of the so-called Eurocrats. In fact, the elaboration of the Treaty has mainly been a task of the experts and diplomats centered around Brussels. The process resembled a classical multilateral *negotiation* between states. Except for the participation of the Commission and the commentary from the EP, little hinted at the struggle for, and the creation of, a *union*. A main political debate—to the extent that this can be called a debate—took place only over the final document, and in a selective manner, country by country. The member states needed a special European Council session in Birmingham to meet the public objections that originated as much in the procedure of elaboration as in the substance of the Treaty.

The narrow rules of the revision clause in Title V of the Maastricht Treaty provide a great temptation to repeat the previous error. Certainly, it would look awkward, at first glance, if a broad EU-wide discussion were launched to discuss some minor alterations of Article J.4. Yet even if the Treaty is not changed at all, the chance for a wider political debate on a major part of the political union should not be missed. Most member countries, with the exception of those who underwent a referendum for the ratification of the Maastricht Treaty, will need such a debate, in order to catch up. Foreign and security policy has been a latecomer in the integration process and was treated as such in the IGCs that led to Maastricht. The sector needs more elaboration in integrationist terms and the EU people need to determine the range of their commitment to a wider, transnational responsibility, sharing in a new international constellation. The seemingly technical revision of Article J.4 needs strategic guidance and a comprehensive political approach.

The Maastricht revision process should therefore be designed as much as a public debate on the external reach of the EU as a negotiation among governments. To achieve this, the discussions need to be started early on, not only by the Revision 96 Working Group, but also by political movements, interest groups, the media, and nongovernmental experts. The contributions of nongovernmental organizations and think tanks would serve such a purpose better than the suggestions of the diplomats for *their* future duties based on *their* report of *their* previous performance. Certainly, the discussion of a draft constitution that includes the foreign and security policy of the Union would serve the need for a broader-based consensus in this area of European integration even better, but it is unlikely to become reality soon. Whether Article J.4 revision or draft constitution, the outcome of the process should be a combination of institutional clarification as well as political acceptance (integration level as well as policy objectives).

The Right Measure of Expectation

In the spring of 1995, the multitude of official statements, demands, and propositions made with respect to IGC 96 raised the question of overload. The net result of the revision process should be realistically anticipated. It could consist of both a larger awareness of the body politic of the EU on issues of international relations (a political Report 96?), and a legal document that can be read and understood by the citizens of the EU. It could help to clarify

- The further pace and scope of integration in Western and Central Europe
- The range of external commitments of the Union (assignment of competencies)
- The nature of the EU's connection with the other European countries and organizations

Concerning security and defense matters, IGC 96 is likely to concentrate on a specification and addition of the present setup of Article J.4, leaving the long-term provisions for a common defense policy and a common defense more or less untouched. In the eyes of many in Europe and especially in Germany, this would further imbalance the parallel development of EMU and Political Union even though the steps for a common currency and a European Central Bank have meanwhile been stretched. A more enlightened appreciation should, however, regard collective security measures, if they were to become a prime responsibility of post-1996 EU, a balance factor within the give-and-take among the major powers of the EU in the European integration process.[30]

The difficulties in ratifying the Maastricht Treaty proved that the method of successive revisions (for deepening and broadening purposes) by means of intergovernmental conferences may be too clumsy in the future and may create a constant uncertainty about the Union's range and stability of action. Hence the idea of choosing another path that would reduce the need for the EU to undergo repeated alterations and amendments of its founding treaties by diplomatic negotiations without the people really knowing what kind of statehood the Union is heading for. The alternative path could be the writing of a "constitution" for the Union. The initiation of a constitutional process would be the foremost task of the European Parliament, in collaboration with the parliaments of the member states. The Fernand Herman Draft Constitution on behalf of the EP Committee on Institutional Affairs could be considered as the starting point. Other initiatives from the European Council, as well as from the European public (see the draft of the European Policy Forum), would enrich such a process. While it avoids the disadvantage of the revision-of-the-revision method, this procedure has tremendous risks of its own.

Notes

1. *Agence Europe,* 22 October 1994, p. 1.

2. Ludgar Kühnhardt and Hans-Gert Pöttering, *Weltpartner Europäische Union* (Osnabrück: Fromm, 1994).

3. This is also the approach that is shared most widely among the integrationist elite in Europe. See Peter Ludlow, "Preparing for 1996 and a Larger European Union: Principles and Priorities," *CEPS Special Report* no.6 (Brussels: Centre for European Policy Studies, 1995).

4. Certainly, the development of the EU had important effects on its environment. See Philippe de Schoutheete de Tervarent, "The Treaty of Maastricht and Its Significance for Third Countries," in *Österreichische Zeitschrift für Politikwissenschaft* 3 (1993), pp. 247–260.

5. For the change in motivation to integrate Europe, see Walter Carlsnaes, ed., *European Foreign Policy. The EC and Changing Perspectives in Europe* (London: Sage Publications, 1994).

6. Michel Korinman and Lucio Caracciolo, eds., *Les Fractures de l'Occident—Eléments de géopolitique* (Paris/Rome: La Découverte, 1994).

7. For the record and the assessment of the process that led to the establish-

ment of CFSP, see Mathias Jopp, "The Strategic Implications of European Integration," *Adelphi Paper* 290 (London: IISS, Brassey's, July 1994).

8. To focus the reform of CFSP on J.4 is "legally" correct in terms of the Treaty and reflects the thinking of the beginning 1990s when common defense was the issue in which some of the member states had wanted to go further and others had opted against intensified integration. The way out of this deadlock was to include a revision clause in Title V. This was all the more appropriate as the WEU Treaty was ending in 1998 and had to be renewed or confirmed in time anyway. Yet, the dynamics of the years that followed the deliberations of Maastricht turned to subjects of collective security and cooperative security rather than to traditional collective defense. Ethnic intrastate conflict and the violation of human rights have since become the prime challenges for the EU. In response, collective security measures and conflict prevention have become growth industries of security policy.

9. Some answers to these questions are to be found in the following report: "Assembly of Western European Union, A European Defence Policy." Report submitted on behalf of the Defence Committee by Mr. Baumel, Doc. 1445, November 1994.

10. The EU would also have to make clear that a member state loses all solidarity if it provokes an attack or danger by its own incautious behavior—for instance, in the event that Greece drags Macedonia or Albania into an armed conflict. See also Theodore A. Couloumbaris, "Greece and European Security in the 1990s," in Charles L. Barry, ed., *The Search for Peace in Europe* (Washington, D.C.: National Defense University Press, 1993), pp. 55–69.

11. Reinhardt Rummel, "The German Debate on International Security Institutions," in Marco Carnovale, ed., *European Security and International Institutions After the Cold War* (London: Macmillan Press, 1995), pp. 177–197.

12. In this context, it may be regretted by France and others that they protected their special relationships in J.5 instead of "communitarizing" it.

13. A set of activities and the development of ties between WEU and the Russian Federation is discussed in the following report: "Assembly of Western European Union, WEU's Relations with Russia." Report submitted to the Political Committee by Baumel, Doc. 1440, November 1994.

14. The assets and constraints of WEU are laid out by its former secretary-general, Willem Frederik van Eekelen, "WEU After Two Brussels Summits," *Studia diplomatica* 2 (1994), pp. 37–48.

15. Peter Schmidt, ed., *In the Midst of Change: On the Development of West European Security and Defense Cooperation* (Baden-Baden: Nomos Verlagsgesellschaft, 1992).

16. See, for the future capacity of the Satellite Centre in Torrejón, the following report: *Assembly of Western European Union, The Development of a European Space-Based Observation System.* Report submitted on behalf of the Technological and Aerospace Committee by Mr. Valleix, Doc. 1436, November 1994.

17. See, for this line of argumentation, Hochrangige Expertengruppe für die GASP, "Die Voraussetzungen für eine glaubwürdige GASP im Jahr 2000," *Erster Bericht,* Brüssel, den 19. December 1994.

18. For the analysis of these and further deficiencies, see Günter Burghardt, "The New Europe." Speech to the 16th World Congress of the International Political Science Association in Berlin; 23 August 1994, Brussels: Directorate-General for External Political Relations, EU, 1994. A slightly different reading of the strength and weaknesses of CFSP is given by the British foreign secretary, Douglas Hurd, "Developing the Common Foreign and Security Policy," in *International Affairs* 3 (July 1994), pp. 421–428.

19. Some scholars have already dared an evaluation after twelve months of CFSP activity. Barbara Christine Ryba, "La politique étrangère et de sécurité commune (PESC). Mode d'emploi et bilan d'une année d'application (fin 1993/1994)," *Revue du marché commun et de l'Union européenne* 384 (January 1995), pp. 14–35.

20. Joint actions have not yet been used for conflict prevention purposes, unless the continuation of the one on election monitoring in South Africa can be regarded as a preventive measure. Martin Holland, *Plus ça change . . . ?: The European Union "Joint Action" and South Africa* (Brussels: Centre for European Policy Studies, 1994).

21. The Commission is not very convincing with its four commissioners who deal with foreign policy (in geographical areas) and with the president holding an additional dossier of foreign policy and a coordination role for himself. Will weekly coordination meetings of the five avoid the danger of compartmentalization of the Commission's external relations?

22. Commission representatives have criticized member countries for the formation of the Contact Group on Bosnia because of their deviation from EU rules of common representation. However, the Commission should not expect that the member states will only consult according to the rules enshrined in the Maastricht Treaty. Member states have many multilateral forums of contact and want to keep them alive. These non-EU forums are useful and should not be regarded as strategies to undermine the EU. The Commission cannot and should not artificially try to narrow down the range of different types of consultations.

23. Next time, the Commission could, for instance, turn the Stability Pact sequence around and ask the French prime minister to take an initiative because the Commission has instruments for an active and urgent policy, as analyzed by the Commission.

24. It should also be different from existing research units on the European level, such as IISS, SIPRI, CEPS or within member states such as SWP in Germany, Analyses et Prévision in France, IAI in Italy, Chatham House in the United Kingdom, Clingendal in the Netherlands, just to mention a few. For a wider elaboration of the concept, see Reinhardt Rummel, *An Assessment Unit for CFSP—Purpose and Features* (Ebenhausen: SWP, 1995).

25. The EP has made propositions to settle the dispute. "Europäisches Parlament, Ausschuß für Auswärtige Angelegenheiten, Sicherheit und Verteidigungspolitik, Entwurf einer Stellungnahme für den Haushaltsausschuß zum Entwurf des Haushaltsplans der Europäischen Gemeinschaften für das Haushaltsjahr 1995," Berichterstatter Gary Titley, 6 September 1994.

26. Arnhild Spence, *Enlargement of the European Union. A Step Towards a Common Foreign and Security Policy* (Oslo: Norwegian Institute of International Affairs, 1994).

27. The answer given to this question by insiders is rather mixed. See Horst G. Krenzler and Henning C. Schneider, "Die Gemeinsame Außen- und Sicherheitspolitik der Europäischen Union. Zur Frage der Kohärenz," *Europarecht* 2 (1994), pp. 144–161. Peter Christian Müller-Graff, "Europäische Politische Zusammenarbeit und Gemeinsame Außen- und Sicherheitspolitik: Kohärenzgebot aus rechtlicher Sicht," *Integration* 3 (July 1993), pp. 147–157.

28. These institutional questions were already at the heart of the debate when CFSP started in November 1993. Geoffrey Edwards and Simon Nuttall, "Common Foreign and Security Policy," in Andrew Duff, ed., *Maastricht and Beyond* (London: Routledge, 1994), pp. 84–103.

29. "Assembly of Western European Union: A European Security Policy." Report submitted on behalf of the Political Committee by Mr. Soell, Doc. 1439, November 1994.

30. Moreover, such a specified CFSP competence for collective security could pave the way for a constructive integration of the countries with a tradition of neutrality into EU security policy. UN-mandated peace operations have traditionally made up the bulk of neutral countries' military activities. For the time being, collective security-related integration of an enlarging EU does not cause severe problems for Moscow, but the EU will have to be more aware of the fact that it already shares a long border with Russia.

Appendix:
Title V, Article J, of the Treaty on European Union: Provisions on a Common Foreign and Security Policy

Article J

A common foreign and security policy is hereby established which shall be governed by the following provisions.

Article J.1

1. The Union and its Member States shall define and implement a common foreign and security policy, governed by the provisions of this Title and covering all areas of foreign and security policy.
2. The objectives of the common foreign and security policy shall be:

- To safeguard the common values, fundamental interests, and independence of the Union;
- To strengthen the security of the Union and its Member States in all ways;
- To preserve peace and strengthen international security, in accordance with the principles of the United Nations Charter as well as the principles of the Helsinki Final Act and the objectives of the Paris Charter;
- To promote international cooperation;
- To develop and consolidate democracy and the rule of law, and respect for human rights and fundamental freedoms.

3. The Union shall pursue these objectives:

- By establishing systematic cooperation between Member States in the conduct of policy, in accordance with Article J.2;
- By gradually implementing, in accordance with Article J.3, joint action in the areas in which the Member States have important interests in common.

4. The Member States shall support the Union's external and security policy actively and unreservedly in a spirit of loyalty and mutual solidarity. They shall refrain from any action which is contrary to the interests of the Union or likely to impair its effectiveness as a cohesive force in international relations. The Council shall ensure that these principles are complied with.

Article J.2

1. Member States shall inform and consult one another within the Council on any matter of foreign and security policy of general interest in order to ensure that their combined influence is exerted as effectively as possible by means of concerted and convergent action.

2. Whenever it deems it necessary, the Council shall define a common position.

Member States shall ensure that their national policies conform to the common positions.

3. Member States shall coordinate their action in international organizations and at international conferences. They shall uphold the common positions in such fora.

In international organizations and at international conferences where not all the Member States participate, those which do take part shall uphold the common positions.

Article J.3

The procedure for adopting joint action in matters covered by the foreign and security policy shall be the following:

1. The Council shall decide, on the basis of general guidelines from the European Council, that a matter should be the subject of joint action.

Whenever the Council decides on the principle of joint action, it shall lay down the specific scope, the Union's general and specific objectives in carrying out such action, if necessary its duration, and the means, procedures, and conditions for its implementation.

2. The Council shall, when adopting the joint action and at any stage

during its development, define those matters on which decisions are to be taken by a qualified majority.

Where the Council is required to act by a qualified majority pursuant to the preceding subparagraph, the votes of its members shall be weighted in accordance with Article 148(2) of the Treaty establishing the European Community, and for their adoption, acts of the Council shall require at least fifty-four votes in favour, cast by at least eight members.

3. If there is a change in circumstances having a substantial effect on a question subject to joint action, the Council shall review the principles and objectives of that action and take the necessary decisions. As long as the Council has not acted, the joint action shall stand.

4. Joint actions shall commit the Member States in the positions they adopt and in the conduct of their activity.

5. Whenever there is any plan to adopt a national position or take national action pursuant to a joint action, information shall be provided in time to allow, if necessary, for prior consultations within the Council. The obligation to provide prior information shall not apply to measures which are merely a national transposition of Council decisions.

6. In cases of imperative need arising from changes in the situation and failing a Council decision, Member States may take the necessary measures as a matter of urgency having regard to the general objectives of the joint action. The Member State concerned shall inform the Council immediately of any such measures.

7. Should there be any major difficulties in implementing a joint action, a Member State shall refer them to the Council which shall discuss them and seek appropriate solutions. Such solutions shall not run counter to the objectives of the joint action or impair its effectiveness.

Article J.4

1. The common foreign and security policy shall include all questions related to the security of the Union, including the eventual framing of a common defence policy, which might in time lead to a common defence.

2. The Union requests the Western European Union (WEU), which is an integral part of the development of the Union, to elaborate and implement decisions and actions of the Union which have defence implications. The Council shall, in agreement with the institutions of the WEU, adopt the necessary practical arrangements.

3. Issues having defence implications dealt with under this Article shall not be subject to the procedures set out in Article J.3.

4. The policy of the Union in accordance with this Article shall not prejudice the specific character of the security and defence policy of certain Member States and shall respect the obligations of certain Member States

under the North Atlantic Treaty and be compatible with the common security and defence policy established within that framework.

5. The provisions of this Article shall not prevent the development of closer cooperation between two or more Member States on a bilateral level, in the framework of the WEU and the Atlantic Alliance, provided such cooperation does not run counter to or impede that provided for in this Title.

6. With a view to furthering the objective of this Treaty, and having in view the date of 1998 in the context of Article XII of the Brussels Treaty, the provision of this Article may be revised as provided for in Article N(2) on the basis of a report to be presented in 1996 by the Council to the European Council, which shall include an evaluation of the progress made and the experience gained until then.

Article J.5

1. The Presidency shall represent the Union in matters coming within the common foreign and security policy.

2. The Presidency shall be responsible for the implementation of common measures; in that capacity it shall in principle express the position of the Union in international organizations and international conferences.

3. In the tasks referred to in paragraphs 1 and 2, the Presidency shall be assisted if need be by the previous and next Member States to hold the Presidency. The Commission shall be fully associated in these tasks.

4. Without prejudice to Article J.2(3) and Article J.3(4), Member States represented in international organizations or international conferences where not all the Member States participate shall keep the latter informed of any matter of common interest.

Member States which are also members of the United Nations Security Council will concert and keep the other Member States fully informed. Member States which are permanent members of the Security Council will, in the execution of their functions, ensure the defence of the positions and the interests of the Union, without prejudice to their responsibilities under the provisions of the United Nations Charter.

Article J.6

The diplomatic and consular mission of the Member States and the Commission Delegations in third countries and international conferences, and their representations to international organizations, shall cooperate in ensuring that the common positions and common measures adopted by the Council are complied with and implemented.

They shall step up cooperation by exchanging information, carrying out joint assessments and contributing the implementation of the provisions referred to in Article 8c of the Treaty establishing the European Community.

Article J.7

The Presidency shall consult the European Parliament on the main aspects and the basic choices of the common foreign and security policy and shall ensure that the views of the European Parliament are duly taken into consideration. The European Parliament shall be kept regularly informed by the Presidency and the Commission of the development of the Union's foreign and security policy.

The European Parliament may ask questions of the council or make recommendations to it. It shall hold an annual debate on progress in implementing the common foreign security policy.

Article J.8

1. The European Council shall define the principles of and general guidelines for the common foreign and security policy.

2. The Council shall take the decisions necessary for defining and implementing the common foreign and security policy on the basis of the general guidelines adopted by the European Council. It shall ensure the unity, consistency, and effectiveness of action by the Union.

The Council shall act unanimously, except for procedural questions and in the case referred to in Article J.3(2).

3. Any Member State or the Commission may refer to the Council any question relating to the common foreign and security policy and may submit proposals to the Council.

4. In cases requiring a rapid decision, the Presidency, of its own motion, or at the request of the Commission or a Member State, shall convene an extraordinary Council meeting within forty-eight hours or, in an emergency, within a shorter period.

5. Without prejudice to Article 151 of the Treaty establishing the European Community, a Political Committee consisting of Political Directors shall monitor the international situation in the areas covered by common foreign and security policy and contribute to the definition of policies by delivering opinions to the Council at the request of the Council or on its own initiative. It shall also monitor the implementation of agreed policies, without prejudice to the responsibility of the Presidency and the Commission.

Article J.9

The Commission shall be fully associated with the work carried out in the common foreign and security policy field.

Article J.10

On the occasion of any review of the security provisions under Article J.4, the Conference which is convened to that effect shall also examine whether any other amendments need to be made to provisions relating to the common foreign and security policy.

Article J.11

1. The provisions referred to in Articles 137, 138, 139 to 142, 146, 147, 150 to 153, 157 to 163 and 217 of the Treaty establishing the European Community shall apply to the provisions relating to the areas referred to in this Title.

2. Administrative expenditure which the provisions relating to the areas referred to in this Title entail for the institutions shall be charged to the budget of the European Communities.

The Council may also:

- Either decide unanimously that operational expenditure to which the implementation of those provisions gives rise is to be charged to the budget of the European Communities; in that event, the budgetary procedure laid down in the Treaty establishing the European Community shall be applicable;
- Or determine that such expenditure shall be charged to the Member States, where appropriate in accordance with a scale to be decided.

The Contributors

David Allen, senior lecturer in European studies, University of Loughborough

Günter Burghardt, director general, Directorate General I.A., European Commission, Brussels

Fraser Cameron, foreign policy adviser, Directorate General I.A., European Commission, Brussels

Jacques Delors, former president of the European Commission, Brussels

Geoffrey Edwards, director of studies, Centre for International Studies, University of Cambridge

Roy H. Ginsberg, associate professor of government, Skidmore College, New York

Thomas Grunert, Secretariat General, Directorate General IV, European Parliament, Brussels

Christopher Hill, Montague Burton Professor of International Relations, London School of Economics and Political Science

Mathias Jopp, director, Institut für Europäische Politik, Bonn and visiting professor, College of Europe, Bruges

Patrick Keatinge, Jean Monnet Professor of European Integration, Trinity College, Dublin

Horst G. Krenzler, director general, Directorate General I, European Commission, Brussels

Barbara Lippert, deputy director, Institut für Europäische Politik, Bonn

Paul Luif, senior researcher, Österreichisches Institut für Internationale Politik, Luxembourg

Jörg Monar, professor and director, Centre for European Politics and Institutions, University of Leicester

Simon J. Nuttall, visiting fellow, Centre for International Studies, London School of Economics and Political Science and visiting professor, College of Europe, Bruges

Elfriede Regelsberger, deputy director, Institut für Europäische Politik, Bonn

Reinhardt Rummel, senior researcher, Stiftung Wissenschaft und Politik, Ebenhausen

Heinrich Schneider, emeritus professor, University of Vienna, chairman of the academic board of the Institut für Europäische Politik, Bonn

Henning C. Schneider, directorate general I.A., European Commission, Brussels

Ambassador Philippe de Schoutheete de Tervarent, permanent representative of Belgium to the European Union, Brussels

Wolfgang Wessels, Jean Monnet Professor, University of Cologne and chairman of the board of the Trans European Policy Studies Association (TEPSA), Brussels

Index

Accession Treaty (1994), 352, 360*n59*
ACP countries, 102, 105; dialogues with, 265, 266–267, 270
Actions: abroad, 147; capacity for, 76; coherence in, 44, 125; collective, 87–88, 89; common, 3, 25, 44, 54, 57, 60, 82, 141, 150*n29,* 150*n30,* 151*n31,* 190, 242; complementary, 310, 312; consistent, 142; coordinated, 309; facilitating, 148; financing, 81, 141–142; government, 112; immediate, 9; intergovernmentalism in, 55; joint, 2, 6, 9, 79, 81, 82, 85, 90, 111, 113, 117, 138–141, 142, 144, 146, 150*n15,* 150*n28,* 185, 198, 210, 214, 230–231, 322, 327, 330–331, 369, 372, 380*n20;* monitoring of, 112; procedures for, 140–141; purposes of, 140; scope of, 140; uniform, 133; unilateral, 371
Afghanistan, 20, 29, 30, 37, 244, 304
Aidid, Mohamed, 287, 288, 291
Albania, 103, 184; dialogues with, 80*tab;* Europe Agreements with, 207*tab;* membership in European Union, 261*n39;* PHARE program in, 222
Albright, Madeleine, 194*n35*
Algeria, 92, 93, 371
Allen, David, 219–234
Andean Pact Group, 265, 268
Angola, 30

Arbitration Commission, 178
Argentina, 20, 32, 33
Armenia, 232
Arms. *See* Weapons
ASEAN. *See* Association of South East Asian Nations
Asolo list, 49, 61, 93
Assistance: development, x, 53, 57, 100, 222, 310; disaster, 156; distribution of, 36; economic, 20, 198; financial, 224; financing, 106; humanitarian, 99, 105–106, 144–145, 156, 161, 180, 183, 185, 188, 227, 288, 298; mutual, 8, 128; refugee, 184; technical, 99, 198, 224, 227
Association Agreements, 28, 163
Association of South East Asian Nations (ASEAN), 80*tab,* 265, 267
Atlantic Alliance, 38, 51, 119, 125, 154, 158, 159, 220, 245, 277
Australia, 80tab, 265, 268, 272
Austria: Christian Democratic Party in, 338, 342, 343; dialogues with, 266; economic growth in, 337, 338; liberalization in, 338; membership in European Union, 88, 104, 163, 252, 261*n39,* 335, 337–339; military capabilities, 358*n22;* modernization in, 338, 339; neutrality of, 339, 342, 343, 344, 350, 359*n56;* peacekeeping contributions, 280, 281*tab;* People's Party, 338, 342; referen-

About the Book

Already an influential actor on the international scene, the European Union continues to debate its foreign policy platform. This collection traces the evolution of an integrated European foreign policy, the actors involved, and recent foreign policy successes and failures. The volume concludes with a discussion of future challenges for—and limitations of—the Common Foreign and Security Policy.

Elfriede Regelsberger is deputy director of the Institut für Europäische Politik (IEP), Bonn. **Philippe de Schoutheete de Tervarent** is Belgium's ambassador extraordinary and plenipotentiary to the European Union. **Wolfgang Wessels** is professor at the University of Cologne and the College of Europe, Bruges, and also chair of IEP's Executive Council.